The
Political Economy
of Agricultural
Pricing Policy

VOLUME 2
ASIA

A World Bank
Comparative Study

The Political Economy of Agricultural Pricing Policy

VOLUME 2
ASIA

A World Bank
Comparative Study

Edited by
- Anne O. Krueger
- Maurice Schiff
- Alberto Valdés

PUBLISHED FOR THE WORLD BANK
The Johns Hopkins University Press
Baltimore and London

© 1991 The International Bank for Reconstruction
and Development/The World Bank
1818 H Street, N.W., Washington, D.C. 20433, U.S.A.

The Johns Hopkins University Press
Baltimore, Maryland 21211, U.S.A.

The text of this book is printed on paper containing
50 percent virgin pulp, 45 percent recycled preconsumer waste,
and 5 percent recycled and deinked postconsumer waste.

Library of Congress Cataloging-in-Publication Data

The Political economy of agricultural pricing policy / edited by Anne
    O. Krueger, Maurice Schiff, and Alberto Valdés.
        p.   cm.
    Contents: —v. 2. Asia.
    Includes bibliographical references.
    ISBN 0-8018-4030-9
        1. Agricultural prices—Government policy—Developing countries—
    Case studies.   2. Agricultural prices—Government policy—Asia—
    Case studies.   I. Krueger, Anne O.   II. Schiff, Maurice W.
    III. Valdés, Alberto, 1935–
    HD1417.P65   1991   90-27232
    338.1'8'091724—dc20   CIP

Contents

Appendix 281

Anne O. Krueger, Maurice Schiff, and Alberto Valdés

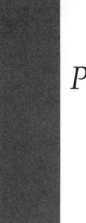

Preface

This is the second of five volumes summarizing the results of the World Bank research project, A Comparative Study of the Political Economy of Agricultural Pricing Policies. The project consisted of eighteen country studies that employed a common analytical framework and entailed close collaboration between the investigators and the project's three codirectors. This volume deals with the six countries studied in Asia: the Republic of Korea, Malaysia, Pakistan, the Philippines, Sri Lanka, and Thailand. The remaining countries are also organized by region in two other volumes, which examine Latin America (Volume 1) and Africa and the Mediterranean (Volume 3). Volumes 4 and 5 present a synthesis and comparative analysis of the findings from each country study.

The purpose of the project was threefold: to provide systematic estimates of the degree of price discrimination against agriculture within individual countries and to explain how it changed over time; to determine how this intervention affected such key variables as foreign exchange earnings, agricultural output, and income distribution; and to gain further insight into the political economy of agricultural pricing policy through a study of the motivations of policymakers, the economic and political factors determining the degree of agricultural intervention, and the attempts to reform unsuccessful policies.

Until recently, analysts were primarily concerned with the direct effect that agricultural pricing policies might have on agricultural product and input prices. According to international trade theory and general equilibrium analysis, however, a policy that protects one particular sector of the economy (in this case, industry) is essentially imposing a tax on other sectors of the economy (in this case, agriculture). The tax is likely to raise the real exchange rate, which will then lower the real return to exportables and unprotected import-competing sectors, which account for most of agriculture. Indeed, a country's general economic policies may have far greater indirect effect on agricultural incentives than its agriculture-specific or direct pricing policies do.

That is why this project proceeded on the premise that it is impossible to judge the impact of a developing country's policies without an understanding of the relative importance of direct and indirect intervention. This approach also provides an effective means of evaluating the political economy of agricultural pricing policies across a number of countries, as explained in the final volumes of this series. The systematic examination of the impact of these policies on output, consumption, government budgets, foreign trade, intersectoral transfers, and income distribution in itself contributes a great deal to our understanding of the workings of these policies in developing countries.

Economic growth is such a complex process that it is extremely difficult to interpret accurately. Because it consists of many phenomena changing simultaneously, the effects of particular policies are hard to isolate, especially if the policies have been in place for a long time. To deal with this problem, we asked the researchers to test three hypotheses in each country study: (a) agricultural pricing policies elicit economic responses (in the market, for example) and political responses (among pressure groups, bureaucratic organizations, and voter blocs) that affect the evolution of those policies; (b) the results of the policies may differ significantly from—and in some cases be opposite to—what was intended when they were adopted; and (c) the costs of price intervention are usually underestimated and tend to rise over time.

Several criteria were used to select the countries for the project. A foremost concern was to represent a reasonable range of country experience. Therefore, some countries in the group are exporters of food, others are exporters of agricultural (but nonfood) commodities, and still others are importers of food. An effort was also made to achieve some balance between low-income and middle-income countries, as well as among geographic regions. The task would have been impossible without able researchers willing to participate in the project and to prepare the country reports (published as individual volumes in the World Bank Comparative Studies series).

The countries included in the project, the participants, and their affiliations were as follows:

Argentina   Adolfo Sturzenegger and Wylian Otrera (assisted by Beatriz Mosquera), Fundación Mediterranea, Buenos Aires

Brazil	José Luiz Carvalho, Universidade Santa Ursula, Rio de Janeiro; Antonio Brandao, Fundaçao Getulio Vargas, Rio de Janeiro
Chile	Hernán Hurtado and Eugenia Muchnik, Catholic University, Santiago; Alberto Valdés, International Food Policy Research Institute (IFPRI), Washington, D.C.
Colombia	Jorge García García, World Bank, Washington, D.C.; Gabriel Montes Llamas, Instituto Colombiano Agropecuario (ICA), Bogotá
Côte d'Ivoire	Achi Atsain, Ministère de l'Industrie; Allechi M'Bet, Centre for Economic and Social Research (CIRES), Université Nationale de Côte d'Ivoire, Abidjan
Dominican Republic	Duty Greene, Sigma One Corporation, Quito; Terry Roe, University of Minnesota, St. Paul
Egypt	Jean-Jacques Dethier, World Bank, Washington, D.C.
Ghana	Dirck Stryker, Associates for International Resources and Development (AIRD), Somerville, Massachusetts
Republic of Korea	Pal-Yong Moon, Kon Kuk University, Seoul; Bong-Soon Kang, Seoul National University, Suwon
Malaysia	Glenn Jenkins and Andrew Lai, Harvard Institute for International Development, Cambridge, Massachusetts
Morocco	B. Lynn Salinger, AIRD, Somerville, Massachusetts; Hasan Tuluy, World Bank, Washington, D.C.
Pakistan	Naved Hamid, Asian Development Bank, Manila; Ijaz Nabi, World Bank, Washington, D.C.; Anjum Nasim, Lahore University of Management Sciences, Lahore
Philippines	Ponciano S. Intal, Jr., University of the Philippines, Los Baños; John H. Power, University of Hawaii

Portugal	Francisco Avillez, Instituto Superior de Agronomia, Lisbon; Timothy J. Finan, University of Arizona, Tucson; Timothy Josling, Food Research Institute, Stanford University, Stanford, California
Sri Lanka	Surjit Bhalla, The Policy Group, New Delhi
Thailand	Ammar Siamwalla and Suthad Setboonsarng, Thailand Development Research Institute, Bangkok
Turkey	Hasan Olgun and Haluk Kasnakoglu (with the cooperation of Arslan Gurkan), Middle East Technical University, Ankara
Zambia	Doris Jansen, Development Technologies Inc., Larkspur, California

An advisory board knowledgeable on the issues and experienced in analyzing agricultural pricing policies was assembled to oversee the project. Board members were asked to comment on all aspects of the project and to review various country reports. Board members, their affiliations, and the countries for which they took primary responsibility were as follows:

Romeo Bautista, IFPRI	Korea, Malaysia, Philippines
Hans Binswanger, World Bank	Pakistan, Sri Lanka
Vinod Dubey, World Bank	Côte d'Ivoire, Morocco
Peter Hopcraft, World Bank	Ghana, Zambia
D. Gale Johnson, University of Chicago	Portugal, Turkey
Yair Mundlak, Hebrew University, University of Chicago, and IFPRI	Argentina, Chile, Thailand
Edward Schuh, University of Minnesota	Brazil, Egypt
Marcelo Selowsky, World Bank	Colombia, Dominican Republic

Many other persons helped to bring the project to a successful conclusion, and we thank them here. Project administrator Celina Bermudez and her predecessor Rosario Seoane handled an endless flow of personnel and communications matters; Anne Muhtasib, the project secretary, processed voluminous correspondence and the numerous edited manuscripts; and word processors Myriam Bailey and

Estela Zamora provided helpful support. Our research assistants—Lilyan Fulginiti, Emmanuel Skoufias, Pierre Nadji, and Claudio Montenegro—reviewed the results in the many country reports and summary chapters and helped us conduct the statistical analysis for the synthesis volumes. The editor for the project was Phillip Sawicki, assisted by Paul Wolman, Vicky Macintyre, and Mary Ellen Buchanan.

Terms and Abbreviations

Below is a list of terms and abbreviations found in some or all of the chapters in this volume. The more technical terms are explained in detail in the appendix.

ACCFA	Agricultural Credit and Cooperative Financing Administration (Philippines)
AFDC	Agricultural and Fisheries Development Corporation (Korea)
APCOM	Agricultural Prices Commission (Pakistan)
CCSF	Coconut Consumer Stabilization Fund (Philippines)
CEC	Cotton Export Corporation (Pakistan)
COCOFED	Philippine Coconut Producers Federation
CPI	Consumer price index
CPI$'$	Consumer price index in the absence of direct price policies
CPI*	Consumer price index in the absence of total price policies
DAP	Democratic Action Party (Malaysia)
e	Real exchange rate
e^*	Equilibrium real exchange rate
E_0	Nominal official exchange rate
E^*	Equilibrium nominal exchange rate
EFSN	Food subsidies
EFSNTC	Ratio of food subsidies to revenue from tree crop taxes
ERP	Effective rate of protection
FCMA	Farmers' Cooperative Marketing Association (Philippines)
FEEC	Multiple exchange rate taxes
FPA	Fertilizer and Pesticide Authority (Philippines)
GDP	Gross domestic product
GIB	Government investment bias
GMP	Guaranteed minimum price

GNP	Gross national product
IFPRI	International Food Policy Research Institute
IMF	International Monetary Fund
ISA	International Sugar Agreement
LPN	Lembaga Padi dan Beras Negara (National Paddy and Rice Board, Malaysia)
MAF	Ministry of Agriculture and Fisheries (Korea)
MARDI	Malaysian Agricultural Research and Development Institute
MCA	Malaysian Chinese Association
MIC	Malaysian Indian Congress
MINFA	Ministry of Food and Agriculture (Pakistan)
MRRDB	Malaysian Rubber Research and Development Board
NACF	National Agricultural Cooperatives Federation (Korea)
NARIC	National Rice and Corn Administration (Philippines)
NEP	New Economic Policy (Malaysia)
NFA	National Food Authority (Philippines)
NLCF	National Livestock Cooperatives Federation (Korea)
NPR	Nominal protection rate
NPR_D	Nominal protection rate due to direct price policies
NPR_I	Nominal protection rate due to indirect price policies
NPR_{LT}	Long-term nominal protection rate
NPR_{ST}	Short-term nominal protection rate
NPR_T	Total nominal protection rate (includes NPR_D and NPR_I)
NUPW	National Union of Plantation Workers (Malaysia)
P_i, P_A	Domestic agricultural producer prices
P_A', P_i'	Producer prices in the absence of direct price policies (which equal the border price evaluated at the official exchange rate, after adjustment for transport and other margins)
P_{NA}	Price index of the nonagricultural sector
P_{NA}^*	Price index of the nonagricultural sector in the absence of interventions (under free trade and at the equilibrium exchange rate)
P_{NAH}	Price index of the nontradable component of the nonagricultural sector
P_{NAT}	Price index of the tradable component of the nonagricultural sector
PAS	Parti Islam (Malaysia)
PCPIA	Adjusted consumer price index
PORIM	Palm Oil Research Institute of Malaysia
PORLA	Palm Oil Registration and Licensing Authority (Malaysia)
PPP	Purchasing power parity

PRCC	Effective consumer price
PRCF	Effective producer price
REC	Rice Export Corporation (Pakistan)
RISDA	Rubber Industry Smallholders' Development Authority (Malaysia)
RRIM	Rubber Research Institute of Malaysia
SLFP	Sri Lanka Freedom Party
t_M	Average equivalent tariff (measuring the effect of tariffs and quotas on imports)
t_{NA}	Effect of trade policies on the price of nonagricultural tradables
t_x	Average equivalent export taxes
TXTC	Tree crop taxes
UCPB	United Coconut Planters Bank (Philippines)
UMNO	United Malay National Organization
UNICOM	United Coconut Oil Mills (Philippines)
UNP	United National Party (Sri Lanka)
VA	Value added expressed in domestic market prices
VA*	Value added expressed in border prices converted at the equilibrium exchange rate
WPI	Wholesale price index
ΔQ_0	Nonsustainable part of the current account deficit
ΔQ_1	Current account deficit that would result from the removal of interventions on imports t_M and on exports t_x at exchange rate E_0
ϵ_S	Elasticity of supply of foreign exchange with respect to the real exchange rate e
η_D	Elasticity of demand for foreign exchange with respect to the real exchange rate e (defined as positive)

1 Measuring the Effects of Intervention in Agricultural Prices

Anne O. Krueger
Maurice Schiff
Alberto Valdés

Most developing countries have adopted policies that affect agricultural prices, either directly or indirectly through industrial protection and macroeconomic policies. These policies have affected production incentives by making agriculture more or less attractive than other sectors of the economy.

Direct, sector-specific measures have often been the equivalent of direct taxation in that they have kept the prices received by agricultural producers below the levels that would have prevailed in their absence. Among the more important interventions of this type have been the procurement of agricultural outputs by government marketing boards (often the only legal buyers), the establishment of quotas on exports of food crops and other agricultural commodities, and the direct taxation of such exports.

Although some direct interventions have kept producer prices lower than they would have been otherwise, others have benefited agricultural producers. Domestic producers of import-competing food products, for example, have often been protected by quantitative restrictions or tariffs on imported commodities. In addition, the government has often subsidized the costs of farm credit and important agricultural inputs, such as fertilizer. Protection for food producers has been a publicly stated objective of many developing countries, which have sought to raise their level of self-sufficiency in response to the perceived unreliability of world markets (see Valdés 1981, chapter 1). Direct intervention has also been used frequently to stabilize domestic producer prices relative to prices on world markets.

In some developing countries, the government has also intervened in agricultural markets by subsidizing the costs of food for urban consumers. Retail food prices have sometimes been fixed by government edict, or ceilings have been imposed on producer prices. Another approach has been to establish dual pricing systems that keep producer prices high and consumer prices low, with the government making up the difference out of its own budgetary resources.

Subsidizing consumer food prices, however, has frequently proved to be unsustainable because of budgetary and balance-of-payments pressures, which have then forced the government to tax agricultural producers directly. In principle, the fiscal costs of cheap food policies can be reduced by targeting the subsidies to specific groups, such as consumers with income below a certain level. But the effectiveness of such programs has often been limited because the institutional structures needed to implement them have been so complex and the target groups have been so large.

Agricultural producers have also been strongly influenced by the indirect effects of economywide policies. The principal indirect effects have been (a) exchange rate misalignment because of macroeconomic policies, which reduces the real purchasing power of income received from sales of export and import-competing commodities; (b) protection for domestic industry, which forces farmers to pay more for agricultural inputs than they would have had to pay for the same goods imported at world prices and also reduces the purchasing power of farm households as consumers of manufactured goods; and (c) appreciation of the real exchange rate because of industrial protection policies, which results in additional taxation of farm producers.

Our comparative analysis of the direct and indirect effects of intervention showed that the effects were similar in most of the eighteen selected countries. Intervention usually reduced agriculture's share of gross national product and led to slower growth in agricultural production and agricultural exports. At the same time, the administrative complexity of intervention increased, and so did illegal activities such as smuggling, as producers and traders sought to evade the costs imposed by price intervention.

Another particularly significant finding was that direct and indirect intervention in combination yielded net taxation of agricultural producers. Even in those countries where direct intervention alone tended to benefit producers, that positive effect was outweighed by the negative effects of indirect intervention.

We found, too, that changing circumstances often forced policymakers to change the policies under which intervention occurred. Apart from their difficulties in foreseeing broad changes in the world prices of agricultural commodities, policymakers often failed to gauge accurately the effects of price intervention on such things as agricultural output, the government budget, and the balance of payments. Moreover, the makers of agricultural pricing policies often failed to anticipate the reactions of specific groups to price intervention. For all these reasons, the policymakers often found it necessary to amend existing policies or to devise new ones.

The rationales for taxing agriculture directly or indirectly include (a) that taxes on agricultural trade are relatively easy to collect in countries where the tax base is thin or the institutional capacity to collect other types of taxes is limited; (b) that not much agricultural output will be forgone by holding down food prices in urban areas, because agriculture is not especially responsive to incentives; and (c) that the terms of trade for primary products seem to be declining over time. Although the dim prospects for exports of primary products prompted early arguments for import-substituting industrialization, a more recent argument has been that markets for agricultural goods are limited not only by the level of final demand but also by the protectionist policies adopted by the industrial countries.

These arguments have now been reappraised by Schultz (1964), Mundlak (1985), Mundlak, Cavallo, and Domenech (forthcoming), and Coeymans and Mundlak (forthcoming). Evidence has accumulated that strongly suggests that agriculture is a dynamic sector that responds positively to price incentives and that "policies which tax agriculture reduce the investment in agriculture, increase outmigration, and reduce the implementation of new techniques" (Mundlak 1985). Much of the earlier pessimism about the trade prospects in agriculture overlooked cost-reducing technological innovations and export growth of nontraditional agricultural commodities, which would give economies of the developing countries more flexibility to cope with changing conditions in the international economic environment.

The Scope of the Project

Since the early 1970s a great deal of research has been done on development strategies and trade regimes in developing countries. (See, for example, Little, Scitovsky, and Scott 1970; Balassa 1971; Bhagwati 1978; Krueger 1978 and 1983; and Krueger, Lary, and Akrasanee 1981.) A recurring finding of such studies is that countries that sought to build their industrial sector through an inward-oriented strategy of import substitution have often been less successful than countries that adopted outward-oriented strategies.

In any case, none of the comparative studies referred to above deals explicitly with the agricultural sector. As a result, the impact of trade and balance-of-payments regimes (and other types of indirect intervention) on agricultural incentives has not been systematically examined.

There are, of course, well-known comparative studies of agricultural pricing policies such as the Stanford Food Research Institute's examination of rice policies in Asia (1975) and the World Bank's case studies of administered agricultural prices, taxes, and subsidies

(1976). These, however, deal essentially with sectoral output and input price policies. And a set of studies on the interaction between industrial protection and agricultural incentives has been conducted by the International Food Policy Research Institute (IFPRI) (Bautista and Valdés, forthcoming).

Studies of individual countries to estimate the short-term effects of sector-specific policies on agricultural output, food consumption, and trade flows are common, and one can also find occasional attempts to determine the political factors underlying the selection of agricultural pricing policies in individual countries. These studies, however, do not use the same methodology, nor do they cover the same time period, and the accompanying changes in such important measures as terms of trade, exchange rates, real interest rates, technology, and government investment in the agricultural infrastructure vary both across countries and time. These studies, therefore, do not lend themselves to useful cross-country comparisons of the effects of either direct or indirect intervention. The IFPRI studies mentioned above deal with the impact of industrial protection policies, but they do not analyze the indirect effects of other macroeconomic policies, the quantitative effects of the policies, or the political economy.

The World Bank's agricultural pricing policy project was designed to fill the gap in the literature by assessing the effects of both direct and indirect intervention in agricultural prices over a long period in eighteen representative developing countries. The project used a common conceptual framework and methodology and analyzed the political economy of these interventions. The first step in the process was to measure the impact of direct and indirect intervention on relative prices within agriculture and then to compare the impact on agricultural prices with the impact on prices in the rest of the economy— that is, in the nonagricultural sector. The next step was to estimate the effects of direct and indirect intervention in agricultural prices on (a) agricultural production, (b) consumption of agricultural products, (c) foreign exchange earnings, (d) the government budget, (e) income transfers between agriculture and the nonagricultural sector, and (f) the distribution of income among the various income groups. These estimates, in conjunction with a history of agricultural price interventions in each country, were the basis for an analysis of the evolution of the country's political economy of agricultural pricing policies.

The provision of public goods (irrigation, rural roads, research and extension, rural electrification) is, of course, important to the progress of the agricultural sector. Although analysis of the provision of public goods to agriculture was not a fundamental part of the project, the project authors were asked to measure the transfer of public expenditures and investment to and from agriculture and the net effects of those transfers on agricultural income.

The project also examined the so-called compensation hypothesis—the argument that taxation of agriculture is not necessarily harmful to the sector because the revenues tend to be reinvested in the sector. That hypothesis was tested by two alternative methods and is fully described in volume 4 in this series. Analyzed by the first method, the hypothesis was rejected for most of the countries studied. In most cases, either no relation was found between the provision of public services to the agricultural sector (that is, investment) and price intervention, or else a positive relation was found. In other words, taxation of the agricultural sector in most cases was either accompanied by a reduction in investment in the sector or else had no impact on investment. Analyzed by a second method, the hypothesis was not rejected, but public investment was found to compensate for only a very small fraction of the income lost because of price intervention.

This project, however, did not address such issues as the optimal investment of public goods in the agricultural sector, the optimal taxation of agriculture, or the role of agriculture in overall development strategy. Important as these questions are, they cannot be examined in an analysis that concentrates, like this one, on a single sector of the economy. A broader analytical framework is necessary.[1]

Measuring the Impact of Agricultural Pricing Policies

The various agricultural commodities of the developing countries are often subject to different pricing policies. Food commodities are usually treated differently from nonfood commodities, and the same is true for exportable and import-competing products. The authors of our studies were therefore asked to identify those farm products that they considered reasonably representative of commodity categories in their countries. Table 1-1 shows the twenty-six products selected. The products most frequently studied were rice, wheat, corn, sugar, and cotton.

To estimate the impact of price intervention, it was necessary to have a benchmark price, and we chose border prices. Border prices can be measured easily and provide a uniform comparator for all of the studies. Moreover, border prices represent the opportunity cost of tradables (allowing, of course, for the costs of processing, storing, marketing, and transport) for countries that are price-takers in the world market. Of course, one objection to using world prices as benchmark prices is that they are subject to a great deal of short-run instability. We do not argue, however, that optimal allocation of resources requires domestic prices to fluctuate in step with world prices, especially in developing countries that have limited abilities to hedge

Table 1-1. Agricultural Product Classification, by Region and Country

| | Latin America | | | | | Asia | | | |
Product	Argentina	Brazil	Chile	Colombia	Dominican Republic	Rep. of Korea	Malaysia	Pakistan	Philippines
Apples	—	—	X	—	—	—	—	—	—
Barley	—	—	—	—	—	M	—	—	—
Beef	X*	—	M*	—	—	M*	—	—	—
Cocoa	—	—	—	—	—	—	—	—	—
Coffee	—	—	—	X	X	—	—	—	—
Copra	—	—	—	—	—	—	—	—	X
Corn	X	X	—	—	—	—	—	—	M
Cotton	—	X	—	X	—	—	—	X	—
Grapes	—	—	X	—	—	—	—	—	—
Hazelnuts	—	—	—	—	—	—	—	—	—
Milk	—	—	M*	—	—	—	—	—	—
Palm oil	—	—	—	—	—	—	X	—	—
Pork	—	—	—	—	—	M*	—	—	—
Potatoes	—	—	—	—	—	—	—	—	—
Rice	—	M*	—	X*	M*	M*	M*	X*	M*
Rubber	—	—	—	—	—	—	X	—	—
Sheep[a]	—	—	—	—	—	—	—	—	—
Sorghum	X	—	—	—	—	—	—	—	—
Soybeans	X	X	—	—	—	M	—	—	—
Sugar	—	—	—	—	X*	—	—	M*	X*
Sunflowers	X*	—	—	—	—	—	—	—	—
Tea	—	—	—	—	—	—	—	—	—
Tobacco	—	—	—	—	—	—	—	—	—
Tomatoes	—	—	—	—	—	—	—	—	—
Wheat	X*	M*	M*	M*	—	—	—	M*	—
Wine	—	—	—	—	—	—	—	—	—

— Not applicable.

Note: M = importable; X = exportable; H = nontradable. Asterisks (*) indicate staple commodities; otherwise, commodities are considered to be nonstaples.

a. Consists of mutton and lamb.

against changes in world prices.[2] Instead, we simply claim that a reasonable way to analyze price intervention is to compare relative domestic prices with long-term trends in border prices. In our studies, the authors show the average deviations of domestic prices from border prices over five-year periods and over the entire period covered by the studies. Where it existed, the price-setting power of a developing country in a world market (for example, cocoa in Ghana) was taken into account.[3]

With border prices as their reference points, our authors then identified various types of intervention in both producer prices and input prices and quantified their effects on producer receipts. For tradable commodities, which included most of those considered, these esti-

Sri Lanka	Thailand	Côte d'Ivoire	Egypt	Ghana	Morocco	Portugal	Turkey	Zambia	Product
				Africa and the Mediterranean					
—	—	—	—	—	—	—	—	—	Apples
—	—	—	—	—	X*	—	M	—	Barley
—	—	—	—	—	—	M*	—	—	Beef
—	—	X	—	X	—	—	—	—	Cocoa
—	—	X	—	—	—	—	—	—	Coffee
X	—	—	—	—	—	—	—	—	Copra
—	X	—	M	M	—	M	—	M*	Corn
—	—	—	X	—	—	—	X	X	Cotton
—	—	—	—	—	—	—	—	—	Grapes
—	—	—	—	—	—	—	X	—	Hazelnuts
—	—	—	—	—	—	M*	—	—	Milk
—	—	—	—	—	—	—	—	—	Palm oil
—	—	—	—	—	—	—	—	—	Pork
—	—	—	—	—	—	H*	—	—	Potatoes
M*	X*	M*	X*	M*	—	M*	—	—	Rice
X	X	—	—	—	—	—	—	—	Rubber
—	—	—	—	—	—	X*	X*	—	Sheep[a]
—	—	—	—	—	—	—	—	—	Sorghum
—	—	—	—	—	—	—	—	—	Soybeans
—	X*	—	M*	—	M*	—	X	—	Sugar
—	—	—	—	—	—	—	—	—	Sunflowers
X	—	—	—	—	—	—	—	—	Tea
—	—	—	—	—	—	—	X	X	Tobacco
—	—	—	—	—	—	X	—	—	Tomatoes
—	—	—	M*	—	M*	M*	M*	—	Wheat
—	—	—	—	—	—	X	—	—	Wine

mates were conceptually straightforward. They are presented as the effects of direct intervention and are the authors' estimates of the percentage by which the producer price (value added) of each crop exceeded or fell short of the adjusted border price (value added) at the official exchange rate.

The next step was to estimate the impact of indirect intervention on relative agricultural prices. Here, the analytic underpinnings were more complex. In effect, the authors first had to estimate what the exchange rate would have been if the country in question had abandoned tariffs and quantitative restrictions while incurring a sustainable current account deficit—that is, a deficit small enough to be financed through foreign aid and long-term capital inflows. These assumptions allowed the authors to estimate the equilibrium exchange rate that would then have prevailed. (See the appendix to this volume for a discussion of the methods used to estimate the equilibrium exchange rate.) Some authors found it necessary to adapt the project methodology to their own specific situations.

To measure the impact of indirect intervention, an estimate was needed of how much the prices of goods purchased by agricultural producers would have declined if there had been no intervention. Thus, an index of nonagricultural prices was adjusted for the difference in that index if farmers had faced border prices at the equilibrium exchange rate for the tradable goods they purchased. (See the appendix for the methodology used.)

The Quantitative Effects of Intervention in Agricultural Prices

There are good reasons to believe that production of individual crops responds in the short run to changes in relative prices between crops, as well as to changes in relative differences between input and output prices. The estimates of supply elasticities available for many agricultural commodities in several developing countries confirm this belief. Based on such estimates of price elasticity, the authors were asked to estimate the short-run effects of price intervention. They were also asked to estimate the long-run effects—that is, the effects that occurred after producers had fully adapted to a new price environment. In addition to determining the effects of price intervention on agricultural output, the authors assessed the impact of intervention on consumption, foreign exchange, government expenditures, intersectoral income transfers, and income distribution.[4]

The Political Economy of Agricultural Pricing Policies

This project was designed not only to measure the effects of agricultural pricing policies on farm prices and production and other important variables, but also to explain how government intervention in agricultural prices was affected by market forces and political factors.

A number of hypotheses can be proposed as possible explanations of the policies that were adopted in the eighteen countries. It is possible, for example, that much of the discriminatory effect of intervention on agricultural prices, and especially indirect intervention, was a byproduct of the theory that claimed that the best way to achieve industrialization was to adopt the inward-oriented strategy of import substitution. As such, price discrimination against agriculture may have been unintentional. As mentioned earlier, one of the project's findings was the surprising magnitude of the discrimination against agriculture and the related income transfers from agriculture because of industrial protection policies and the exchange rate over-valuation associated with import-substitution regimes.

Another argument is that price intervention that discriminates against agricultural producers was a natural consequence of the political dominance of urban populations. In many countries, policy-makers are under pressure to design policies that will benefit urban populations. (For analyses of related policies, see Bates 1981, 1983.)

Discrimination against agricultural prices may also have other causes. Such discrimination might, for example, be an unintended byproduct of transfers of income to the urban poor when budgetary resources are inadequate. Or a government might intervene in domestic agricultural prices because of a desire to protect producers from instability in world prices. This well-intended intervention might have become discriminatory against agriculture as circumstances changed. Another plausible hypothesis is that intervention, which originally discriminated against agriculture, might develop a life of its own as market reactions and political pressures alike prompt further intervention.

To test these hypotheses, the authors were asked to provide an analytical history of pricing policies. One aspect of the task was to evaluate the degree to which announced policies achieved their stated objectives; another was to identify those who gained and those who lost because of price intervention. A surprising degree of inconsistency was found in many countries between stated and actual outcomes. As the two synthesis volumes for this project show, the comprehensive evaluation of the political economy of agricultural pricing policy is a difficult task.

The authors of the country studies were also asked to examine reforms of agricultural pricing policies that occurred during the period studied. This meant, among other things, identifying groups that supported or opposed the existing system, as well as sketching the positions taken by national political parties. In many of the countries, issues of reform played a critical role in the analysis.

The International Economic Environment

The international economic environment played a large role in shaping agricultural pricing policies in the eighteen countries. The period covered in most of the studies runs from the early 1960s to the mid-1980s—a period marked by significant volatility in the prices of major agricultural goods.

Until 1970, the period was one of rapid growth in the international economy under reasonably stable conditions. That was followed by a commodity price boom in the first half of the 1970s, which affected both agricultural and nonagricultural commodities. Although the prices of both agricultural and nonagricultural commodities were differentially affected, the prices of many of the agricultural products studied in this project reached historical peaks at some point in the first half of the decade, often followed by sharp drops. The oil price shock of 1973 played a significant role, of course, in many commodity markets during this time.

The second half of the 1970s was a period of rising worldwide inflation, and commodity prices were affected again. In 1977–78, for example, coffee prices soared but then fell sharply.

In hindsight, the latter half of the 1970s can be described as a permissive period in the world economy. Although inflation rates rose steeply, international interest rates stayed in the range of 6 to 8 percent. As a result, the real value of the developing countries' debts did not increase, despite substantial increases in their borrowing, and debt-servicing obligations did not rise as swiftly as export earnings or real incomes.

With the second oil price shock in 1979 and the ensuing worldwide recession of the early 1980s, the world economy was transformed. Among other things, most commodity prices plunged downward, eventually reaching lows that had not been seen since the 1930s. These lows occurred at the same time that many developing countries began to experience great difficulty in servicing their international debts because of much higher interest rates and a fall in capital inflows that occurred almost overnight. In short, the permissive environment of the 1970s became the harsh environment of the 1980s. Policies that seemed sensible in the earlier decade incurred large penalties in the 1980s. These comparative studies allow the reader to assess the relative importance of domestic and external factors in shaping agricultural pricing policies. Just as important, they demonstrate how a representative sample of the developing countries responded when confronted by the same external stimuli and the same difficulties.

Regional Findings

Three volumes in this series are case studies grouped by region. The first one deals with Latin America, the second with Asia, and the third with Africa and the Mediterranean. Each of these examines the experience of selected countries in the region in regard to the impact of price policies on agricultural incentives, as reflected in direct, indirect, and total nominal protection rates. A broad view of the similarities and differences in the causes, implementation, and effects of agricultural pricing policy across countries and regions is the subject of volumes 4 and 5, which present syntheses of the case studies from the perspective of economics and political economy.

Our sample consists of eighteen countries, with the following regional distribution. Latin America: Argentina, Brazil, Chile, Colombia, and the Dominican Republic; Asia: the Republic of Korea, Malaysia, Pakistan, the Philippines, Sri Lanka, and Thailand; Mediterranean: Egypt, Morocco, Portugal, and Turkey; and Sub-Saharan Africa: Côte d'Ivoire, Ghana, and Zambia.

Average measures of price intervention for the products selected in the studies are presented in Table 1–2. A number of similarities across regions are immediately apparent. First, over the period examined, direct intervention on importables was positive on average in each of the four reigons, and direct intervention on exportables was negative in all regions. Second, direct intervention on all selected products was negative in all regions, indicating that the direct tax on exportables dominated protection on importables. Third, the rate of indirect taxation (due to industrial protection policy and overvaluation of the real exchange rate) was large in all regions (usually exceeding 20 percent), and it dominated the rate of direct taxation in all regions. And fourth, total taxation exceeded 25 percent in all regions.

The impact of price interventions on agricultural incentives also differs among regions. First, indirect taxation over the period studied was largest in Sub-Saharan Africa, amounting to 28.6 percent (it was more than 30 percent in Ghana). This was followed by Asia and Latin

Table 1-2. Direct, Indirect, and Total Nominal Protection Rates, by Region, 1960–84
(percent)

Region	Indirect protection	Direct protection	Total	Direct protection of importables	Direct protection of exportables
Asia[a]	−22.9[b]	−2.5	−25.2	22.4	−14.6
Latin America[c]	−21.3	−6.4	−27.8	13.2	−6.4
Mediterranean[d]	−18.9	−6.4	−25.2	3.2	−11.8
Sub-Saharan Africa[e]	−28.6	−23.0	−51.6	17.6	−20.5

Note: The period covered is generally from 1960 to 1984, but it varies somewhat in a number of countries.

a. Republic of Korea, Malaysia, Pakistan, Philippines, Sri Lanka, and Thailand.

b. In South Asia (Pakistan, Sri Lanka), the indirect nominal protection rate was − 32.1 percent, while in East Asia (Korea, Malaysia, Philippines, Thailand) it was − 18.1 percent.

c. Argentina, Brazil, Chile, Colombia, and Dominican Republic.

d. Egypt, Morocco, Portugal, and Turkey.

e. Côte d'Ivoire, Ghana, and Zambia.

America (between 21 and 23 percent), with the Mediterranean region the lowest (about 19 percent).

In Latin America, the indirect taxation rate in each country was quite close to the regional average of 21.3 percent. In Asia, there was a significant difference between South Asia (Pakistan and Sri Lanka) and East Asia (Korea, Malaysia, the Philippines, and Thailand). The indirect taxation rate by region was largest in South Asia (32.1 percent) and lowest in East Asia (18.1 percent). In the Mediterranean region, the indirect taxation rate was close to the reigonal average for Egypt and Morocco, although Turkey's rate was the highest in our sample and Portugal's was the lowest.

Like indirect taxation, direct taxation was also largest in Sub-Saharan Africa (where agriculture in our sample is dominated by export crops), amounting to 23 percent. That region was followed by Latin America and the Mediterranean, with 6.4 percent each, and Asia with 2.5 percent. The average direct taxation rate in Asia was low because of high direct protection in Korea (39 percent). Without Korea, the average rate of direct taxation in Asia was close to 11 percent (with a rate of 25 percent in Thailand). In Latin America, the highest direct taxation rates were found in Argentina and the Dominican Republic (about 18 percent), while in the Mediterranean region, the highest direct taxation rate was in Egypt (about 25 percent). Finally, the total taxation rate was larger than 25 percent in all regions, but was about twice as large in Sub-Saharan Africa as in the other regions.

The remaining chapters in this volume provide self-contained summary accounts of agricultural pricing policies in Korea, Malaysia, Pakistan, the Philippines, Sri Lanka, and Thailand. Volume 1 of this series covers the five Latin American countries, and volume 3 covers six countries in Sub-Saharan Africa and the Mediterranean. In all cases, the chapters are based on longer and much more detailed country reports published in the World Bank Comparative Studies series, The Political Economy of Agricultural Pricing Policy.[5]

Notes

1. Good reference materials on taxation and public finance in developing countries and the relation between public finance and economic development are the World Bank's 1988 *World Development Report,* and Toye (1979).

2. Valdés and Siamwalla (1988) claim that it may be optimal to shift some of the risk to the government, which may be better able to pool risks from a variety of activities than individual farmers are.

3. In general, world prices for agricultural commodities are highly distorted as a result of price interventions by the European Communities, Japan, the United States, and others. But for the national policymaker in most small and medium-size economies, and for most commodities, the world's oppor-

tunity cost of producing these products is irrelevant. We submit that the world price does reflect the economic opportunities a country faces and thus should be used as a reference. Of course, there may be circumstances when a divergence between domestic and world prices is called for, such as a need to protect low-income consumers against short-term world price instability and monopoly power on world markets or a need to protect producers against temporary foreign export subsidies strong enough to cripple the import-competing sector.

4. Computable general equilibrium models are available for several of the eighteen countries included in the project. These were considered by the country authors, who decided not to use them because they found that the particular models for their countries were not satisfactory for the purposes of these studies.

A more complete analysis would also have included measuring the effects of agricultural price intervention on rural-urban migration, wages, and investment flows. Although it was recognized that these long-run effects are important, the authors were not requested to measure them, on the grounds that doing so would have substantially lengthened the time needed to complete the studies. Several authors, however, sought to assess the impact of agricultural price intervention on rural wages over time (see the appendix). Moreover, in the case of Chile, the impact of policy on intersectoral migration and investment flows was estimated. See Mundlak, Cavallo, and Domenech (forthcoming) and Coeymans and Mundlak (forthcoming) for analyses that incorporate such measurements.

5. Data and conclusions from the study of Côte d'Ivoire are used in volumes 4 and 5. That study is being published in Côte d'Ivoire and not in the World Bank Comparative Studies series or in volume 3 of this series.

References

Balassa, Bela. 1971. *The Structure of Protection in Developing Countries.* Baltimore, Md.: Johns Hopkins University Press.

Bates, Robert H. 1983. *Essays on the Political Economy of Rural Africa.* Berkeley: University of California Press.

———. 1981. *Markets and States in Tropical Africa.* Berkeley: University of California Press.

Bautista, R., and Alberto Valdés, eds. Forthcoming. *Trade and Macroeconomic Policies in Developing Countries: Impact on Agriculture.* Washington, D.C.: International Food Policy Research Institute.

Bhagwati, Jagdish N. 1978. *Foreign Trade Regimes and Economic Development: Anatomy and Consequences of Exchange Control Regimes.* Lexington, Mass.: Ballinger Press for the National Bureau of Economic Research.

Coeymans, Juan-Eduardo, and Yair Mundlak. Forthcoming. "Agricultural and Sectoral Growth: Chile, 1962–1982." In R. Bautista and Alberto Valdés, eds., *Trade and Macroeconomic Policies in Developing Countries: Impact on Agriculture.* Washington, D.C.: International Food Policy Research Institute.

Krueger, Anne O. 1983. *Trade and Employment in Developing Countries:* Vol. 3, *Synthesis.* Chicago: University of Chicago Press.

————. 1978. *Foreign Trade Regimes and Economic Development: Liberalization Attempts and Consequences.* Lexington, Mass.: Ballinger Press for the National Bureau of Economic Research.

Krueger, Anne O., Hal B. Lary, and Narongchai Akrasanee. 1981. *Trade and Employment in Developing Countries,* Vol. 1. Chicago: University of Chicago Press.

Little, I. M. D., T. Scitovsky, and M. Scott. 1970. *Industry and Trade in Some Developing Countries.* London: Oxford University Press.

Mundlak, Yair., 1985. "The Aggregate Agricultural Supply." Working Paper 8511. Center for Agricultural Economic Research. Rehovot, Israel.

Mundlak, Yair, D. Cavallo, and R. Domenech. Forthcoming. "Agriculture and Growth: The Experience of Argentina, 1913–84." In R. Bautista and Alberto Valdés, eds. *Trade and Macroeconomic Policies in Developing Countries: Impact on Agriculture.* Washington, D.C.: International Food Policy Research Institute.

Schultz, T. W. 1964. *Transforming Traditional Agriculture.* New Haven: Yale University Press.

Timmer, C. P., and W. Falcon. 1975. "The Political Economy of Rice Production and Trade in Asia." In L. G. Reynolds, ed., *Agriculture in Development Theory.* New Haven: Yale University Press.

Toye, J. F. J., ed. 1979. *Taxation and Economic Development.* London: Frank Cass.

Valdés, Alberto, ed. 1981. *Food Security for Developing Countries.* Boulder, Colo.: Westview Press.

Valdés, Alberto, and A. Siamwalla. 1988. Chapter 7 in J. W. Mellor and R. Ahmed, eds., *Agricultural Price Policy for Developing Countries.* Baltimore, Md.: Johns Hopkins University Press.

World Bank. 1988. *World Development Report 1988.* New York: Oxford University Press.

2 The Republic of Korea

Pal-Yong Moon
Bong-Soon Kang

One of the notable features of the Republic of Korea's development strategy during the 1950s and 1960s was its emphasis on rapid industrial growth. Consequently, the government paid little attention to the agricultural sector and instead focused on maintaining low food prices, to the benefit of the industrial sector. As industrial development progressed, industries became heavily concentrated in urban areas, and many people seeking better income opportunities moved there from the rural areas. Until the late 1960s the government did not do much to improve the economic situation in rural areas. Then, in the early 1970s, the government made two critical policy decisions concerning agriculture. It began to improve the terms of trade for agricultural products and it substantially increased the level of investment in the agricultural sector. This chapter is about the political and economic factors that spurred Korea's policymakers to change the direction of the country's agricultural pricing policies and the effects of that decision (see Appendix Table 2-14). The study covers the period from 1960 to 1986.

Overview of the Economy

An important factor to consider in reviewing the changes in Korea's economy since 1960 is the decline in its population growth rate, which fell from 2.9 percent in 1960–61 to 1.9 percent in 1970–71 and to 1.2 percent in 1985–86. This decline was the result of a government-sponsored program of family planning, combined with changes in economic opportunities and greater emphasis on restricting family size. Nonetheless, population density—at 416 persons per square kilometer in 1986—remains a serious problem. This pressure on limited space is largely due to rapid urbanization, which has been one of the most conspicuous changes of the third quarter of the twentieth century in all the developing countries. In Korea, urbanization (defined here as the rate of growth of the percentage of population in cities

15

of 50,000 or more) has proceeded at a rate of 4.1 percent per year. This high rate of urbanization has been closely linked to the country's rapid economic growth, particularly in the urban-oriented and labor-intensive manufacturing and service sector.

The Economy

Korea has managed to sustain its high growth rate since the early 1960s, except in a few years when production temporarily declined. Between 1962 and 1986, real GNP grew at an average annual rate of 8.2 percent. Even during the worldwide recession of 1974–75, the growth rate remained at 7–8 percent. With the rapid growth of output and the decline in the population growth rate during this period, per capita GNP (in 1975 constant prices) increased eightfold in two decades, from US$144 in 1960 to US$1,262 in 1986 (see Table 2-1).

The strength of the economy in this period derived largely from Korea's export-oriented industrialization strategy. Until the early 1960s, exports accounted for a small proportion of GNP—only 2 percent in 1962. Thereafter, the rate of export growth surpassed that of GNP. Merchandise exports increased at an average annual rate of about 40 percent, from US$55 million in 1962 to US$1,624 million in 1972. Between 1972 and 1986, exports increased at a rate of about 27 percent per year. The nominal value of merchandise exports in 1986 reached US$34.7 billion, or roughly 36 percent of GNP. Since 1962 the real value of exports has increased at an average annual rate of 25 percent. In contrast, imports of goods and nonfactor services have grown at a rate of about 15 percent.

This level of economic growth could not have been achieved without a sustained increase in domestic capital formation. In fact, gross domestic investment rose from less than 15 percent of GNP in the early 1960s to nearly 30 percent after the mid-1970s. To finance this increase, the country had to import a significant amount of foreign capital, which was needed to fill the domestic savings gap. However, the inflow of foreign savings fluctuated during the study period relative to the balance of payments situation and the domestic saving/investment gap. The ratio of savings to GNP increased from a three-year average of 7.7 percent in 1954–56 to nearly 10 percent in 1961–63 but then declined to 6.6 percent in 1981–82, mainly as a result of the sharp increase in world oil prices in 1979–80. Although domestic savings increased at a fairly slow pace initially—from about 5 percent of GNP in the mid-1950s to over 7 percent in the mid-1960s—the rate shot up to 20 percent in the mid-1970s and almost 30 percent in the mid-1980s.

Table 2-1. Economic Indicators 1960–86

Year	Real GNP in constant 1975 won (billions)	Per capita GNP (U.S. dollars)		Percentage of GNP				
		Nominal	Real[a]	Gross investment[b]	Domestic savings	Foreign savings	Imports	Exports
1960	2,846	79	144	10.9	0.8	8.6	17.2	1.6
1965	3,885	105	177	15.0	7.4	6.4	15.4	5.8
1970	6,363	248	341	26.8	17.3	9.3	24.8	10.5
1975	10,092	591	591	30.0	19.1	10.1	34.9	24.4
1980	14,359	1,605	1,130	31.3	21.9	9.4	36.4	28.6
1984	18,979	1,999	1,124	30.0	27.4	2.3	37.8	36.1
1986	23,174	2,296	1,262	30.2	32.8	-2.8	33.0	36.5

a. Nominal U.S. dollars deflated by the U.S. wholesale price index (1975 = 100).
b. Domestic and foreign savings may not add to gross investment owing to statistical discrepancy.
Source: The Bank of Korea, National Income Statistics, various issues.

Relative Importance of Agriculture

Until the 1960s Korea was a typical agrarian country. Almost half of its GNP was generated by agriculture, and an overwhelming proportion of its population was engaged in farming. But the vigorous industrialization and export drive that began in the early 1960s rapidly transformed the character of the economy. Between 1960 and 1986, the share of agriculture in GNP declined from 36.5 percent to 12.7 percent, and agriculture's share in total employment declined from 60.2 percent to 22.7 percent (Table 2-2). During this period, the non-agricultural sector expanded far more rapidly than the agricultural sector. Whereas total GNP expanded at an average annual rate of 8.2 percent during 1962–86, the agricultural sector grew at a rate of about 3.6 percent.

Overall, GNP increased by 20,103 billion won (in 1975 constant prices) between 1962 and 1986. Agriculture accounted for 1,856 billion won of this amount, or roughly 9.2 percent, whereas the manufacturing sector contributed 7,696 billion won in value added, or 38.3 percent. The service sector expanded because its assistance was needed in handling the increased volume of manufactures.

Although agriculture's contribution to GNP growth appears relatively small, its performance since 1962 has actually exceeded the world average. Korea probably has one of the highest levels of land productivity in the world, largely because it has a good supply of farm workers relative to its scarce land resources. However, the amount of cultivable land per household—which has remained at about 1 hectare since 1960—is probably the lowest in the world. Given the poor land resources and the limited substitutability of capital and labor, it was inevitable that agriculture would lag behind the other sectors.

Although the 3.6 percent annual increase in agricultural production has more than kept pace with the population growth rate, Korea was unable to produce enough foodgrains, feedstuff for livestock, oilseeds, and other agricultural goods to meet the growing demand created by population pressures and rising incomes. By the early 1980s Korea had almost attained self-sufficiency in rice, but its overall self-sufficiency in all grains declined from 94.5 percent in 1960 to 44.5 percent in 1986, by which time the country was relying on imports to fill more than half of its total grain requirement. In 1965 the total value of grain imports amounted to US$51 million, but by 1975 it had increased to US$722 million, and by 1986 it was up to US$1,016 million. If livestock products and processed foods are added, the country's recent bill for food imports comes to US$1.6–2.0 billion, which is roughly 5 to 8 percent of total imports.

Table 2-2. Agriculture's Share of Gross National Product, Employment, Imports, and Exports for Selected Years, 1960–86

Year	Percentage of GNP	Percentage of total employment	Agricultural imports		Agricultural exports		
			Millions of U.S. dollars	Percentage of total imports	Millions of U.S. dollars	Percentage of total exports	Percentage of total agricultural output
1960	36.5	60.2	32	9.3	4	15.2	0.3
1965	37.6	56.1	64	13.8	15	8.6	1.3
1970	26.4	49.5	319	16.0	30	3.6	1.3
1975	24.7	43.3	947	13.0	176	3.5	3.4
1980	14.4	32.3	1,797	8.1	459	2.6	5.2
1984	13.9	25.9	1,622	5.3	489	1.7	4.3
1986	12.7	22.7	1,421	4.5	541	1.6	4.5

Source: The Bank of Korea, *Economic Statistics Yearbook* and *National Income Statistics* (various issues); Ministry of Agriculture and Fisheries, *Agricultural Statistics Yearbook* (various issues).

The Macroeconomic Environment

Since the early 1960s, Korea has been governed by a highly author-
itarian and centralized government, whose principal objective has
been to achieve economic growth. The macroeconomic environment
in which this has taken place merits close attention.

Basic Government Interventions

Policymaking is in the hands of a relatively small group, which has
shaped the course of development largely through top-down planning mechanisms. The government has the authority to use any type
of instrument or intervention policy whenever it considers them
useful.

TRADE. Because Korea has few natural resources and a relatively small
domestic market, it has relied heavily on foreign trade to ensure the
success of its industries. The government's commitment to growth
through export-oriented industrialization can be seen in the continuous expansion of various export incentives, notably (a) tariff exemptions on imports of raw materials for export manufacturing (since
1959), (b) domestic indirect tax exemptions on intermediate imports
used for export production and on export sales (since 1961), (c) direct
tax reductions on income earned from exports and other foreign exchange earnings (since 1961), (d) tariff and tax exemptions for domestic supplies of intermediate goods used in export production
(since 1961), (e) wastage allowance subsidies (since 1965), (f) low-
interest preferential loans for exports (since 1965), and (g) the provision of local letters of credit and standby credit (since 1965) (Westphal and Kim 1977).

In 1973 Korea began to reduce the scope of these export incentives,
first by eliminating the reductions in direct taxes on profits from exports. Since then, wastage allowances have been decreased, and dis-
counted utility rates for exporters have been withdrawn. With the
decline in interest rates, which dropped sharply in 1982, the government decided to eliminate the credit subsidy to exporters (Yang 1986).
At the same time, the government took various steps to liberalize
imports. For example, it reduced both tariff and nontariff protection
of domestic industries and announced plans to raise the import liberalization ratio to 95.2 percent by 1988. By then, most manufactured
goods were expected to be off the restricted import list.

CENTRAL MARKET. Korea has relied on monetary policy in particular
to control aggregate demand. Its annual financial stabilization program, which focuses on monetary management, specifies year-end

money supply targets along with goals for coordinating short-run stabilization policies. In addition, most of Korea's financial institutions are under strict government supervision. Monetary authorities directly control ceilings and quotas on the size of bank loans and changes in required reserve ratios; they also oversee the deposit banks' stabilization accounts with the central bank, and handle forced sales of stabilization bonds to these banks and institutional investors. Until recently, money banks, which dominate Korea's capital market, have been no more than branches of the central bank. Their main role has been to mobilize deposits and allocate these resources, along with new credit supplies from the central bank, to the sectors, industries, and even individual borrowers designated by the government. Consequently, banks have had little say in the allocation of resources. In recent years more than 50 percent of their total loans have been classified as "directed policy loans," which means that the government itself specifies the amount and states how it is to be disbursed, often without regard to monetary stabilization (Park 1984).

LABOR MARKET. Since the early 1970s the government has also kept a close check on labor. The relatively open system of collective bargaining that had begun to unfold in the 1960s was suspended in 1971 by the enactment of the Special Law on National Security, which remains in force today. It requires labor unions to secure government approval before engaging in contract negotiations with management, and it prohibits strikes. Despite the ban on strikes, each year seems to bring numerous labor disputes, although most of them have to do with workers' rights rather than wages or working conditions. Unions have been organized in only a few industries, notably the long-established textile companies and public enterprises such as the railway, telephone, and electricity corporations. Union workers who are classified as civil servants are not permitted to strike. Even the newly emerging giant corporations have only a few unions. Consequently, unions have had little success in raising the wages of either nonorganized workers or their own members. Until the late 1970s it was market forces, not labor unions, that secured wage increases. Because Korea had an abundant supply of labor—an unlimited supply in the Lewsian sense—during the initial stages of economic development, real wages did not keep pace with labor productivity. During the 1960s, real wages rose only 5.8 percent per year in comparison with a 12.0 percent increase in the labor productivity index. After the effects of the 1973 oil shock subsided, however, real wages began to increase faster than productivity, as recovery had created an excess demand for high-quality labor. In the late 1970s the government became concerned about the possible impact of wage increases on prices and on Korea's competitiveness in international markets, since many of Korea's exports were still labor-intensive. The government there-fore decided to intervene in the wage determination process by in-troducing de facto wage guidelines. Although these guidelines did help to control the wage rates for civil servants and government-controlled banking institutions, they had little effect on private firms (Kim 1984).

Public Enterprises

Although Korea appears to lean more toward capitalism than any other developing country, its public enterprises—which handle everything from the railways, electricity, and telephones to tobacco and coal—constitute a "leading sector" in the national economy. Moreover, they have grown much faster than the economy as a whole. From 1970 to 1980, value added in the public sector grew at the rate of 14.5 percent a year, whereas the total economy grew 9.5 percent a year and the nonagricultural sector grew 12.2 percent. During these years the public sector absorbed an average of 25 percent of the country's annual gross investment.

Most public enterprises in Korea are large firms located in monop-olistic or oligopolistic markets. Since their goods and services are usu-ally priced to cover costs and yield a certain rate of profit, the private enterprises purchasing these goods and services are not indirectly subsidized. The earnings of public enterprises make a sizable con-tribution to government revenue. The tobacco monopoly alone ac-counts for about 7 percent of total government revenue every year. Approximately 10 percent of the value added by public enterprises has been sold in competitive markets, but these enterprises concen-trate mainly on import substitution and deal mostly in nontradables. Capital intensity is also high in these firms (see Mason and others 1980).

Price Control

Korea has been only partly successful in achieving its twin objectives of growth and stability. Despite its extensive system of price controls, which has been in effect since the 1960s, the rate of inflation during 1962–86, measured by the wholesale price index (WPI), has averaged more than 14.0 percent per year (it ranged from 0.2 percent to 42.1 percent). If the GNP deflator is taken into account, the rate of inflation averaged 17.0 percent per year for this period.

The Law of Price Stability passed in 1963 was designed to strengthen the government's control over prices by allowing it to have a say in practically all prices—including rents, real estate, and ser-vices. It was also permitted to prosecute anyone engaged in unfair trading activities (such as charging more than the ceiling price) or in excessive profit taking. The law also required businesses to post the prices of essential products, such as foodstuffs, medical supplies, and building materials. As the price of imported commodities began to shoot up after the oil shock, price controls merely created additional problems. Resource allocation became increasingly inefficient, supply shortages grew worse, and black markets expanded.

To deal with these problems and to reduce the impact of the oil crisis, the government in February 1974 announced a comprehensive policy package designed to stabilize prices. One of the measures was a system of moderate wage controls. In addition, greater emphasis was placed on demand management. These measures marked an important change in economic policy as they signaled a move toward overall liberalization. The comprehensive policy package left little doubt that the government now placed economic stability ahead of growth, that it wished to restore market mechanisms to guide the allocation of resources, and that it intended to give the private sector a greater role in the economy. In keeping with this market-oriented philosophy, the government relaxed price controls and reduced the number of products regulated under its price stability and fair trade laws (Park 1984).

Exchange Controls and Currency Overvaluation

During the 1950s and the first half of the 1960s, Korea maintained a complicated system of multiple exchange rates. These rates were applied in allocating both government-owned foreign exchange and U.S. aid dollars under a bidding system. In May 1964 Korea devalued its currency by 100 percent, from 130 to 256 won to the U.S. dollar. At the same time, it announced that the existing fixed rate of exchange would be converted to a unitary floating rate. The exchange rate continued to float until June 1971, when there was a 13 percent devaluation (from 326 to 370 won to the U.S. dollar). The rate remained pegged at that level until the end of 1971, but then was allowed to depreciate until June 1972, when it was again fixed, this time at 400 won to the U.S. dollar.

This rate remained in effect until December 1974, when the government announced a 21 percent devaluation (from 400 to 484 won to the U.S. dollar), which was more or less parallel with changes in purchasing power parity. After this sizable devaluation, Korea maintained a fixed exchange rate of 484 won to the U.S. dollar until the end of 1979, despite the gradual overvaluation of the won and the resulting deterioration in the country's balance of payments. To improve this balance and to slow down the rate of inflation, which was again picking up speed, Korea introduced another package of stabilization measures in 1980. This time the won was devalued by 20 percent (from 484 to 580 won to the U.S. dollar), and the exchange rate was put under a managed floating system, which is still in effect today.

Despite these various devaluations, the official exchange rate was overvalued throughout the 1960–85 period. Korea has been able to maintain the current exchange rate at a low level despite its chronic trade imbalance because of the inflow of nontrade foreign exchange and its quantitative restrictions on imports. From the mid-1950s to the late 1960s, foreign grant aid, especially from the United States, financed the bulk of imports. Other sources of foreign capital, such as short-term and long-term capital inflows and private transfers, were relatively unimportant during this period. By the early 1970s, however, foreign grant aid had also become negligible, and other forms of external financing, such as long-term loans and remittances from Korean emigrants working abroad (mainly in Japan and the United States) had begun to fill the trade gap.

Agricultural Pricing Policies

Foodgrains play such an important role in the Korean economy that the pricing of these commodities, particularly rice, has long been a central issue in the formulation of agricultural policies. It was not until the mid-1970s that a few selected noncereal products were included in the government's support programs.

History

Before 1939 Korea was a rice-exporting country, and Japan was its principal export market. The government did not intervene in grain pricing, and the prices of all agricultural products, including staple foodgrains, were determined largely by market forces. With the outbreak of the Sino-Japanese war in 1939, however, Korea found itself hard-pressed to meet Japan's military demand, and the government was forced to intervene in the grain market. Thus, it assigned grain quotas to all farmers and rationed supplies to all consumers, but it paid such low prices that farmers kept production to a minimum. This system of complete control continued until the end of World War II.

When Korea was liberated in August 1945, the U.S. military government discontinued food rationing and restored free-market transactions for all grain, even though the country's transportation, communication, banking, and market facilities were completely inadequate to meet the needs of a free economy. The U.S. military authorities apparently believed that Korea had a substantial surplus of foodgrains owing to the country's past record of rice exports. Consequently, this liberalization merely served to increase the imbalance between supply and demand. With the repatriation of approximately 1.2 million Koreans from abroad and the influx of about 2 million refugees from the Democratic People's Republic of Korea, both consumption and grain prices began to rise sharply. Fearing that this sudden switch to a peacetime system would lead to political, economic, and social confusion, the U.S. military government was obliged to impose a ceiling on the retail prices of 11 major consumer items, including rice, barley, and cotton cloth, in order to stabilize general prices and give urban consumers some protection. But these ceilings were not observed in the market; instead, hoarding and black-marketing prevailed. Consumers who had earlier depended on government rations for their staple food supplies suddenly found themselves without any source of food.

Recognizing that the ceiling prices had failed, the U.S. military authorities revised the grain policy yet again. They closed the free grain market, made rice collections from farmers compulsory, and reinstituted rationing for all urban consumers, which was continued until the period of military government ended in 1948. Although this policy helped to balance the overall supply of and demand for staple foods and to some extent alleviated the inflationary forces arising from the grain sector, it reminded the public of the rationing system that had existed during the period of Japanese rule.

The Republic of Korea was established in August 1948, and in November the new government enacted a new Grain Purchase Law. Grain producers and landowners were required to sell the government all their grain other than that required for home consumption and seed, and they were not allowed to sell on the open market. The purpose of the Grain Purchase Law was to improve farm income through government purchase at an adequate price level and to secure a stable supply of foodgrain for urban consumers. However, the government was unable to procure enough grain to fully implement rationing. The main reason was undoubtedly the low purchase price (much lower than the market price), which was all that the government could afford because it had underestimated the funds available for grain procurement, not to mention grain production costs.

Under the circumstances, a fundamental policy change was inevitable. Controls were lifted, free-market transactions were allowed, and the general rationing system was converted into a priority rationing system. First claim to the limited government-controlled grain supply was given to the military, police, government employees, and workers in critical industries, such as coal mining and the railroads. Urban consumers not receiving rations were able to purchase rice in the open market.

While continuing to enforce the partial rationing system, the govment in February 1950 enacted a Grain Management Law, which ay is the basic legal authority for Korea's foodgrain policy. The mary purpose of this law was to enable the government to secure sufficient grain from farmers to stabilize the economy. The main provisions of the law were reaffirmed in 1963, 1967, and 1970, when additional authority was given to the government, but its basic direction remained the same.

Following the outbreak of the Korean War in June 1950, the government found itself faced with the task of securing grain for the armed forces and distributing relief grain to war refugees. However, the enormous budgetary requirements of the war, together with monetary inflation and spiraling grain prices, forced it to discontinue the direct purchase of grain. Instead, an attempt was made to secure grain through a land tax in kind and a scheme to barter fertilizer for rice. In addition, farmers were reimbursed for land distributed to tenant farmers at the time of the 1950 land reform. The land tax was considerably more successful than the fertilizer barter program, primarily because the price of grain under the latter was lower than the market price.

In 1955 American grain became available under U.S. Public Law 480. These supplies enabled Korea to keep the price of staple foodgrains down. The quantity of grain imported under this program between 1956 and 1965 equaled about 8–12 percent of Korea's annual grain production. Because the aid grain was purchased with local currency, Korea was able to obtain the supplies it needed without draining its foreign exchange.

In the early 1960s the country was occupied with postwar rehabilitation, which in the view of many policymakers at the time hinged on industrialization. Thus the emphasis in both the first (1962–66) and the second (1967–71) five-year economic development plan was on rapid industrial growth. This industry-oriented strategy required massive investment in the nonagricultural sector. As a result, the government concentrated on maintaining low prices for staple foodgrains and preventing wide seasonal price fluctuations, rather than on supporting farm incomes. Government purchase prices were below market prices in almost every year of both plans. Although the low food prices for urban workers were rationalized as being an instrument of equitable income distribution, they served primarily to increase industrial profits and capital formation at the expense of farm producers. These adverse terms of trade not only impoverished the already poor rural economy but also hindered efforts to increase food production. Furthermore, they stimulated rice consumption and thus helped to widen the food gap.

Faced with an ever-increasing food shortage, a foreign exchange problem, and income disparity between urban and rural households, policymakers were obliged to give serious consideration to expanding foodgrain production and to promoting a more equitable distribution of income between the agricultural and nonagricultural sectors. The pressure for more emphasis on agriculture mounted in the early 1970s as the world food crisis worsened and grain prices soared on the world market. By then, however, the government had already begun to turn things around.

In 1969 it attempted to improve the terms of trade in favor of farm producers by raising the real purchase prices for rice and barley, and after 1970 the prices of agricultural products received by farmers rose more rapidly than the prices farmers paid for nonfarm products. These measures signaled a drastic change in farm price policy, which was now geared toward stimulating the domestic production of foodgrains and upgrading farm incomes. Because of the intermediate handling costs incurred by the government, a higher purchase price would, under normal circumstances, have led to higher consumer prices, which in turn would have pushed up the cost of living in general, particularly in urban areas. Thus, to protect the interests of farm producers and urban consumers alike, the government introduced a two-tier system for major foodgrains, with higher selling prices for farmers and lower purchase prices for urban consumers.

As the government quickly discovered, this two-tier system conflicted with its other main objectives—financial and monetary stability—because it rapidly depleted the Grain Management Fund. Inasmuch as a large portion of the deficit was being financed by an inflationary method, or long-term overdraft from the Bank of Korea, this policy became a major factor in the government's decision to increase the money supply. Since the government also had to contend with enormous budget requirements for developing heavy industry and expanding social overhead capital, the cost of the two-tier system was almost more than it could tolerate. Thus, the expanding scale of the government deficit emerged as one of the serious drawbacks of the grain price policy.

From the mid-1970s on, the government turned its attention to reducing the grain deficit. This task fell largely to farm producers, although consumers had to share some of the burden. After 1976, annual increases in the purchase price of rice began to fall behind the rate of inflation; that is, the purchase price in real terms gradually fell.

Relative Importance of Policy Objectives

Policymakers are seldom faced with simple choices when it comes to identifying economic objectives, which are usually in competition to one degree or another. Therefore, they tend to choose some combination of these objectives. In general, this is how agricultural price policy has been formulated and implemented in Korea. The price of foodgrains—especially rice, by far the most important commodity in Korea—is closely tied to various economic objectives. Those considered to have the greatest effect on agricultural pricing policy are the desire to enhance farm income, achieve food self-sufficiency, reduce foreign exchange expenditures on food imports, maintain general price stability, improve urban consumer welfare, and reduce government costs.

The first three of these objectives obviously complement one another, but are in competition with the last three. That is, a higher grain price motivates farm producers to expand their production and at the same time improves farm income. Expanded production and reduced consumption due to higher prices may help to reduce a country's imports of foreign grain. However, the higher grain price may have just the opposite effect on prices in general, as well as on government costs and urban living expenditures.

Depending on how the government operates the foodgrain program, these competitive objectives need not always be in conflict. For instance, a two-price system for grain may simultaneously achieve two seemingly conflicting objectives. At the same time, the overall result may conflict with yet another objective, for example, that of reducing government costs. Which objective will be given the highest weight depends upon the policymakers' preferences. These in turn tend to be governed by the social, political, and economic situation at any given time.

Within the context of the tradeoff between rural and industrial concerns in major policy decisions, the Korean government has historically given higher priority to general price stability, to the benefit of the urban and industrial sector, except during the support period of 1969–75. Table 2-3 shows how the relative importance of four types of policy objectives changed in Korea between 1950 and 1986 by numerical weight.

Table 2-3. Relative Importance of Policy Objectives, 1950–86
(by numerical weight)

Objective	1950–69	1970–75	1976–86
Farm income, food self-sufficiency	0.3	0.5	0.2
Foreign exchange	n.a.	0.2	0.2
Price stability, urban consumer welfare	0.5	0.3	0.3
Government costs	0.2	n.a.	0.3

n.a. Not available.
Source: Authors' estimates.

Price Intervention

To achieve its objectives, the government has intervened in agricultural affairs at all levels and has established an extensive system of public and semipublic institutions to deal with agricultural issues.

The Ministry of Agriculture and Fisheries (MAF) has primary responsibility for formulating agricultural policies and various development programs in rural areas. Other ministries—such as the Ministry of Home Affairs, the Ministry of Social Affairs, the Economic Planning Board, and the Ministry of Construction—are also concerned with improving rural infrastructure, employment, rural industrialization, and living conditions. Various bureaus within the Ministry of Agriculture and Fisheries are in charge of planning budgets, foodgrain and other price support programs, land and water resource development, fertilizer distribution, credit programs, marketing, and imports and exports of agricultural products.

Three other organizations that are directly concerned with agricultural pricing policies and product marketing are the National Agricultural Cooperatives Federation (NACF), the National Livestock Cooperatives Federation (NLCF), and the Agricultural and Fisheries Development Corporation (AFDC). The agricultural cooperatives act more as a monopolistic arm of the government than as a farmers' voluntary organization. Farmers exercise little control over the activities of these organizations and have only a small investment in their capital structure.

The NACF is a national organization consisting of 1,476 local primary cooperatives for the producers of the country's primary grains and 42 special-purpose cooperatives for the marketing of primarily horticultural products. The NACF handles matters connected with part of the grain supply for which the MAF supervises price support and distribution. For example, it was given a monopoly in fertilizer distribution. It also provides farm credit, markets farm products, and provides various agricultural inputs on its own account. Economic and political conditions at the time the NACF was formed in 1961 made it heavily dependent on the government for financial support.

The NLCF was established in 1980, after being consolidated with the Livestock Industry Development Corporation, which was established as a government agency in 1978. The NLCF has the authority to provide livestock development loans to its members and to import and export livestock products under the MAF-determined supply and demand program. It has control of livestock development funds, which are used to finance technological and infrastructural support for livestock development and credit to farmers for the purchase of dairy and beef cattle.

The AFDC, which was created in 1968, provides loans for the development of facilities for processing, storing, and marketing agricultural, forestry, and fisheries products. It obtains most of its resources from the government and from international organizations such as the World Bank. In addition to supervising loans, the AFDC has control over the agricultural products price stabilization funds used to manage buffer stocks of selected agricultural commodities, such as peanuts, red pepper, sesame seeds, soybeans, garlic, and onions. Yearly specified amounts are procured at harvest time and are stored in AFDC warehouses for sale during the off-season, when prices are higher. The AFDC has complete authority to import and export the quantities needed to maintain buffer stocks, depending on the domestic crop situation. In most cases, it incurs a loss in handling domestic products, but makes a profit on imports.

Major Instruments of Price Intervention

The Korean government relies on several instruments to carry out its price policies: (a) purchase and price controls on staple foodgrains, (b) a monopoly on fertilizer distribution, (c) agricultural credit controls, (d) a buffer stock of noncereal farm products, (e) ceiling prices on beef and pork, and (f) quantitative import restrictions and tariffs.

The government acquires grain from farmers through various programs at prices set during or after the harvest season. The major acquisition programs consist of direct purchase, rice-fertilizer barter, and the collection of harvest taxes in kind. In recent years almost all grains have been acquired through direct cash purchases. The government's supplies are directed mainly toward military use, government institutions, prisoners and detainees, relief programs, seed grain distribution, grain loan, price stabilization, and contingency or emergency programs. The wide range of grain programs in Korea is a reflection of the chronic shortages experienced by a population dependent on a cereal diet. Most Koreans believe that direct government intervention in grain procurement and distribution is necessary to maintain economic stability and to ensure a steady flow of grain supplies to consumers. Many also believe that the government should take whatever action may be appropriate or necessary for this end.

In the early years of the program, the government acquired mainly rice, but it recently has expanded the share of barley substantially. Whenever the government has been unable to secure sufficient supplies of domestic grain, the gap has been filled by imports. During the 1950s the government share of total rice marketed was less than 10 percent, but since then it has expanded to 30–50 percent. The government handled almost 90 percent of the barley marketed in 1986.

The Monopoly on Fertilizer Distribution

In view of Korea's limited land resources, the only means of improving overall agricultural production is to increase land productivity. In part, this means increasing the use of fertilizer. Since the early 1960s the government has made an all-out effort to do just that by providing price subsidies and purchase credits. As a result, fertilizer consumption (in nutrient terms) more than doubled between 1965 and 1986, from 393,000 metric tons to 825,000 metric tons, which equals an average annual growth rate of 5 percent.

This rapid increase in fertilizer consumption led to the construction of a series of large-scale fertilizer plants. Consequently, by the mid-1970s the country had surpassed self-sufficiency and was producing export surpluses. In the early 1980s production averaged 1.4 million metric tons (in nutrient terms) a year, which exceeded the annual domestic requirement by more than 600,000 metric tons. From 1976 on, 35 percent of fertilizer production was exported.

Since the enactment of the Fertilizer Control Law in 1962, all fertilizer marketing, including the determination of procurement requirements and pricing, has been completely under government control. The government purchases fertilizer from the manufacturers and then sells it at a lower price to farmers. Fertilizer exports are sold at a still lower price. This scheme is exactly the same as the two-price system for major foodgrains discussed earlier.

Agricultural Credit Control

The NACF has sole responsibility for administering the government's agricultural loans. No other institution is authorized to borrow from the government or the central bank for agricultural purposes, and almost all NACF programs are required to follow procedures and guidelines issued by the government. For instance, NACF's annual business program must be approved by the Ministry of Agriculture and Fisheries and the Ministry of Finance, which also determine the level of resources that will be made available to the NACF. They then allocate credit to specific programs and activities in accordance with government priorities at interest rates also set by the government. Agricultural credit is financed from government funds, borrowings from the Bank of Korea, agricultural bonds, deposits received, and the foreign loan fund. Although the government's financial support for agricultural development has expanded steadily in absolute terms, it has been insufficient to meet the rapidly rising demands for medium- and long-term farm loans brought about by the acceleration of agricultural development.

BUFFER STOCK PROGRAM. The buffer stock program is intended primarily to prevent excessive price fluctuations during the marketing season. This program was set in motion in 1970, when the government began to purchase set amounts of selected agricultural commodities at government-set prices during the harvest seasons. They were then sold during the off-season, when their prices were higher. The selling prices are determined on the basis of the purchase prices plus handling and storing costs, but the prevailing market prices are also taken into consideration. The products stockpiled under the program in 1971 included red pepper, garlic, and sesame seeds. Later, peanuts, eggs, soybeans, onions, and laver (processed seaweed) were added to the list.

Because the stockpiling program requires a lump-sum release of government funds (through the Agricultural and Fisheries Development Corporation) so that crops can be purchased in a short period of time, the government initiated a marketing-regulation program in 1972 to complement the stockpiling program. Under this program, the AFDC makes advance payments to producers—instead of buying crops directly from them—to enable them to hold their products off the market during the harvest seasons, when prices tend to be depressed.

CEILING PRICE SYSTEM FOR BEEF AND PORK. In order to stabilize prices, the government for a long time subjected the prices of beef and pork to controls under an "administration-guided" price system. This system linked the consumer price of beef and pork to the price of live cattle and hogs in the producing areas as well as to the wholesale price of carcasses at the auction markets. However, meat prices failed to stabilize owing to illegal transactions caused by oscillations in demand and supply and by the inadequate marketing structure.

In August 1981 the government deregulated the consumer prices of meat, leaving market forces to determine the outcome. At the same time, it decided to restrict the sale of imported meat, mainly beef, to auction at the wholesale markets; that is, meat retailers were allowed to set consumer prices by adding marketing costs and appropriate profit margins to wholesale prices at auction. The government apparently believed that the level of domestic beef production plus the 25,000 metric tons imported in 1979, combined with a sizable decline in domestic demand due to a prolonged economic recession, caused the price of beef to drop considerably. As a result, domestic supplies fell sharply in 1981 and beef prices soared, despite large imports.

In response, the government introduced "posted prices," which set a ceiling on the retail prices of beef and pork. This system is still in effect, although the ceiling has occasionally been raised, depending on the demand and supply situation. Whereas the wholesale price of carcasses is determined at the daily auctions held at the livestock wholesale markets (located at slaughterhouses) in major cities, the retail price of beef and pork is directly controlled by the government.

QUANTITATIVE IMPORT RESTRICTIONS AND TARIFFS. Despite the substantial liberalization of imports of manufactured items in recent years, most important agricultural products are still on the restricted list under Korea's highly protective agricultural policy. Out of 793 CCN eight-digit agricultural commodities, 250 items were still subject to quantitative restrictions in 1986. Included in these categories were rice, feed corn, corn for industrial use, soybeans, milo, compound feeds, beef, and pork. Only eligible importers who are licensed by the relevant ministries, mainly the MAF and Fisheries, are allowed to import these items. However, such licenses are issued only when domestic producers cannot adequately meet demand.

As for tariffs, a uniform rate of 10 percent had been levied on all imports until 1950, when the government introduced a multitariff system with different rates for different commodities. The legal tariffs now range from 5 to 30 percent or more of the import value, including 5 percent for rice and wheat, 7 percent for feed corn, 10 percent for soybeans, 22 percent for meatstuffs, and 30 percent for corn for industrial use. In actuality, however, a significant proportion of the tariffs on imports of major grains, such as rice, wheat, and feed corn, are manipulated on the grounds that it is necessary to stabilize prices in the domestic market.

Historically, tariffs on agricultural imports have not been used as a policy tool to raise government revenue, nor to maintain domestic producer prices by insulating domestic prices from world prices. Therefore, as far as agricultural commodities are concerned, tariffs per se have not been a deterrent to imports. Rather, quantitative import restrictions have become the chief mechanism used to ensure that domestic price targets will not be undercut by competition from cheaper imports.

Phases of Intervention

The evolution of price intervention in Korea can be divided into five phases, according to the extent to which price interventions were used, their complexity, and their direction. In most countries, these phases proceed as follows. Phase 1 is characterized by government intervention in a limited number of important products and/or inputs, but the rates of subsidization or taxation on the products are relatively low. In phase 2, the complexity of the interventions increases, both with respect to the number of subsidized or taxed products and the types of instruments used. Phase 3 is a period of transition in which

government attempts to reform the system of agricultural price
tervention. This may be part of a more general reform effort to
emedy the distortions in other economic policies, such as international trade, the exchange rate, monetary policies, and so on. This
type of reform effort may result in the elimination of price controls
for some products, so that their relative price will be brought into line
with their equivalent border prices. If phase 3 is successful, it is normally followed by phase 4, which is marked by a reduction in the
number and/or severity of interventions. Phase 5 is characterized by
a virtual absence of direct price interventions. In this phase, the relative internal prices of agricultural products at the producer and consumer levels are approximately equal to their equivalent relative border prices (Krueger, Schiff, and Valdés 1985).

Korea's agricultural pricing policies during 1950–69 belong to phase
1. Price interventions were limited to staple foods, notably rice and
barley, and fertilizer. The prices of these commodities were by far the
most important ones under government control, although the degree
of market control varied from year to year. The Grain Management
Law enacted in 1950 gave the government full authority to regulate
the prices of staple foods through its procurement program. The market share of government-controlled rice in total marketing was less
than 10 percent during the 1950s but expanded to 20–25 percent during the 1960s.

From the early 1970s on, price intervention moved into phase 2 as
an increasing number of products and inputs came under government
regulation. In addition to rice and barley, buffer stocks of noncereal
products such as red pepper, garlic, sesame seeds, peanuts, and eggs
were established in 1970. Pesticides and farm machinery were added
to the list of subsidized inputs. The government steadily increased
the purchase price of rice and barley with a view to increasing food
production and reducing the urban-rural income gap. As a consequence, the average effective rate of protection for rice rose from −26
percent in 1962–69 to 39 percent in 1970–79. However, the government did not call for a comparable rise in the prices of rice and barley
on urban markets. As a result, the grain account showed a substantial
deficit, which had to be made up out of overdrafts from the central
bank. Although the government had begun to liberalize imports of
a wide range of manufactured commodities, imports of most tradable
agricultural products remained under the import quota system.

In the early 1980s the government took a great leap forward by
reducing both tariff and nontariff protection of manufacturing industries. It announced a plan to raise the import liberalization ratio
to 95.2 percent by 1988. With the adoption of a floating system in
1980, foreign exchange rates began to depreciate and have continued
to do so ever since. In this sense Korea can be said to be in a stage

of transition between phase 4 and phase 5 with respect to industrial policies. In contrast, the level of protection for agriculture has been steadily increasing in Korea. Producer prices of farm products continue to be maintained at levels far above border prices, and most agricultural commodities are still on the list of restricted imports. In 1980–86 the effective rate of protection for rice rose to 81 percent and that for beef to 87 percent.

At present, the government seems to be making no effort to reduce government intervention in pricing policies and to move to phase 3. Hence, as far as agricultural pricing policy is concerned, Korea is still in phase 2.

Measures of Intervention

Three crops and two livestock products were selected for the analysis: rice, barley, soybeans, beef, and pork. Together, these five products constituted almost 70 percent of the total value of Korea's agricultural output in 1986. Border prices for each commodity were calculated using the f.o.b. export prices for those years in which Korea exported (after subtracting transport costs to major ports to get the producer-price equivalents) and the c.i.f. import prices for those years in which Korea imported. The import prices of Japan or Hong Kong were used as the proxies for border prices for those years in which Korea did not export or import significant quantities.

DIRECT PRICE INTERVENTION. In measuring the net effect of direct intervention, we converted both c.i.f. and f.o.b. prices into domestic currency at the official exchange rate (not at the effective exchange rate.[1] The average estimated nominal rate of protection (NPR_D) for producer prices and consumer prices for six subperiods between 1960 and 1986 are presented in Table 2-4. The results indicate that throughout much of this period the government protected the production of rice, barley, soybeans, and beef relative to the production of nonagricultural goods. Only in the case of pork did the producer price policy cause a decline in the nominal rate of protection; this occurred during 1980–86. The average nominal rate of protection NPR_D for rice rose from 45.4 percent during 1960–64 to over 100 percent during 1985–86, while that for beef rose from 14.2 percent to 25.6 percent. In contrast, the NPR_D for pork declined from 33.4 percent to 27.3 percent during the same period. This decline implies that the efficiency of Korea's swine-raising industry has steadily improved.

The picture for consumer prices of the same products is somewhat similar. Rice, soybeans, beef, and pork were protected throughout 1960–86, which means that consumers were persistently taxed with

Table 2-4. Effect of Direct Price Intervention, 1960–86
(percent)

Subperiod	Relative producer price						Relative consumer price					
	Rice	Barley	Soybeans	Beef	Pork		Rice	Barley	Soybeans	Beef	Pork	
1960–64	45.4	82.9	65.8	14.2	33.4		25.8	29.1	32.8	42.4	24.0	
1965–69	3.2	2.8	51.3	19.2	42.5		11.0	-4.8	22.4	33.1	43.8	
1970–74	44.5	34.8	61.2	35.2	59.6		17.6	3.0	30.7	55.4	61.8	
1975–79	108.5	86.6	90.0	111.0	33.9		45.9	-7.3	40.2	76.6	36.6	
1980–84	99.5	117.6	-238.2	138.4	11.1		35.8	-5.5	89.5	95.5	6.7	
1985–86	101.8	220.4	271.6	25.6	27.3		29.4	24.1	105.5	39.8	12.2	

Source: Moon and Kang (1989).

respect to these four products. Only in the case of barley were consumers subsidized (in 1965-69, 1975–79, and 1980–84).

INDIRECT PRICE INTERVENTION. The relative prices of agricultural products in Korea were also affected by exchange rate overvaluation, import tariffs, and quantitative restrictions on both exports and imports. Table 2-5 shows the effect of this indirect intervention (NPR$_I$) for producer prices and consumer prices for six subperiods between 1960 and 1986. Since producers and consumers are equally affected by trade and exchange rate policy, the magnitude of the indirect effects in relative terms is the same for both producer and consumer prices. It appears that indirect price interventions had a negative effect on both producer and consumer prices throughout the period 1960–86. In other words, the equivalent border prices used in measuring the effect of direct price intervention were underestimated by the ratios calculated in the last column of Table 2-5, owing to overvaluation of the won. As a result, the border prices of the five products selected for study were on average 40 percent lower during 1960–64 than they would otherwise have been; they were about 28 percent lower during 1970–74, and 1.5 percent lower during 1985–86.

A new series of product prices and a nonagricultural price index, adjusted to indirect price interventions, were used to calculate the effect of direct and indirect intervention combined (NPR$_T$) for each product (see Table 2-5). The estimated results indicate that all five products were subjected to negative protection during the 1960s. But under the increasing subsidy in effect since the early 1970s, the NPR$_T$ has been steadily increasing for rice, barley, soybeans, and beef, but not for pork. The NPR$_T$ for rice rose from -21.0 percent during 1960–64 to 101.1 percent during 1985–86, that for soybean from -12.1 percent to a high of 267.3 percent, and that for beef from -39.7 percent to 22.8 percent. In the case of pork, the protection rate increased from -27.1 percent during 1960–64 to 25.6 percent during 1985–86.

The combined effects of product and input price intervention (including exchange rate policy) on value added can be measured as the percentage difference between the value added (VA) expressed in domestic market prices and the value added (VA*) expressed in border prices converted at the equilibrium exchange rate (E^*). Three tradable inputs were considered in this study: fertilizer, pesticides, and farm machinery. These items account for approximately 85 percent of the inputs purchased for the production of rice, barley, and soybeans (excluding the costs of hired labor and irrigation water). Other costs for items such as seeds, miscellaneous materials, and depreciation on farm facilities were excluded because they are nontradable and because these costs are negligible as individual items. Cornfeed was the only input considered for beef and pork in this analysis.

Table 2-5. Effect of Total Intervention, 1960–86
(percent)

Subperiod	Relative producer price					Relative consumer price					Indirect effect (NPR_I)
	Rice	Barley	Soybeans	Beef	Pork	Rice	Barley	Soybeans	Beef	Pork	
1960–64	−21.0	1.7	−12.1	−39.7	−27.1	−27.1	−10.1	−15.0	−10.4	−23.1	−39.8
1965–69	−32.8	−29.9	2.9	−19.2	−3.5	−35.9	−36.6	−7.4	−1.1	8.3	−32.0
1970–74	3.5	−3.2	15.1	−3.1	14.1	−21.8	−21.5	2.3	20.8	27.0	−28.2
1975–79	73.1	55.3	57.9	75.8	10.2	24.2	−22.7	24.5	62.5	17.1	−17.8
1980–84	73.9	91.4	178.2	110.5	−5.3	42.0	−17.6	78.9	79.1	−4.2	−12.4
1985–86	101.1	217.8	267.3	22.8	25.6	27.9	22.4	103.6	37.6	11.0	−1.5

Source: Moon and Kang (1989).

For prices of fertilizer, the average unit value (per metric ton) was used for both domestic and border prices obtained from the total value of consumption divided by the total quantity used. The c.i.f. import price was used for imports of fertilizer (before 1972) and the f.o.b. export price for exports (after 1972). For pesticides, the domestic and border prices were simply assumed to be the same, for it is almost impossible to obtain reasonably comparable prices when a large number of different kinds are in use and traded. In the case of farm machinery, the widely used 8-horsepower tiller was thought to be representative of both domestic and border prices. In the actual calculations, we used the depreciation cost inclusive of all types of farm implements in use, owing to the difficulty of isolating the depreciation for each type. For feed corn, the border price (evaluated at official rate E_0) plus 7 percent tariff was taken as the domestic price paid by livestock farmers. The estimated results are given in Table 2-6.

The estimated effective rates of protection (ERPS) for rice, barley, and soybeans did not differ significantly from the NPR$_T$s for all corresponding subperiods. This is because the distortion in the price of fertilizer was not large enough to alter the ERPs, which had only a negligible share in the total value of production. In the case of rice, for instance, the cost of fertilizer constitutes only 4 to 5 percent of the producer price. In the case of beef and pork, the estimated ERPs were higher than the NPR$_T$s for all subperiods. This implies that livestock farmers by and large benefited from using the feed mix containing cheaper imported corn. Overall, trade and exchange rate policies exerted a squeeze on agriculture in the 1960s, while agricultural pricing and trade policies since the early 1970s indicate increasing protection.

The Effects of Price Intervention

Price intervention in Korea has had noticeable effects throughout the agricultural sector—on output, consumption, foreign exchange earnings, intersectoral transfers, and income distribution.

Table 2-6. Effect of Total Intervention on Relative Value Added (ERP), 1962–86
(percent)

Period	Rice	Barley	Soybeans	Beef	Pork
1962–64	−16.4	0.6	−5.8	−31.5	11.7
1965–69	−31.8	−27.3	6.0	−12.7	11.7
1970–74	4.9	−0.2	17.0	1.1	24.1
1975–79	72.6	54.3	56.7	78.2	13.4
1980–84	73.7	90.3	196.8	111.9	−3.6
1985–86	98.7	212.5	262.3	23.5	26.9

Source: Moon and Kang (1989).

Agricultural Output

Given the elasticity of supply of each product with respect to the various relative prices, one can estimate the effect of government intervention on the output of each product, both in the short run and long run. The supply elasticity was measured by fitting the Nerlovian lagged supply function to the observed data (see Moon and Kang 1989, chap. 4).

The estimated elasticity coefficients were used to measure both the direct and total effects of price intervention on aggregate output. Estimates of the total long-run effect were based on the cumulative effects of past price changes rather than on long-run elasticity.

Direct intervention appears to have had positive short-run effects on all five products from 1962 to 1986, and the magnitude of these effects increased over this period (Table 2-7). During 1962–64 the average direct short-run output effects were 11.7 percent for rice, 30.7 percent for barley, 10.7 percent for soybeans, and 2.7 percent for beef. As nominal protection intensified, the output effects rose to 22.4 percent, 66.2 percent, 73.0 percent, and 25.4 percent, respectively. In the case of pork, however, the effect on output was somewhat different. Pork output increased by an average 16.3 percent during 1962–64 and 39.2 percent during 1970–74, but the increase in output then declined to only 10.4 percent in 1985–86. The cumulative effects were even greater than the short-run effects. In 1985–86, for example, rice output increased by an average 44.0 percent, barley output by 204.1 percent, soybean output by 231.0 percent, beef output by 82.4 percent, and pork output by 21.0 percent.

When the effects of both direct and indirect intervention are combined to take into account the overvaluation of the won, the output effects are negative for all products throughout the 1960s; for the remaining years, the effects are substantially reduced. Estimates of total short-run output (Table 2-8) indicate that rice production during the 1962–64 period decreased by an average of about 11.0 percent, barley production by 7.7 percent, soybean production by 8.0 percent, beef production by 3.7 percent, and pork production by 20.3 percent. Overvaluation of the exchange rate more than offset the effect of direct price intervention in this period. Although overvaluation persisted throughout the remaining period, it did not offset the effect of direct price intervention after the mid-1970s, with the result that the overall effect of intervention on output was positive. During 1985–86 the total short-run output effect averaged 20.6 percent for rice, 66.4 percent for barley, 70.3 percent for soybeans, 22.9 percent for beef, and 8.7 percent for pork.

Table 2-7. Change in Agricultural Production Due to Direct Price Intervention, 1962–86
(percent)

Subperiod	Short-run effect					Long-run (cumulative) effect				
	Rice	Barley	Soybeans	Beef	Pork	Rice	Barley	Soybeans	Beef	Pork
1962–64	11.7	30.7	10.7	2.7	16.3	16.0	31.8	18.3	5.0	25.0
1965–69	2.2	5.6	15.8	2.4	18.8	7.0	44.4	41.2	3.0	39.0
1970–74	12.8	18.6	20.0	10.0	39.2	20.0	43.8	66.0	21.8	93.0
1975–79	22.0	23.0	19.6	22.0	23.2	34.8	58.2	63.2	42.0	69.8
1980–84	32.4	58.6	60.8	34.6	5.2	62.6	168.2	154.6	82.2	26.0
1985–86	23.4	66.2	73.0	25.4	10.4	44.0	204.1	231.0	82.4	21.0

Source: Moon and Kang (1989).

Table 2-8. Change in Agricultural Production Due to Total Price Intervention, 1962–86
(percent)

Subperiod	Short-run effect					Long-run (cumulative) effect				
	Rice	Barley	Soybeans	Beef	Pork	Rice	Barley	Soybeans	Beef	Pork
1962–64	−11.0	−7.7	−8.0	−8.0	−20.3	−8.0	3.3	−5.3	−15.0	−18.0
1965–69	−11.6	−13.8	−2.2	−9.4	−9.4	−14.4	−13.0	2.4	−19.6	−15.0
1970–74	−0.8	−1.4	4.8	−2.6	10.0	−2.4	−10.8	21.0	−5.8	25.2
1975–79	14.2	12.8	12.2	14.0	9.6	17.4	14.5	30.0	19.0	26.2
1980–84	22.8	43.0	48.8	25.4	−4.8	45.0	118.8	117.4	60.0	−0.4
1985–86	20.6	66.4	70.3	22.9	8.7	28.9	173.8	201.0	68.3	6.0

Source: Moon and Kang (1989).

Consumption

The estimated magnitude of the effects of direct and total intervention on aggregate consumption of each product is given in Table 2-9. The effect of direct price intervention was to reduce the consumption of rice, soybeans, and beef in nearly all years from 1962 to 1986. Although pork consumption declined until the mid-1970s, it increased thereafter. However, the total effect (direct plus indirect) resulted in quite a different pattern. In earlier years, when the exchange rate overvaluation was relatively high, rice and soybean consumption increased, but as overvaluation declined the level of consumption also declined. In the case of beef, consumption declined in most years, whereas for barley and pork it fell in the earlier years of the study period but increased in the later years.

Foreign Exchange Earnings

In a country like Korea, which has long depended on imports of food and feedgrain, changes in the production and consumption of tradable agricultural products, along with changes in the use of tradable inputs, inevitably affect foreign exchange spending. In order to isolate the direct foreign exchange implications of these various changes, we assumed that agricultural price policy is not affected by the magnitude of foreign exchange availability. We also assumed that nonagricultural imports and exports are independent of agricultural price policies.

The direct short-run and long-run effect on foreign exchange gain or loss due to price interventions was measured for each product under the above assumptions (see Table 2-10). Changes in the use of tradable inputs (fertilizer for rice and barley, and soybeans and corn for beef and pork production) are assumed to be proportional to the change in output of each product.

Direct price intervention had a positive effect on foreign exchange earnings, both in the short run and long run throughout 1962–86 (Table 2-11). The amount of foreign exchange gained due to direct long-run intervention reached about 155.0 percent of total exports during 1962–64, but dropped to 5.2 percent of total exports in 1985–86. Although this helped increase the use of inputs (fertilizer and feed corn), the positive effect on output more than offset this negative effect, so that a positive effect was registered for the overall study period.

When the effects of direct intervention are combined with those of indirect intervention, the results show a loss of foreign exchange, or an increase in imports, until the mid-1970s, but a gain thereafter through 1986. In other words, without direct and indirect intervention, there would have been a saving in foreign exchange until the

Table 2-9. Effect on Consumption Due to Direct Price Intervention, 1962–86
(percent)

Subperiod	Short-run effect					Long-run (cumulative) effect				
	Rice	Barley	Soybeans	Beef	Pork	Rice	Barley	Soybeans	Beef	Pork
1962–64	−2.0	1.7	−6.7	−11.0	−1.3	4.7	−6.3	1.3	−0.7	2.7
1965–69	−0.6	0.6	−6.6	−2.8	−6.6	6.2	−5.2	1.4	5.4	−2.2
1970–74	−5.8	7.6	−7.4	−10.2	−8.8	3.6	−3.4	−0.4	−1.6	−4.4
1975–79	−14.8	23.4	−21.2	−48.2	3.2	−12.6	17.8	−6.6	−39.6	5.2
1980–84	−14.6	17.4	−23.0	−73.2	13.2	−12.2	16.8	−20.2	−64.2	13.0
1985–86	−5.0	5.8	−25.1	−57.6	9.9	−4.3	5.0	−23.8	−54.0	10.1

Source: Moon and Kang (1989).

Table 2-10. Effect of Price Intervention on Foreign Exchange Earnings, as a Percentage of Total Exports, 1962–86

Period	Annual export[a]	Direct effect		Total effect	
		Short-run	Long-run	Short-run	Long-run
1962–64	86.9	113.5	155.0	− 120.7	− 83.3
1965–69	364.7	7.6	29.4	− 40.8	− 51.0
1970–74	2,242.5	9.8	15.4	− 1.6	− 2.4
1975–79	10,121.8	7.3	10.0	4.7	5.5
1980–84	22,860.4	5.8	8.2	4.4	6.2
1985–86	32,498.8	3.5	5.2	3.5	4.1

a. Millions of U.S. dollars.
Source: Moon and Kang (1989).

mid-1970s, owing to the increased production in most years, but foreign exchange spending would have increased thereafter. During 1962–64, for example, the net loss of foreign exchange due to total long-run effects was about 83.3 percent of total exports, but during 1985–86 there was a 4.1 percent gain.

Intersectoral Transfer of Resources

The transfer of resources to the agricultural sector from the nonagricultural sector was quantified for two main categories: price-related transfers and nonprice transfers. The former category includes implicit price subsidies and agricultural credit subsidies that would have been realized in the absence of government intervention (or under the free-trade situation), and the latter includes actual public expen-

Table 2-11. Real Transfers into (+) and out of (−) Agriculture as a Percentage of Agricultural GDP, 1962–86

Period	Nonprice transfer		Price-related transfer		Total transfer	
	Direct effect	Total effect	Direct effect	Total effect	Direct effect	Total effect
1962–64	0.5	0.3	22.1	− 16.9	22.6	− 16.5
1965–69	2.7	2.4	4.4	− 29.9	7.1	− 27.5
1970–74	5.4	5.0	16.9	− 1.4	22.3	3.6
1975–79	5.3	5.2	28.7	21.0	34.0	26.2
1980–84	8.2	8.0	30.2	26.1	38.4	34.1
1985–86	7.3	7.0	24.8	23.9	32.1	30.9

Source: Moon and Kang (1989).

ditures in the agricultural sector. The farmland tax and miscellaneous public charges are the only types of direct income transfer out of agriculture. Table 2-11 presents the estimated "real" transfer of resources (expressed by the ratio of the transfer to total agricultural GDP) between the agricultural and nonagricultural sectors under a free-trade situation.

The results show a modest flow of resources into the agricultural sector owing to direct price intervention throughout the study period. The sum of price-related transfers to the agricultural sector due to value added in real terms (1980 = 100.0) accounted for 22.1 percent of the GDP originating in the agricultural sector during 1962–64, but the relative share increased to 24.8 percent during 1985–86. If non-price transfers (or public investment in agriculture) are included, the relative share in agricultural GDP was 22.6 percent during 1962–64 and 32.1 percent during 1985–86.

However, if one takes into account the impact of overvaluation of the exchange rate, the pattern of resource flow is completely different. The negative figures throughout the 1960s indicate that resources were extracted from the agricultural sector and channeled into the nonagricultural sector during these years. As a share of agricultural GDP, the resource flow from the agricultural to the nonagricultural sector totaled 16.5 percent in 1962–64 and 27.5 percent in 1965–69. This reverse flow of resources in the 1960s is due mainly to the persistent overvaluation of the domestic currency. Between 1970 and 1986 the overvaluation gradually decreased, with the result that price subsidies for major food crops intensified, and resources flowed back to the agricultural sector and consistently increased thereafter. The relative share of price-related transfers in agricultural GDP reached a peak of 23.9 percent in 1985–86. When added to the public investment portion, the share increased to 30.9 percent in the same period, which implies that nearly one-third of agricultural GDP came from the non-agricultural sector during 1985–86.

Overall, Korea's agricultural pricing policies produced a modest financial flow from the nonagricultural to the agricultural sector throughout the 1962–86 period, but the country's trade and exchange rate policies more than offset this flow into agriculture.

Income Distribution

One concern in this analysis is the income distribution that occurred between small and large farms in rural areas and between low- and high-income groups in urban areas. Although the same price was applied, the relative benefits or loss due to changes in relative prices differed among these categories. The distributional effects were measured by the proportional changes in real income of each farm and urban group due to price intervention. The household was taken as the basic unit in our calculations. Farm producers were classified into three groups on the basis of farm size: small-scale farms (less than 0.5 hectares), medium-scale farms (0.5–1.5 hectares), and large-scale farms (1.5 hectares or more).[2] Urban households were classified into three groups on the basis of the size of income: the lowest three deciles were considered the low-income group, the middle four deciles the middle-income group, and the highest three deciles the high-income group. Table 2-12 presents the real income effect of both direct intervention and total intervention in rural areas. Table 2-13 gives the real income effect of both direct intervention and total intervention in urban areas.

PRODUCER INCOME. The benefits of a government's protection policy can be measured by the proportional changes in real income to farmers beyond what they would have received in the absence of that policy. Large farms normally produce more and sell a larger portion of what they produce than do small farms. Hence, the benefits of price support tend to be more heavily concentrated among large farms. The results presented in Table 2-12 support this hypothesis.

The immediate distributional benefit that small farmers gained through an increase in real income during 1962–64 amounted to 12.3 percent of the increase in the absence of protection, whereas the benefit to the large farmer was 15.0 percent. The difference in the absolute amount of the gain in real income (1980 prices) was much greater. The net increase in real income for small farmers was 73,900 won per household, whereas that for large farmers was 340,000 won, or more than four times more. Over time, the immediate distributional impact has become greater as more and more producer prices have become subsidized. The relative net benefit to small farmers during 1985–86 was 7.8 percent of 301,000 won per household in absolute amounts, and that for the large farmer was 36.9 percent of 1,437,300 won (Moon and Kang 1989).

If overvaluation of the exchange rate is taken into account, the size and pattern of the distributional impact changes during the study period. As shown in Table 2-12, the distributional effects for small farmers were negative during most of the 1960s and were negative for medium and large farmers throughout the decade, but they became positive for all three groups after the early 1970s. During 1965–69 the immediate distributional loss for small farmers in terms of the decrease in real income was 7.0 percent of what it would have been in the absence of price support and the exchange rate policy, whereas the loss for the large farmer was 24.5 percent. During 1985–86 the real income of small farmers rose 6.6 percent and that of large farmers 34.3 percent.

Table 2-12. Change in Rural Real Income Due to Direct and Total Price Intervention, 1962–86
(percent)

Period	Instantaneous effect			Short-run effect			Long-run effect		
	Small-scale farmers	Medium-scale farmers	Large-scale farmers	Small-scale farmers	Medium-scale farmers	Large-scale farmers	Small-scale farmers	Medium-scale farmers	Large-scale farmers
Direct intervention									
1962–64	12.3	20.0	15.0	16.4	26.8	34.7	16.1	25.8	31.4
1965–69	5.9	8.3	8.9	8.2	12.8	16.1	11.3	15.3	17.9
1970–74	15.7	28.6	35.2	16.4	35.9	47.4	21.0	41.9	55.4
1975–79	12.3	23.0	40.0	16.7	40.3	60.9	17.5	39.9	59.7
1980–84	15.7	37.1	57.7	18.5	44.0	73.8	16.6	41.7	73.5
1985–86	7.8	22.5	36.9	10.3	28.4	46.7	12.4	33.3	55.4
Total intervention									
1962–64	9.9	-2.7	-8.8	7.3	-5.9	-12.6	6.2	-7.3	-14.2
1965–69	-7.0	-17.8	-24.5	-9.3	-22.9	-30.3	-12.8	-26.9	-34.3
1970–74	9.3	9.3	9.6	9.0	8.9	8.9	6.2	5.4	5.5
1975–79	9.1	20.3	30.2	10.7	24.2	37.4	11.6	26.1	40.2
1980–84	14.0	30.4	47.9	15.9	35.7	56.0	17.7	39.9	64.5
1985–86	6.6	20.7	34.3	8.9	26.1	43.5	9.5	27.7	45.9

Source: Moon and Kang (1989).

**Table 2-13. Change in Urban Real Income Due to Direct
and Total Price Intervention, 1962–86**
(percent)

Period	Low-income group	Middle-income group	High-income group
Direct intervention			
1962–64	−1.9	−1.1	−1.5
1965–69	0.6	0.6	0.0
1970–74	−2.4	−1.8	−1.3
1975–79	−5.0	−3.7	−2.5
1980–84	−6.1	−4.2	−2.8
1985–86	−5.8	−3.9	−2.5
Total intervention			
1962–64	10.8	6.6	3.9
1965–69	8.9	5.4	3.0
1970–74	3.1	1.9	1.0
1975–79	−2.9	−1.8	−1.3
1980–84	−4.3	−3.1	−2.0
1985–86	−6.3	−4.7,	−3.5

Source: Moon and Kang (1989).

When changes in output and the quantity of purchased inputs are taken into account, real income gains show a similar pattern in all categories. The effect is much greater both in percentage and absolute terms among larger farms than smaller farms, with the result that income distribution worsens throughout the agricultural sector. Moreover, the smallest farms were hurt by price support programs that aimed at maintaining domestic market prices above international market prices, because many farmers with marginal holdings are net purchasers of food during the off-season. Insofar as these farmers purchase for cash, they are affected by price supports primarily as consumers, and consequently their real income declines.

CONSUMER INCOME. The effect of price intervention on income distribution among urban consumers is almost the reverse of its effect in rural areas. Food prices affect urban consumers in proportion to the ratio of expenditure on food to income. In general, lower-income urban consumers spend a much higher proportion of their incomes on food items than do those with higher incomes.

In the immediate and short term, direct intervention (or nominal protection) caused real income for all income groups to fall in most years between 1962 and 1986 (Table 2-13). In 1985–86 alone, direct intervention reduced real income by 5.8 percent in the low-income group and by 2.5 percent in the high-income group. In contrast, when the effects of indirect intervention are added, the real income for all groups shows an increase until the mid-1970s. The reason is that urban groups consumed food at lower prices than would have prevailed in the absence of government intervention, especially under the exchange rate regime. Since the late 1970s, however, government intervention has tended to reduce the real income of all urban consumers. During 1985–86 the real income of the low-income group fell by 6.3 percent and that of the high-income group by 3.5 percent. But the incremental expenditure in absolute amounts is much larger for the high-income group because of a larger initial expenditure.

In sum, the present price support programs tend to provide benefits primarily for larger farms and upper-income urban consumers. Conversely, small farmers and urban lower-income earners receive relatively little help from these support programs. Thus, agricultural price policy in Korea has tended to benefit the higher-income group in the rural and urban sectors, in both absolute and relative terms.

As the economy continues to grow, however, product lines will become increasingly diversified and the pattern of consumption will change substantially. As a result, the variety and volume of non-agricultural goods in the domestic market will increase, while the relative share of food in household expenditure will undoubtedly fall. The average share of rice in the cost of living was almost 20 percent in 1975, but it declined to 8 percent in 1986. It is expected to decline even further as real incomes grow. Consequently, the distributional impact of Korea's grain price support policy on urban wage-earners will be much smaller than it is on farm producers.

Policy Reform Efforts

Although the Korean economy is basically oriented toward a free-market system, government intervention in the farm products market, especially the grain market, has steadily intensified since 1960. Various types of price controls, trade restrictions, and demand and supply adjustments have been used to this end. Historically, government intervention has been readily accepted because it is widely believed that the government would not be able to achieve its national economic objectives if agricultural prices were determined by market forces.

What are these policy objectives and what would stand in the way of their achievement? The answer to this question depends on how Korea's policymakers view political and economic conditions at any given time. The following objectives are considered important in formulating agricultural price policy: (a) enhancing farm income, (b) food (especially rice) self-sufficiency, (c) reducing foreign exchange expenditures on food imports, (d) price stability and urban consumer welfare, (e) minimizing government costs, and (f) seasonal price stabilization.

Since 1960 a number of changes have taken place in the economic and political climate of Korea. These changes have affected the degree of emphasis placed on the objectives underlying Korea's agricultural policy and development strategy. A multitude of constraints have also affected policy direction. To understand the shift in priorities and how it affected price policy, one must compare the intended objectives and actual outcomes of policies from a historical perspective.

Negative Protection

As already mentioned, during the 1950s the government was mainly interested in rehabilitating the war-wrecked economy and alleviating the spiraling postwar inflation. Policymakers were particularly concerned about the effects of agricultural prices on the urban wage-earner's cost of living and on inflation. The government's investment in and loans to agriculture were severely limited because budgetary resources were being drained by rehabilitation works and defense expenditures. About all that the budget could do for the agricultural sector was to help it maintain existing irrigation facilities and import fertilizer. The fact that American grain was readily available on concessionary terms under the U.S. Farm Surplus Importation Agreement concluded in 1955 did little to strengthen an already weak agricultural price policy. Although the importation of grain greatly helped to stabilize Korea's food supply and general economic situation, it created a disincentive for policymakers to increase domestic production of foodgrain.

By the early 1960s the economy had gradually recovered from the war, and the major objectives of economic policy had shifted from rehabilitation to expansion. The basic goal of the policy as envisaged in the first (1962–66) and the second (1967–71) economic development plans was to lay the foundation for self-sustaining economic growth. "Increased domestic food production" and "rural-urban income equity" appeared as economic objectives in almost every policy document. Thus the Farm Products Prices Maintenance Law was promulgated in 1961 "to maintain proper prices of agricultural products to ensure the stability of agricultural production and the rural economy." The law covered rice, barley, and other agricultural products specified by the Ministry of Agriculture and Forestry (now the Ministry of Agriculture, Forestry, and Fisheries).

Although the stated objectives of Korea's economic policy were food self-sufficiency and farm income support, the government continued to emphasize general price stability. Because grain was one of the country's wage goods, the increase in the price of foodgrain was

believed to be a major cause of the general increase in prices. Therefore, the government concluded that by stabilizing foodgrain prices
through a moderate increase in imports it would be able to stabilize
prices in general. But the law remained nothing more than a slogan.
Low food prices for urban workers, whose expenditures on food items
accounted for almost 60 percent of their total living costs in the mid-
1960s, were rationalized as an equitable means of distributing income,
but their principal function was to protect industrial interests and
capital formation in the nonagricultural sector.

Much of the literature on economic development views savings in
the rural sector as essential sources of investment financing in the
initial stage of industrialization, whether they accumulate through
voluntary savings of farm surplus or are obtained through such compulsory measures as land taxes. This hardly seems to have been the
case in Korea, for there is little evidence to suggest that the agricultural
sector provided sizable financial resources for investment in the nonagricultural sectors during the 1950s and 1960s. To begin with, there
was not much farm surplus to use as rural savings. Second, the political atmosphere in Korea after World War II was such that it did
not permit heavy taxation of the rural sector. In the 1950s, farmers
in general had a negative cash flow. In the 1960s, farmers were able
to save a portion of their income, but relatively little of their savings
went into the nonagricultural sector. Beginning in the 1970s, Korean
farmers achieved substantial cash savings, but evidence from various
sources indicates that most farm savings remained on the farm in the
form of farm equipment purchases, housing improvements, and the
like. Moreover, the country's financial policy did not call upon the
government to transfer substantial sums of money out of agriculture
to other sectors (Ban, Moon, and Perkins 1980).

Agricultural price policy was a different story. In the initial stage
of industrialization, the supply of labor was highly elastic, since the
rural areas were overpopulated. Low food prices helped keep labor
costs down in two ways: directly, they reduced the cost of living in
urban areas and thus made it possible to maintain industrial wages
at a lower level; indirectly, a continual flow of rural laborers seeking
urban jobs exerted downward pressure, or at least alleviated an upward pressure, on urban wage rates.

The persistently negative price policy for major foodgrains eventually hindered farmers' efforts to increase food production.[3] As the
food shortage intensified and the income disparity between rural and
urban families increased, the government realized that it had to expand foodgrain production and enhance the income position of farmers. Since a large portion of the foodgrain shortage was met by local
currency under the PL 480 agreement, the food gap itself did not

impose a serious burden on the country's foreign exchange position, that is, not until the importation of inexpensive aid grain declined and U.S. assistance began to be phased out. Thereafter, foodgrain imports caused a substantial drain on the foreign exchange reserves.

A rapid influx of rural migrants into urban areas—especially large cities like Seoul and Busan—was another stimulant for rural development. By one estimate, approximately 400,000 rural people moved to urban areas every year during the 1950s and 1960s. Government officials became concerned that the urban infrastructure would collapse in the face of the growing numbers of migrants, all of whom required basic services. These migrants were by and large young and poor, and in most cases faced long waits for job opportunities. Thus, rural poverty was being transformed directly into urban poverty.

Another change of a more political nature that occurred in the late 1960s also impelled the regime to reorient economic policy toward agriculture. Rural people had become increasingly conscious of the widening gap between the standard of living in the cities and the standard of living in rural areas. Historically, beginning in 1948, rural voters tended to support whichever regime happened to be in power, despite the regime's emphasis on urban-biased economic policies. The rural landlord class that might earlier have organized into a political pressure group had been completely disintegrated by the land reform of 1950, and the government felt no immediate concern about the political allegiances of rural voters.

Although Korean farmers have organized one group—the Catholic Farmers' Association, which is the only grass roots organization in Korea—its membership is not large enough to influence government policies. The National Agricultural Cooperative Federation, although cooperative in name, has not been organized by farmers from the bottom up but rather is totally controlled by the bureaucracy. In this respect Korea contrasts strongly with Japan, where cooperatives not only exert political pressure directly on their elected representative but also are able to make their demands for protection felt through their cooperative activities (Anderson and Hayami 1986).

As a foreign cynic has pointed out, the political impotence of Korean farmers used to be so great that the state could manage agriculture as "one farm" (Wade 1982). But that situation has now changed. Declining support for the late President Park in rural areas in the 1971 presidential vote was perceived as an ominous popular reaction to the bias against agriculture in Korea's economic development policy. The world food crisis in the early 1970s and soaring grain prices in the world market forced the government to shift its emphasis toward agriculture in its development strategy.

Shift to Positive Protection

Beginning in the early 1970s, the government steadily increased the purchase prices of rice and barley with a view to improving the terms of trade for farm producers. In another major shift in policy, it initiated a massive investment in rural infrastructural development under the Saemaul (New Community) Movement. In particular, high priority was given to enhancing overall productivity through the expansion of irrigation facilities and paddy field consolidation projects. The rice self-sufficiency program—which was designed to increase production through the use of high-yielding varieties, combined with higher prices and input subsidization—became the main focus of rural income policy.

The change in the government's agricultural policy was also reflected in the drastic shift from negative protection to positive protection for major agricultural commodities. Although the government had begun liberalizing imports of a wide range of industrial items by the early 1970s, most tradable agricultural products were controlled by means of the Trade Notice, surveillance list, or special laws such as the Grain Management Law and the Livestock Development Law. Thus agricultural trade was strictly managed on the basis of supply and demand projections to ensure that certain commodities would be imported only to fill domestic shortages (Yang 1986). The average effective rate of protection for rice rose from −16.4 percent in 1960–64 to 4.9 percent in 1970–74 and then to 98.7 percent in 1985–86. The rate for beef rose from −31.5 percent in 1960–64 to 1.1 percent in 1970–74 and to 23.5 percent in 1985–86 (see Table 2-6). The total price-related and nonprice transfers from the nonagricultural to the agricultural sector amounted to 3.6 percent of total GDP in 1970–74, 26.2 percent in 1975–79, and 30.9 percent in 1985–86. The investment bias rose from 0.4–0.8 in the 1960s to 1.0–1.3 in the 1970s and reached a high of 2.0 by the mid-1980s. This trend indicates that the agricultural sector was receiving more and more investment resources relative to its contribution to the growth of national output (Moon and Kang 1989, Table 16). In short, the agricultural sector, which was once a major contributor to industrialization, became a major beneficiary of the expanding economy.

What about the food self-sufficiency and the farm income objective that the government was so eager to pursue? Owing to the expanded cultivation of high-yielding varieties, improved farming techniques, and expanded investment in the rural infrastructure, a remarkable increase has been recorded in aggregate farm output, especially in grain production. The total food production measured in index terms increased from 55–60 in the early 1960s to 120–130 in the early 1980s (Moon and Kang 1989, Table 4). Despite this rapid growth in overall food production, self-sufficiency in all grains declined from 93.9 percent in 1965 to 73.0 percent in 1975 and 44.5 percent in 1986; over half of the total grain requirement was filled by imports. This decline in the rate of self-sufficiency was due mainly to increasing demand for wheat, corn, and soybeans, which in turn was caused by rapid changes in food consumption patterns (Moon and Kang 1989).

The actual effect on farm income can be measured by the growth of farm household income relative to that of the urban wage-earner's household income over time. During the 1960–69 period, when the government's economic policy favored urban areas, the annual average growth rate of income for urban wage-earners was 14.6 percent, whereas that for farm households was only 3.5 percent. During 1970–76 the situation was reversed: Farm household income increased at an annual rate of 9.5 percent, while that of urban wage-earners increased only 4.6 percent. Although protective policies continued after the late 1970s, farm income rose at a slower pace than that of wage-earners in the ensuing years, and thus the pressure for agricultural protection intensified.

The Government Deficit as a Constraint

In pursuing the government's protective agricultural policies, officials of the Ministry of Agriculture and Fisheries gained a strong position vis-à-vis industrial interests and other ministries. Although price increases for wage goods posed something of a threat to the industrial sector, they were not strong enough to block the agricultural price increase related to the devastating world food crisis of 1973–74. But the urban interest in cheap food, particularly for lower-income groups, and the need to keep labor-intensive manufacturing competitive, were not totally neglected as the government recognized that the burden of supporting agriculture by means of higher prices could not be shouldered by food consumers alone. Thus both food producers and consumers were subsidized under a two-tier system for staple foodgrains. That is, producers were allowed to charge higher purchase prices and urban consumers to buy at lower selling prices, and the difference was paid by the government.

A two-tier system for barley was put into effect in the summer of 1969, and for rice in the fall of 1969. Until 1968 the selling prices of rice were determined by adding intermediate handling costs to the original acquisition prices. Beginning with the 1969 crop, the selling prices (except for the 1971 crop) were below the cost of acquisition and intermediate handling. After 1973 the difference between the purchase and selling prices continued to widen, and the loss incurred by the government amounted to 20–25 percent per 80-kilo bag every year.

In the case of barley, the price difference was even greater. Government efforts to keep barley prices low for consumers were motivated by a desire to induce consumers to substitute barley for rice in their diet. Before 1969 the market price of barley had been maintained at a level that was about 65 percent of the price of rice. But as the price subsidy for barley increased, the consumer price of barley dropped to 50 percent or less of the rice price. In another administrative measure taken to save rice, all restaurants were required to serve nonrice items on Wednesdays and Saturdays. However, as per capita income grew, the average consumer became less responsive to changes in the relative price of barley. The two-tier policy for barley no longer exerted an effect on the marginal rate of substitution between rice and barley. Thus administrative efforts to influence consumption had to be abandoned by the late 1970s.

The two-tier policy for rice and barley may have helped save rice and at the same time alleviated the upward pressure on consumer prices, but it also pushed up the costs of operating the government's grain program. During 1970–86 the total financial loss amounted to 2,707 billion won (approximately US$4.5 billion).

The deficit arising from this grain operation was compensated in large part by inflationary financing. If funds for the deficit had been taken from the general budget account, there would have been a reduction in expenditures for other sectors. Faced with increasing demands for limited resources from the nonagricultural sectors, especially for defense purposes, the government found it necessary to rely on inflationary financing. Most of the deficit was financed through long-term grain bonds with a one-year maturity period. The outstanding balance of the long-term borrowing totaled 1,577 billion won (approximately US$2.5 billion) at the end of 1986. The repayment of grain bonds has been financed either by long-term overdrafts or the reissue of grain bonds. Whichever method was used to finance the deficit, the money supply increased. This increase contributed to overall monetary expansion during the study period. It accounted for about 22 percent of the total increase in the money supply in 1972 and rose to 98 percent in 1975. Thereafter, approximately one-fourth of the total increase in money supply occurred in the grain sector.

Given the importance placed on protecting consumer welfare and enhancing the socioeconomic status of farmers, who still account for a large proportion of the population, the government grain operation and grain pricing policy must be viewed from a broader perspective than that of monetary policy alone. However, the government's policy of relying on a long-term overdraft from the central bank to finance the grain deficit is inconsistent with the policy goal of fiscal and financial stability.

A net increase in the money supply resulting from the current inflationary financing of the government grain operation is bound to cause upward pressure, with some time lag, on the general price level, the reason being that lump-sum funds released at the time of grain acquisition are likely to be spent immediately by farmers, whose cash demand is usually high. Thus, a two-tier policy is obviously self-defeating and fails to stabilize prices in general. The expanding government deficit has emerged as one of the serious constraints to agricultural pricing policies.

As long as the government makes grain purchases from farmers, there are two ways to narrow the price differential: through a relative reduction in the purchase price or a relative increase in the selling price. Whichever method is chosen, the problem boils down to one of determining the purchase price, high or low. According to an analysis of the effects of grain prices, a 10-percent rise in the real price of grain would have the positive effect of increasing rice production by 2–3 percent and boosting farm household income by 7–8 percent. The same percentage rise in the real price of grain would result in only a 0.5-percent increase in the general price level and a 1.0-percent increase in the consumer cost of living. One easily concludes that government selling prices must be raised to the point where they eliminate the deficit caused by the grain program. This would probably save the government more than it would cost the private sector.

Seeking Substitutes for Price Supports

Are there less expensive ways to achieve farm income objectives? Many economists and nonagricultural public officials argue that farm income needs to be improved over the long run through programs other than those that subsidize the prices of agricultural products. One possibility would be to increase agricultural productivity, particularly labor productivity, and thereby reduce the domestic cost of producing food. However, there is limited scope for doing this because of the small size of farms in Korea, which average only 1 hectare, and thus it would be difficult to substitute capital for labor. Since the early 1960s the government has been striving to improve the agrarian structure, but it has been unable to do much to enlarge the scale of farming operations because land resources are also limited.

Many people have begun to advocate an easing or even a repeal of the 3-hectare ceiling on individual holdings of farmland. Their rationale is that this would expedite the movement of landholdings into the hands of a smaller number of farmers. Because the market price

mland is much higher than the value of the land determined
gh the capitalization of income obtained by farming, there is a
g tendency to hold agricultural land as an asset. Also, this ten-
y is most conspicuous among medium-size farmers because they
are in a position to achieve relative financial stability by supplementing their incomes by off-farm earnings. This suggests that the
average farm size in Korea will likely remain almost static for some
time to come, and that the existing smallholder structure must be
accepted as a given condition in formulating agricultural policy.

Another way to achieve rural/urban income parity would be to expand the sources of nonagricultural income by encouraging industries
to locate in rural areas. As of 1984, the share of farm income from
nonagricultural activities in Korea remained slightly higher than 30
percent, whereas it reached 80 percent in Japan and 70 percent in
Taiwan.[4] This suggests that as far as rural/urban income parity is
concerned, increased access to nonagricultural employment in rural
areas could substitute for agriculture price supports. This approach
is not new. In fact, such a rural industrialization program was
launched in Korea in the early 1970s under the Saemaul (New Community) Factory Program. According to official statistics, a total of 741
factories ranging from food processing and handicrafts to textile manufacturing had been established in rural areas by 1980. But because
of inefficient marketing practices and poor management, among other
problems, only about 400 factories remain in operation.

Recognizing the importance of nonagricultural employment opportunities in rural areas, the government enacted the Farm Household Income Source Development Act in 1981. The Off-farm Income
Development Planning Group was established in 1981 as a national
planning and coordinating organization as part of the rural industrialization program.

Given the unfavorable infrastructural conditions in rural Korea,
however, off-farm employment sources cannot be expanded in a short
period of time. It will take long-term regional planning and a diverse
physical and institutional infrastructure. Nor can it be achieved simply by means of an industry relocation plan with financial incentives
or an agro-related supplementary program, as has been the case in
Korea so far. The present institutional framework for decisionmaking
is another factor limiting the pursuit of rural industrialization. Six
ministries are currently responsible for policies affecting the rural
population: the Economic Planning Board; the Ministry of Finance;
the Ministry of Agriculture, Forestry and Fisheries; the Ministry of
Commerce and Industry; the Ministry of Construction; and the Ministry of Health and Social Affairs. Although Korea does have a co-
ordination group on the Economic Planning Board, it appears to be
extremely difficult to reach agreement on how to carry out compre-

hensive programs that would include agricultural and nonagricultural rural investments. Another factor to consider is that the expansion of off-farm employment opportunities may cause farmland prices to rise further, owing to the increased demand for residential and industrial sites, overinvestment in farm machinery because of a rise in rural wages, and a decrease in incentives for farming. Thus, paradoxically, rural industrialization, which is thought to be a good substitute for agricultural price increases, may exert upward pressure on agricultural prices. As pointed out by Anderson and Hayami (1986), however, the political costs of higher food prices for urban consumers will decline as the share of food costs in urban household budgets declines.

Conclusion

Throughout much of the 1950s and 1960s, the government of Korea was concerned with curbing inflation. Therefore, one of its main goals was to stabilize agricultural prices at a low level. Low agricultural prices were made more possible by the easy availability of American grain on concessionary terms. The government's trade and exchange rate policies (that is, its monopoly on grain imports and exports and its overvaluation of the domestic currency) also put a squeeze on agriculture. Low food prices helped to keep labor costs down by reducing the cost of living in urban areas.

In the early 1970s, however, the government began to use grain prices to improve the agricultural terms of trade with a view to enhancing farm incomes and stimulating production, even at the cost of some increase in inflationary pressure. Food producers and consumers alike were subsidized by means of a two-tier scheme for staple foodgrains, and the financial cost was borne by the government. In another major policy shift, the government began investing in rural infrastructural development on a massive scale under the Saemaul (New Community) Movement program. Thus, the flow of resources between the agricultural and nonagricultural sectors also changed. Once a major contributor to industrialization, the agricultural sector had now become a major beneficiary of the expanding economy. With the introduction of high-yielding varieties of seed, improved farming techniques, and greater investment in the development of land and water resources, total food production increased in the late 1970s, and self-sufficiency in rice was nearly attained. Since then, the expanding government deficit has emerged as a serious constraint to the highly supportive agricultural price policy. Furthermore, present agricultural price policy tends to benefit primarily larger farms and upper-income urban consumers, and does little for small farmers or lower-income urban groups.

By the early 1980s policymakers were showing enthusiasm for rural industrialization as a substitute for agricultural price supports. Given the current unfavorable infrastructural conditions in rural Korea and inefficient industrial linkages, however, the government will have difficulty expanding such sources of off-farm employment quickly. Consequently, farmers will continue to seek income increases through price supports.

Appendix Table 2-14. Main Events Affecting Agricultural Price Policies in Korea, 1950–86

Period	Agricultural factors and policies	Macroeconomic factors and policies	Political factors
1950–59	Enactment of the Land Reform Law, 1949: Tenant-farmed land distributed to tenants and landlords paid in government bonds with the face value stated in terms of rice. Enactment of the Grain Management Law, 1950: Government given full authority to control food market, including purchase and selling prices, imports and exports of grain, etc. Signing of the U.S. Farm Surplus Importation Agreement (PL 480), 1955: Importation of 10 percent or more of total grain requirement made it easier to control grain market and to pursue low-price policies for staple foodgrains through supply management.	Policy emphasis on the rehabilitation of the war-wrecked economy and alleviation of postwar inflation. Annual average rate of inflation rises to 17.5 percent in 1955–59. Domestic currency (won) substantially overvalued under the fixed exchange rate system.	Outbreak of Korean War, 1950. Armistice agreement signed, 1953.
1960–69	Newly established National Agricultural Cooperatives Federation given sole authority to distribute chemical fertilizer, 1962.	Ojectives of economic policy shifted to expansion; export-oriented industrialization strategy pursued.	Rhee's government ousted by student revolution, 1960. Chang's regime ousted by military coup, 1961.

Table 2-14 *(continued)*

Period	Agricultural factors and policies	Macroeconomic factors and policies	Political factors
	Two-price policy initiated for rice and barley, 1969. Market share of government-controlled rice rises from 10 percent in 1950–59 to 20–25 percent in 1960–69. Effective rate of protection for rice rises from −28.8 percent in 1962 to −22.4 percent in 1969, and that for beef from −23.9 percent to −2.6 percent. Rural-urban income gap aggravated. U.S. supply of aid grain (PL 480) terminated. Food gap widened.	Exchange rate devalued by 100 percent, 1964. Annual average GNP growth rate 8.5 percent for 1961–69. Annual average rate of inflation 13.0 percent for 1960–69.	Park's regime comes into power. Presidential election, 1963 and 1967.
1970–79	Government begins using price incentives to increase food production. Grain Management Law reinforced to intensify government control on food market, 1973. Saemaul Movement initiated, 1972. Buffer-stock operation initiated for noncereal farm products, including red pepper, sesame, peanuts, garlic, 1972; number of products steadily increases.	Comprehensive policy package for price and wage controls implemented, 1974. Annual average GNP growth rate 9.6 percent for 1970–79. Annual average inflation rate 15.6 percent for 1970–79. Exchange rates devalued by 13 percent in 1971 and 21 percent in 1974.	Presidential election, 1971. Yushin revolution (coup by Park's regime), 1972. Political opposition strengthened by minor party. Presidential Park assassinated; political and social instability follows.

1980–86	Rice-saving measures enforced (e.g., no rice served for two days a week), 1973. Ceiling price system for beef and pork implemented, 1979. Government deificit due to two-price system compensated by inflationary financing (overdraft from the Bank of Korea). Market share of government controlled rice rises to 35–40 percent by the early 1980s. Rice self-sufficiency nearly attained by the early 1980s. Agricultural protection rates rise steadily; effective rate of protection for rice rises from −16.9 percent in 1970 to 52.0 percent in 1984, and that for beef from 0.0 percent to 151.5 percent. Off-farm Income Development Program initiated, 1981.	Exchange rate control reduced by adopting floating system, 1980. Exchange rate devalued by 20 percent in 1980. Annual average GNP growth rate 6.5 percent for 1980–86. Annual average inflation rate 9.1 percent for 1980–86. Import liberalization ratio of manufactured goods increased to 90 percent by 1985.	Chun's regime takes over the government, 1980. Political opposition intensifies and student riots become widespread.

Notes

1. In measuring the nominal protection rate (NPR) for Korea for 1955–64, Anderson and Hayami (1986) used the purchasing-power-parity effective exchange rate on imports obtained from Frank, Kim, and Westphal (1975, pp. 70–73) to convert the domestic prices of nine agricultural products to the border price equivalents. Frank, Kim, and Westphal estimated the purchasing-power-parity exchange rate after adding the actual tariff and foreign exchange tax per dollar of imports to the official exchange rate. Since in our view the actual tariff belongs to a direct measure and the foreign exchange tax to an indirect measure, it is doubtful that Anderson and Hayami's calculation could be appropriately defined as the "nominal protection rate." Moreover, they used the purchasing-power-parity effective rate expressed in real terms (deflated by Korea's WPI: 1965 = 100) for 1955–64 and the nominal official exchange rate for 1965–82, which we consider to be a conceptual inconsistency. Also, a question has been raised as to whether the measure of direct intervention should be based on the effective exchange rate on exports or the official exchange rate. The effective exchange rate on exports cannot be applied to measure NPR$_D$ for two reasons: First, we are dealing with the agricultural products that Korea has had to obtain almost entirely from imports. Second, even in the few years in which Korea exported rice (mostly in small amounts), farm producers had nothing to do with the effective exchange rate because the government had sole monopoly on rice exports. The effect of this government restriction on rice exports must be captured in an indirect measure (NPR$_I$).

2. Not all large farms have large sales, and not all farms with large sales are large-size. Therefore, even in judging the relative distribution of benefits, farms must be classified by income size, not by acreage size. But since the data on income are limited, we had to rely on the acreage size.

3. One may well ask how the government could implement a "low food price policy" or "negative protection" in the 1950s and 1960s, when the nominal protection rates (NPRS) were positive in those years. Even though the degree of overvaluation had not been calculated or officially announced, policymakers and academicians were well aware that the Korean won was highly overvalued in those years and that this was putting a squeeze on agriculture. The fact that the curb market exchange rates were almost three times as high as official rates and that the effective exchange rates on exports (though not applied to rice farmers) were substantially higher than the official rates indicates the extent of the overvaluation.

4. This wide difference in the share of nonagricultural income is due in part to differences in the approach to industrialization and in part to Korea's relative neglect of rural development throughout the two postwar decades. In the course of stepping up its industrial activities, Korea concentrated heavily on the urban areas. In contrast, Japan and Taiwan, China, utilized much of the farm labor force in rural industrialization, and so fewer workers were forced to move their location. A number of factors are responsible for the urban concentration of industrialization in Korea. First, from the outset, Korea pursued an outward-looking development strategy, which emphasized

exports. Instead of developing domestic markets, entrepreneurs focuse
marily on export markets, for which generous incentives were provided.
readily available port facilities and other conveniences, Seoul and Busan
easier access to export markets and thus offered a more favorable loca
for business activities (Ho 1982). Second, the highly centralized system of
government—and this is still the norm—has added to the geographical concentration of industries. Seoul is where major governmental decisions affecting all facets of business operations are made. Under these circumstances,
concentration seems inevitable (Park 1986).

Bibliography

The word "processed" describes works that are reproduced from typescript
by mimeograph, xerography, or similar means; such works may not be cataloged or commonly available through libraries, or they may be subject to
restricted circulation.

Anderson, K. 1986. "Food Price Policy in Korea, 1955 to 1985." Paper read
at the Workshop on Food Price Policies in Asia, Stanford University, Stanford, Calif. Processed.

Anderson, K., and Y. Hayami. 1986. *The Political Economy of Agricultural Protection: East Asia in International Perspective.* Sydney: Allen & Unwin.

Ban, S. H., P.-Y. Moon, and D. H. Perkins. 1980. *Rural Development. Studies
in the Modernization of the Republic of Korea: 1945–75.* Cambridge, Mass.:
Harvard University Press.

Bierman, R. W. 1964. "Procurement and Supply Programs, Grain Management Special Account." Seoul: U.S. Agency for International Development/
Korea. Processed.

Braverman, Avishay, Choong Yong Ahn, and Jeffrey S. Hammer. 1983. *Alternative Agricultural Pricing Policies in the Republic of Korea: Their Implications
for Government Deficits, Income Distribution, and Balance of Payments.* World
Bank Staff Working Paper 621. Washington, D.C.

Burmeister, L. L. 1985. "Agricultural Policy in a Developmental State: The
Case of South Korea." Processed.

Food and Agriculture Organization. 1954. *Rehabilitation and Development of
Agriculture, Forestry, and Fisheries in South Korea.* New York: Columbia University Press.

Frank, C. R., K. S. Kim, and L. Westphal. 1975. *Foreign Trade Regimes and
Economic Development: South Korea.* New York: Columbia University Press.

Ho, Samuel P. S. 1982. "Economic Development and Rural Industry in South
Korea and Taiwan." *World Development*, vol. 10, pp. 971–90.

Kim, K. S. 1984. *The 1964–65 Exchange Rate Reform, Effective Export Promotion
Measures, and Import Liberalization Program.* Korean Economic Policy Case
Studies. Honolulu, Hawaii: East-West Population Institute.

Koo, B. Y. 1986. "The Role of the Government in Korea's Industrial Development." In K. U. Lee, ed., *Industrial Development Policies and Issues.* Seoul:
Korea Development Institute.

Krueger, A. O. 1979. *The Developmental Role of the Foreign Sector and Aid: Studies in the Modernization of the Republic of Korea, 1945–75.* Cambridge, Mass.: Harvard University Press.

———. 1983. *Exchange Rate Determination.* London: Cambridge University Press.

Krueger, Anne O., Maurice Schiff, and Alberto Valdés. 1985. "A Comparative Study of the Political Economy of Agricultural Policies: A Framework for the Country Studies." World Bank, Country Economics Department, Trade Policy Division, Washington, D.C. Processed.

Lee, D. S. 1983. "A Study of the Effects of Fertilizer Price Policy in Korea." Master's thesis, Konkuk University, Seoul.

Mason, E. S., and others. 1980. *The Economic and Social Modernization of the Republic of Korea: Studies in the Modernization of the Republic of Korea, 1945–75.* Cambridge, Mass.: Harvard University Press.

Mellor, J. W. 1978. "Food Price Policy and Income Distribution in Low-Income Countries." *Economic Development and Cultural Change,* vol. 27, p. 1.

Moon, Pal-Yong. 1975. *The Evolution of Rice Policy In Korea.* Stanford University Food Research Institute Studies 14:4. Stanford, Calif.

———. 1979. "The Impact of Industrialization on Agriculture in Korea." *Journal of Rural Development* (Seoul), vol. 2, p. 2.

———. 1982. "Reforming Foodgrain Policy." *Korea Agricultural Policy Review,* vol. 9, p. 1.

Moon, Pal-Yong, and Bong-Soon Kang. 1989. *Trade, Exchange Rate, and Agricultural Pricing Policies in the Republic of Korea.* A World Bank Comparative Study. Washington, D.C.

Nam, S. W. 1985. "Semi-annual Model of the Korean Economy." Korea Development Institute Staff Working Paper. Seoul. Processed.

Park, H. S. 1986. "Off-farm Employment in Korea: Current Status and Future Prospects." In R. T. Shand, ed., *Off-Farm Employment in the Development of Rural Asia.* Sydney: Australian National University, Center for Development Studies.

Park, Y. C. 1984. *Price Controls and Stabilization Measures.* Korean Economic Policy Case Studies. Honolulu, Hawaii: East-West Population Institute.

Ruttan, V. W., and A. O. Krueger. 1986. "The Impact of External Economic Assistance to Korea." *Journal of Rural Development* (Seoul), vol. 9, p. 2.

Tolley, George S., Vinod Thomas, and Chung Ming Wong. 1982. *Agricultural Price Policies and the Developing Countries.* Baltimore, Md.: Johns Hopkins University Press.

U.S. Agency for International Development/Korea. 1967. *Report on Rural Development Program Evaluation.* Seoul.

Wade, R. 1982. *Irrigation and Agricultural Politics in South Korea.* Boulder, Colo.: Westview Press.

Westphal, L. E., and K. S. Kim. 1977. "Korea." In Bela Balassa and others, eds., *Development Strategies in Semi-industrial Economies.* Baltimore, Md.: Johns Hopkins University Press.

Yang, S. G. 1986. "Korea's Foreign Trade Policy and Economic Development." In K. U. Lee, ed., *Industrial Development Policies and Issues.* Seoul: Korea Development Institute.

3 Malaysia

Glenn P. Jenkins
Andrew Kwok-Kong Lai

Since 1960 Malaysia has become a highly efficient producer of natural rubber, thanks to its agricultural and trade policies. The primary purpose of these policies has been to maintain political and economic balance. Consequently, Malaysia's leaders have concentrated on modifying agricultural pricing policies in degree (for example, by adjusting to fluctuating world prices) rather than in kind, and their policy goals have remained fairly constant. In particular, they have endeavored to keep the producer price of rice stable and thus maintain the real purchasing power of the country's politically powerful paddy farmers; help rubber and palm oil farmers improve productivity; set taxes on rubber and palm oil at levels that provide funds for public investment; maintain an economy with fairly low and uniform tariffs on imported consumer goods and with very low or no tariffs on imported inputs; and distribute significant amounts of the revenues obtained from exports of oil to the agricultural sector. The policies used to achieve these goals from 1960 to 1983, and their impact on Malaysian agriculture, are the subjects of this chapter.

Overview of the Economy

Malaysia consists of two land masses in Southeast Asia that together cover an area of 330,434 square kilometers. One of these lies on the southern end of the Malay Peninsula, and the other lies some 650 kilometers across the South China Sea on the northeastern part of the island of Borneo. Peninsular Malaysia comprises 11 states and a federal territory; the island region, which constitutes about 60 percent of Malaysia's total land area, comprises only two states, Sabah and Sarawak.

The population of Malaysia in 1983 was about 14.8 million (see Table 3-1). During the 1960s the population grew at a rate of about 3.0 percent per annum, but the rate fell to 2.6 percent during the 1970s. In 1980 the labor force totaled 5.3 million (or 39 percent of the pop-

Table 3-1. Selected Demographic Characteristics for Selected Years, 1960–83

Year	Total population (millions)	Urban population (percentage of total population)	Total labor force in agriculture (percentage)
1960	8.113	25.2	n.a.
1965	9.422	26.1	n.a.
1970	10.864	28.8	46.6
1975	12.248	32.0	42.4
1980	13.764	35.0	38.4
1983	14.802	n.a.	n.a.

n.a.   Not available.
Source: Fourth Malaysia Plan 1981–85; Malaysia Department of Statistics.

ulation); about 2.0 million (or 38 percent of all labor) were employed in agriculture.

Almost 83 percent of the population lives in Peninsular Malaysia. The ethnic mix there—54 percent Malay, 35 percent Chinese, 10 percent Indian, and 1 percent other (Eurasians, Europeans, other Asians)—has remained relatively stable since 1970. The principal ethnic groups in Sabah and Sarawak are Kadazans, Ibans, Chinese, Muruts, Malays, and Melanus. Malaysia's ethnic composition and the distribution of the various ethnic groups have been prominent political issues, particularly since the racial riots in 1969.

In 1980 about 65 percent of the population lived in rural areas. Malays make up two-thirds of the rural population, Chinese about a quarter, and Indians and other races the rest. The Chinese have become the largest racial group in urban areas as a result of the forced resettlement of rural Chinese in 1952–54, during the communist insurgency (see Young, Bussink, and Hassan 1980, p. 15).

To even out the distribution of the three principal ethnic groups, the government has promoted the urbanization of Malays. Thus between 1970 and 1980 the urban Malay community increased 6.7 percent a year, in comparison with 3.7 percent for the Chinese community and 4.2 percent for the Indian community.

One of the most significant changes in the Malaysian economy since 1960 has been the move toward greater diversification of exports, which in the past were dominated by agricultural commodities, particularly rubber. Although rubber is still important, crude oil and petroleum products, along with manufactures, have become large contributors to exports since the late 1970s.

The principal imports are intermediate and capital goods, in addition to food. From time to time there have been a few quantitative restrictions on imports of manufactured and industrial goods. Rice and cabbages are the only agricultural products under import restrictions. There have been no subsidies for imports or exports. Although import licenses are mandatory, they are used primarily for statistical purposes.

Another important change during the study period was a shift away from a laissez-faire, market-oriented economy toward greater intervention, as a result of the New Economic Policy (NEP) incorporated into the Second Malaysia Plan (1971–75). Fundamentally, the NEP was designed to prevent the recurrence of race riots, and therefore one of its principal objectives was to correct the economic imbalance between Malays and non-Malays. Accordingly, it encouraged more Malays to participate in commerce and industry to compensate for the perceived inroads the Chinese had made in the political sphere (Anand 1983, pp. 8–9). The second major objective of the plan was to "eradicate poverty among all races." These two objectives were to be achieved by 1990, and it was hoped that the association between race and economic function would eventually disappear. The imbalance in income distribution, employment, ownership, and control of wealth was to be corrected through a rapid expansion of the economy (Rudner 1971, p. 41).

In implementing the new policy, however, the authorities have given more attention to rural Malay poverty than to urban Chinese poverty. Although nearly two-thirds of Malays were below the poverty-level household income of M$180 per month in 1980 (in 1970 prices), 39 percent of the Indian community and 26 percent of the Chinese were also classified as poor (see Young, Bussink, and Hasan 1980, p. 61).[1] Consequently, the NEP has come to be considered a policy for the transfer of resources from the urban to the rural economy. In addition, non-Malays have begun to feel uneasy about the proposed restructuring, which they fear will greatly reduce their wealth and their ownership of corporate assets. Since Malay savings have been scarce, the government has established state-owned and state-controlled enterprises and financial institutions to acquire share capital in existing and new companies and industries, which will be held in trust for the Malays.

Also in accordance with the NEP, Malays are given preference when import licenses are issued. Importers with the necessary license can readily obtain letters of credit for their transactions from any commercial bank. Furthermore, there are no restrictions on the transfer of funds in and out of the country for legitimate business purposes, except that amounts of M$1 million or more need prior approval of the central bank.

Between 1960 and 1983, real GNP climbed from a low of 3.1 percent per year to a high of 10.5 percent, for an average of 6.8 percent. In monetary terms, real GNP increased from M$11,837 million to M$53,382 million (in 1980 prices), while per capita real GNP rose from M$1,541 in 1960–64 to M$3,560 in 1980–83, for an average growth rate of 4.0 percent a year (see Table 3-2). This growth was achieved without high rates of inflation, as indicated by the consumer price index (CPI), which rose only about 4 percent a year over the entire study period.

Real gross investment also grew at a fast pace, starting at 5.1 percent a year in 1960–70 and then jumping to 16.2 percent in the next decade, followed by a rate of 13.9 percent in 1980–83. Real gross investment as a share of real GNP increased from 13 percent in 1960–64 to 34 percent in 1980–83, for an average of about 22 percent over the entire period (Table 3-2). This growth was directly related to huge investments made during the 1970s to reduce poverty and restructure Malaysian society. Some of the growth in the early 1980s was also related to investment in the petroleum industry.

Gross savings in Malaysian national accounts, calculated as the sum of gross domestic capital formation and the balance on the current account, grew at an average rate of 9.4 percent a year in the 1960s, rose to 19.7 percent in the 1970s, and then dropped to −3.0 percent in 1980–83. As a share of real GNP, savings rose from an average of 12 percent in 1960–64 to 18 percent in 1965–69, 21 percent in 1970–74, and 28 percent in 1975–79, closing the period of study at 25 percent (Table 3-2).

The value of total imports, as a share of real GNP, declined from 43 percent in 1960–64 to 36 percent in 1965–69 but then climbed up to 48 percent by 1983. Total real imports followed a slightly different pattern, rising from 2 percent a year during the 1960s to 12 percent during the 1970s, but then dropping to 4 percent in 1980–83. The sharp rise in imports during the 1970s was due in part to capital needs in the crude oil industry and to the emergence of other industries dependent on imported inputs. The mix of imports also changed, with investment and intermediate goods replacing consumer goods as the dominant components.

The behavior of exports has also been somewhat uneven. Real exports grew at an annual rate of 3.1 percent in the 1960s and then shot up to 15 percent in the 1970s. By 1983, however, the rate had declined to −2 percent. The share of exports in real GNP fluctuated between 35 and 56 percent, averaging about 46 percent for the entire period.

The Importance of Agriculture

Although the value and volume of agricultural production have not declined since the beginning of the 1960s, the position of agriculture has changed. Thus far the change has been moderate, with agricul-

Table 3-2. Economic and Agricultural Indicators, 1960–83

| Period | Per capita GNP (Malaysian ringgit) | Percentage of GNP | | | | | Agricultural output | Agricultural exports as percentage of agricultural ouput |
		Gross savings	Gross investments	Total imports	Total exports	Agricultural output	
1960–64	1,541	12	13	43	49	28	49
1965–69	1,767	18	16	36	42	24	49
1970–74	2,130	21	23	37	41	23	50
1975–79	2,818	28	26	38	49	20	85
1980–83	3,560	25	34	48	51	17	91
Average	2,313	21	22	40	46	22	64

Source: Jenkins and Lai (1989).

tural GDP as a proportion of GNP falling from 28 percent in the early 1960s to 17 percent in the early 1980s (see Table 3-2). Even though real agricultural imports rose by 22.2 percent a year in the 1970s—as a result of rising food imports, especially rice, wheat, meat, live cattle, and temperate fruits and vegetables—exports in the same period climbed to 25 percent a year. Agriculture is expected to contribute substantially to the national economy up to the end of the century.

The three crops chosen for this study—paddy rice, rubber, and palm oil—play a large role in Malaysian agriculture. Paddy is still the principal food crop, although per capita consumption declined from 135.1 kilograms in the early 1960s to 112.4 kilograms in the early 1980s. Rubber and palm oil are the main export crops. Palm oil is considered a nonfood export crop, although it is consumed as a vegetable oil in other countries. In recent years, however, Malaysians have begun to consume small quantities in cooking. If palm oil were considered a food commodity in Malaysian trade statistics, the country would be a net exporter of food. In 1981 the prices of rubber and palm fell and their share in GDP declined—rubber dropped to 5.5 percent after hitting 14.4 percent in 1974, while palm oil fell from 6.3 percent to 4.4 percent. The relative importance of export crops over food crops can be seen in the acreage devoted to the former. In 1983 the total cultivated area equaled 4,676,000 hectares; rubber was planted on 42.4 percent, oil palm on 26.8 percent, paddy on 14.3 percent, coconuts on 7.4 percent, cocoa on 4.9 percent, and other crops on 4.4 percent (Ministry of Agriculture 1985). The ratio of nonfood crops to food crops in Malaysia is approximately 1:0.13, compared with 1:3 for the Philippines and 1:16 for Thailand.

Exchange Rates

The average nominal exchange rate between 1960 and 1983 was M$2.71 to the U.S. dollar (see Table 3-3). This rate remained fairly constant over the entire study period except for a slight fluctuation when the rate went down to M$2.18 per U.S. dollar in 1979 and then up to M$2.34 in 1983. The real exchange rate—which is calculated by adjusting the nominal exchange rate by the ratio of the trade-weighted wholesale price indices (WPIS) of Japan, the United Kingdom, and the United States to the Malaysian consumer price index—also remained quite stable. It started out at an average of M$1.87 to the U.S. dollar in the early 1960s and then moved close to M$2.00, where it remained until 1979. By 1983 it had moved to about M$2.20 per U.S. dollar.

To estimate the real exchange rate in the absence of deficits or surpluses in the current account and in the absence of trade distortions, the equilibrium nominal exchange rate E^* is first estimated (see

Table 3-3. Budget Deficit and Exchange Rates, 1960–83

| Period | Budget deficit | | Nominal exchange rate (ringgit per U.S. dollar) | Trade-weighted real exchange rate (ringgit per U.S. dollar) | Equilibrium real exchange rate (ringgit per U.S. dollar) | Divergence of actual and equilibrium real exchange rates (percent) | Inflation rate (percent) |
	As percentage of total budget	As percentage of GNP					
1960–64	11	2	3.05	1.87	1.91	−1.9	0.5
1965–69	23	6	3.06	2.09	2.10	−0.8	1.0
1970–74	25	7	2.70	2.01	2.06	−2.2	6.9
1975–79	26	8	2.37	2.07	2.08	−0.4	4.1
1980–83	37	17	2.27	2.17	2.30	−5.7	6.5
Average	24	8	2.71	2.04	2.08	−2.0	3.7

Source: Jenkins and Lai (1989).

73

the appendix to this volume for the E^* formula; see Jenkins and Lai 1989 for parameter values).

This equilibrium real exchange rate is obtained as follows. The equilibrium nominal exchange rate E^* is multiplied by the ratio of the trade-weighted WPI for Japan, the United Kingdom, and the United States to the Malaysian CPI, which has been adjusted to remove the effect of trade distortions by the following formula:

$$\text{CPI}^* = \alpha(E^*/E_0) P_t + (1 - \alpha) P_{nt}$$

where α is the share of the CPI made up of tradable goods, E_0 is the nominal exchange rage, P_t is the price index for the tradable component of the CPI, and P_{nt} is the price index for the nontradable component of the CPI.

The equilibrium real exchange rate varied somewhat more than the trade-weighted rate, going from M\$1.83 per U.S. dollar in 1960 to M\$2.32 in 1982 and averaging M\$2.09 over this period. The equilibrium real value of the ringgit (e^*) depreciated by 10 percent between the early 1960s and the late 1960s and then remained stable at about M\$2.10 per U.S. dollar until the early 1980s, when it depreciated to M\$2.30 per U.S. dollar. Thus, e^* depreciated by 19.7 percentage points over the entire study period.

Until 1979 the trade-weighted and the equilibrium real exchange rate differed by no more than -1.9 percent (see Table 3-3). By 1983, however, the divergence was -5.7 percent. The absence of any significant degree of exchange rate disequilibrium was a result of stable macroeconomic policies and the low degree of trade intervention.

Agricultural Pricing Policies

Since the 1950s, intervention in agricultural prices has remained at a fairly low level in Malaysia, although this basic policy has been modified from time to time. Two of Malaysia's economic objectives have been to raise the standard of living of Malay paddy farmers and to achieve self-sufficiency in rice production. In the case of rubber and oil palm, the emphasis has been on stabilizing the price of the products at the farmgate while making sure that the government has a share in any surplus, particularly when world prices are high.

Rubber

One reason for the lack of intervention in rubber—for example, through a market board, which was a popular instrument in several British colonies in Africa—was the strong opposition of British and local investors (see Edwards 1970, p. 55). For its part, the Malaysian government was reluctant to interfere because the rubber industry was contributing a great deal to the economy. Although the world price of rubber fluctuated considerably during the 1950s and 1960s, it remained high, and no price support mechanism was deemed necessary. Graduated and progressive export taxes were able to capture enough of the windfall profits when prices were high or to reduce the tax burden as prices fell.

RUBBER EXPORT TAX. A rubber export tax was introduced in 1907, just after rubber became an important crop, in order to generate revenues for public expenditures. Although the tax has undergone many transformations—from a flat rate tax to a variable (ad valorem) levy and then a specific rate based on the export price—it has remained an important source of revenue for the government.

The current export tax on rubber evolved during the 1950s and has remained in place since then (for details, see Jenkins and Lai 1989). The tax is paid at the point of export by the exporters. The price that the exporter pays to the supplier is net of the export tax (and a tax on research and replanting) and of his own marketing margin. This net price is reflected all the way down the marketing chain to the producer, with each link in the chain deducting its own marketing margin from the price received.

The base for the export tax is the weekly posted price of rubber, which is calculated from the f.o.b. price. Before October 1977 the posted price was a two-week moving average of the f.o.b. price for top-grade rubber quoted up to the previous week. The export tax fluctuated with the world price, but there was a time lag, which exporters took advantage of for speculative purposes. To discourage such activity, the government began basing the posted price on a four-week moving average. This reduced the week-to-week movements of the posted price and the gains that could be realized from accelerating or holding back shipments of rubber (Lim 1975, p. 30).

Although Malaysia is the world's largest producer and exporter of natural rubber (in 1983 it supplied 13 percent of world output of natural and synthetic rubber), world demand is highly elastic because of the competition of synthetic substitutes. Since Malaysia is only one of several suppliers, the export duty can only be shifted backward to the relatively immobile factors of production, land, and labor. The burden on labor is reduced somewhat by the alternative opportunities available to rubber plantation workers, who also have a strong voice in labor matters through the National Union of Plantation Workers (NUPW). As a group, however, these workers have had a long attachment to the plantations, and they lack opportunities for training in other types of work. The situation is now changing, owing to a steady flow of labor (particularly young workers) from the rural to urban areas. This migration has created a shortage of workers and has put pressure on the rubber plantations to increase wages and improve working conditions.

Malaysian rubber plantations can be divided into smallholdings, which cover less than 100 acres (40 hectares), and estates, which cover 100 acres or more. Although it need not be in contiguous parcels, an estate must be under one owner or manager. Smallholders find it difficult to shift part of the export tax burden to hired labor simply because they do not employ wage labor outside the household, and if they do, wage payments are usually set by employment in other fields. In the short run, increases in the export tax merely increase the burden on the owners of land, and on labor, because it is not easy to shift resources in and out of rubber production. In the longer run, there would be some impact on the price of land, although the fact that oil palms can be planted on land used for rubber will eventually put a floor on the price of land. Hence, the export tax on rubber will stimulate the conversion of rubber estates into oil palm estates.

The rubber export tax does not have the same impact on estates and smallholdings. Although smallholders are not very responsive to short-term price movements, they can vary tree-tapping frequency more easily than the estates can. Furthermore, smallholders have traditionally supplemented family income through off-farm work and thus have greater flexibility than the estates in applying labor to rubber production.

RESEARCH, REPLANTING, AND GOVERNMENT POLICY. Soon after rubber became an important crop in Malaysia, the estate owners pushed for more research. They were particularly impressed by the success achieved in plant breeding in the Dutch East Indies (Indonesia), which had led to higher productivity. They also feared that their rubber crops might be seriously damaged by pests and disease, as their coffee and coconut crops had been earlier. On the advice of the Rubber Growers' Association of Malaysia, the government in 1925 established the Rubber Research Institute of Malaysia (RRIM) and placed a special tax on the sale of rubber to fund the institute. The government recognized that the private sector would have difficulty sustaining both rubber research and replanting activities. Thus, in addition to creating the special tax on rubber, and subsequently on palm oil, the government administered the research and financial arrangements for replanting, although in both cases the industry played a leading role in determining what was to be done. The research tax is levied according to the volume of rubber exported, which in 1983 amounted to 1.563 million tonnes. The rate, which has been amended many times since the 1920s, began at 0.025 sen per pound and is now 1.75 sen per pound. In 1983 the tax generated M$60.176 million for research on rubber.

The research tax is administered by the Malaysian Rubber Research and Development Board (MRRDB), which coordinates and allocates funds for the work of the RRIM and a research unit in England. This work is complemented by that of research units operated and funded by the major plantation agencies in Malaysia. The findings of these private research units are disseminated at the discretion of the agencies, whereas the results of RRIM projects are freely available to the entire industry. Owing to the technological advances resulting from these efforts, the natural rubber industry continues to attract investment, even though the relative price of rubber has fallen since the early 1960s.

RUBBER REPLANTING TAX. The rubber industry in Malaysia recovered rapidly from the ravages of World War II, and by 1948 production was some 150,000 tonnes above that of 1940 (Barlow 1978, p. 76). Output was bound to drop, however, because most estates and smallholdings had low-yielding and aging trees. Thus, by 1954 nearly two-thirds of Malaysia's rubber trees had exceeded their economic life. The annual replanting rate among smallholders between 1947 and 1952 was a mere 0.2 percent; it was only 15 percent among the estates.

In 1951 the government introduced a tax to build up funds for replanting. The tax was levied on export volume on a sliding scale, based on a price formula. A year later the rate was amended to 4.5 sen per pound irrespective of the export price of rubber (this rate is still used). In actuality the tax was collected only from smallholders, since the tax collected from the estates was refunded unconditionally until 1973 (for more details, see Jenkins and Lai 1989).

The proceeds from the tax were paid into a so-called Fund B and were used in conjunction with allocations of general revenues to finance replanting grants. Fund A was created for the estates, which until 1967 also received financial assistance from general revenues for replanting up to a maximum of 21 percent of planted acreage. Thus, by 1973 about 91 percent of the estates planted in 1946 had been replanted with high-yielding clonal material and about 67 percent of the smallholdings had been rejuvenated. The industry is now undergoing another round of replanting (see Barlow 1978, p. 86).

Palm Oil

The area planted with oil palms in 1983 totaled 1,253,000 hectares, up from 54,630 hectares in 1960 and 201,000 hectares in 1970. Part of this increase was due to the conversion of rubber estates to oil palm and to plantings on newly cleared jungle land.

PALM OIL EXPORT TAX. Palm oil has been exported from Malaysia since the 1920s, but for many years commercial interest in the crop was only moderate. Then in 1960 the private sector began to recognize the need to diversify the agricultural sector and saw oil palm as a promising alternative to rubber. The government encouraged this move by planting the new crop extensively in new settlements developed from jungle land. During the late 1950s and early 1960s the shift to oil palm also received impetus from the declining price of rubber. In contrast, the current and prospective price of palm oil was high. Moreover, the tax burden was negligible compared with that on the rubber industry. The tax on oil palm was calculated to be 4 to 8 percent of gross revenue per hectare, compared with 17 to 24 percent for rubber (Lim 1979, p. 22, table 6). Another attractive feature of oil palm was that the trees take only four years to mature after field planting (whereas rubber trees take six to seven years), and they are quite resistant to indigenous pests and diseases.

To take advantage of the prevailing prices for palm oil, the government upped its export tax from the flat rate of 5 percent ad valorem. In 1960 the tax on exports of palm oil was raised to 7.5 percent. In 1972 the tax was converted into a graduated tax designed to tap into the excess profits of the industry. It progressed at the rate of 2.5 percent for every M$49.20 per tonne increase in the f.o.b. price of palm oil above a threshold price of M$344.37 per tonne up to a price of M$688.75 per tonne. At that level, the tax was 30 percent ad valorem.

The tax on exports of palm oil is based on a monthly published price calculated as a moving average of the f.o.b. price during the preceding four weeks. The impact is shifted backward to the producers, as is also the case for rubber, since the commodity is traded in a perfectly competitive market. Although some of the effect may be shifted to land that is particularly suited to oil palm, other factors of production are unlikely to be affected, least of all the workers on oil palm estates. Palm oil production is less labor-intensive than rubber production, and most workers have alternative employment opportunities.

PALM OIL RESEARCH TAX. Research has been instrumental in identifying the economic potential of oil palm. The level of support that Malaysia's private sector—notably the industry itself—provides for research is unusual in a developing country. Much of the research in palm oil prior to 1969 was carried out by the leading plantation agencies at their own research stations. Although the results of such efforts were proprietary, much of the information was released in scientific papers at a number of conferences held in Malaysia during the 1960s. Government-supported research was conducted by the Department of Agriculture and was mainly concerned with the development and testing of new varieties. In 1969, however, responsibility for the government's oil palm research was handed over to the Malaysian Agricultural Research and Development Institute (MARDI), which is funded by a research tax.

Because oil palm was only one of many crops investigated by MARDI, producers argued that an agency specializing in oil palm research, modeled along the lines of the Rubber Research Institute, was needed. In response, the government in 1979 set up the Palm Oil Research Institute of Malaysia (PORIM), which was not only to conduct research of its own but also to coordinate oil palm research throughout Malaysia. Private research stations also do some work for PORIM. Its research program is drawn up by a joint committee of industrial and government representatives and covers all aspects of production research—including processing, storage, delivery systems, marketing, consumption, and end-uses in both the food and nonfood industries. One area of research that has been neglected is the treatment of the effluent from Malaysia's palm oil mills, which has now become a serious pollutant. The effluent is difficult to treat prior to discharge.

In 1980 the research tax on oil palm was raised from M$1.00 to M$4.00 per tonne, irrespective of price. The fund gives PORIM access to more than M$12 million annually for its research. Recurrent costs, including the salaries of the research staff and operation of the research facilities, are covered by a budgetary allocation.

PALM OIL REGULATORY POLICY. In 1980 the government established the Palm Oil Registration and Licensing Authority (PORLA) and put it in charge of regulating, coordinating, and promoting all aspects of palm oil production. These activities are financed by a tax of M$1.75 per tonne of palm oil. Representatives of the industry and the government sit on PORLA's board of directors. Those involved in the industry are required to obtain a license from PORLA before beginning their business. The licenses are used mainly for statistical purposes.

One of PORLA's principal functions is to oversee the quality of palm oil exported from Malaysia. The authority has the power to enforce strict measures against anyone whose practices do not meet contract specifications or established standards. Another of its functions is to develop new markets for palm oil and to promote the commodity in order to maintain Malaysia's share of the world market for vegetable oils. PORLA also acts as the mediator in contractual disputes between shippers and consignees.

Paddy Rice

As already mentioned, rice is the main food crop in Malaysia. Cultivation systems range from traditional methods to modern forms of plantation agriculture. Price intervention dates back to World War II.

PADDY PRICE SUPPORT POLICY. The paddy price support policy in Malaysia came about because of rice shortages during the Japanese occupation (1941–45) and immediately after the war. At that time, Malaysia was wholly dependent on rice imports, so that the disruption in supply caused by the war and then by a shortfall in Burma was devastating. The British colonial government therefore declared rice to be a strategic good and made the attainment of self-sufficiency in rice a policy goal. To promote domestic rice production, the government in 1949 introduced a guaranteed minimum price (GMP). The GMP was linked to the world market price and was fixed one season at a time, so that the difference between the GMP and the domestic market price would not become too distorted and force the government to buy all the paddy produced in the country. The government pledged to buy all paddy at the prevailing minimum price.

The GMP was set at M$265 per tonne of paddy in 1949 and was increased to M$381 per tonne in 1973 because the world price had risen steeply. To complement the GMP (and in effect increase its level), the government also introduced a price support scheme sponsored by the Lembaga Padi dan Beras Negara (LPN, or National Paddy and Rice Board). There have been several increases in the support price since 1973, the most recent being a cash subsidy of M$168 per tonne announced in 1980, which raised the support price to M$598 per tonne. Initially, the cash subsidy amounted to only M$33 per tonne of paddy sold. However, Malaysia's rice farmers organized demonstrations to protest the manner in which the subsidy was paid—namely, through coupons cashable only at post offices and at the national savings bank for the sole purpose of opening savings accounts—and the subsidy was withdrawn in 1980. The subsidy scheme introduced the next season offered a generous M$168 for each tonne of paddy sold.

The government buys paddy at the support price and mills it into rice. It also buys from private rice millers, provided they are able to certify that they paid the support price. The rice is stored in the government stockpile. Originally intended to be a strategic source to safeguard against shortages, it now functions more as a buffer stock that helps to stabilize prices. (Note, however, that rice cannot be stored for more than six months without a serious loss in quality.)

Until 1974 the minimum price mechanism consisted of an import-mixing regulation and import licensing that required the importer to purchase a certain proportion of rice from the government stockpile for every unit of rice imported. This made it possible to turn over the stockpile quickly and allowed the government to recover the cost of maintaining it. Part of the revenue from domestic rice sold to importers is used to cover storage and administrative costs. By and large, importers have found the price of domestic rice to be much higher than that of imported rice, even though the quality of stockpile rice is lower. Nevertheless, rice importers are able to recoup this price differential on locally grown rice from the profits made on the sale to domestic consumers of the high-quality imported rice, which commands a premium price in the Malaysian market.

The government began to import rice on a government-to-government basis through the LPN in 1974, when the high world price eliminated from the market those importers who could not make the cash deposits demanded by exporters. Thereafter, the agency was given a monopoly, and rice dealers were required to buy the imported rice from the LPN instead of importing it themselves. The producer price is now supported entirely by the government, which makes up losses through general revenue allocations. In 1975 and 1977 major irrigation programs became operational in Kedah and Kelantan and helped to increase the domestic output of rice. Imports were reduced, and the cost of maintaining the producer price rose in proportion to the degree of self-sufficiency achieved.

Under the GMP scheme, farmers are guaranteed a single price for good, clean, dry paddy delivered to the mill. Deductions are made for high moisture content (in excess of 14 percent), the presence of dirt and foreign matter, and immature grains. Because the policy emphasizes quantity, farmers are encouraged to produce low-quality varieties, which most consumers do not want, and to sell the best-quality paddy to private millers for premium prices. A price differential was introduced into the GMP in 1964 to persuade farmers to double-crop their paddy land and to plant recommended varieties, but it was withdrawn in 1974 because double-cropping was being adopted in irrigated areas as well.

Also in 1974, the LPN decided to try a grading system based on grain length, which turned out to be somewhat more successful. Producers of long-grain rice are paid a premium of M$33 per tonne of paddy more than producers of medium-grain rice and M$66 more than producers of short-grain varieties. Although the market favors long-grain rice, there is a demand for lower-quality rice. The high end of the market is then satisfied by imported rice, and the profit from selling this rice at a premium is used to support the paddy price policy.

This policy has reduced some of the risks of paddy growing in Malaysia as it guarantees a minimum price and hence stabilizes incomes. A cash subsidy introduced in July 1980 also raised paddy farmers' incomes, but it had two unintended side effects. First, it made paddy farming operations more profitable, with the result that large farmers began buying up small farms, displacing both owner-operators and tenants and increasing the number of landless laborers (Tamin 1986, p. 22). Second, because the amount of the cash subsidy is based on the amount of paddy sold, the marketable surplus has increased since 1982. The rational paddy farmer sells all his paddy to obtain the cash subsidy and then buys his rice from the market. Before 1980, rice farmers kept up to 60 percent of their output for their own consumption (Rudner 1971, p. 86).

With farmers selling all their output to the government for the cash subsidy, many small rice mills in rural areas have closed for lack of business. Meanwhile, the LPN has had to expand its facilities to handle the larger volume of paddy being marketed by farmers. By 1980 the LPN was operating 28 integrated rice-milling complexes and was handling 33 percent of the paddy produced locally. Private rice mills processed the rest.

PADDY INPUT SUBSIDY POLICY. The subsidy for paddy inputs evolved from Department of Agriculture fertilizer demonstrations in the early 1950s. The purpose of these demonstrations was to inform farmers of the recommended rates of fertilizer use and the benefits of urea and other chemical fertilizers. The favorable response of the paddy farmers led the Department of Agriculture to launch a fertilizer subsidy scheme in 1955 in a few selected states in which the cost of the fertilizers was reimbursed by the federal government. In 1961 the scheme was expanded to all 10 states of Peninsular Malaysia.

In the first year, the subsidy amounted to 50 percent of the cost. It then declined by 10 percentage points annually until 1965, when it reached 10 percent. However, the quantities of fertilizer bought by paddy farmers increased—from 3,882 tonnes in 1961 to 12,682 tonnes in 1965—as the farmers came to recognize the benefits of using such inputs. In 1966 a uniform subsidy of 30 percent was announced and was extended to 1970. A budgetary allocation of M$10 million was approved to provide fertilizer for about 89,000 hectares of paddy land. In practice, however, only about a third of the area received subsidized fertilizer in any one year, and the farmers received only enough fertilizer for 2 hectares. These shortfalls occurred because of a great increase in demand for subsidized fertilizer to an estimated 25,400 tonnes per year.

In 1971 the fertilizer subsidy was replaced by a credit program in irrigated areas, since paddy farmers had by then become familiar with the use of urea, the principal nitrogenous fertilizer used in paddy growing, and other chemical fertilizers. The fertilizer subsidy was continued in nonirrigated areas. The success of the subsidy is evident from the willingness of paddy farmers to purchase their own fertilizer after the subsidy was terminated (Lee 1978, p. 250). Consequently, a market for urea and other chemical fertilizers was established in all paddy areas, and the dealers and agents of the fertilizer firms found themselves supplementing the work of the government's extension agents.

In 1973 the price of urea in the world market rose by 50 percent, and in 1974 it rose by 233 percent. In Malaysia the price increased by 278 percent between 1972 and 1974. To help paddy farmers cope with this increase, the government introduced a price support scheme in 1974. It was believed that if farmers were forced to stop using urea because the price was too high, domestic output would decline, farmers' incomes would be reduced, and the country would need to import more rice.

Under the scheme, farmers paid a nominal price of M$10 for a 20-kilogram bag of urea, and any difference between this nominal price and the market price was subsidized (the difference ranged from M$10.58 to M$14.58 per bag). The scheme was to be terminated automatically if the price of urea fell below the threshold price, as it did in 1976. Despite this support, the use of urea declined in 1975 and 1976. Between 1972 and 1976, Malaysia's farmers purchased 59,365 tonnes of subsidized urea at a cost of about M$61 million. But the estimated crop loss at the farm level during this period was M$48.5 million, and rice valued at M$59.6 million had to be imported to make up the loss. Thus it appears that the subsidy failed to stop rice production from declining.

In 1980 a different fertilizer subsidy scheme was introduced. This scheme provides a 100 percent subsidy for the fertilizer required by the average paddy farm in Malaysia (2.4 hectares or less). This size limit was imposed to ensure that only small paddy farmers would benefit, but many larger farms were then subdivided into units well within the threshold size in order to benefit from the scheme (Tamin 1986, p. 22). Farm records are often incomplete, but it is not unusual for a paddy farm to have multiple owners under the Islamic law of inheritance.

Subsidized fertilizer is distributed to paddy farmers through rural organizations. Each organization is paid a commission based on the quantity of fertilizer handled, and most of the organizations (for instance, the farmers' associations participating in the Muda irrigation scheme in Kedah) have benefited financially under the system. However, the network of commercial fertilizer agents disappeared after the subsidy was put into effect, and Malaysian farmers now have to depend solely on government extension workers.

Two criticisms have been leveled against the current subsidy program. First, it is argued that farmers' incomes could have been enhanced by a higher minimum price or through financial assistance for other costs, such as land preparation for poor farmers who do not own tractors. The generalized fertilizer subsidy, it is held, is an inefficient means of transferring income to poor paddy farmers. A second criticism is that the Department of Agriculture has too easily assumed that its recommended fertilizer rates are appropriate for given areas and soil types. Despite evidence to the contrary provided by farmers, the department has not examined the economics of fertilizer use for alternative relative prices of fertilizer and paddy. Farmers generally apply only the amount of fertilizer that will optimize their income. Furthermore, the Department of Agriculture has not considered changing the recommended level of subsidized fertilizer, even when the price of paddy has changed.

INFRASTRUCTURE TO SUPPORT PADDY PRODUCTION. The new high-yielding varieties of paddy have greatly improved the prospects for self-sufficiency. Because these varieties need regular water supplies, it was decided in the early 1960s to increase expenditures on drainage and irrigation for paddy production to 26 percent of all infrastructure investment, a sharp rise from the 17 percent of the 1956–60 period (Tan 1987, p. 7). The amount allocated for these purposes fell to 21 percent in the First Malaysia Plan (1966–70), and in the subsequent plans for 1971–75, 1976–80, and 1981–85 the proportion going to drainage and irrigation was reduced to 16, 12, and 18 percent, respectively. Because suitable land for further irrigation schemes is in short supply, production under the Fifth Malaysia Plan (1986–90) will be concentrated in the existing paddy-growing areas (Tan 1987, p. 33), and efforts to achieve rice self-sufficiency will be relaxed. The proportion of expenditures allocated to drainage and irrigation has fallen to about 3 percent.

Effects of Pricing Policies

Malaysian agricultural and trade policies have been remarkably consistent since 1960. They have protected food production and helped to develop the nonagricultural sector. But these policies, along with certain taxes, have discriminated against the country's best export crops–rubber and oil palm. This conclusion is supported by data on the impact of intervention on relative prices, production, consumption, foreign exchange, the budget, transfers of resources, and income distribution.

Relative Prices

The relative prices of rubber and palm oil are the ratio of their producer prices (their f.o.b. price less marketing and transport costs and taxes) to the nonagricultural price index (P_{NA}). Between 1960 and 1983 there was a downward trend in the relative prices of estate and small-holder rubber owing to the competition from synthetic rubber as well as natural rubber from other countries, notably Indonesia. (For the indices used to calculate P_{NA}, see Jenkins and Lai 1989.) The relative producer price during 1980–83 was 60 percent of that during 1960–64. In contrast, the relative price of palm oil showed no systematic pattern, fluctuating between 8.8 and 11.5 and averaging 9.8 over the study period.

The producer price that was used to calculate the relative price of paddy was the guaranteed minimum, or support, price at the farm level. Since 1960 there has been an upward trend of about 25 percent in the relative price of paddy. The increases were most pronounced in 1970–74, when the price moved up 10.1 percent, and in 1975–79, when the price rose 14.8 percent.

Nominal Protection for Crops

Pricing policies in Malaysia have had a direct effect on incentives to invest in the agricultural sector, as can be seen in the nominal protection rates for rubber, palm oil, and paddy. These rates were calculated by comparing border prices relative to the nonagricultural price index with actual prices relative to the same nonagricultural price index. For rubber and palm oil, border prices are the f.o.b. prices less marketing and transport costs. For imported rice, the border price is its c.i.f. price less the costs of milling, drying, and transport, with conversion to paddy at the farm level calculated at 65 percent. As shown in Table 3-4, these rates were negative for rubber and oil palm in each five-year period of the study and therefore suggest that Malaysia's pricing policies discriminated against these crops.

Table 3-4. Nominal Protection Rates, 1960–83

	NPR				
Period	*Estate rubber*	*Smallholder rubber*	*Palm oil*	*Paddy*	NPR$_I$
1960–64	−8	−15	−8	20	−9
1965–69	−7	−15	−8	−1	−9
1970–74	−9	−19	−12	4	−10
1975–79	−23	−25	−16	39	−4
1980–83	−19	−20	−15	76	−10
Average	−13	−19	−10	26	−8

Source: Jenkins and Lai (1989).

The direct nominal protection rate for estate rubber averaged −13 percent between 1960 and 1983, ranging from −0.07 percent in the early 1960s to −0.23 percent in the early 1970s. The rate was higher for rubber produced by smallholders (on average, −19 percent) because agricultural policy was biased against this group. Until 1981 the export tax was based on the top grade of rubber, which smallholders were seldom able to produce. In addition, as already mentioned, they had to pay the replanting tax instituted in 1951, whereas the estates had the tax rebated until 1975. The direct nominal rate of protection for palm oil production was also negative, averaging about −10 percent between 1960 and 1980.

In contrast, the direct nominal rate of protection for paddy was positive—except in 1967–69 and 1973–75, when the world price of rice was high—and averaged 26 percent over the 1960–83 period. Abnormally low rice prices for imported rice pushed the nominal protection rate to 160 percent in 1983.

The impact on agricultural incentives of indirect intervention (industrial protection and exchange rate policies) is measured by NPR$_I$, the indirect nominal protection rate (defined in the appendix), and is shown in Table 3-4.

Indirect intervention, which affects all tradable agricultural products equally, had a negative impact, as can be seen from the negative protection rate (−0.08) for the study period. Two factors account for this negative rate. First, the (low) degree of overvaluation of the currency in Malaysia has a greater impact on the agricultural sector, which is almost entirely tradable, than on the nonagricultural sector, which is only partly tradable. Second, the tariffs on imported goods in the nonagricultural sector made nonagricultural investments relatively more attractive than they would otherwise have been.

Total intervention, which includes the impact of both direct and indirect policies, is shown in Table 3-5. Total nominal protection rates averaged −20 percent for rubber estates and −25 percent for rubber

Table 3-5. Total Nominal Protection, 1960–83

Period	Estate rubber	Smallholder rubber	Palm oil	Paddy
1960–64	−17	−23	−16	9
1965–69	−15	−23	−16	−10
1970–74	−18	−27	−20	−5
1975–79	−27	−28	−19	33
1980–83	−27	−28	−14	59
Average	−20	−25	−17	15

Source: Jenkins and Lai (1989).

smallholders from 1960 to 1983. In both cases the negative rate of protection increased somewhat over time, as indicated by the rates for selected years in Table 3-5. In the case of palm oil, however, there was no noticeable trend in the negative protection rate, which averaged − 17 percent for the period.

In contrast, paddy production was highly protected by total intervention (because NPR$_D$ dominated NPR$_I$), except during the seven years of high rice prices, as noted earlier. Total nominal protection averaged about 15 percent between 1960 and 1983, but in recent years has risen to levels in excess of 100 percent of the c.i.f. price of imported rice. The effective protection rates were found to be similar to the nominal protection rates both in sign and magnitude.

Production and Consumption

In response to lower net prices, rubber and palm oil producers have been planting smaller acreages, particularly in the case of rubber, which has been more heavily taxed than palm oil and competes with it for land. Meanwhile, the price support given to paddy has encouraged farmers to grow more paddy and less of other crops. Consequently, fewer workers are leaving rural areas, and the abandonment of unirrigated paddy has slowed down.

To determine how the supply of rubber responds to changes in pricing policies, it is necessary to consider how price changes affect tapping frequencies and fertilizer practices (which in turn affect the short-run response in output) and price expectations (which affect decisions concerning replanting and new planting). Given that rubber and oil palm are alternative crops for the same land and are often grown by the same producers, a higher price for palm oil will result in less replanting and new planting of rubber, and vice versa. Hence, long-run supplies of rubber and palm oil will be affected by the output price of both crops.

The change in the quantity supplied due to changes in the prices of rubber and palm oil, relative to the nonagricultural price index (P_{NA}), can be expressed as a function of the short- and the long-run elasticities of supply. The short-run elasticities of supply describe the production response over time through more intensive tapping of the rubber trees or shorter intervals between harvesting rounds for oil palm, and the frequency of fertilizer applications. The long-run elasticities of supply reflect the lagged response of output due to the effect that higher prices have on decisions related to replanting and expansion of acreage. Cross-price elasticities will also influence the long-run production response through their impact on decisions regarding replanting and acreage expansion. The following formula was used to describe the change in the supply of rubber arising from a series of price changes in both rubber and palm oil:

$$(3\text{-}1) \quad dQ_t^R = \left(\sum_{i=0}^{t} Q_t^R \cdot E_{Si}^{RR} \cdot dP_i^R / P_i^R \right) + \left(\sum_{i=0}^{t-k} Q_t^R \cdot E_{Li}^{RR} \cdot dP_i^R / P_i^R \right)$$

$$+ \left(\sum_{i=0}^{t-k} Q_t^R \cdot E_{Li}^{RO} \cdot dP_i^O / P_i^O \right)$$

where dQ_t^R is the change in the supply of rubber in period t caused by cumulative changes in the price of rubber and palm oil from period 1 to t; Q_t^R is the quantity of rubber produced in year t in the absence of price changes; E_{Si}^{RR} is the elasticity of the supply of rubber with respect to the change in the price of rubber that occurred in period i; dP_i^R / P_i^R is the proportional change in the price of rubber (relative to nonagricultural goods) that has occurred in period i; E_{Li}^{RR} is the long-run elasticity of supply of rubber with respect to the change in the price of rubber that occurred in period i; E_{Li}^{RO} is the long-run elasticity of supply of rubber with respect to a change in the price of palm oil; dP_i^O / P_i^O is the proportional change in the price of palm oil (relative to nonagricultural goods) that has occurred in period i; and k is the time lag in years between a price change and the initial year when the long-term elasticity takes effect.

The equation describing the production response of palm oil to changes in the prices of palm oil and rubber can be written as

$$(3\text{-}2) \quad dQ_t^O = \left(\sum_{i=0}^{t} Q_t^O \cdot E_{Si}^{OO} \cdot dP_i^O / P_i^O \right) + \left(\sum_{i=0}^{t-k} Q_t^O \cdot E_{Li}^{OO} \cdot dP_i^O / P_i^O \right)$$

$$+ \left(\sum_{i=0}^{t-k} Q_t^O \cdot E_{Li}^{OR} \cdot dP_i^R / P_i^R \right).$$

If one wants to determine the immediate impact of a change in pricing policy, only the short-run elasticities are relevant, and only for the periods in which response is to be measured.

It is likely that the supply of paddy will respond more quickly to a price change than the supply of rubber or palm oil. Paddy can be planted and harvested within six months, and two crops can be grown in one year if sufficient water is available. In addition, paddy does not compete for the same land as rubber or oil palm. The relationship between changes in paddy production, dQ_t^f, and the prices of paddy and other crops can be expressed as follows:

$$(3\text{-}3) \quad dQ_t^f = \sum_{i=0}^{t} \left[\left(Q_t^f \cdot E_i^{ff} \cdot dP_i^f / P_i^f \right) + \left(\sum_m Q_t^f \cdot E_i^{fm} \cdot dP_i^m / P_i^m \right) \right]$$

where E_i^{ff} is the elasticity of supply of paddy with respect to the price of paddy (relative to the price of nonagricultural goods) in period i; Q_t^f is the quantity of paddy produced in period t in the absence of any change in price policy; dP_i^f/P_i^f is the proportional change in the price of paddy in year i; E_i^{fm} is the elasticity of supply of paddy with respect to the price of other crops that could be grown on paddy land; and dP_i^m/P_i^m is the proportional change in price of these other crops in period i.

The elasticity of supply for paddy was assumed to be 0.2 in the year of the price change, 0.3 in the following year, and fully adjusted at 0.4 by the third year. This figure is based on studies by Arromdee (1969), Squire and Barnum (1976), Sahathavan (1974), and Haughton (1983), all of which imply that despite the price and input incentives provided, the supply response of paddy is relatively insignificant.

Other studies have indicated that the short-run elasticity of supply of rubber is quite low. However, the estimated elasticity for small-holders is larger than that for estates because it is easier for the former to allocate their time between tapping rubber and other activities than for the latter, which have permanent work crews. In this study, 0.3 is assumed to be the short-run elasticity for rubber. Because it takes rubber trees six years to become productive, there is a lag between a change in pricing policies and increased production. Hence, the long-run supply elasticity for rubber was estimated to be 0.8, based on assumptions for short-run elasticity. A number of other studies have also reported a low estimate (see Chan 1962; Cheong 1962; Chow 1965; Behrman 1975; Pee 1977).

The cross-price elasticity of the supply of rubber with respect to the price of palm oil is negative because an increase in the price of palm oil will provide an incentive to replace rubber with oil palm. If the price of palm oil falls, however, relatively more new land will be planted in rubber. The same own- and cross-price elasticities of supply were used for oil palm, since there are no empirical studies on these elasticities.

Output response to changes in trade policies is measured in two ways. First, the impact on prices and the values of elasticity parameters are calculated. The changes in producer prices are obtained by multiplying the values of the effective rates of protection for the total and the direct effects of trade policies with the ratio of the producer prices of the commodity to the value added of the commodity adjusted for the total effects. Second, the elasticities of supply of commodities with respect to their nonagricultural prices and the prices of other goods are estimated.

Table 3-6 shows the short-run direct and total effects of pricing policies on output of rubber, palm oil, and paddy. The response is defined as the response occurring in the year following that in which the policy change occurred. Between 1960 and 1974 the short-run

Table 3-6. Short-run Effect of Direct and Total Intervention on Output of Estate and Smallholder Rubber, Palm Oil, and Paddy

Period	Direct effect				Total effect			
	Estate rubber	Smallholder rubber	Palm oil	Paddy	Estate rubber	Smallholder rubber	Palm oil	Paddy
1960–64	−1	−3	−1	4	−2	−4	−2	2
1965–69	−1	−4	−1	−1	−2	−5	−2	−3
1970–74	−1	−5	−2	1	−3	−7	−3	−3
1975–79	−4	−7	−3	7	−5	−8	−3	−5
1980–83	−3	−6	−1	14	−5	−8	−2	9
Average	−2	−5	−2	4	−3	−7	−3	2

Source: Jenkins and Lai (1989).

impact on estate rubber was a 1 percent reduction in output. When the export tax on rubber was raised in 1974, the impact increased to a 4 percent reduction, which then declined to 3 percent when the tax rates were reduced in 1981. Between 1960 and 1983 short-run direct intervention reduced estate rubber production by an average 2 percent annually.

Because short-run elasticity of supply is larger for smallholders, it is estimated that the direct effects of pricing policies reduced the output of this group by an average 5 percent annually over the study period. During the years of high taxation (1975–79), smallholder rubber production declined by up to 7 percent a year. This trend moderated to 6 percent a year after tax policy was changed in 1981. The short-run direct impact on output of palm oil was only a 1 percent reduction in annual output between 1960 and 1982. When the export tax on this commodity was raised in 1974, the short-run impact rose to 3 percent. When tax policy was amended in 1981, the short-run impact dropped to 1 percent again. In the case of paddy production, removal of the direct effects of pricing policies would have had a greater short-run impact. The short-run impact amounted to 4 percent in 1960–64, −1 percent in 1968–69, and 7–14 percent in 1975–83. In general, the short-run direct impact of the policies was somewhat greater (in absolute value) when the world prices of rubber and palm oil were high (and hence the export tax was large), while for paddy the impact was greater when world prices were low.

The short-run total effect of pricing policies was a 3 percent annual decline in average production of both estate rubber and palm oil, and a 7 percent decline in production of smallholder rubber. Because the direct and indirect effects on paddy production are of the opposite sign, the short-run total effects are 3–4 percentage points per year less than the short-run direct effects.

Table 3-7 shows the cumulative direct and total effects of intervention on all three crops. The cumulative direct impact between 1960 and 1983 amounted to a 9 percent reduction for estate rubber and a 16 percent reduction for rubber smallholders. In the case of cumulative total effects, output declined by 13 percent on the estates and by 20 percent on the smallholdings. These findings strongly suggest that the rubber export tax in Malaysia has been biased against smallholders. During the same period, palm oil production declined by an average 7 and 11 percent, respectively, as a result of cumulative direct and total effects of intervention. In the case of paddy, the indirect effects of changes in the exchange rate largely offset the effects of direct intervention. Thus, the output of paddy increased by an annual average of 6 percent over the study period as a consequence of direct intervention, but increased by only 2 percent when the cumulative effects of total intervention were considered.

Table 3-7. Cumulative Effect of Direct and Total Intervention on Output of Estate and Smallholder Rubber, Palm Oil, and Paddy

Period	Direct effect				Total effect			
	Estate rubber	Smallholder rubber	Palm oil	Paddy	Estate rubber	Smallholder rubber	Palm oil	Paddy
1960–64	−9	−15	−4	8	−12	−18	−8	5
1965–69	−8	−15	−5	1	−12	−18	−8	−2
1970–74	−6	−16	−7	1	−11	−20	−12	−4
1975–79	−8	−18	−9	7	−13	−22	−14	4
1980–83	−12	−18	−11	16	−17	−23	−17	10
Average	−9	−16	−7	6	−13	−20	−11	2

Source: Jenkins and Lai (1989).

Table 3-8. Effect of Direct and Total Intervention on Quantity of Rice Demanded and Consumer Price of Rice

Period	Proportional change in quantity of rice demanded due to intervention		Proportional change in consumer price of rice due to intervention	
	Direct	Total	Direct	Total
1960–64	−3	−2	7	4
1965–69	1	2	−1	−5
1970–74	−1	2	1	−6
1975–79	−5	−3	12	8
1980–83	−14	−10	34	24
Average	−4	−2	10	4

Source: Jenkins and Lai (1989).

Changes in pricing policies also affect demand. Since the domestic consumption of rubber and palm oil is negligible, we focus attention on the consumption of rice, the basic food crop of the country. The own-price elasticity of demand for rice in Malaysia is low (Arromdee 1969; Goldman 1975; Sahathavan 1974). A value of −0.4 is assumed in this study.

Table 3-8 shows that the direct effect of pricing policies in Malaysia between 1960 and 1983 was a 4 percent decline in the demand for rice, whereas the total effect was only a 2 percent decline. The most significant impact of the pricing policies was that they smoothed out the pattern of consumption in years when the world price of rice was highly volatile. In the late 1960s, the direct effects of the policies reduced rice consumption by 2 to 4 percent, and by 1 to 22 percent in the late 1970s. In the intervening decade, consumption increased in some years and declined in others. Total intervention also reduced rice consumption, although somewhat less. In addition, the consumer price of rice increased by an average of 10 and 4 percent, respectively, owing to direct and total intervention.

Foreign Exchange Earnings

Export taxes and exchange rate adjustments have served to discourage exports of Malaysian rubber and palm oil. In the case of rice, the direct effects of intervention on production have by and large reduced the need to import rice. However, these effects have been partly offset by the indirect effect of an overvalued exchange rate.

For rubber and oil palm, pricing policies reduced the amount of foreign exchange earned by an average of 2 and 4 percent of the total agricultural exports during 1961–83 as a result of the short-run direct and total effects, respectively. The cumulative direct and total effects were reductions in the foreign exchange earnings of these crops by annual averages of 11 and 18 percent. Foreign exchange was lost because the production of export crops declined, even though fewer imports of inputs were required. In the case of paddy, there were savings from reductions in rice imports. Another important factor here is that the prices of rubber and palm oil are exogenously determined. In the world market, Malaysian natural rubber has to compete with synthetic rubber made from petroleum. Similarly, palm oil has many substitutes among the vegetable oils, particularly soya bean oil. In the case of rice, the short-run and cumulative direct effects were foreign exchange savings of about 1 percent of total agricultural imports for 1960–83. There was no impact on foreign exchange earnings for paddy.

The average short-run direct effect of pricing policies was to reduce the amount of foreign exchange available to Malaysia by slightly more than 1 percent of the total value of agricultural exports, while the reduction due to the total effects was about 4 percent. The reduction in foreign exchange owing to the cumulative direct effects of pricing policies was about 9 percent of total agricultural exports for 1961–83, and 15 percent in the case of the cumulative total effects (see Table 3-9).

The Government Budget

The principal source of government revenue from the agricultural sector is the tax on exports of rubber, palm oil, and less important agricultural crops. Little from the budget has been spent directly to subsidize the production of paddy. Most of the budgetary allocations have gone into the infrastructural development of irrigation systems, dams, roads, and processing facilities. Since 1980 Malaysia's policy has been to subsidize local paddy production directly, in the form of a cash grant per unit of paddy sold. This is in addition to a direct input subsidy equal to M\$45.45 per tonne of paddy produced.

The overall impact on the budget of this taxation and the pricing policies has been positive. Net revenues from the tax on agricultural crops as a proportion of total government revenues have fluctuated considerably, from 12 percent in the early 1960s to 2 percent in the early 1980s, with an average of 7 percent for the period. Since the introduction of the cash subsidy for paddy in 1980, the relative importance of the agricultural sector as a source of government revenue has declined (see Table 3-10). The government investment bias— which was estimated by dividing the ratio of government investment in agriculture to total government investment by the ratio of value

Table 3-9. Short-run and Cumulative Effects of Direct and Total Intervention on Foreign Exchange Earnings of Rubber, Palm Oil, and Paddy

Period	Short-run direct intervention			Short-run total intervention			Cumulative direct intervention			Cumulative total intervention		
	Change in output of export crops (1)	Reduced imports of rice (2)	Change due to (1) + (2)	Change in output of export crops (3)	Reduced imports of rice (4)	Change due to (3) + (4)	Change in output of export crops (5)	Reduced imports of rice (6)	Change due to (5) + (6)	Change in output of export crops (7)	Reduced imports of rice (8)	Change due to (7) + (8)
1960–64	−2	2	0	−3	1	−2	−12	3	−8	−17	1	−13
1965–69	−2	−1	−3	−3	−2	−5	−11	0	−10	−16	−2	−15
1970–74	−3	0	−2	−5	−2	−6	−10	0	−8	−17	−2	−16
1975–79	−4	2	−2	−5	0	−4	−12	1	−9	−18	0	−15
1980–83	−3	5	1	−5	3	−2	−14	5	−8	−23	3	−17
Average	−3	1	−1	−4	0	−4	−11	1	−8	−18	0	−15

Source: Jenkins and Lai (1989).

Table 3-10. Effect of Intervention on Government Budget, Investments, and Expenditures

Period	Net tax revenues as a proportion of total budget	Net tax revenues as a proportion of budget deficit	Ratio of value added in agriculture without price interventions to GDP (1)	Ratio of government investment in agriculture to total government investment (2)	Government investment bias (2) ÷ (1)	Ratio of current expenditure in agriculture to total government expenditure	Government expenditure bias
1960–64	12	−72	31	13	44	2	7
1965–69	5	−23	25	26	107	2	9
1970–74	6	−27	28	25	91	2	6
1975–79	9	−34	25	21	85	2	10
1980–83	2	−6	21	13	64	4	13
Average	7	−33	26	20	79	3	10

Source: Jenkins and Lai (1989).

added in agriculture (without intervention) to GDP—averaged 0.79 for the period 1960–83. This bias was higher during the late 1960s and early 1970s, when huge investments were made in irrigation infrastructure and land development schemes. Although still substantial, government investment in agriculture declined in the late 1970s and continued to decline after 1980 as the nation shifted its emphasis to industrial development and the petroleum industry.

The government expenditure bias—which is the ratio of current development expenditure to total expenditure and the ratio of the GDP in agriculture (in the absence of intervention) to GDP—averaged 0.10 for the period of study. In the early 1970s this indicator began to rise, moving to 0.10 in the late 1970s and 0.18 in the early 1980s. This reflected a shift in government expenditures toward subsidies and service-oriented activities. Accordingly, the paddy price support scheme is currently being financed from budget allocations instead of income earned from rice exports.

Changes in the transfer of resources due to pricing policies have been beneficial to paddy farmers and detrimental to the rubber and oil palm industries (see Table 3-11). On average, the direct effects of these policies reduced the producer surplus accruing to farmers by about 10 percent of total agricultural GDP between 1960 and 1983, while the total effects reduced it by 16 percent. If the nonprice transfers and only the direct effects of pricing policies are considered, the net transfer to the agricultural sector has averaged 1 percent of total agricultural GDP. When the combined effects of all price and nonprice policies are taken into account, the net transfer for the period averages −6 percent of agricultural GDP. This move to a negative value is due to the exchange rate effect.

Table 3-11. Real Transfers into (+) and out of (−) Agriculture Due to Direct and Total Intervention

Period	Share of value of agricultural output (CPI unadjusted)		Share of value of agricultural output (CPI adjusted)		Tranfers from price and nonprice policies as a share of value of agricultural output	
	Direct	Total	Direct	Total	Direct	Total
1960–64	−3	−16	−10	−13	−2	−10
1965–69	−9	−15	−11	−14	−1	−7
1970–74	−9	−17	−11	−14	−1	−9
1975–79	−15	−18	−18	−19	−3	−5
1980–83	−5	−14	−9	−13	13	4
Average	−10	−16	−12	−15	1	−6

Source: Jenkins and Lai (1989).

Income

Although the impact of pricing policies on income distribution can be evaluated both before and after production and consumption have had an opportunity to adjust, this analysis concentrates on the situation before output has had a chance to adjust. Therefore, only instantaneous change is discussed here. This change is measured by the difference between the domestic value added at the producer level and the value added for the commodity, adjusted for either the direct or the total effects; the result is multiplied by the actual output of the commodity. (For short-run and cumulative cases, see Jenkins and Lai 1989.)

If the direct effects of pricing policies on paddy are considered alone, paddy farmers' incomes increased by 16 percent over the period 1960–83, although the impact varied from year to year. In the late 1960s, for example, when the consumer price of rice was high, the incomes of paddy farmers declined 4 percent. It was not until the cash subsidy for paddy was introduced in 1982 that the incomes of paddy farmers increased significantly (see Table 3-12). The effect of total intervention on the incomes of paddy farmers was less than the effect of direct intervention, owing to the exchange rate. On average, the pricing policies increased incomes by only 9 percent over the study period.

Farmers were assumed to retain 60 percent of their paddy output for home consumption during 1960–74. After 1975 this proportion was assumed to decline by 10 percent a year until a level of 30 percent was reached. This assumption was made on the grounds that paddy output increased after the major irrigation schemes came onstream. Income from paddy was estimated to be 65 percent of total farm income. After adjusting for home consumption, the instantaneous change in income due to the direct intervention averaged 7 percent for 1960–83. This was 9 percent lower than the direct effect on the unadjusted income. A similar difference was observed in the total effect of pricing policies on the adjusted and unadjusted income. The instantaneous change in income due to total intervention declined from 9 percent to 5 percent during 1960–83.

In the case of estate rubber, the effect of direct intervention was a reduction in income in each year of the study, the average being − 19 percent in the instantaneous case. The total effect on the incomes of estate workers was higher—an average − 28 percent for the period—since the output is exported. Similarly, the incomes of rubber small-holders during 1960–83 were substantially reduced by the direct and total intervention in the instantaneous case. The average for direct intervention was − 28 percent, and for total intervention − 38 percent.

Palm oil producers saw their incomes reduced by an average 13

Table 3-12. Instantaneous Income Changes in Rubber, Palm Oil, and Paddy Due to Direct and Total Effects of Policies

Year	Estate rubber		Smallholder rubber		Palm oil		Paddy		Paddy	
	Direct intervention	Total intervention	Direct intervention	Total intervention	Direct intervention	Total intervention	Direct intervention	Total intervention	Direct intervention[a]	Total intervention[a]
1960–64	−11	−21	−21	−31	−10	−20	18	11	5	3
1965–69	−8	−16	−21	−29	−10	−17	−4	−11	−1	−3
1970–74	−12	−23	−27	−40	−16	−28	2	−8	0	−2
1975–79	−37	−39	−39	−42	−23	−26	24	22	11	10
1980–83	−28	−44	−31	−47	−6	−19	45	39	21	18
Average	−19	−28	−28	−38	−13	−22	16	9	7	5

a. Adjusted for home consumption and other income earned.
Source: Jenkins and Lai (1989).

percent during 1960–83 owing to the direct impact of pricing policies and by an average 22 percent owing to total intervention. The largest declines occurred in years of good prices for palm oil, indicating that pricing policies effectively siphoned off producer income during boom years.

The Political Economy of Agricultural Pricing Policies

Agricultural pricing policies in Malaysia between 1960 and 1983 were designed to promote rice self-sufficiency, obtain the political support of paddy farmers, and provide revenues for economic development. Only a few adjustments were made to meet changing economic circumstances or the political pressures exerted by various groups with agricultural interests. These groups have not joined forces because the pricing policies that affect rubber planters, for example, are not the same as those that affect paddy farmers. Consequently, opposition to existing pricing and investment policies has not been strong, and change has been gradual, even in the wake of the New Economic Policy introduced in 1971. The emphasis in the NEP is on the corporate sector, which is dominated by non-Malay and foreign interests. The government wants to restructure the sector to allow more Malays to be involved.

This goal points to one of Malaysia's problems—its ethnic diversity. The government is a coalition of ethnic-based parties that strive to promote the interests of their communities. A coalition of the country's three main parties has been returned to power at the federal level in all general elections since 1955. The government uses a consensus approach to arrive at decisions and minimize conflict among the parties. However, in the aftermath of the racial riots on May 13, 1969, and the adoption of the New Economic Policy, this approach seemed to break down as the Malay party in the coalition, the United Malay National Organization (UMNO), grew in electoral strength. Meanwhile, the main Chinese party, the Malaysian Chinese Association (MCA), lost out to the multiracial opposition party, the Democratic Action Party (DAP). The Indian community is represented in the coalition by the Malaysian Indian Congress (MIC), while other ethnic groups in Sabah and Sarawak are represented by a number of small parties. Since electoral strength is weighted in favor of the rural areas, and Malays form a majority of the rural population, UMNO is often under political pressure to meet the demands of rural areas.

Before the adoption of the NEP in 1971, the government practiced a noninterventionist approach to the economy. Since then, the NEP has become the basis of public policies affecting the entire nation. Of the NEP's objectives, the desire to eradicate poverty has had the greatest effect on Malaysia's agricultural pricing policies. Note, however, that poverty in Malaysia is relative, as there is no malnutrition or hunger. The poverty line is defined as the minimum income needed to obtain food, housing, clothing, utilities, transport, health care, education, and recreation.

By 1975 the paddy price supports introduced by the British colonial government in 1949 had outgrown their usefulness. Under pressure from the Malay paddy farmers, the government agreed to increase the guaranteed minimum price for paddy, starting in 1973. Further increases were made in 1974, 1979, and 1980, all of which were meant to raise and maintain the income of paddy farmers above the poverty line. In 1980 paddy farmers were also given a cash subsidy for every tonne of paddy sold. This direct subsidization grew out of the government's desire to distribute some of the oil wealth of Malaysia to the farmers.

Besides price supports, paddy farmers receive a subsidy on inputs, which in 1980 equaled 100 percent of costs. Farmers' incomes are directly increased by the subsidy because it reduces the amount they would have spent on fertilizers and other production costs. Free fertilizers are intended to increase output directly and farm incomes indirectly. Consequently, the government was indignant when it discovered that paddy farmers were selling the fertilizer they had obtained free of charge. Moral persuasion has been used to discourage the practice, but there has been no report on the result.

Before farmers can receive subsidized fertilizer, their applications must be examined by a village leader, who is usually a member of UMNO. Paddy farmers who belong to the opposition Parti Islam (PAS), particularly in Kelantan, often have their applications delayed, mislaid, or investigated more thoroughly than do others. Entire villages have been excluded from the subsidy scheme until political leaders intervened.

The decision to implement a urea price support scheme for paddy farmers in 1972–76 was also an effort to maintain the income level of paddy farmers. Although the scheme failed to prevent a decline of rice output, the government considered this tactic politically necessary to demonstrate that it was trying to help the paddy farmers.

It is not surprising that the government took a long time to react to the pressure of rubber smallholders seeking relief from pricing policies. Although the government was aware of the impact of the export tax on this group, it was reluctant to abolish the tax because such action would have led to a substantial loss of revenue. Furthermore, rubber smallholders are more dispersed geographically than paddy farmers; hence, their political influence is not as great.

In 1980 the government amended the old method of estimating the price of rubber for export tax purposes and began basing it on the f.o.b. prices of lower grades of rubber. This in effect reduced the export tax on rubber. Another move to assist the smallholders was the cost-plus principle instituted in 1982 to calculate the rate at which the export tax became payable. These two changes were possible because the government wished to share its growing revenues from exports of crude petroleum with the rubber smallholders in the form of a reduced export tax rate. Indirectly, the estates also benefited from this move.

The government has yet to act on the rubber industry's request that the replanting tax be removed or reduced. Although the tax, together with a government grant from general tax revenues, is returned to the smallholder to help him replant, not all smallholders qualify to receive the replanting grant (they must have title to their holdings, although this regulation has since been relaxed for those with very small holdings, who are mainly Malays). In addition, owners with holdings of 10 hectares or more were only allowed to receive replanting grants for a third of their holdings, but this ruling was removed in 1981.

Until the 1980s, private oil palm plantations in Malaysia were owned mainly by non-Malaysians. The government then intervened to purchase the equity of plantation companies in order to increase the Malays' share of equity capital. The income from oil exports provided the funds for these purchases. Nationalization of these companies was thereby avoided. The government considers the oil palm industry a source of revenue and thus the direct effects of its pricing policies did little to stabilize palm oil prices. Since there are no smallholders, the government is less concerned about the oil palm industry in any case.

To reiterate, the pricing policies analyzed in this study have been highly consistent since 1960. In accordance with these objectives, the government has attempted to use the increasing income from crude petroleum exports to raise the incomes of the small farmers, either directly, through subsidies, or indirectly, through reductions in the export tax. To this end, the policies reflect cultural, political, and economic conditions in the country.

The agricultural sector, particularly its export crops, has been a consistent source of revenue for economic development. Although the importance of these taxes has declined in recent years, the government has been careful to encourage the growth and development of export crops. Transfers out of agriculture in the form of taxes have been offset in part by infusions of capital into the infrastructure of rural areas, rubber replanting grants, paddy price support, input subsidies for paddy and other crops, research facilities, extension services, and processing facilities.

Malaysia's particular blend of policies is the product of tension between the politically strong paddy farmers and the economically strong plantations and emerging industrial sector. Between 1960 and 1983 rubber production was taxed fairly heavily, although the government made every effort to maintain its competitiveness by establishing a research organization. Although this research effort was financed by the industry, the government made certain that the proceeds went into rubber research and thus benefited the producers. Similarly, the replanting of new varieties of rubber trees and the diversification program from rubber to oil palm were largely financed by the rubber industry, but the programs were implemented by the government.

The stable (and high) rice price that has been the cornerstone of Malaysia's agricultural policy since the mid-1940s has also contributed to the country's general stability. Although urbanization has been rapid, it has been educated youths rather than landless laborers who have been moving from the rural areas to the cities. The country's pricing policy has also helped the more moderate and highly pragmatic Malay political party to stay in power. In the case of rice, however, the policy has incurred a direct economic cost in the form of additional investment in infrastructure and the additional labor retained in rice production in marginal paddy-growing areas. Overall, the policy has enabled a multiracial country to achieve rapid economic development without serious ethnic conflicts.

Notes

1. All monetary values reported in this chapter are in Malaysian ringgit (M$). The market exchange rate in 1983 was US$1.00 = M$2.3382, which in December 1987 had depreciated to M$2.52 per U.S. dollar.

Bibliography

The word "processed" describes works that are reproduced from typescript by mimeograph, xerography, or similar means; such works may not be cataloged or commonly available through libraries, or they may be subject to restricted circulation.

Allott, D. H. N, and Ivan C. H. Wong. 1977. "Evolution of Palm Oil Marketing from Malaysia." In D. A. Earp and W. Newall, eds., *International Developments in Palm Oil. Proceedings of the Malaysian International Symposium on Palm Oil Processing and Marketing, Kuala Lumpur, 17–19 June, 1976*. Kuala Lumpur: Incorporated Society of Planters.

Anand, Sudhir. 1983. *Inequality and Poverty in Malaysia: Measurement and Decomposition.* New York: Oxford University Press.

Arromdee, V. 1969. "Can West Malaysia Become Self-Sufficient in Rice by 1975?" *Malayan Economic Review*, October.

Bank Negra Malaysia. 1985a. *Quarterly Economic Bulletin*, vol. 18, no. 4 (December).

———. 1985b. *Annual Report*. Kuala Lampur.

Barlow, C. 1978. *The Natural Rubber Industry: Its Development, Technology, and Economy in Malaysia*. Kuala Lumpur: Oxford University Press.

Behrman, J. 1975. "Mini Models for Eleven International Commodity Markets." Paper read at the United Nations Conference on Trade and Development, December. Processed.

Chan, F. K. 1962. "A Preliminary Study of Supply Response of Malayan Rubber Estates between 1948 and 1959." *Malayan Economic Review*, vol. 7 (October), pp. 77–94.

Cheong, K. C. 1962. *An Econometric Study of the World Natural and Synthetic Rubber Industry*. Ph.D. dissertation, University of London. Processed.

Chow, C. S. 1965. "Some Aspects of Price Elasticities of Rubber Production in Malaysia." *International Rubber Conference, 1975*. Kuala Lumpur: Rubber Research Institute of Malaysia.

Edwards, C. B. 1975. "Protection, Profits and Policy—Industrialization in Malaysia (Parts I and II)." Thesis submitted to the School of Development Studies, University of East Anglia, Norwich, England.

Edwards, C. T. 1970. *Public Finance in Malaysia and Singapore*. Canberra: Australian National University Press.

Fertilizer Advisory, Development, and Information Network for Asia and the Pacific. 1984. *Report: Marketing, Distribution, and Use of Fertilizer in Malaysia*. Bangkok.

Gibbons, David S. 1984. "Padi Poverty and Public Policy." Preliminary Report. University Sains Malaysia, Centre for Policy Research. Kuala Lumpur. Processed.

Goldman, R. 1975. "Staple Food, Self-sufficiency and the Distributional Impact of Maylasian Rice Policy." *Food Research Institute Studies*, vol. 14, no. 3.

Goldman, R., and L. Squire. 1982. "Technical Change, Labor Use, and Income Distribution in the Muda Irrigation Project." *Economic Development and Cultural Change*, vol. 30, no. 4 (July), pp. 753–75.

Haughton, Jonathan. 1983. "Rural Development in Peninsular Malaysia: The Case of Single Crop Padi Cultivators." Ph.D. dissertation, Harvard University, Cambridge, Mass. Processed.

Huang, Yukon. 1972. "Some Reflections on Padi Double-Cropping in West Malaysia." *Malayan Economic Review*, vol. 17, no. 1 (April).

Jackson, J. C. 1964. "Smallholding Cultivation of Cash Crops." In Wang Gangwu, ed., *Malaysia: A Survey*. London: Pall Mall Press.

Jenkins, Glenn P., and Andrew Lai. 1989. *Trade, Exchange Rate, and Agricultural Pricing Policies in Malaysia*. A World Bank Comparative Study. Washington, D.C.

Lai, Andrew Kwok-Kong. 1983. "An Economic Analysis and Evaluation of the Urea Price Support Scheme, 1974–1976." Processed.

Lee, Aun Nee. 1982. "Institutional Innovation and Competition in Malaysian Smallholder Rubber." Council for Asian Manpower Studies Discussion Paper 82-10. University of the Philippines, Quezon City. Processed.

Lee, Hock Lock. 1978. *Public Policies and Economic Diversification in West Malaysia, 1957–1970*. Kuala Lumpur: Penerbit University, Malaya.

Lim, Chong Yah. 1960. "Export Taxes on Rubber in Malaya—A Survey of Post-War Development." *Malayan Economic Review*, vol. 5, no. 2 (October).

———. 1961. "The Malayan Rubber Replanting Taxes." *Malayan Economic Review*, vol. 6, no. 2 (October), pp. 43–52.

Lim, David. 1973. *Economic Growth and Development in West Malaysia, 1947–1970*. Kuala Lumpur: Oxford University Press.

Lim, Sow Ching. 1975. "An Analysis of Export Duty and Cesses on Rubber." *Selangor Planters' Association Annual Report*, pp. 27–31.

———. 1979. "The Current Malaysian Supply." *Malaysian Rubber Review*, vol. 2, no. 2, pp. 14–23.

Lim, Sow Ching, and Thiam Hock Tay. 1977. "A Note on the Restructured Export Duty on Rubber." *Malaysian Rubber Review*, vol. 1, nos. 2 & 3 (December), pp. 21–31.

Malaysia, Ministry of Agriculture. n.d. "National Rice Campaign and Rice Economy." Kuala Lumpur. Processed.

Malaysia, Ministry of Finance. 1980. *Economic Report, 1980–81*. Kuala Lumpur: National Printing Department.

———. 1985. *Economic Report, 1985–86*. Kuala Lumpur: National Printing Department.

Nik, Fuad Kamil. 1985. "Modelling the Operations of the Malaysian Rice Sectors." *Malaysian Journal of Agricultural Economics*, vol. 2, no. 2 (December).

Peacock, F. 1980. "The Failure of Rural Development in Peninsular Malaysia." In J. C. Jackson and M. Rudner, eds., *Issues in Malaysian Development*. Singapore: Heinemann.

Pee, Teck-Yew. 1977. *Social Returns from Rubber Research*. Ph.D. dissertation, Michigan State University, East Lansing.

RISDA (Rubber Industry Smallholders' Development Authority). n.d. "RISDA Replanting Grant." Kuala Lumpur. Processed.

Rubber Industry (Replanting) Board, Fund B. 1973. *Report on Operations, 1972*. Kuala Lumpur: Government Printer.

Rudner, M. 1971. "The Malayan Quandary: Rural Development Policy under the First and Second Five-Year Plans." *Asian Studies*, vol. 1. Reprinted in 1975 in David Lim, ed., *Readings on Malaysian Economic Development*. Kuala Lumpur: Oxford University Press.

Sahathavan, Meyanthan. 1974. "Analytical Aspects of West Malaysian Rice Price Stabilization and Support." Master's thesis, University of Malaya, Kuala Lumpur.

Selvadurai, S. 1972. *Padi Farming in West Malaysia*. Kuala Lumpur: Ministry of Agriculture.

Squire, Lyn, and H. N. Barnum. 1976. "An Econometric Model of an Agricultural Household." Cited in Pasquale L. Scandizzo and Colin Bruce, *Methodologies for Measuring Agricultural Price Intervention Effects* (1980). World Bank Staff Working Paper 394. Washington, D.C.

Stubbs, R. 1983. "Malaysia's Rubber Smallholding Industry: Crisis and the Search for Stability." *Pacific Affairs*, vol. 56, no. 2 (Spring), pp. 84–105.

Tamin, Mohktar. 1979. "Output Supply and Factor Demand Functions for Padi Farms: A Case Study of the Muda Region." *Kajian Ekonomi Malaysia*, vol. 14, no. 2 (December), pp. 1–32.

————. 1986. "Past Government Policies on the Rice Industry." Persidangan Padi Kebangsaan (National Padi Conference, January 20–22). Working Paper 1. Kuala Lumpur.

Tan, C. Suan. 1984. *World Rubber Market Structure and Stabilisation: An Econometric Study*. World Bank Commodity Working Paper 10. Washington, D.C.

Tan, Siew Hoey. 1987. *Malaysia's Rice Policy: A Critical Analysis*. Kuala Lumpur: Institute of Strategic and International Studies.

Tan, Tat Wai. 1982. *Income Distribution and Determination in West Malaysia*. Kuala Lumpur: Oxford University Press.

Tang, Loon Boon. 1982. "Price Support and Procurement for Paddy and Rice in Peninsular Malaysia." Working Paper of the Regional Workshop on the System of Price Support, Kuala Lumpur, May 3–7. Processed.

Thoburn, J. T. 1977. *Primary Commodity Exports and Economic Development: Theory, Evidence and a Study of Malaysia*. London: Wiley & Sons.

U.S. Department of Agriculture. 1985. "Malaysia—Oilseeds and Products." Attaché Report, Foreign Agricultural Service Report MY5017. Kuala Lumpur. Processed.

Visaria, Pravin. 1981. *Incidence of Poverty and the Characteristics of the Poor in Peninsular Malaysia, 1973*. World Bank Staff Working Paper 460. Washington, D.C.

Young, K., W. F. Bussink, and Parvez Hasan. 1980. *Malaysia: Growth and Equity in a Multiracial Society*. Baltimore: Johns Hopkins University Press.

4 Pakistan

Naved Hamid
Ijaz Nabi
Anjum Nasim

Despite signs of dynamism, agricultural growth in Pakistan over the past 30 years or so has been uneven. After stagnating in the 1950s, agriculture surged during the 1960s, stagnated again during most of the 1970s, and moved forward again after 1978. The central question in this chapter is, to what extent can these trends be attributed to transfers of resources between sectors and to other government policies?

It is widely accepted that substantial resources in Pakistan were transferred out of agriculture into industry, and that agricultural development suffered as a result. However, the repercussions of these actions have not yet been fully studied. In this chapter we attempt to quantify the transfers between sectors and to assess the impact of relevant policies on agricultural output, exports, and income distribution; determine the degree to which interest groups and ideology influenced the scope of price intervention; identify the groups with the greatest influence; and explain the process by which the intragroup conflicts were resolved. The period of study is 1960 to 1987.

Previous studies of agricultural pricing policies in Pakistan have given special attention to the terms of trade between the agricultural and nonagricultural sectors. The reason for this interest, according to Cheong and D'Silva (1984), is that agriculture's terms of trade indicate "whether income is being transferred out of agriculture" and signal "the strength of incentives to the agricultural sector to adopt innovations and produce more." Kazi (1987), in examining the terms of trade phases identified by Lewis and Hussain (1966) and Lewis (1970), notes that "the first phase 1951–52 and 1954–55 is marked by a decline in the prices of farm goods vis-à-vis nonagricultural goods. This is followed by a period of continuous improvement in the terms of trade in favor of agriculture from the mid-1950s to 1967–68, tapering off till 1970–71. The final phase up to the late seventies is characterized by wide fluctuations in the series along a sharply increasing trend." Kazi's own indices for the period 1970–71 to 1981–82, which are based on a different methodology, show that agricultural terms of trade improved by an average of 0.5 percent annually from 1970–71 to 1981–82, but these indices fluctuate as well. As for the relationship between the terms of trade and agricultural output, Gotsch and Brown (1980) and Kazi (1987) argue that it is statistically insignificant. (For information on output supply response at a disaggregated level, see Falcon 1964; Gotsch and Brown 1980; Ashiq 1981; Nuzhat, Bengali, and Iqbal 1983; Tweeten 1985.)

After reviewing these earlier results, we decided to use Tweeten's (1985) supply response estimates (output elasticities) to obtain estimates of output in the absence of government price intervention. We considered output response under two scenarios: (a) farmers receive border prices (appropriately adjusted) at the official exchange rate (see the appendix to this chapter for details), and (b) farmers receive border prices, but the exchange rate is the rate that would have prevailed if tariffs, quotas, and other trade restrictions had been replaced by a free-trade regime. Our study therefore goes beyond indices and trends in agricultural terms of trade to the magnitude of output losses or gains in agriculture that can be attributed to the price policy pursued by various governments. We also consider demand and compare actual consumption with consumption at border and free-trade prices. (Demand elasticities were obtained from Hamid and others 1987.) The new output and consumption figures provide a measure of potential exports (or imports) at border and free-trade prices and an estimate of foreign exchange earnings foregone.

Although income distribution has received considerable attention in the literature (for a review, see Qureshi 1987), we expand upon earlier work by comparing rural incomes in the presence and absence of price intervention. We then calculate the extent to which the actual 1980 incomes of small, medium, and large farmers were below potential incomes. Potential income is the income that farmers would have received if free-trade prices had prevailed. Indices of actual prices (P), border prices (P'), and free-trade prices (P^*) are constructed for both the rural and the urban sectors. A comparison of the indices provides a direct measure of the loss or gain in real income due to price intervention.

The chapter also contains a discussion of transfers from agriculture to the rest of the economy. These include budgetary transfers (notably, government tax revenues received from the agricultural sector) and price-related transfers arising from the differences between actual prices, border prices, and free-trade prices of inputs and outputs. Whereas Gotsch and Brown (1980), Cheong and D'Silva (1984), and Qureshi (1987) estimate transfers at border prices, we in addition estimate transfers at free-trade prices and take into account the cost of tradable inputs at border and free-trade prices. We provide estimates for five crops: wheat, basmati (traditional) rice, irri (new variety) rice, cotton, and sugarcane.

One of the main concerns in this chapter is to explain how different interest groups have helped shape agricultural pricing policies in Pakistan. Consequently, information is also provided on the phases, types, and changing priorities of intervention, the decisionmaking process involved in formulating pricing policies for Pakistan's important crops, the accommodation of conflicting interests and changing ideological positions, and some of the administrative problems related to pricing policies that have led to smuggling and corruption.

Overview of the Economy and Agricultural Sector

Pakistan covers an area of 804,000 square kilometers, or 79.6 million hectares, of which about 20.3 million hectares (26 percent) are cultivated. Most of the cultivated area lies in the provinces of Punjab (11.9 million hectares) and Sind (5.4 million hectares) in the Indus Basin, which is a vast plain formed by alluvial deposits from the Indus River and its five tributaries. The climate in this basin ranges from subtropical to semiarid and arid, with hot summers and fairly cold winters. Rain is concentrated in two seasons (the summer monsoons arrive in July and August, and the winter rains in January and February). These coincide with the basin's two crop seasons: rabi (winter) and kharif (summer). Because of low rainfall and extreme seasonality, farmers in the basin depend heavily on artificial irrigation. Indeed, Pakistan today possesses what is probably the largest canal irrigation network in the world. Wherever feasible, canal irrigation is supplemented by tubewell water.

The population of Pakistan in 1987 totaled more than 100 million, which was up from 84 million in 1981. Arable land per person employed in agriculture declined from about 4 hectares in 1961 to 2.75 hectares in 1981 (see Table 4-1). During the same period, the share of urban population in the total population increased from 22.5 percent to 28.3 percent, although concentration declined. In 1981, 54 cities accounted for 75 percent of the urban population (the seven largest accounted for 51 percent of the urban population), in comparison with 41 in 1951.

The level of education and literacy in Pakistan is still extremely low. In 1981 only 26.2 percent of the adult population was literate, and only 7.4 percent had 10 years or more of schooling.

The Economy

On the economic front, Pakistan has a strong record. Between 1960 and 1988, GNP increased to just under 6 percent a year, and real per

Table 4-1. Demographic Indicators, 1951–81

Census year	Population (thousands)			Urban (percent)	Concentration index[a]	Agricultural labor force (thousands)	Arable land per person[b] (hectares)	Cultivated area per person[b] (hectares)
	Total	Urban	Rural					
1951	33,780	6,019	27,761	17.8	41	10,324	3.39	2.45
1961	42,880	9,654	33,226	22.5	45	13,893	4.04	2.40
1972	65,309	16,593	48,716	25.4	52	19,527	3.01	1.90
1981	84,253	23,840	60,413	28.3	54	22,623	2.75	1.75

a. Number of cities accounting for 75 percent of urban population.
b. "Arable land" is the total culturable land and "cultivated area" is the net sown area plus current fallow. These have been divided by the number of persons in the agricultural labor force.
Source: *Pakistan Economic Survey; Pakistan Statistical Year Book; Agricultural Statistics of Pakistan.*

capita income (at 1959–60 prices) increased from Rs 373 to Rs 856 (see Table 4-2). In 1986 Pakistan's per capita income (US$380) was the highest in South Asia. This growth has been spurred by substantial capital inflows in the form of workers' remittances and foreign aid, but domestic investment and savings have been relatively low. Since the early 1970s, Pakistan's economy has been fairly open. Although this openness is not fully reflected in official trade statistics, exports plus imports account for more than 30 percent of GNP.

Between 1970 and 1987, investment as a proportion of GNP fluctuated between 13 and 18 percent (the average was about 16 percent), while the savings rate, except for a slight decline in 1973–74 and 1974–75, has been fairly stable. Imports as a share of GNP increased sharply in 1973–74 and again in 1978–79, in response to the oil shocks of those periods, and exports declined as a result of the worldwide recession of the 1970s, reaching their lowest level in 1978. However, the resulting disequilibrium in the trade account was offset by rapid growth in worker remittances, which in 1982–83 amounted to almost US$3 billion, or about 10 percent of GNP. That was through official channels alone. The amount entering the country through informal channels was thought to be almost as large. Since then, worker remittances have declined steadily and by 1988 were down to about US$2 billion.

Pakistan's average annual rate of inflation during the 1960s was only 3.3 percent, but between 1970 and 1982 the figure rose to 12.7 percent. In the period 1972–75, after the first oil shock, the inflation rate shot up beyond 20 percent, but it then declined to 8.4 percent by 1977–78. Since then, the government has kept the inflation rate well below 10 percent a year by managing demand better and relying on domestic nonbank borrowing to finance the deficits.

The Agricultural Sector

As already mentioned, agricultural growth in Pakistan has been uneven since independence. In 1950 agriculture accounted for 53 percent of real GNP, but by 1960 this figure had dropped to 46 percent as a result of Pakistan's emphasis on industrialization through import substitution. Large-scale public investment in irrigation and drainage and the introduction of high-yielding varieties of wheat and rice during the 1960s pushed the agricultural growth rate up to 5 percent per annum. Even so, industry continued to grow more rapidly, so that by 1970 the share of agriculture in GNP had declined to about 37 percent. Between 1971 and 1978, agricultural growth slowed to 1.7 percent a year. Although industry did not grow much faster, the noncommodity sectors expanded rapidly, so that by 1978 agriculture's share had come down to 30 percent. Since then, agriculture has grown

Table 4-2. GNP, Investment, Savings, and Trade, Selected Years, 1950–88

| Fiscal year[a] | Real GNP 1959–60 prices (rupees) | Real GNP per capita (rupees) | Percentage | | | | | |
			Investment	Savings[b]	Imports	Exports	Net factor income
1950	12,380	351	n.a.	n.a.	n.a.	n.a.	n.a.
1955	14,464	363	n.a.	n.a.	n.a.	n.a.	n.a.
1960	16,803	373	13.5	7.4	13.2	7.2	−0.1
1965	23,299	450	22.8	12.6	17.0	7.1	−0.2
1970	32,339	542	15.8	13.1	10.3	7.6	0.0
1975	40,188	574	16.2	8.3	20.5	11.6	1.0
1980	54,976	676	17.1	14.5	21.6	11.7	7.2
1985	75,586	798	15.6	12.0	20.7	9.7	7.4
1988	88,887	856	15.7	12.8	19.3	12.2	4.3

n.a. Not available.
a. In Pakistan the fiscal year is from July 1 to June 30. Thus fiscal year 1988 would run from July 1987 through June 1988.
b. Savings = investment + (exports − imports) + net factor income from abroad.
Source: Pakistan Economic Survey.

112

at 4 percent a year, but its share in GNP has continued to decline. In 1988 agriculture accounted for only 22.5 percent of GNP (Table 4-3).

Nonetheless, agriculture has contributed significantly to other spheres of Pakistan's economy. In 1988, 49 percent of the labor force was employed in agriculture, and more than 30 percent of the country's exports consisted of agricultural products. If cotton yarn, textiles, and other agrobased manufactures are included, agriculture accounts for 80 percent of total exports. In contrast, agricultural imports have been declining, owing to increasing self-sufficiency. In 1980 agricultural imports accounted for about 12 percent of total imports.

Between census years 1961 and 1981, food production outpaced the growth of population, and per capita consumption improved greatly. The output of major nonfood items also increased. When production is broken down according to categories of imported, exported, and nontraded crops, growth in the first two categories has been much the same, but it has been much slower in the third.

The cropping pattern in Pakistan has changed somewhat since 1960. The area devoted to food grains, cash crops, vegetables, fruit, and condiments has increased steadily, whereas that devoted to pulses, oilseeds, and other crops (mainly fodder) has declined. At the same time, land utilization has increased. Since 1972, cropped area has increased by 3.51 million hectares and cropping intensity by 11.4 percent.

Pakistan's agricultural growth since 1960 has been due largely to technological improvements. The number of tractors, for example, jumped from about 20,000 in 1960 to more than 200,000 by 1986, and total fertilizer used increased from less than 100,000 nutrient tonnes in 1966 to more than 500,000 nutrient tonnes in 1976 and 1.5 million nutrient tonnes in 1986. In addition, there was a large increase in the number of tubewells and water storage facilities, which made it possible to increase the availability of farmgate water from 64 million acre-feet in 1966 to 105 million acre-feet in 1986. Support for these improvements has come from government institutions, cooperatives, and commercial banks. The credit disbursed to the agricultural sector from these sources rose from just over Rs 3 billion (in 1986 prices) in 1976 to about Rs 13 billion in 1986.

Although tenancy is still widespread in Punjab and Sind provinces, it has been declining since independence. Between 1960 and 1980 the area cultivated by tenants declined from 37 percent to 19 percent in the Punjab and from 54 percent to 36 percent in Sind. At the same time, the rented area of owner-cum-tenants increased somewhat. This class of cultivators has been the most successful in innovating and deriving benefits from technological change. Tenurial arrangements appear to be changing, however, as there is now a greater tendency to rent out land on fixed cash rents as opposed to sharecropping.

Table 4-3. The Agricultural Sector, Selected Years, 1960–88

Fiscal year[a]	Percentage		Agricultural imports		Agricultural exports		
	Of GDP	Of employment	Millions of U.S. dollars	Percentage of total imports	Millions of U.S. dollars	Percentage of total exports	Percentage of agricultural output
1960	45.82	60	n.a.	n.a.	n.a.	n.a.	n.a.
1970	36.82	59	n.a.	n.a.	n.a.	n.a.	n.a.
1980	29.52	53	591	12.5	1,087	46.0	17.2
1988	22.53	49	n.a.	n.a.	n.a.	n.a.	n.a.

n.a. Not available.

a. In Pakistan the fiscal year is from July 1 to June 30. Thus fiscal year 1988 would run from July 1987 through June 1988.

Source: Pakistan Economic Survey.

Data on landownership in Pakistan is unreliable because of the widespread practice of registering land under false names. The information that can be gathered from the agricultural censuses of 1972 and 1980 indicates that the distribution of land is fairly unequal. In 1972, for example, about 40 percent of holdings were smaller than 5 hectares and accounted for less than 10 percent of the cultivated area, whereas 1 percent of the holdings were 100 hectares or more and accounted for about 25 percent of the cultivated area. However, there were slightly more medium-size farmers in 1980 than in 1972, and the area they owned was somewhat larger in 1980. The size of operated holdings in the Punjab and Sind increased slightly between the two years. (For a more detailed discussion of the agrarian economy, see Nabi, Hamid, and Zahid 1986.)

History of Agricultural Pricing Policies

When Pakistan became independent, its sources of revenue were limited mainly to taxes on foreign trade, in keeping with its emphasis on import substitution as a means of achieving rapid industrial development. Import duties on manufactures and export taxes on raw cotton and jute, in particular, provided revenue as well as protection for domestic industry. In addition, foreign exchange earnings from cotton, jute, and other agricultural commodities were made available to the fledgling industrial sector for the import of machinery and equipment. During the 1950s, these commodities accounted for 80–90 percent of foreign exchange earnings.

To implement its development strategy, the government set up an elaborate system of import controls that allowed it to maintain an overvalued currency, which in effect imposed an indirect tax on agriculture. Broadly speaking, these controls passed through three phases, which coincided more or less with the regimes of Ayub Khan (1958–69), Ali Bhutto (1971–77), and Mohammad Zia ul-Haq (1977–88). However, the pattern was first set in 1953, during the balance of payments crisis that followed the collapse of the Korean war boom, when the government resorted to direct import controls rather than a devaluation. The resulting overvaluation of the rupee turned the terms of trade in favor of industry and against agriculture, and thus precipitated the transfer of resources out of agriculture.

Some trade liberalization took place under the Bonus Voucher Scheme, essentially a system of multiple exchange rates introduced by Ayub Khan. However, it provided support only for industry, and agricultural exports continued to receive the least favorable exchange rate. When Bhutto's government devalued the rupee in 1972, agriculture's prospects should have improved, but the government also levied heavy duties on agricultural exports to raise revenues and control inflation and then made rice and cotton exports a state monopoly. Thus, direct controls and exploitation of the agricultural sector reached a peak during this period. Zia's military government, which came to power in 1977, began a serious attempt to dismantle the system of government intervention by denationalizing agricultural processing, liberalizing imports, adjusting the exchange rate, derationing sugar and wheat, and allowing the private sector to participate in the export of cotton and rice. These measures have tended to reduce the distortions in the economy.

The overall impact of Pakistan's commercial policy and exchange rate distortions between 1960 and 1985 can be assessed by comparing the free-trade equilibrium exchange rate with the actual exchange rate. We used the elasticity approach to calculate the equilibrium exchange rate. That is, we used the import equation for Pakistan to calculate the uniform equivalent tariff, which (given import and export elasticities) in turn gave the exchange rate in the absence of government intervention. The distortions in the exchange rate that have prevailed at different times during the study period are indicated in Table 4-4. Before 1970 the distortion was high, owing to the regime of import restrictions, high tariffs, and multiple exchange rates. With the devaluation of the rupee in 1972, the distortion declined, although direct intervention increased up to the mid-1970s. In the 1980s the distortion again declined, after the rupee was delinked from the U.S. dollar in 1982 and devalued. During this period, direct intervention was also reduced.

Many of Pakistan's direct interventions in agriculture came into being during World War II, when the British government in India introduced price controls and rationing because of wartime shortages.

Table 4-4. The Evolution of Exchange Rates in Pakistan, 1960–87
(rupees per U.S. dollar)

Period	Nominal actual exchange rate	Nominal equilibrium exchange rate	Exchange rate distortion[a] (percent)
1960–65	4.76	10.87	−56.2
1966–70	4.76	13.53	−64.8
1971–75	7.98	17.56	−54.5
1976–80	9.90	21.44	−53.8
1981–85	12.37	24.32	−49.1
1986–87	16.65	28.34	−41.3
Average	8.60	18.34	−53.1

a. (Nominal equilibrium exchange rate ÷ nominal actual exchange rate) − 1.
Source: Hamid, Nabi, and Nasim (1990).

After independence, the new government kept these measures in place to cope with the disruptions of partition. Table 4-5 presents Pakistan's interventions in agricultural producer prices, while Table 4-6 contains a description of Pakistan's recent history in tabular form. The phases of that history are described below.

Phase 1, 1961–71

During the first half of the 1960s, the exchange rate was used to keep the domestic prices of food and agricultural raw materials low in order to promote industrialization. At the same time, large public invest-ments were made in irrigation and drainage works, in accordance with the terms of the Indus Water Treaty with India signed in 1960. These projects were sponsored by the World Bank. However, after the hostilities with India in 1965 (which resulted in the suspension of U.S. aid) and the drought in 1965–66, the government could no longer ensure that food grains would be available at the old prices. This in turn made clear the hazards of excessive dependence on aid-financed food imports. Therefore, in the mid-1960s food security was added to the objectives of government policy. To this end, the gov-ernment raised the producer price of wheat and increased its ex-penditure on input subsidies. Just at this time, high-yielding varieties of wheat became available and precipitated what is popularly known as the Green Revolution. Thus, for the rest of the period, lack of food grain was no longer a problem.

Nonetheless, the entire period should be designated phase 1 be-cause *direct* government price intervention was restricted to a single crop—wheat—and existed for only a short time. Otherwise, the mar-ket was allowed to operate more or less unhindered, and private traders were free to buy and sell in the domestic market as well as to export. During this phase producer prices were fairly close to bor-der prices at the official exchange rate (nominal protection rates were low), except in the case of sugar, which was heavily protected.

The government intervened in pricing primarily through *indirect* means, namely, by overvaluing the currency. Thus, all crops were affected, although wheat and edible oils were imported under the PL 480 program, and agrobased domestic industries such as textiles, sugar, and vegetable ghee (hydrogenated oil) were highly protected.

Phase 2, 1972–76

In December 1971, Bhutto's People's Party took office and placed rad-ical socialists at the head of the Ministries of Finance and Agriculture.

Table 4-5. Effect of Price Intervention on Relative Producer Prices, 1961–87
(percent)

Years	Direct					Indirect all crops	Total[a]				
	Basmati	Cotton	Irri	Sugarcane	Wheat		Basmati	Cotton	Irri	Sugarcane	Wheat
1961–65	−16	−14	n.a.	279	−3	−39	−43	−47	n.a.	133	−41
1966–70	−10	−15	n.a.	448	27	−42	−48	−51	n.a.	218	−26
1971–75	−42	−26	−27	16	−15	−31	−62	−49	−55	−26	−45
1976–80	−46	−22	−38	−26	−26	−31	−63	−46	−57	−49	−49
1981–85	−54	−21	−32	−26	−30	−28	−67	−43	−51	−46	−50
1986–87	−61	−14	−2	20	−21	−23	−70	−34	−25	−8	−40
1961–87	−38	−19	−29	124	−10	−33	−60	−46	−51	39	−42

n.a. Not available.

a. The direct and indirect measures of intervention do not add up to the total measure because of a change in the denominator. For further details, see the appendix to this chapter.

Source: Hamid, Nabi, and Nasim (1990).

Party leaders feared that the country's capitalists, who had controlled the country since independence and exploited its poor people, would make every effort to topple the new government by sabotaging the economy. The government saw every price rise—or, where prices were fixed by the government, every shortage in the market—as a capitalist conspiracy and responded by taking over the activity and restricting or eliminating the role of the private sector. As a result, the number of parastatals dealing with agriculture increased rapidly and government intervention in this sector expanded. In 1972 the government banned the sale of sugar on the open market and began distributing it through ration shops. It took over fertilizer distribution and set up several parastatals at the provincial level to handle it. The government also nationalized firms involved in tractor import, assembly, and distribution and placed them under the control of the Pakistani Tractor Corporation. In 1973 rice exports became a state monopoly under the newly established Rice Export Corporation (REC), as did cotton exports. In addition, the consumer subsidy on wheat rose to almost Rs 2 billion, or about 10 percent of the government's current budget. Compulsory procurement of wheat in the Punjab was also attempted. In 1974 all private ghee mills were nationalized, and a government monopoly on the purchase of cottonseed oil was established under the control of the Ghee Corporation of Pakistan. In 1975 two new parastatals were established at the federal level for the procurement, storage, and marketing of agricultural commodities. And in 1976 all flour mills, rice mills, and cotton ginning factories, which numbered several thousand, were nationalized.

Thus, by the end of phase 2 the government had intervened in the pricing and trade of almost all major agricultural commodities (wheat, rice, cotton, sugar, and edible oils) and inputs (fertilizer, pesticides, diesel fuel, and credit). The role of private traders was greatly reduced, and the open market almost eliminated. This pattern was reflected in a widening gap between producer prices and border prices for all crops during this period. The nominal protection rate ranged from -0.25 to -0.60, in comparison with 1.91 to -0.15 in the 1960s.

Phases 3 and 4, 1977–88

On coming to power in 1977, the Zia government began dismantling the controls that had been established during the previous period. Although this was a slow process, Zia made substantial progress in this direction during his 11 years in office. The first step was to denationalize the flour mills, rice mills, and cotton ginning factories. Next, the ban on private investment in the vegetable ghee, tractor, and fertilizer industries was lifted. Then in 1980 the government an-

Table 4-6. Phases of Government Intervention

Phase and period	Producers	Consumers
Wheat		
Phase 1, 1960–71	Domestic production handled mostly by private traders before 1968. From 1968, government procurement on voluntary basis also important.	Ration shop system, supplied by PL–480 imports, worked as fair price shops. Open market remains important.
Phase 2, 1972–1976	Voluntary (and at times compulsory) procurement. Nationalization of flour (atta) mills in 1976.	Ration shop system expanded and flour (atta) provided at a subsidized price.
Phases 3 and 4, 1977–88	Voluntary procurement. Denationalization of flour mills in 1977.	Declining importance of the ration shop system, particularly after derationing of sugar in 1983. Rationing of atta discontinued as of April 1987.
Rice		
Phase 1, 1960–71	Government intervenes only through exchange rate distortion.	
Phase 2, 1972–76	Compulsory procurement. Monopoly of exports, RECP (parastatal), set up. Domestic prices kept below world prices at official exchange rate. Rice mills nationalized in 1976.	Quotas (a percentage of the amount procured) retained by private traders for sale in the domestic market.
Phases 3 and 4, 1977–88	Rice mills denationalized in 1977. Compulsory procurement abolished in 1986. Restricted export by private sector permitted in 1987.	From 1986, private traders free to sell as much as they like in the domestic market.
Cotton		
Phase 1, 1960–71	Government intervenes only through exchange rate distortion.	
Phase 2, 1972–76	Voluntary procurement. Monopoly on exports, CEC (parastatal) set up. Ginning nationalized in 1976.	Forward trading in Cotton abolished. Domestic market free otherwise.
Phases 3 and 4, 1977–88	Ginning denationalized in 1977. Restricted export by private sector permitted in 1987.	

Sugar

Phase and period	Cane procurement	Sugar marketing
Phase 1, 1960–71	Sugar mills buy cane from growers in their zone only, at price fixed by the government. High import duties, and restriction on imports and investment sanctions.	Sugar mills sell on open market and to the government. Government supplies minimum requirement through ration shops (no subsidy but price below that on open market).
Phase 2, 1972–76	As above.	Sugar mills can sell only to government, which supplies entire amount through ration shops (open market sale illegal; black markets develop).
Phases 3 and 4, 1977–88	System of mill zones abolished in 1987. Sugarcane growers free to sell to anyone. (Competition among mills raises prices above government fixed prices in some areas.) Restrictions on investment sanctions reduced.	Sugar derationed (1983) and mills sell entire output in open market. Government imports sugar and makes periodic bulk sales in open market to stabilize prices when domestic output fluctuates. Private import of sugar allowed in 1985.

Phase and period	Fertilizers	Pesticides	Tractors
Phase 1, 1960–71	Subsidy on fertilizer. Private sector allowed to set up industry, handle distribution.	n.a.	n.a.
Phase 2, 1972–76	New industry restricted to public sector. Marketing of fertilizer taken into public sector and parastatals established.	Subsidy on pesticides. Government monopoly on import and distribution.	Import, assembly, and distribution of tractors made government monopoly.
Phases 3 and 4, 1977–88	Private sector allowed to set up industry; given greater role in fertilizer distribution. Price controls/subsidy on urea eliminated in 1986.	Subsidy eliminated, and private sector free to import and distribute pesticides in 1984.	Private sector allowed to set up assembly, manufacture, and distribution facilities.

n.a.   Not available.
Source: Authors' analysis.

nounced its New Agricultural Policy, which was to promote agricultural development by gradually increasing domestic agricultural prices and bringing them up to par with world prices. At the same time, it proposed to reduce subsidies on agricultural inputs and in the future limit their use only to promoting new inputs, technologies, or crops. Also, the role of the private sector in general was to be expanded and that of the government reduced.

Accordingly, an Agricultural Prices Commission (APCOM) was established in 1981 to advise the government on setting support prices for all major crops. In its annual recommendations, APCOM takes into account the relative profitability of certain crops (at market prices of inputs and outputs) and their export/import parity prices. As a result of APCOM's recommendations, agricultural prices have been regularly increased to bring them in line with border prices.

Besides reducing direct price distortions, the government took steps to eliminate other forms of intervention in the agricultural sector. Beginning in 1978, sugar mills were allowed to sell a part of their production on the open market, but the bulk of the output continued to be purchased by the government at a fixed price and sold through the ration shops. In 1983 the government derationed sugar by allowing the sugar mills themselves to sell their product on the open market. Since 1983 the price of sugar has not been directly fixed, but if at any time the government feels that an increase in the price of sugar is excessive, it releases sugar into the market from its own stocks and then replenishes them through imports. The private sector is also allowed to import sugar, and the import duty is adjusted from time to time to ensure that the domestic price remains in the desired range. Because the domestic price of sugar has remained substantially higher than the world price since 1977, the government has not run into any problems so far.

In 1984 the import and distribution of pesticides was completely opened to the private sector and the subsidy on public sector operations eliminated. The use of pesticides has grown rapidly since then as competition among the large multinational chemical companies has prompted them to launch massive publicity campaigns and thus increase the size of the market. This strategy has had an enormous impact on the cotton crop. Yields have increased by over 50 percent since the deregulation.

Since 1985 a number of additional deregulatory measures have been introduced. In 1986 the monopoly of the Ghee Corporation on edible oil imports and the purchase of local cottonseed oil was eliminated, the government's monopoly procurement of rice was replaced by voluntary procurement, and all price controls on urea fertilizer were abolished. In 1987 the government discontinued the rationing of wheat *atta* and permitted the private sector to participate in principle in the export of cotton and rice.

However, if we take the nominal rates of protection as a measure of indirect intervention, the improvement during the 1980s has not been as large as expected because substantial depreciation of the rupee during this period (from Rs 9.90 to the U.S. dollar in 1982 to Rs 18.20 currently) has forced the government to move cautiously in freeing domestic agricultural prices.

Trends and Movements in Crop Prices

For convenience, direct intervention is discussed on a crop-by-crop basis. In reality, of course, the intervention has had more general objectives and reflects a certain uniformity across crops.

WHEAT. The domestic producer (procurement) price of wheat, adjusted for inflation, declined steadily from about Rs 2,150 in 1961–65 to Rs 1,900 in 1987. In contrast, wheat output and consumption have expanded steadily. Thus, the increase in the supply of wheat appears to be the result of a reduction in unit costs coming from government investment in agriculture, subsidies on green revolution inputs, and technological change.

Two questions immediately arise here: Was the domestic producer (procurement) price too low? Could output have been larger had farmers received a "better" (border) price? On the average, the inflation-adjusted border price for wheat, at Rs 2,561.71 per ton between 1961 and 1988, was about 30 percent higher than the corresponding procurement price. But not always so. In the late 1960s, for instance, it was lower, which suggests greater variability of border prices in comparison with procurement prices. In fact, the coefficient of variation of the inflation-adjusted border price and procurement price was 0.29 and 0.09, respectively. Thus, border prices may have resulted in greater price uncertainty for the farmer, and it is not clear what the supply response would have been. We must view the nominal rates of protection with this in mind. In most years since 1960 there was negative nominal protection; that is, price policy taxed wheat growers (on average, the negative nominal rate of protection was around 25 percent). Thus it appears that the government used direct intervention to maintain lower consumer prices. However, in setting the procurement price, it may have had an additional objective, namely, price stabilization.

On the demand side, the consumption of wheat expanded steadily (keeping pace with output), mainly because of population growth. However, the inflation-adjusted consumer price of wheat was kept within a narrow range, with a mean of Rs 2,019.15 per ton and a coefficient of variation of 0.07, which was even lower than that of procurement prices. Thus, consumer price stability appears to have been an important consideration in the government's price policy.

BASMATI RICE. The producer price of basmati rice, adjusted for inflation, was on average less than half the corresponding border price during the study period. The nominal protection rate was -0.55, which suggests a fairly high rate of tax on rice growers. This high rate persisted throughout the study period, except during the 1960s, and tended to increase over time. The border price, although higher, was also more unstable (the coefficient of variation for the two price series is 0.18 and 0.36, respectively). Thus government intervention not only lowered the domestic producer price but also reduced price instability.

Since basmati rice output nearly doubled in this period, farmers appear to have done well despite high taxation. Basmati is essentially an export crop, and domestic consumption is not a primary concern of government policy. The government appears to have passed on some of the international price instability to domestic basmati consumers (the coefficient of variation for the basmati consumer price, at 0.21, falls between the variations for producer and border prices).

IRRI RICE. In many ways, the story of irri rice (rice developed at the International Rice Research Institute) is similar to that of basmati. Nominal rates of protection have been negative and high (-42 percent), while the procurement price has been more stable (coefficient of variation = 0.11) when compared with the border price (coefficient of variation = 0.54). Similarly, the supply response of farmers has been quite good (output doubled) despite (or because of) government intervention.

However, one important difference, owing to world price movements, is that the implicit tax on basmati rice has been high and increasing since the 1960s, whereas that on irri rice has been declining. Although the inflation-adjusted border price of basmati rice increased between 1960 and 1987, that of irri rice declined. The consumer price of irri, although higher than the producer price, has been fairly stable (coefficient of variation = 0.09). Like basmati, irri was considered a revenue earner for the government, as can be seen in its pricing decisions, but the decline in world prices in the mid-1980s forced the government to subsidize its rice exports.

COTTON. The producer price of cotton, adjusted for inflation, increased until the 1980s and then declined, but remained below the border price throughout the study period. In other words, there was a tax on cotton growers (on average, the nominal rate of protection was −21 percent), but it was not as high as that on rice. The tax on cotton reached a peak in the 1970s under the Bhutto government, which employed both export taxes and an export monopoly to obtain maximum revenues.

Cotton output increased fourfold over the period 1960–86, but the slowest increase was in the 1970s, possibly because of the adverse pricing policies of the government. As in the case of other crops, the border price for cotton was more unstable than the domestic price (the coefficients of variation were 0.26 and 0.19, respectively), but the difference was not as great as in the case of rice and sugarcane.

SUGARCANE. The producer price of sugarcane, adjusted for inflation, has declined steadily since 1960. The border price, on the other hand, has fluctuated wildly. The coefficient of variation was 0.16 for the producer price, as against 0.79 for the border price. The average nominal rate of protection for the period as a whole was −0.27. In the 1960s the sugarcane growers experienced a large implicit subsidy, and then (until recently) a substantial tax.

Since 1960, sugar production has increased two and a half times, but consumption has increased even more rapidly as refined sugar has replaced the farm-produced *gur*. The inflation-adjusted price of sugar was remarkably stable over the entire period at an average Rs 9,138 per ton (1985–86 prices), with a coefficient of variation of only 0.09. In the 1960s government policies were criticized for encouraging "inefficient" sugar production, but the large fluctuations in world price since then seem to indicate that the policy was not without merit. Nonetheless, the government has without doubt favored sugarcane above all other crops and thus at times has misallocated its resources.

Effects of Price Intervention

Price intervention in Pakistan has had effects on output, consumption, exports, and foreign exchange earnings. These effects, in turn, have had important implications for the government budget, transfer of resources, income distribution, and agricultural price stability.

Direct effects refer to the impact of border prices calculated at the official rate of exchange. Total effects refer to the impact of border prices calculated at the equilibrium rate of exchange. In the discussion that follows, we distinguish between the short-run and long-run (cumulative) effects of price intervention.

Output

The short-run and cumulative effects on output were calculated using a Nerlovian-type model. The results are reported in Tables 4-7 and

4-8. The five-year averages in Table 4-7 suggest that the short-run output was below potential for all crops except sugarcane in each of the five subperiods between 1963 and 1987. In the case of sugarcane, actual output exceeded the level that would have been achieved without direct intervention for most of the period, especially during the 1960s, when actual output was 50 to 75 percent above nonintervention output. In part this reflects the extremely low international price of sugar during those years and also the high protection given to the domestic sugar industry as part of the government's overall strategy of import-substituting industrialization. The average direct effects of negative protection on output of basmati, cotton, irri, and wheat were -9, -7, -5, and -1 percent, respectively. Thus, the direct effects were relatively small, and the five-year averages were remarkably stable over the 25-year period.

The short-run effects of total intervention (Table 4-7) were substantially larger than the effects of direct intervention but were equally stable over the period. Output fell short of potential output by an average of 7 percent for wheat to 20 percent for cotton, and the positive effect of direct intervention on sugarcane was transformed over time into a small negative effect.

The cumulative effects of direct and total intervention (Table 4-8) were two to four times as large as the short-run effects. The five-year averages for the cumulative effects are more unstable than the corresponding short-run series, with sugarcane being the most unstable of all crops.

To sum up, agricultural output since 1963 has been below its potential because of government price intervention, both direct and indirect. However, the extent of the shortfall must be considered an approximation, since demand and supply elasticities of inputs and outputs do not fully capture the dynamics of technological change and the implications of different levels of private investment in Pakistan's agricultural sector. Government intervention, in the form of subsidies on inputs and direct investment in irrigation, probably had a positive impact on the former and, because of the output price policies, a negative impact on the latter. Therefore, it is difficult to say whether the numbers presented above tend to underestimate or overestimate the actual effect of government intervention on agricultural output.

Consumption

Price intervention also affects consumption. The difference between actual and nonintervention consumption depends upon the difference between consumer prices under the two regimes and on own- and cross-price elasticities.

Table 4-7. Short-Run Effect on Output Due to Price Intervention, 1963–87
(percent)

Period	Basmati rice		Cotton		Irri rice		Sugarcane		Wheat	
	Direct	Total	Direct	Total	Direct	Total	Direct	Total	Direct	Total
1963–65	n.a.	n.a.	−4	−21	n.a.	n.a.	47	2	−1	−8
1966–70	−4	−14	−8	−23	n.a.	n.a.	74	29	3	−7
1971–75	−8	−14	−8	−21	−5	−13	6	−15	−2	−8
1976–80	−9	−14	−6	−19	−7	−13	−7	−18	−3	−8
1981–85	−11	−14	−7	−18	−6	−12	−8	−17	−4	−8
1986–87	−12	−15	−5	−14	−0	−7	6	−6	−3	−6
Average[a]	−9	−14	−7	−20	−5	−12	−13	−5	−1	−7

n.a. Not available.

Note: Direct effect for 1967–68 and 1968–69 values added for sugarcane at transport-adjusted border prices was negative. For these years the non-intervention output of sugarcane was taken to be zero. The output effect, $(X_t − X'_t)/X'_t$, is not defined for these years.

a. Basmati rice does not include 1963–65. Irri rice does not include 1963–70.

Source: Hamid, Nabi, and Nasim (1990).

Table 4-8. **Cumulative Changes in Output Due to Price Intervention, 1963–87**
(percent)

Period	Basmati rice		Cotton		Irri rice		Sugarcane		Wheat	
	Direct	Total	Direct	Total	Direct	Total	Direct	Total	Direct	Total
1963–65	n.a.	n.a.	−6	−26	n.a.	n.a.	60	5	−1	−10
1966–70	−7	−19	−17	−57	n.a.	n.a.	113	62	4	−16
1971–75	−16	−35	−24	−69	−5	−24	64	13	2	−19
1976–80	−25	−40	−25	−65	−22	−38	−13	−46	−9	−21
1981–85	−30	−42	−22	−59	−21	−37	−28	−55	−9	−19
1986–87	−34	−44	−19	−52	−10	−28	1	−34	−9	−18
Average[a]	−23	−38	−20	−59	−15	−32	−26	−8	−3	−18

n.a. Not available.

Note: Direct effect for 1967–68 and 1968–69 values added for sugarcane at transport-adjusted border prices was negative. For these years the non-intervention output of sugarcane was taken to be zero. The output effect, $(X_t - X'_t)/X_t$, is not defined for these years.

a. Basmati rice does not include 1963–65. Irri rice does not include 1963–70.

Source: Hamid, Nabi, and Nasim (1990).

Between 1960 and 1987, consumption of the five crops, unlike production, was generally higher than it would have been in the absence of price intervention. On the average, the differences between actual consumption and consumption if intervention had been removed were 17, 22, -2, -1, and 8 percent for basmati, cotton, irri, sugar, and wheat, respectively. The impact on irri rice was negative because it is a substitute for basmati rice, which had greater negative protection.

It seems that per capita consumption of food and clothing was much higher than it would have been in the absence of intervention. However, that does not take into account the income effect of the larger output that higher producer prices would have generated. Nevertheless, consumption in urban areas would undoubtedly have been lower under a nonintervention scenario, and that could have created political problems for the government. Note that the public demonstrations that led to the fall of Ayub Khan's government in 1969 were triggered by urban protests over a sharp increase in the price of sugar.

Exports and Foreign Exchange

The difference between output and consumption in the absence of intervention provides an estimate of the exports (or imports) that would have resulted under those conditions. Given that in most cases the nonintervention output would have been higher and consumption lower, it should come as no surprise that price intervention would have had a large adverse impact on foreign exchange earnings.

To estimate this impact, we assumed that changes in Pakistan's exports would not affect world prices. This assumption is not appropriate in the case of basmati rice, since Pakistan enjoys a virtual monopoly over this crop. In all likelihood, greater output as a result of passing nonintervention prices on to farmers would have allowed the international price of basmati rice to fall, and this in turn would imply lower output, higher domestic consumption, and lower exports of basmati rice than those reported above. However, since no estimates of the export price elasticity of basmati rice are available, it is not possible to correct for this effect.

The potential gains from nonintervention, which manifest themselves either as a decline in imports or an increase in exports of individual crops, were used to calculate foreign exchange earnings. These earnings were then subtracted from actual foreign exchange earnings to obtain the "foreign exchange earnings foregone," which are presented as a proportion of total foreign exchange earnings from all exports (Table 4-9). The results are striking. Direct price intervention produced an average net foreign exchange loss of about 21 percent in the short run and 50 percent in the long run. When both direct

Table 4-9. Actual and Foregone Exchange Earnings Due to Intervention, 1963–87

Period	Actual earnings (millions of U.S. dollars)		Foregone foreign exchange earnings for all crops (percent)			
			Short-run		Cumulative	
	All crops	Total exports	Direct	Total	Direct	Total
1963–65	−0.04	232.57	3.24	110.32	3.18	123.71
1966–70	42.44	313.10	−16.08	111.41	−5.81	285.26
1971–75	80.12	800.09	60.35	124.84	58.25	317.76
1976–80	264.29	1,532.57	40.03	98.07	76.73	268.92
1981–85	666.56	2,684.82	22.01	71.62	63.22	216.43
1986–87	694.00	3,379.66	−16.72	31.62	4.31	100.22
Average	277.29	1,411.56	20.87	78.27	49.92	218.99

Source: Hamid, Nabi, and Nasim (1990).

and indirect price interventions are taken into account, the loss in foreign exchange earnings increases to 78 percent in the short run and 219 percent in the long run. The loss in foreign exchange earnings under intervention reached a maximum in the first half of the 1970s, and since then has tended to decline, although even now the loss is substantial.

Income Distribution

The impact of price intervention on income distribution can be assessed from its effect on farm, rural nonfarm, and urban households.

FARM HOUSEHOLDS. As we have seen, for four out of the five major crops, farmers received lower output prices than they would have received in the absence of intervention. However, inputs, especially fertilizer, were heavily subsidized for most of the period from 1960 to 1987. Thus a nonintervention price regime would have implied higher output prices and higher input prices for farmers. Their incomes would also have been higher, even if we ignore the effect of prices on production. The income effects would be amplified when production effects are taken into account. However, such interventions would not affect all farmers equally. For example, small farmers who produce only for their own consumption would have been less affected than large farmers producing primarily for the market. Also, insofar as all crops were not equally affected, there would be regional differences based on crop specialization.

Without intervention, the income of small farmers in 1980 would have been 2.4 to 2.8 times higher and that of large farmers 3 to 3.5 times higher. In the unirrigated areas, incomes would have been 1.5 to 2.3 times higher. In view of the wide gap between the actual incomes of small and large farmers, and between irrigated and non-irrigated areas, a noninterventionist policy would have accentuated both the interpersonal and the interregional income differences, while improving the living standards of the poor.

To obtain more detailed information on income distribution effects in rural Pakistan, we divided farmers into three groups (small, medium, and large) and the country into 10 agroclimatic zones. The results for 1980 are presented in Table 4-10. The incomes of small, medium, and large farmers were all below what they would have been in the absence of intervention. This holds true even if we disregard the effect of nonintervention on output prices. Thus, the instantaneous effects $(y - y' / y')$, which disregard the output effect, are negative for all income groups and for all regions. Similarly, the short-run effects $(y - y' \ sr / y' \ sr)$ and the cumulative effects $(y - y' \ lr / y' \ lr)$, which take into account the effect of prices on output, are also negative throughout. As expected, short-run effects are stronger than instantaneous effects, and long-run effects are stronger than short-run effects, whether in the absence of direct or of total intervention. Furthermore, the effects of total intervention dom-

Table 4-10. Effect of Price Intervention on Rural Income, 1980
(percent)

1980 zones	Instantaneous		Short-run		Cumulative	
	Direct	Total	Direct	Total	Direct	Total
Barani, Punjab	−18	−33	−20	−37	−23	−45
Mix, Punjab	−37	−54	−43	−61	−48	−75
R/W, Punjab[a]	−42	−56	−46	−62	−54	−73
Low-density, Punjab	−27	−47	−32	−55	−39	−71
C/W, Punjab[a]	−25	−48	−31	−56	−39	−75
C/W, Sind[a]	−21	−46	−26	−55	−34	−75
Rice, Sind	−43	−59	−48	−65	−55	−75
Irrigated, North-West Frontier Province	−48	−62	−54	−69	−59	−80
Unirrigated, North-West Frontier Province	−27	−43	−31	−48	−36	−59
Baluchistan (except Sibi)	−21	−37	−23	−41	−27	−50

a. C/W = cotton/wheat; R/W = rice/wheat.
Source: Hamid, Nabi, and Nasim (1990).

inate the effects of direct intervention. These conclusions apply to every farm size and each agroclimatic zone.

In addition, price intervention may alter the regional distribution of income. Our estimates suggest that incomes in the unirrigated areas—Barani Punjab, North-West Frontier Province, and Baluchistan—were not as adversely affected as those in the irrigated areas of Punjab and Sind. Since the incomes in the latter regions were higher, one can conclude that price intervention tended to reduce regional inequalities.

RURAL NONFARM HOUSEHOLDS. Direct intervention appeared to benefit hired labor by keeping consumer food prices below nonintervention prices during the 1970s. From 1971 to 1975 the annual benefit was 16 percent; afterward, it dropped to about 13 percent. If we adjust for the equilibrium exchange rate, the benefit is more than 10 percent in the pre-1970 period and around 30 percent in the first half of the 1970s. The five-year averages since then indicate some narrowing of the gap between actual prices and free-trade prices, but the benefit for rural hired labor is still substantial.

At nonintervention prices, agricultural output would have been larger, and demand for farm labor would have been greater. This would have meant higher rural wages. However, these effects are not captured in the framework of our analysis. Therefore, the benefits of price intervention for hired labor are overestimated.

URBAN HOUSEHOLDS. Urban price indices indicate that direct intervention was beneficial to urban consumers during most of the post-1970 period, but that the actual benefits were extremely small. It appears that intervention benefited low-income and middle-income groups only. This result is to be expected because spending on agricultural commodities, particularly food, as a proportion of total income tends to decline as income rises. On the average, the actual incomes of low- and middle-income groups exceeded nonintervention levels by 6 and 3 percent, respectively. For both groups, benefits were highest in the 1970s and then declined somewhat.

The Government Budget

Intervention produces revenues for the government (through taxes on exports), but it also usually includes government expenditures (subsidies for food producers and raw materials). For example, the government may provide subsidized irrigation water, seeds, credit, fertilizer, and extension services. In Pakistan most of these inputs have had a positive effect on agricultural growth, but it is not possible

Table 4-11. Effect of Direct Price Intervention on the Budget, 1960–87
(millions of 1985–86 rupees)

Fiscal year	Total revenue	Total expenditure	Net expenditure[a]	Net expenditure as a percentage of budget
1960–65	108	340	232	n.a.
1966–70	18	586	568	n.a.
1971–75	1,504	4,020	2,515	6.07
1976–80	1,609	6,554	4,946	9.04
1981–85	1,800	5,798	3,998	4.72
1986–87	− 1,520	7,843	9,363	7.54
Average	821	3,784	2,964	6.59

n.a. Not available.
a. Total expenditure minus total revenue.
Source: Hamid, Nabi, and Nasim (1990).

to quantify the effect. Therefore, we can only present their budgetary costs and compare them with the effects of intervention on revenues.

Table 4-11 shows government revenues obtained from explicit export taxes on cotton and rice and implicit taxes in the form of profits for government monopolies in cotton and rice exports. It also shows government expenditures, consisting of explicit subsidies on imported food crops; subsidies for consumers of wheat, edible oils, and sugar; and direct subsidies for inputs, mainly on fertilizer, water, and credit. The differences between government revenues and government expenditures are the budgetary effects of price intervention.

Unfortunately, without data on (West) Pakistan's budget for the period prior to 1971, it is impossible to calculate the proportion of net revenues (or more appropriately, net expenditures) to the budget or the budget deficit for the 1960s. In the 1970s, however, net expenditure on agriculture as a proportion of the government budget increased somewhat, and in the second half of the 1970s it reached peaks of 9 percent of the total budget and almost 20 percent of the budget deficit. By this time the government had begun to realize that subsidies were getting out of control and took steps to reduce them. Fertilizer prices and water rates were adjusted upward, and the subsidy for pesticide purchases was discontinued. As a result, the proportion of net government expenditures associated with agricultural price policy fell to an average 4.7 percent a year in the first half of the 1980s. Since then, it has begun to increase once again, with the decline in the subsidy on fertilizer being more than offset by increased subsidies for water and credit. As a percentage of the budget deficit, net expenditure on agriculture (after declining in the early 1980s) was again around 20 percent in 1986–87.

Transfer of Resources from Agriculture

The five-year average of total transfers from agriculture owing to price intervention and other government expenditures increased from about 5 percent of GDP in the 1960s to 20 percent in the first half of the 1970s (Table 4-12). Since then, the transfers have gradually declined. These trends indicate not only reductions in direct and indirect taxation of agriculture, but also a decline in agriculture's share in GDP. One might conclude that by the 1980s the agricultural sector had by and large fulfilled its historical role of providing capital resources for industrial development and that therefore the need for previous levels of transfers no longer existed.

To determine whether the government attempted to compensate the agricultural sector for these transfers, we calculated indices of government investment and expenditure bias as ratios between government resources going to agriculture and the share of agriculture in GDP (Table 4-13). These results show that during the latter half of the 1960s, government investment favored the agricultural sector, as shown by massive investment in water resources. Thus, transfers out of agriculture through the price mechanism were partly compensated by government investment, which probably explains the extremely good performance of the agricultural sector during this period. A bias against agriculture then emerged in the early 1970s and continued to increase during the second half of the 1970s. Transfers out of agriculture through price policy also reached their maximum (almost 8 percent of GDP) at this time. This was a product of the People's Party's industry-oriented public investment policy. Since then, the bias toward industry has been reduced somewhat by an increased emphasis on rural infrastructure.

Price Variability

Government intervention in agricultural pricing is often defended on the grounds that it reduces the impact of world price instability on domestic prices. Our calculations of the coefficient of variation for producer and consumer prices (that is, actual, border, and equilibrium prices deflated by the nonagricultural sector) show that the government succeeded in stabilizing prices. Price intervention reduced the coefficient of variation of the producer prices of all five crops. Moreover, the coefficient of variation of consumer prices was considerably less than that of free-trade, nonintervention, consumer prices. In

Table 4-12. Transfers into (+) and out of (−) Agriculture, 1961–87
(millions of 1985–86 rupees)

Fiscal year	Total nonprice transfers	Price-related transfers		Total of price and nonprice transfers		Total of price and nonprice transfers as a percentage of GDP	
		Direct	Total	Direct	Total	Direct	Total
1961–65	2,762	5,166	−8,868	7,928	−6,106	6.19	−4.77
1966–70	5,986	4,999	−21,176	10,985	−15,190	6.19	−8.56
1971–75	6,463	−11,816	−53,391	−5,353	−46,927	−2.35	−20.56
1976–80	7,946	−9,548	−48,098	−1,602	−40,152	−0.55	−13.77
1981–85	8,901	−14,569	−58,080	−5,669	−49,179	−1.43	−12.37
1986–87	9,615	−6,027	−31,733	3,589	−22,118	0.71	−4.40
Average	6,649	−5,218	−37,464	1,430	−30,815	0.54	−11.69

Source: Hamid, Nabi, and Nasim (1990).

Table 4-13. The Bias in Government Investment, 1960–87

Period	AGDP-NI[a]	GIA/GI[b]	GIB[c]
1960–65	0.47	0.32	0.70
1966–70	0.42	0.46	1.08
1971–75	0.57	0.39	0.71
1976–80	0.50	0.22	0.44
1981–85	0.45	0.26	0.58
1986–87	0.35	0.23	0.66
Average	0.47	0.32	0.70

a. Nonintervention agricultural GDP.
b. Government investment in agricultural sector ÷ total government investment.
c. Index of investment bias (GIA/GI ÷ AGDP-NI).
Source: Hamid, Nabi, and Nasim (1990).

other words, the government reduced price instability both for producers and consumers.

The Political Economy of Agricultural Price Intervention

Three factors appear to have governed direct price intervention in Pakistan: (a) balance of payments considerations, which led the government to emphasize foreign exchange earnings in the case of export crops (cotton and rice) and to reduce imports of deficit crops (wheat and sugar); (b) political considerations, which prompted the government to shield urban consumers against increases in food prices; and (c) budgetary considerations, which imposed an upper limit on subsidies. These factors were often in conflict. For example, there was political pressure to keep food prices low, but if subsidies were used to do so, the budget suffered. Meanwhile, if producer prices were depressed, supplies dwindled, and the government was forced to turn to imports and thus aggravate balance of payment problems. Similarly, although taxes on export crops generated fiscal revenues, they also adversely affected supply and thus the surplus available for export, and therefore the balance of payments.

Which of these considerations was uppermost depended on the situation at the time. During the commodity boom of the early 1970s, for example, the government attempted to protect urban consumers by keeping the procurement price of wheat low and subsidizing imported wheat. To finance the import subsidy, the government monopolized export trade in cotton and rice, and created a wedge between their international and domestic prices. Because of stagnation in agricultural production, however, wheat imports rose while exports of cotton and rice declined. Thus the balance of payments came under pressure. Also, since imported wheat was much more expensive than that produced domestically, the amount of the import subsidy increased rapidly. Balance of payments and budgetary pressures in 1974–75 then forced the government to increase the producer prices of all crops substantially.

Although various considerations affected the agricultural sector as a whole, the resulting price policies tended to be fairly crop-specific. The procurement price fixed for an individual crop each year depended on whether it was an importable or an exportable, whether surpluses or shortages were increasing or decreasing, whether the world price was high or low, and so on. Since all these factors seldom moved in the same direction at the same time for all crops, actual pricing decisions were made on a crop-by-crop basis. Therefore, it is useful to examine the interactions between different economic and political actors, and the administrative implications for each crop.

Wheat

The government's primary objective in intervening in the price of wheat was to provide urban consumers with *atta* (flour) at low prices. The secondary objective was to protect wheat farmers against seasonal price fluctuations. The latter became important in 1968, when high-yielding varieties of wheat were introduced and generated large surpluses that the existing system was unable to handle. The government feared that because most farmers did not have storage capacity, private traders would take advantage of the seasonal glut to push down the price. Therefore, it decided to purchase directly from farmers, in competition with private traders. The private traders found it difficult to compete, and the government's share of wheat trade expanded. By 1982 the government was procuring 73 percent of the marketable wheat surplus in the Punjab (Cornelisse and Naqvi 1984). In other words, what was initially conceived as a backup system to ensure a minimum price to the farmer became the major system for the marketing of wheat.

Since wheat is a staple and its price a politically sensitive issue, all Pakistani governments have attempted to insulate urban wheat consumers from the market. As a result, wheat *atta* has been supplied through a government-controlled system at a fixed price. This control over the timing of the price increase has been politically important, for it has enabled the government to announce price increases at the same time it announces wage increases for workers.

In the 1970s the procurement price of wheat (and other crops) was set on an ad hoc basis. In 1981, however, APCOM was established to advise the Ministry of Food and Agriculture (MINFA). Each year in August, APCOM presents a paper on the support price policy for wheat to MINFA. This paper, along with the recommendations of MINFA, is discussed by the cabinet, and the procurement price of wheat is announced before wheat sowing begins in November. The government then commits itself to purchase, at harvest time, all the wheat offered to it at the announced procurement price.

The rationing system for wheat consumers was first established by the British in 1942 in response to wartime shortages of goods. The ration shops consisted of licensed private retail outlets through which the government distributed a fixed quantity of wheat per person per day. Other commodities—such as sugar, tea, matches, kerosene, and cloth—were also available through ration shops. After independence in 1947, the rationing of commodities other than wheat and sugar was discontinued. In 1960 rationing was replaced by a partial provisioning and price stabilization policy. Within a certain price band, private wheat traders were allowed to operate freely. Under the partial provisioning system, the ration shops continued to distribute *atta* supplied by the government without limiting the quantity purchased. This situation continued until 1965–66, when war with India, bad weather, and reduced food aid from the United States forced the government to reinstitute rationing.

The People's Party government greatly expanded the ration shop system in the early 1970s and established a government monopoly on sugar. However, it had difficulty providing basic food items at low prices. In the face of inflationary pressures, the government attempted to maintain the procurement price of wheat and reinstituted the monopoly procurement of wheat in the Punjab, but farmer opposition forced it to abandon that policy fairly quickly and to increase the procurement price. The government then attempted to maintain the ration shop price of *atta* at the old level, but the subsidy became very large (about Rs 2 billion a year in 1973–74 and 1974–75, or more than 10 percent of the government's expenditure). Consequently, the government was forced to increase the price of *atta*.

After Zia's government took over in 1977, the ration system lost its hold. In 1976–77, more than 75 percent of the urban population obtained *atta* from the ration shops, but by January 1986 the proportion had declined to less than 30 percent. In April 1987, wheat flour was derationed as the government took advantage of a comfortable wheat stock position (about 5 million tons) that had resulted from the record crop of 1986 and substantial imports in 1985.

The system as it exists today gives the private sector little marketing incentive because the government is committed to maintaining the same price for wheat at all times in the year throughout the country. However, plans are under way to gradually increase the gap between the procurement price and the sale price and thus encourage the private sector.

The direct administrative cost of operating the wheat procurement and rationing system has not been great (about Rs 150 million in 1985). The more important costs were those entailed in the subsidy and the corruption that the procurement system engendered, particularly following the derationing of sugar in 1983. According to a recent study, only 20 percent of the subsidized wheat supplied by the government to the flour mills was actually purchased by consumers from the ration shops. According to Alderman, Chaudhry, and Garcia (1987), the benefit received by consumers (that is, the difference between the open market price and the ration shop price times the quantity purchased) was only Rs 250 million in 1985–86. However, the cost of the subsidy to the government was Rs 1,800 million. That is to say, under the program, Rs 1,550 million of the subsidy was lost because of corruption and waste. This is equivalent to two and a half times the annual expenditure on research and extension.

The principal beneficiaries of the system were obviously not the consumers but the shop owners, the flour mill operators, and provincial food departments (which were supposed to police the system). These groups became the main lobbyists for continuing the rationing system. When, for example, the government announced that it was considering derationing *atta*, the 45,000 or so shop owners began a campaign against the plan and threatened to demonstrate in the streets if it was carried out.

Although insufficient evidence is available to indicate the extent of wheat smuggling, newspaper reports and interviews with persons in the government suggest that wheat was being smuggled to India on a large scale during most of the 1960s and the first half of the 1970s because the price of wheat there was substantially higher than in Pakistan. But smuggling did not reach alarming proportions between 1965 and 1975 because India and Pakistan were fighting each other, and for most of the period there were armies stationed on both sides of the border, making smuggling difficult.

From time to time the government has introduced regulations to prevent smuggling. For example, it restricted the free movement of wheat between districts and provinces, required that wheat be transported between provinces (when permitted) by rail and not road, and called upon all private traders to declare their stocks. Most of these restrictions have been withdrawn. The price of wheat in Pakistan is no longer below that in neighboring countries, and smuggling is not a problem now.

Sugarcane

Pakistan has only a few areas in which the climate and soil are suited to sugarcane cultivation. Even before independence, however, most farmers planted sugarcane and made a coarse brown sugar called *gur* for their own use. In 1949–50, about 200,000 hectares—that is, 1.6 percent of the cropped area—was under sugarcane. To reduce its balance of payments problem while pursuing an import substitution strategy, the government imposed high tariffs and import restrictions on sugar. This made it more attractive to cultivate sugarcane than other crops, with the result that by 1959–60 about 400,000 hectares were devoted to cane. However, only five sugar mills were in operation at that time, and these consumed only 10 percent of the cane produced; the remaining 90 percent of the cane was still being converted into *gur*.

In the 1960s sugar production continued to be highly profitable, both for the growers and the industrialists. The industry was highly regulated, and the government's decisions on new sugar mills were often made on political grounds. By 1969–70, Pakistan had 19 mills in operation, and these utilized 27 percent of the sugarcane produced. In 1987 the area under sugarcane was about 800,000 hectares, there were about 40 sugar mills in operation, and these crushed about 40 percent of the cane produced in the country.

Government regulations on sugar pricing, production, and distribution can be summarized as follows. The government announces the price of sugarcane each year before the sowing season. The prices vary slightly from one province to another. In recent years the mills have been required to pay the growers a quality premium based on actual average amounts of sugar recovered by the mill. Until 1986 a certain geographic area surrounding a new mill was designated the mill zone, and the mill had to buy all sugarcane offered to it by growers in its zone at the price fixed by the government. Growers in one mill zone were not allowed to sell their sugarcane to another mill, nor were they allowed to convert it into *gur*. However, these regulations were abolished in 1987.

Until 1983 the government also fixed the retail price of sugar. It purchased a proportion of the total production and sold it at this price through the ration shops. The mills were allowed to sell the rest on the open market (except during the People's Party rule, when open market sales were declared illegal). Now the mills must sell their product in the open market, and the government intervenes only when it feels that price increases are unwarranted.

There are three major groups in the sugar economy: farmers, consumers, and sugar mill owners. The farmers can be further divided into those who are near a sugar mill and those who are not. Although farmers outside the mill zones are affected by sugar price policies through their effects on the price of *gur*, sugarcane is not an important crop for them and they do not attempt to influence price policy. However, since sugarcane production in a mill zone is several times as profitable as any other crop, farmers outside the sugar mill zones often seek to gain approval for a new mill in their neighborhood.

The farmers inside mill zones, the mill owners, and consumers are often at loggerheads over the price of sugarcane. The farmers would like high prices, the mill owners want to keep costs down, and consumers would like low prices. Before 1983, as mentioned earlier, the government fixed the price of sugarcane as well as the price of sugar. The consumers were the losers but were given the impression that the government was concerned about their welfare. By creating artificial scarcities and keeping the ration shop price below the open market price (although it was substantially above the import price), the government was able to keep consumers satisfied.

Since 1983, sugar farmers have been lobbying unsuccessfully for an increase in the producer price, but the mill owners have opposed it. In 1986 sugar farmers in Sind refused to deliver sugarcane to the mills at the fixed price, but the government convinced the farmers to end their strike by promising to increase the price of sugarcane during the next crushing season. The price of sugarcane was increased by 22 percent, and the system of zoning was abolished. As a result, competition among mills caused producer prices during the 1987–88 season to be generally higher than those fixed by the government.

The rationing of sugar has led to widespread corruption. As long as the open market price was above the ration shop price, shop owners and others found it profitable to divert a part of the quota to the open market. This was done through false ration cards, which may have amounted to 20 percent of the total number of cards issued. However, the cost of corruption here was not borne by the government, since there was no subsidy on sugar sold through the ration shops.

From 1972 to 1977 open market sales were illegal, and an active black market developed. In 1974–75 the black market price was Rs 8–10 per kilogram, compared to the ration shop price of Rs 4.60 per kilogram. Although it is impossible to guess what proportion of sugar was sold on the black market, it seems to have increased over time.

Rice

The procurement of rice, particularly the basmati variety, has been strongly influenced by revenue considerations, as the government believed that the elasticities of supply and international demand for basmati rice were low. Revenue was obtained both through an export tax and profits from the government monopoly on rice exports.

Bhutto's government decided to put a halt to what it saw as the exploitation of farmers by traders, and it nationalized the rice export trade (along with cotton and vegetable oil) in 1973–74. In 1976 rice milling was also nationalized.

Rice had been marketed by small traders who, along with private rice mills, provided employment to a large section of the rural non-farm middle and lower middle classes in Central Punjab. The reforms put many out of work and sparked a decline in Pakistan's rice exports in 1972–73, which did not pick up again until 1975–76, despite growth in output. It is widely believed that much rice was smuggled out of the country.

Nationalization generated strong political opposition from the vocal middle class in rural towns, which played a crucial role in the National Alliance Movement of 1977. Bhutto could not survive these pressures, and his government fell to a military coup in July 1977. The Zia government then returned the rice mills to the private sector.

Since 1981 the Agricultural Prices Commission has presented a report on rice to the Ministry of Agriculture. This report reviews the most recent information on the domestic situation for rice (area, production, costs of production, stocks, imports, exports, and border prices) and forms the basis of the price recommendations that MINFA submits to the cabinet. The most important considerations seem to be the cost of production for the average farmer and the size of the previous year's harvest relative to the expected one. Prices are generally adjusted upward to bring them in line with increases in production costs. In a poor harvest year, farmers and traders lobby for price increases through newspaper articles and appeals to the government. These groups also lobby the federal cabinet directly by sending delegations to the ministers of agriculture, commerce, and finance. However, lobbying affects only the following year's price. Rarely does the government revise the current year's procurement price.

More and more farmers have become aware that the prices they receive are below the international prices. This implicit taxation is resented, particularly when the government attempts to remove input subsidies. Farmers also point to this implicit taxation in arguing against an income tax on agricultural activities.

The relationship between the Rice Export Corporation (REC) and the rice traders is also an uneasy one. The corporation was originally given a monopoly over all trade in rice, but after the 1977 military coup the middlemen were allowed to operate again. The REC, however, regulates the activity of private traders through a large number of measures.

Nonetheless, corruption arose after 1977 because the REC monopolized exports. Food inspectors are required to ensure that procured rice meets quality standards, but (in collusion with superior officers), many inspectors allowed greater contamination in exchange for bribes. This resulted in lower prices for Pakistani rice in the international market. The dealers' quota for sales in the local market also gave rise to corruption. By bribing food inspectors, rice dealers were able to exceed their quotas.

In 1986 the Rice Dealers' Association helped to bring about fundamental reform. The free market in the domestic rice trade was restored, and the private sector was also allowed to export basmati rice in packages of 20 kilograms or less. However, an extremely high export tax has prevented the private sector from making significant exports.

Cotton

Before independence, Pakistan had a sophisticated pricing mechanism and a system of intermediaries between growers and users of cotton. The intermediaries included local village middlemen who supplied raw cotton to the ginning mills. These, in turn, operated in the international market through the Karachi Cotton Exchange, which was linked to the London Cotton Exchange. The only direct government intervention was an export tax. Market forces determined prices, and agents responded to these.

Then, in 1959, Pakistan adopted a system of multiple exchange rates, primarily as a means of fostering industrialization and encouraging manufactured exports. Under this system, the government allowed raw cotton to be exported at the official exchange rate (which was unfavorable to exporters), introduced a somewhat better exchange rate for yarn, and gave the best rate to cloth manufacturers. Three distinct groups emerged: cotton growers and ginners, yarn manufacturers, and cloth manufacturers. Until 1972 these groups were concerned mainly with pressuring the government into altering the exchange rate in their own favor.

In 1972 things changed drastically, with the devaluation of the rupee and abolition of the multiple exchange rate regime. At the same time, a commodity price boom in the international market allowed cotton exporters to make substantial profits. The government of Pakistan saw this as an opportunity to raise additional revenue. At first it levied an export duty on raw cotton. It then decided to establish a government monopoly on cotton exports. The Cotton Export Corporation (CEC)—set up for this purpose—was rather different from the Rice Export Corporation. Although it had a monopoly on the export of cotton, it relied on voluntary procurement, in deference to Pakistan's large domestic textile industry, which also purchased cotton directly from the ginners. The CEC bought cotton from private sector ginneries and also created its own ginneries, thus moving into all spheres of the cotton trade. The government, through the CEC, also operated a support price system for raw cotton.

The process of liberalization that has been taking place since 1977 in the case of other crops has not affected cotton significantly. The CEC continues to be directly involved in export trade and in the implementation of the government's support price policy. However, private sector traders still dominate the domestic trade.

The government's price intervention policies have exacerbated the conflicts between cotton growers, manufacturers of yarn, and yarn users. In 1986, for example, when the international price of lint cotton fell below the government's procurement price, the government was forced to incur a loss on exports. As a result, the domestic textile industry complained that it could not compete internationally because the local prices of lint cotton were higher than the international prices. The government agreed to provide subsidized cotton to exporters, but budgetary considerations later forced the government to withdraw the offer.

In 1987 the international price of cotton rose much higher than the domestic price, and the government was forced to impose an export tax on cotton yarn. This was done after intensive lobbying by the textile industry. In this case, the government earned substantial revenues, and these taxes are likely to continue as long as international cotton and yarn prices remain high.

Conclusion

Since the late 1970s Pakistan has made a sustained effort to reduce direct and indirect price intervention in the agricultural sector. To this end, it has increased procurement prices, deregulated trade and industry, reduced input subsidies, and eliminated rationing. Also, the overvaluation of the rupee has been substantially reduced. However, reformers have experienced considerable difficulty in eliminating the de facto state monopolies on rice and cotton exports.

Pakistan's experience clearly demonstrates that a gradual process of reform stands a better chance of success in the face of bureaucratic opposition than a dramatic reform simultaneously encompassing all aspects of intervention. Moreover, the most difficult areas of reform are those that result in the loss of revenue or the loss of jobs. However, it appears that if a reform effort first deals with the relatively easy problems, it may be able to build up the momentum and credibility needed to tackle the more difficult issues later.

It seems that agriculture may pass through several phases as a country develops. In the early stages, when agriculture is the largest sector in the economy, it is heavily taxed to finance the development of other sectors. When other commodity-producing sectors become as large as agriculture, it then faces a more neutral regime. Subsequently, when agriculture becomes only a small proportion of the economy, the country can afford to subsidize it in pursuit of equitable income distribution. Pakistan, having passed through the "primitive accumulation" phase during the first 30 years of its existence, may now be approaching the intermediate phase. If that is the case, the current trend toward less government intervention can be expected to continue for the next decade or so.

Appendix: Domestic and Transport-Adjusted Border Prices

Producer Prices

All producer prices were adjusted to reflect prices at the farmgate. This implies, for example, that if we consider the procurement price as the typical price that the farmers receive for their produce at the procurement center, the farmgate price is obtained by subtracting the transport cost from the farm to the procurement center.

The border prices also have been adjusted to reflect the prices at the farmgate. In this context, the distinction between importables and exportables is important. If a commodity is an exportable, then the price the farmers would receive in the absence of direct intervention would equal the f.o.b. price minus the cost of transport from the farmgate to the border. Thus, if P_g = the producer price at the farmgate, P_x = the f.o.b. price of exportables, and C_{gx} = the cost of transport from the farmgate to the border, then the farmer would receive the following farmgate price for an exportable crop:

$$(4A\text{-}1) \qquad\qquad P_g = P_x - C_{gx}.$$

If a commodity is an importable, then the domestically produced and the imported crop would fetch the same price at any point in the marketing chain (see Westlake 1987). The following relationship therefore holds:

$$(4A\text{-}2) \qquad\qquad P_g + C_{gf} = P_m + C_{mf}$$

where P_g = the producer price at the farmgate, P_m = the c.i.f. price of importables in rupees, C_{gf} = the handling and transportation costs from the farmgate to point f in the marketing chain, and C_{mf} = the handling and transportation costs from the "port" to point f in the marketing chain. From Equation 4A-2 it follows that in the absence of direct intervention, farmers would receive the following price at the farmgate for an importable crop:

$$(4A\text{-}3) \qquad\qquad P_g = P_m + C_{mf} - C_{gf}.$$

The main export crops—cotton, basmati rice, and irri rice—were treated as exportables in our analysis, whereas sugarcane was treated as an importable. Pakistan has been a net importer of sugar for most of its history, although for some years in the 1970s and early 1980s a degree of self-sufficiency was achieved. By the mid-1980s it was again importing about one-third of its white sugar requirements. Wheat was treated as an importable for the years in which imports were greater than 10 percent of output. For the years for which imports were less than 10 percent, we assumed that at the export parity price (given in Equation 4A-1) wheat would therefore have been imported, and at the import parity price (given in Equation 4A-3), it would have been exported. The domestic market would therefore have cleared at a price between the import and export parity prices. We took this price to be the average of the import and export parity prices.

The producer prices for wheat were taken to be the procurement prices from 1968–69 onward. For the earlier years, when very little wheat was procured, we took the wholesale price of wheat and adjusted it downward by 13 percent to account for the marketing margins. The figure of 13 percent was obtained by comparing the ratio of procurement to wholesale prices in the normal years in the 1970s and early 1980s (1971–72 to 1976–77 and 1978–79 to 1981–82) and taking the average markup.

The producer price of seed cotton was obtained from the prices of lint cotton and cottonseed and from the ginning cost. A ton of seed cotton is converted into one-third ton of lint and two-thirds of a ton of cottonseed. The producer price of seed cotton was obtained by adding one-third of the average wholesale price of lint and two-thirds of the average wholesale price of cottonseed, and then subtracting the ginning cost.

The producer price of basmati from the 1970s was taken as the procurement price, and for the 1960s the wholesale price was adjusted downward, as was done for wheat. Irri was introduced in the late 1960s, and the appropriate producer price is the procurement price. For sugarcane, too, the procurement price was considered the appropriate producer price.

Consumer Prices

The domestic consumer prices were either average wholesale prices or the prices in the market where the bulk of the consumption takes place.

The transport-adjusted border prices for importables is the c.i.f. price plus the transport cost from the border to the consumption center. For exportables, the appropriate price was the border prices minus the transport cost from the farm to border plus the cost from the farm to the consumption center.

The consumer price of wheat was taken to be a weighted average of procurement price, ration shop price, and open market price. The procurement price reflects the implicit price of wheat which is not marketed.

The consumer price of cotton was obtained by adding back the transport and ginning costs to the farmgate price of seed cotton.

The consumer prices of basmati and irri were taken as the wholesale price at Lahore and Hyderabad, respectively, which is where the bulk of these crops are produced and consumed.

The price of sugar was the weighted average of wholesale and ration shop price for the period for which it was rationed and as the wholesale price for the years after that.

Bibliography

Alderman, H., M. G. Chaudhry, and M. Garcia. 1987. "Household Food Security in Pakistan with Reference to the Ration Shop System." Washington, D.C.: International Food Policy Research Institute.

Ashiq, M. 1981. "Area Allocation Decisions: A Study of Pakistani Farmers' Responsiveness to Changes in Prices." Publication 186. Lahore: Punjab Economic Research Institute.

Cheong, Kee-Cheok, and Emmanuel H. D'Silva. 1984. *Prices, Terms of Trade, and Role of Government in Pakistani Agriculture*. World Bank Staff Working Paper 643. Washington, D.C.

Cornelisse, P., and S. Naqvi. 1984. *The Anatomy of the Wheat Market in Pakistan*. Islamabad: Pakistan Institute of Development Economics.

Falcon, W. P. 1964. "Farmer Response to Price in a Subsistence Economy: The Case of West Pakistan." *American Economic Review*, Papers and Proceedings, vol. 54.

Gotsch, C., and G. Brown. 1980. *Prices, Taxes, and Subsidies in Pakistan Agriculture, 1960–1976*. World Bank Staff Working Paper 387. Washington, D.C.

Hamid, Naved, Ijaz Nabi, and Anjum Nasim. 1990. *Trade, Exchange Rate, and Agricultural Pricing Policies in Pakistan*. A World Bank Comparative Study. Washington, D.C.

Hamid, N., T. Pinckney, S. Gnaegy, and A. Valdés. 1987. "The Wheat Economy of Pakistan: Setting and Prospects." Washington, D.C.: International Food Policy Research Institute.

Kazi, S. 1987. "International Terms of Trade for Pakistan's Economy: 1970–71 to 1981–82." *Pakistan Development Review*, vol. 26.

Lewis, S. R. 1970. "Recent Movements in Agricultural Terms of Trade in Pakistan." *Pakistan Development Review*, vol. 10.

Lewis, S. R., and S. M. Hussain. 1966. "Relative Price Changes and Industrialization in Pakistan." Karachi: Pakistan Institute of Development Economics.

Nabi, I., N. Hamid, and S. Zahid. 1986. *The Agrarian Economy of Pakistan: Issues and Policies*. Karachi: Oxford University Press.

Nuzhat, A., K. Bengali, and F. Iqbal. 1983. "Long Run Demand and Supply of Major Agricultural Products." Karachi: Applied Economics Research Centre.

Pakistan, Agricultural Census Organization. *Pakistan Census of Agriculture 1972 and 1980.* Statistics Division, Lahore.

Pakistan, Federal Bureau of Statistics. *Household Income and Expenditure Survey, 1972 and 1980.* Statistics Division, Karachi.

———. *Pakistan Statistical Yearbook* (various issues). Statistics Division, Karachi.

———. *Ten Years of Pakistan's Statistics, 1972–82.* Statistics Division, Karachi.

Pakistan, Ministry of Finance. *Pakistan Economic Survey* (various issues). Economic Adviser's Wing, Islamabad.

Pakistan, Ministry of Finance, Planning and Development. *Twenty-Five Years of Pakistan in Statistics, 1947–72.* Economic Affairs Division, Karachi.

Pakistan, Ministry of Food and Agriculture. *Report of the National Commission on Agriculture, 1988.* Islamabad.

Pakistan, Ministry of Food, Agriculture and Cooperatives. *Agricultural Statistics of Pakistan* (various issues). Food and Agriculture Division, Islamabad.

Qureshi, S. K. 1987. "Agricultural Pricing and Taxation in Pakistan." Islamabad: Pakistan Institute of Development Economics.

Saleem, M. A., and M. Haq. 1985. "Farm Accounts, Family Budgets of Rural Families and Cost of Production of Major Crops in the Punjab, 1982–83." Publication 214, Lahore: Punjab Economic Research Institute.

Tweeten, L. 1985. "Supply Response in Pakistan." Islamabad: Food and Agriculture Organization Consultancy Report to Pakistan Agricultural Prices Commission.

Westlake, M. J. 1987. "The Measurement of Agricultural Price Distortion in Developing Countries." *Journal of Development Studies*, vol. 23.

5 The Philippines

Ponciano Intal, Jr.
John H. Power

This chapter is concerned with Philippine trade and agricultural pricing policies from 1960 to the mid-1980s and their effects on agricultural incentives, output, and incomes. The study encompasses not only direct intervention in particular crop prices but also a constellation of policies that affected the exchange rate and thus indirectly affected agriculture. These indirect effects, which were closely tied to the Philippines' overall development strategy, accounted for a substantial part of the total policy bias against agriculture during this period.

The chapter begins with an overview of the Philippine economy and agricultural sector. Next it describes how the nation's macroeconomic and agricultural policy regime affected performance in the agricultural sector. The third section describes our measures of government intervention in agriculture. Later sections present estimates of the effects of intervention on agricultural output, consumption, foreign exchange, the budget, internal transfers, and income distribution. Finally, the history and political economy of intervention are discussed and conclusions are offered.

An Overview of the Philippine Economy and Agricultural Sector

The Philippines is an archipelago of about 7,100 islands in Southeast Asia. The two largest islands, Luzon and Mindanao, account for two-thirds of the total area of about 300,000 square kilometers. With a total population of about 55 million in the mid-1980s, the Philippines had a higher population density than Indonesia, Malaysia, or Thailand.

The Philippine Economy

The Philippines is a lower middle-income developing country. In the 1950s it had one of the highest per capita incomes in Asia, but today it is regarded as an economic "basket case." Between 1960 and 1985, the average rate of growth of real GNP per capita was the lowest among the countries of Southeast Asia and was lower than the average growth rate of all lower middle-income countries. Its growth rate declined from an average of 8 percent per year in 1950–56 to 5 percent in 1957–72, and from 6.8 percent in 1973–79 to a negative rate in 1984–85. The secular deterioration in per capita income was caused by a combination of lagging economic growth and rapid population growth.

Intermittent balance of payments crises during the post–World War II period have shaped both policy and economic performance. The first crisis, in 1949–50, ushered in a decade of foreign exchange and trade controls. The second, around 1960, led to a de facto peso devaluation in 1962. The third, which culminated in 1969, led to a devaluation in 1970. The most recent and serious crisis was that of 1983–85, when another substantial devaluation was required and, for the first time, resulted in lower real incomes.

The international economic environment, which turned from very favorable during the 1950s to very unfavorable during the early 1980s, contributed substantially to the weak growth performance. The Philippines' external terms of trade deteriorated secularly from the 1950s onward, particularly in the latter 1970s and early 1980s under the impact of volatile world commodity prices and oil price hikes, which raised the nation's fuel bill from 11 percent of imports before 1974 to about 25 percent by 1980–82. Another blow to the economy was the sharp rise in real interest rates throughout the world during the early 1980s, which substantially raised the nation's debt service burden.

Whatever the influence of world economic events and periodic crises in payments, the fundamental reason for the lagging growth performance of the Philippines may have been government intervention in the economy. Because this intervention worked against the dictum of comparative advantage, it led to serious misallocation and underutilization of scarce capital and foreign exchange resources. Estimates indicate that the growth in total productivity in manufacturing, which was marginally positive in the 1960s, turned negative during the 1970s, primarily because excessive resources were allocated to poor performers among manufacturing industries. In addition, although total agricultural productivity increased during the 1970s, that growth was confined largely to rice production. The traditional export crops, sugar and coconut, remained stagnant. Inconsistent agricultural productivity, combined with overriding foreign exchange constraints, gave rise to the "stop-go" economic and export performance characteristic of the study period as a whole (see Hooley 1984; David, Barker, and Palacpac 1984).

The Agricultural Sector

Agriculture is an important part of the Philippine economy. Crops and livestock account for about 20 percent of the country's GNP, and the fishery and forestry industries contribute an additional 5 percent. Collectively, these activities employed about 60 percent of the work force during the late 1950s and still accounted for about 50 percent in the 1980s.

Until the early 1960s, agricultural crop exports accounted for more than 60 percent of merchandise exports, and forestry products accounted for an additional 20 percent. During the latter 1970s, however, the share of agricultural goods in exports declined to only about 30 percent. In the same period, Philippine exports of garments and electronic components (principally semiconductors) rose commensurately, although a large share of the gross value of these exports came from imported raw materials. In terms of net value, the share of agriculture in total exports remained substantial.

Philippine agriculture is dominated by rice, corn, sugar, and coconut, which accounted for 55 percent of the value added of agricultural crops and for 86 percent of the total harvested area in 1986. Rice and corn are the main foodgrains, sugar and coconut the principal export crops. Among the minor crops, banana and pineapple are the main nontraditional exports, followed by tobacco and abaca (also known as Manila hemp). Recently, mango and coffee have emerged as export crops. The rest of the country's agricultural production is made up of root crops (such as sweet potato and cassava), tropical fruits and vegetables, and some crops of less commercial importance such as ramie, maguey, and rubber. Hogs and poultry are the principal livestock.

The gross domestic product from agricultural crops at constant prices grew at an average of 4 percent per year during 1956–85. High growth rates in agricultural crop output occurred mainly during or after a peso devaluation (1961–62 and 1970–73) or world commodity price increases (1974–76 and 1980). Low rates of growth of crop output appeared to be associated with low world commodity prices in the early 1980s, with bad weather in 1983, and with intercrop substitution under tight land constraints. The average annual rates of growth of the gross value added at constant prices during 1973–84 were about 3.7 percent for rice, 3.4 percent for corn, 3.0 percent for sugar, and 0.1 percent for coconut.

In general, Philippine farms are small. About 85 percent of the 3.42 million crop and livestock farms in 1980 covered less than 5 hectares and accounted for 50 percent of the total farm area. Only about 60 percent of all farms and farm area were fully owned by the farmers. The unequal distribution of land and ownership of farms has been a

central cause of agrarian unrest and recurring agitation for land reform in the Philippines in the post–World War II period. Rice and
corn farms, the most numerous, have been the focus of government
reform programs. Since the end of martial law, the government has
begun to seek an expanded land reform that would include areas
outside of rice and corn, but the mechanics of this reform have not
been decided upon by the legislature.

The Macroeconomic Environment

Philippine agriculture has been affected significantly by the country's
system of protection and its exchange rate regime, and, to a lesser
extent, by interest and wage rate policies.

The Protection System, 1950–80

Most analysts agree that the government's use of "essentiality" criteria in allocating foreign exchange during the 1950s encouraged import substitution at the finishing stages of primarily nonessential and
semiessential consumer goods. These controls were clearly biased
against exports and agriculture because they supported an overvalued
peso. The tariff system, promulgated in 1957, remained an instrument
of protection until the 1970s, when export taxes, free-trade zones and
bonded warehouses for export firms, and fiscal incentives administered by the Board of Investments were added. There was also a
resurgence of nontariff barriers for the protection of manufactured
intermediate goods.

The trade regime of the 1970s remained biased toward import substitution at the intermediate goods level, although it provided some
openings for a few nontraditional manufactured exports. The extent
of protection is illustrated by the fact that the Philippines had the
highest average tariff rate in Southeast Asia during the 1970s. Disprotection of the traditional export sector worsened, however.

Tariff rate reduction and an import liberalization program were
started in 1981 and continued until 1985. The crisis of 1983–85 stalled
these initiatives, however, and the government's reliance on foreign
exchange allocation and nontariff barriers during 1983–84 made the
tariff reductions ineffective. In 1986 the new government of Corazon
Aquino revived the import liberalization program, first by substitut-
ing equivalent tariffs for nontariff barriers (until April 1988) and then
by gradually reducing tariffs. This program was expected to run into
the early 1990s.

Exchange Rate Policy

Philippine governments have tended to delay adjustments in the exchange value of the peso. When the government imposed trade and

Table 5-1. Actual and Free-Trade Equilibrium Exchange Rates, 1960–86

Period	Actual	Free-trade equilibrium	Degree of divergence[a]
Nominal exchange rate			
1960–61	2.02	2.53	−20.19
1962–66	3.90	4.55	−14.31
1967–69	3.93	4.89	−19.54
1970–74	8.51	7.72	−15.60
1975–79	7.37	9.57	−22.99
1980–82	7.98	10.58	−24.55
1983–86	16.70	20.62	−19.51
Real exchange rate			
1960–61	3.12	4.12	−24.18
1962–66	5.09	6.25	−18.58
1967–69	4.70	6.08	−22.73
1970–74	6.31	7.89	−19.98
1975–79	5.84	7.98	−26.90
1980–82	5.30	7.35	−27.90

a. ([Actual exchange rate ÷ free-trade equilibrium exchange rate] −1) × 100.
Source: Intal and Power (1989).

exchange controls in 1950, it was attempting to maintain the official exchange rate in the face of an exchange shortage at the prevailing rate. Since that time the real exchange rate has followed a characteristic pattern: a few years of depreciation followed by a nominal peso devaluation (Table 5-1).[1]

The Philippine peso would have been about 22 percent higher under free-trade exchange rates than under the actual official exchange rate during 1960–86. Under free-trade and balanced current account conditions, it would have been about 24 percent higher on average than the actual official exchange rate during the period. These estimates of peso overvaluation are probably conservative because the methodology applied in this study did not fully capture the restrictive trade effect of nontariff barriers, which were especially important before 1962, during the late 1970s, and from 1983 to 1985.

Interest Rates and Wage Rates

Until the 1970s, bank deposit and loan rates were set by the Philippine government, in a system that was a legacy of the 1916 Anti-Usury Law. Thus, since the 1950s, rising inflation led to declining real interest rates. By the 1970s the real interest rate on loans was negligible and at times negative, and the real deposit rate was negative on average. Moreover, because the peso was overvalued, the real private interest rate was lower than the real social interest rate for foreign loans. Consequently, the domestic investment rate rose substantially, the private saving rate slackened, and external debt rose rapidly to help finance the investment saving gap.

Low to negative real interest rates led to a substantial increase in capital investments, particularly in intermediate goods, electric power, and other large infrastructural items. These rates also led to the misallocation of capital resources because they encouraged the rent-seeking activities of individuals and firms close to President Ferdinand Marcos.

Measures of Price Intervention

Price intervention is measured by the nominal protection rate, which has three variants: the effects of direct intervention alone (NPR_D), the short-term effects of direct intervention and peso overvaluation (NPR_{ST}), and the long-term effects of intervention and overvaluation (NPR_{LT}).[2]

In the following analysis, the Philippines is considered a small, open economy. That is, the Philippines takes as given, world, or border, prices.[3]

Domestic and Border Prices

The prices of rice, corn, sugar, and copra were measured in relation to the nonagricultural price index (P_{NA}).

Domestic rice prices were found to have been relatively stable in comparison with the border price. When the world rice price was extremely high, as in 1973–74, the domestic retail price of rice was much lower than the border price, even though rice was an importable. Domestic retail, wholesale, and producer prices of rice tended to rise relative to P_{NA} during periods of domestic rice shortfalls (the early 1960s, early 1970s, and 1984–85) and to decline relative to P_{NA} during periods of domestic rice self-sufficiency or marginal surplus (the late 1960s, late 1970s, and early 1980s).

A regression of the producer price of rice with respect to the border price in peso terms over the study period, excluding the years 1973–75, indicates that the elasticity of the domestic producer price with respect to the border price (in peso terms) was 0.81. This suggests that movement in the border price was not fully reflected in the domestic producer price even during the more "normal" periods. A decomposition of the movement of the producer price of rice during 1960–86 indicates that except for 1973–75, peso devaluations contributed nearly 74 percent of the increase in the producer price, whereas the rise in the world price of rice in dollar terms contributed only 20 percent.

The border price of corn followed somewhat the same path as the border price of rice. The domestic price of corn relative to P_{NA} tended to rise during the 1960s and early 1970s. The main difference between the two price regimes was that domestic corn prices were higher than the border price (except in 1973–74), as a result of the government's protectionist policy toward corn, an importable crop.

Over the whole period, devaluations of the peso and the rise in the world price of corn in dollars accounted for 74 percent and 25 percent, respectively, of the rise in the producer price of corn. In the subperiod 1970–86, the devaluations of the peso accounted for 54 percent of the rise in the producer price, whereas the rise in the world price accounted for another 26 percent.

The domestic price of sugar was by and large more stable than the border price. The elasticity of the producer price with respect to the border peso price was only 0.35 during 1960–86. The International Sugar Agreement (ISA) price was more volatile than the Philippine export unit value. This reflected not only the fact that the ISA price was akin to a world dumping price, but also that U.S. sugar policy in the 1960s and the Philippines' long-term export contracts had a stabilizing effect on prices. A decomposition shows that peso depreciation and the border price in dollars accounted for 27 percent and 14 percent, respectively, of the producer price movement during 1960–86.

The domestic and border prices of copra differed from the prices of rice, corn, and sugar in at least two ways. First, there were more frequent peaks and troughs in copra prices. Second, the producer price of copra was lower than the border price adjusted to the producer level during the 1970s and 1980s. That is, coconut farmers experienced no price stabilization during the period.

Regression analysis indicates that the producer price was highly responsive to the movements of the border peso price. Moreover, considering that the compound growth rate of the border dollar price of copra was zero during 1960–86, the increases in the producer price over the whole period were accounted for by the decline in the peso/dollar rate.

Nominal Protection Rates

Table 5-2 presents estimates of the rate of direct nominal protection (NPR$_D$) and the rate of total nominal protection (NPR$_T$). Total nominal protection includes the protection arising from nonagricultural trade policies and from exchange rate policies.

For rice, NPR$_D$ averaged 8 percent during the period 1960–86 (but

Table 5-2. Effect of Direct and Total Intervention on Relative Producer Prices, 1960–86
(percent)

Period	Rice	Corn	Sugar xup[a]	Sugar isa[b]	Copra
Direct (NPR_D)					
1960–61	68	126	−4	138	12
1962–63	−9	11	−12	19	−3
1964–66	27	43	−16	105	−5
1967–69	6	51	−13	168	−5
1970–72	34	35	−21	24	−16
1973–75	−36	−5	−44	−42	−14
1976–79	−6	31	1	11	−11
1980–82	−9	38	−22	0	−36
1983–86	11	42	−29	65	−20
Total (NPR_T)					
1960–61	28	71	−17	106	−4
1962–63	−26	−10	−35	−13	−28
1964–66	3	16	−36	60	−28
1967–69	−18	16	−33	107	−27
1970–72	6	8	−37	−1	−33
1973–75	−49	−24	−55	−54	−31
1976–79	−32	−6	−27	−20	−36
1980–82	−35	−2	−45	−28	−55
1983–86	−16	9	−44	31	−40

a. Border price is export unit value, f.o.b.

b. Border price is average daily price under International Sugar Agreement multiplied by average ratio of Philippine export unit value to New York c.i.f. price for centrifugal sugar.

Source: Intal and Power (1989).

only 1 percent when the peak years of 1961 and 1971 are excluded). The rates were highly variable, averaging 29 percent during 1960–66 and −36 percent during 1973–75. Rice was protected when it was an importable during the 1960s and early 1970s but was neglected, or disprotected, during periods of self-sufficiency, such as the late 1960s, or during periods of export surplus, in the late 1970s and early 1980s. Nonetheless, when border prices rose sharply, either because of a sharp increase in world prices (for example, in 1973–75) or because of a peso devaluation (as in 1962–63), domestic rice prices were not allowed to rise as much as the border price, primarily through the stricter imposition of price controls, antihoarding measures, or quantity queuing regulations.

Corn production, in contrast to rice, was protected during virtually the entire 1960–86 period. In particular, after corn import substitution became a policy concern in the 1970s, NPR$_D$ for corn increased from an annual average of 18 percent in 1970–74 to 42 percent in 1983–86.

If the export unit value is used, the sugar industry was disprotected during the 1960–86 period. But if the ISA daily price is used, sugar was protected during most of the period, particularly in the 1960s. This anomaly is due to the fact that during the 1960s the Philippines exported its sugar almost exclusively to the United States, whose sugar import prices were substantially higher than the world price. During the 1970s—on the whole, years of high world prices—the government imposed export premium taxes or lower composite prices to prevent high world prices from being fully transmitted to the domestic market. ISA prices during the 1980s reveal a positive protection, which was due to the higher U.S. sugar prices and to the fact that the price negotiated by the government trading monopoly in medium-term contracts turned out to be higher than the prevailing price. Although this suggests that the 1980s were similar to the 1960s, the problem in the earlier period was how to meet U.S. sugar quotas, whereas in the latter period the country was faced with an excess of production and milling capacity and declining exports.

The disprotection of copra, which had been marginal during the 1960s, increased during the 1970s and early 1980s. The primary causes were government attempts at price stabilization when world copra prices were high in 1974–75 and the monopsonistic practices of United Coconut Oil Mills (UNICOM) in the early 1980s.

The rate of total nominal protection (NPR$_T$) includes both the direct (NPR$_D$) and indirect (NPR$_I$) rates of protection. The NPR$_I$ is the result of industrial protection policies and exchange rate disequilibrium; it was negative throughout the study period.

A comparison of the rates of direct and total protection shows the importance of indirect protection (NPR$_I$) as a cause of disprotection. For example, the NPR$_D$ for rice averaged 8 percent per year. When indirect protection is taken into account, however, the total protection rate was about -13 percent in the short run and -17 percent in the long run. Similarly, the relatively large average annual NPR$_D$ for corn, 39 percent, was reduced by the rate of NPR$_T$ to 6 percent on average. For sugar, a relatively large disprotection of -18 percent became even larger, -37 percent; for coconut, the rate jumped from -12 percent to -33 percent.

When the increases in nominal producer prices are decomposed into the change in the dollar border price and the depreciation of the peso vis-à-vis the U.S. dollar is taken into account, peso depreciation becomes the dominant influence for the entire 1960–86 period. This means that if the peso had not been overvalued, the producer prices of the four crops would have been higher by as much as about 20 percent per year. In view of the decline in crop prices relative to the prices in the nonagricultural sector during the latter 1970s and early 1980s, elimination of the peso overvaluation would have tempered, if not fully reversed, the deterioration in agricultural terms of trade.

Note that because the current account imbalance was important mainly during the late 1970s and early 1980s, the primary source of overvaluation of the peso (and thus of taxation of agriculture relative to nontradables) during the 1960–86 period was the industrial protection system. This suggests that reducing the disprotection of agriculture would have required a liberalization of the industrial protection system.

Effects of Price Intervention

Price intervention in the Philippines has had a noticeable effect on output, consumption, foreign exchange, the agricultural budget and bureaucracy, resource transfers, income distribution, and price variability and stabilization.

Output Effects

What were the short-run and cumulative effects of direct and total intervention on the output of rice, corn, sugarcane, and coconut?[4] To answer this question, it was necessary to estimate the proportionate effect on the output of crop i. This was the sum of the product at the relevant nominal rate of protection and the own-price elasticity of supply of crop i, as well as the cross-price elasticities of supply of crop i with respect to the prices of the other three crops. A matrix of own-price and cross-price elasticities of supply was constructed from supply regressions performed on the published estimates of other analysts and on rough estimates of cross-price elasticities.

Estimates of the short-run and cumulative direct and total output effects are given in Table 5-3.[5] In 1961–86, direct government intervention boosted the output of rice an average of 0.3 percent per year higher than it would have been without direct intervention. The effects can be divided into roughly three phases: In 1961–73 output effects were largely positive (averaging 3.3 percent annually); in 1974–82 they were by and large negative (averaging −3.9 percent); and in 1983–86 they were positive (averaging 1.4 percent). The cumulative output effect of direct intervention was negative in most years but was a positive 4 percent in 1986, whereas the cumulative effect of total price intervention on output was −3 percent of the nonintervention output by 1986. The short-run and cumulative effects suggest that direct price intervention had little effect on rice output during the period 1961–86 and that the small disincentive to rice production was the result of indirect intervention in prices.

Table 5-3. Effect of Direct and Total Intervention on Agricultural Output, 1961–86
(ratio of nonintervention output)

Period	Rice	Corn	Sugar xup[a]	Sugar isa[b]	Copra
Short-run, direct					
1961–64	0.0364	0.1083	0.0022	0.2612	—
1965–69	0.0223	0.0743	−0.0062	0.3167	—
1970–74	0.0127	0.0446	−0.0299	0.0320	—
1975–79	−0.0317	0.0249	−0.0689	−0.0280	—
1980–82	−0.0434	0.0396	−0.0230	−0.0534	—
1983–86	0.0139	0.0632	−0.0648	0.2115	—
1961–86	0.0034	0.0586	−0.0325	0.1282	—
Short-run, total					
1961–64	0.0034	0.0586	0.0021	−0.0097	—
1965–69	−0.0006	0.0340	−0.0065	0.2145	—
1970–74	−0.0080	0.0098	−0.0474	−0.0122	—
1975–79	−0.0398	−0.0169	−0.1037	−0.0793	—
1980–82	−0.0504	−0.0112	−0.0900	−0.1117	—
1983–86	−0.0126	0.0120	−0.1070	0.1180	—
1961–86	−0.0165	0.0147	−0.0568	0.0274	—
Cumulative, direct					
1964	−0.0261	0.1115	0.0000	0.2431	—
1969	−0.0035	0.1880	−0.0390	0.8018	−0.1426
1974	−0.0590	0.0785	−0.0745	0.5434	−0.2166
1979	−0.0552	0.0889	0.0233	0.0592	−0.2779
1982	−0.0773	0.0743	−0.1172	−0.0420	−0.2189
1986	0.0401	0.1188	−0.1129	0.4087	−0.2050
Cumulative, total					
1964	−0.0279	−0.0158	0.0088	0.1248	—
1969	−0.0370	0.1064	−0.0551	0.4697	−0.0791
1974	−0.0801	−0.0466	−0.1123	0.2129	−0.1526
1979	−0.0952	−0.0256	−0.0662	−0.0401	−0.1948
1982	−0.1127	−0.0479	−0.1685	−0.1229	−0.1247
1986	−0.0287	0.0383	−0.1537	0.2473	−0.0937

— Not applicable.
a. Border price is export unit value.
b. Border price is average daily price under International Sugar Agreement.
Source: Intal and Power (1989).

In the case of corn, direct intervention pushed actual output ahead of nonintervention by an average of 4.7 percent a year during 1968–86, the period in which the government became more conscious of the import substitution possibilities for yellow corn for the domestic livestock industry. The positive effect of total intervention was almost nil (0.2 percent on average). Under direct and total intervention, corn output during 1960–86 increased about 12 percent and 4 percent, respectively, over nonintervention output. On balance, then, intervention resulted in a greater actual output of corn.

In the 1970s sugar and coconut were expressly taxed to increase government revenues, to encourage processing, to stabilize domestic prices, and apparently to yield monopsony rents. Not surprisingly, the negative effects on sugar and coconut output during the 1970s were on average higher than the effects on rice and corn. The cumulative effects on sugar of direct and total price intervention were −11 percent and −15 percent of the nonintervention output, respectively. The corresponding figures for coconut were about −20 percent and −9 percent, respectively. Thus, the two export crops were the ones most adversely affected by intervention.[6]

It may seem surprising that total cumulative output effects for coconut were smaller (in absolute value) than the direct cumulative output effects, even though NPR_T was larger than NPR_D in absolute value. The reason for this result was that the effect on trees planted was based on both the own-price elasticity (0.124) and the cross-price elasticity (−0.160); the latter was assumed to be larger (in absolute value) than the former (for details, see Intal and Power 1989).

Consumption and Foreign Exchange

The effects of intervention on consumption were computed in the same way as the effects on output. The gap between actual consumption and nonintervention consumption was estimated as a proportionate consumption effect, defined as the sum of the product of the relevant NPR at the retail level (wholesale for coconut) and the own- and cross-price elasticities of demand for good i with respect to its own price and the prices of the other three goods, respectively, and the product of the income elasticity and the change in income caused by price intervention.

Estimates of the effects on consumption are presented in Table 5-4. The average annual effect of direct price intervention during 1963–82 was about −3.0 percent for rice, 5.8 percent for corn, 10.5 percent for sugar, and 2.9 percent for copra. The effect of total price intervention during 1963–82 was about 5.8 percent for rice, 6.0 percent for corn, 16.0 percent for sugar, and 41.0 percent for copra.

Overall, price intervention affected consumption and output quite differently. Implicit protection for rice during the 1960s reduced domestic consumption compared with the consumption that would have prevailed without direct intervention. Yet the implicit taxation from direct intervention in rice, sugar, and coconut prices during the 1970s made actual consumption, on average, greater than it would

Table 5-4. Effect of Direct and Total Intervention on Consumption
(ratio of nonintervention consumption)

Period	Rice	Corn	Sugar xup[a]	Sugar isa[b]	Copra
Direct					
1960–64	−0.1147	0.1312	0.0902	−0.1429	−0.0565
1965–69	−0.0775	0.0926	0.1079	−0.4981	0.0396
1970–74	0.0011	0.0904	0.1699	0.0889	0.0476
1975–79	0.0279	−0.0141	0.1145	0.0756	−0.1290
1980–82	0.0101	0.0208	0.1201	0.0335	0.2277
1983–84	−0.0290	0.0179	0.0129	−0.2088	0.1217
1960–84	−0.0304	0.0611	0.1128	−0.1080	0.0205
Total					
1960–64	−0.0252	0.1285	0.1489	−0.0633	0.3113
1965–69	0.0103	0.0961	0.1668	−0.3281	0.4040
1970–74	0.0685	0.0834	0.2058	−0.1408	0.3326
1975–79	0.1145	−0.0128	0.1482	0.1215	0.3472
1980–82	0.1132	0.0300	0.1904	0.1268	0.6404
1983–84	0.0754	0.0311	0.1062	−0.0677	0.5403
1960–84	0.0565	0.0625	0.1660	−0.0160	0.4027

a. Border price is export unit value.
b. Border price is average daily price under International Sugar Agreement.
Source: Intal and Power (1989).

have been without intervention. Corn appears to be an exception because cross-price demand and intercommodity substitution had a greater impact than own-price in this case. Indirect intervention depressed the prices of the four crops further. Because domestic prices were depressed relative to border prices at the free-trade equilibrium exchange rate (relative to P_{NA}), domestic consumption was higher than it would have been in the absence of intervention.

In turn, the changes in output and consumption caused by direct and indirect price intervention affected the volumes of imports and exports and therefore the net foreign exchange. Table 5-5 presents the estimates of the foreign exchange effects. Direct and indirect intervention reduced net foreign exchange earnings from all four commodities, if the unusual year of 1961 is excluded. As a result of direct intervention, foreign exchange earnings declined by an average of 1.7 percent per year during 1962–84. The effects of direct and indirect intervention on earnings averaged about −8.3 percent during the same period. By 1984, the cumulative foreign exchange effect of direct price intervention, including 1961, was about −8.4 percent of export earnings. The cumulative foreign exchange effect of direct price in-

Table 5.5. Effect of Direct and Total Intervention on Foreign Exchange, 1961–84
(ratio of actual export earnings)

Period	Sugar border price is XUP[a]					Sugar border price is ISA[b]				
	Rice	Corn	Sugar	Copra	Total	Rice	Corn	Sugar	Copra	Total
Short-run, direct										
1961–64	0.1372	−0.0002	−0.0074	0.0171	0.1467	0.1780	0.0095	0.0442	0.0018	0.2335
1965–69	0.0517	0.0002	−0.0121	−0.0016	0.0384	0.0900	0.0329	0.0492	−0.0121	0.1600
1970–74	−0.0150	0.0006	−0.0288	0.0049	−0.0382	−0.0283	−0.0012	−0.0346	0.0064	−0.0578
1975–79	−0.0083	0.0030	−0.0454	0.0050	−0.0457	0.0160	0.0094	−0.0083	0.0045	0.0217
1980–82	0.0187	0.0029	−0.0155	−0.0025	0.0036	−0.0078	0.0104	−0.0019	−0.0017	0.0009
1983–84	−0.0168	0.0010	−0.0138	−0.0030	−0.0326	0.0191	0.0561	−0.1071	0.1470	0.1151
1961–84	0.0302	0.0016	−0.0218	0.0040	0.0140	0.0517	0.0159	0.0013	0.0117	0.0806
Short-run, total										
1961–64	0.0367	−0.0052	−0.0120	−0.0082	0.0113	0.0585	0.0031	0.0009	−0.0182	0.0443
1965–69	−0.0076	−0.0042	−0.0171	−0.0157	−0.0445	0.0091	0.0212	0.0283	−0.0200	0.0386
1970–74	−0.0509	−0.0038	−0.0388	−0.0081	−0.1017	−0.0632	−0.0059	−0.0494	−0.0072	−0.1258
1975–79	0.0019	−0.0028	−0.0537	−0.0101	−0.0647	−0.0348	0.0026	−0.0235	−0.0094	−0.0651
1980–82	0.0499	−0.0034	−0.0318	−0.0066	0.0081	0.0302	0.0023	−0.0161	−0.0056	0.0107
1983–84	−0.0208	−0.0048	−0.0270	−0.0075	−0.0183	−0.0250	0.0300	−0.0280	0.3616	0.3387
1961–84	0.0026	−0.0037	−0.0305	−0.0100	−0.0417	0.0094	0.0069	−0.0129	0.0177	0.0211

Cumulative, direct

1964	0.0240	−0.0015	−0.0077	−0.0037	0.0111	0.1067	0.0164	0.0217	−0.0027	0.1421
1969	0.0152	0.0216	−0.0182	−0.0542	−0.0357	0.0079	0.0163	0.0850	−0.0622	0.0470
1974	−0.1670	0.0244	−0.0683	−0.0859	−0.2969	−0.1086	−0.0063	0.1477	−0.0631	−0.0304
1979	0.0284	0.0071	−0.0027	0.1832	−0.1503	0.0471	0.0093	−0.0067	−0.0897	−0.0400
1982	−0.0196	−0.0041	−0.0252	−0.0521	−0.1011	−0.0159	0.0220	0.0273	−0.0595	0.0057
1984	−0.0118	0.0116	−0.0078	−0.0994	−0.1075	0.0578	0.0963	−0.2329	0.3014	0.2226

Cumulative, total

1964	−0.0205	−0.0155	0.0111	−0.0170	−0.0642	0.0226	−0.0019	−0.0021	−0.0196	−0.0010
1969	−0.0644	0.0109	−0.0318	−0.0447	−0.1300	−0.0570	0.0018	0.0604	−0.0451	0.0741
1974	−0.1877	−0.0004	−0.0912	−0.0766	−0.3560	−0.1283	−0.0309	0.0466	−0.0509	−0.1635
1979	0.0662	0.0032	−0.0083	−0.1323	−0.0712	0.0913	−0.0035	−0.0370	−0.0623	−0.0115
1982	0.0376	−0.0133	−0.0422	−0.0291	−0.0471	0.0395	0.0102	0.0081	−0.0359	0.0219
1984	0.0459	−0.0054	−0.0179	−0.0579	−0.0352	−0.0717	0.0541	−0.0634	0.7361	0.6551

a. Export unit value.
b. Price under International Sugar Agreement.

Source: Intal and Power (1989).

tervention and the peso overvaluation after 1961 amounted to −12.7 percent of 1984 export earnings.

The Agricultural Budget and Bureaucracy

In general, direct intervention in agricultural prices takes place through taxes on, or subsidies to, outputs and inputs. Thus, the result is almost invariably a gain or loss in government revenue, or an increase or decrease in government expenditure. Tax revenues accrue directly from agriculture, as well as indirectly from the share of agriculture in general taxes, such as the income tax. Similarly, government expenditures on agriculture may be direct, but may also be indirect. Indirect expenditures are those made on rural infrastructure, research and extension, agrarian reform, and administration.

Before 1970, direct intervention comprised tariffs on imports of agricultural inputs and products, tobacco inspection fees, millers' taxes, and the estimated share of agriculture in general taxes. During the 1970s, the government added export taxes, an export premium tax, and the Coconut Consumer Stabilization Fund (CCSF) levy. Explicit agricultural taxation in the Philippines constituted only 4.4 percent of total tax revenue during 1960–69 and 8.5 percent during 1970–82 (or 1.9 percent and 7.0 percent, respectively, if the estimated share of agriculture in general taxes is excluded). Because the Philippines does not have an adequate system of land titling or cadastral surveys, land valuations tend to be inaccurate and intervention is costly to administer. The government has therefore relied mainly on indirect intervention.

Expenditures on agriculture are particularly difficult to determine because the agricultural portion of such general government services as communications, highways, and schools is unclear. Therefore, we only discuss direct expenditures on programs specifically concerned with or largely related to agriculture.

Table 5-6 presents the agricultural budget in selected years. Note that during the 1960s and 1970s government expenditures on agriculture barely increased as a share of total government expenditures, although they did increase markedly as a share of agricultural output. Some adjustments took place during this time, notably a sharp rise in spending on irrigation, from less than 25 percent to almost 66 percent. This growth reflected the importance of rice and the government's desire to promote new high-yielding varieties, which require good water control. A drop in domestic rice production in the early 1970s, just when the world price of rice was escalating, motivated the government to provide infrastructural support to domestic rice production, via long-term loans from international development agencies.

During most of the 1960s and 1970s, the government spent more on agriculture than it gained from the taxation of agriculture (Table 5-6). This explicit net transfer is misleading, however, given the implicit taxation of agriculture discussed below.

When government intervention increases, the government work force almost always expands. Often, the more rapid its growth, the less coordinated and effective a bureaucracy becomes—a pattern typical of the Philippines during the 1970s.

Although it is difficult to quantify the expansion of the bureaucracy vis-à-vis total government expenditure, that growth took place is evident in the proliferation of new agricultural institutions during the 1970s. A Philippine Coconut Authority and other crop-specific "authorities" were created—all with different pay scales and boundaries of responsibility. Consequently, the function of the Ministry of Agriculture and Food became unclear. Organizational dysfunction may have reached its zenith when the head of the new National Food Authority became a member of the cabinet, alongside the minister of agriculture and food.

Resource Transfers

A country's development strategy usually pays close attention to the resource transfers that government price and nonprice intervention can generate between agriculture and the rest of the economy. Real transfers in the Philippines were estimated on the basis of the difference between the actual per unit value added deflated by the actual GNP deflator and the nonintervention per unit value added deflated by the nonintervention GNP deflator. Transfers caused by fertilizers not allocatable to the four crops of concern or by agricultural machinery and credit were added to transfers caused by output and input price intervention in rice, corn, sugar, and coconut to find the sum of price-related transfers.

Table 5-7 presents estimates of nonprice transfers and price-related transfers caused by output and input price intervention as a share of agricultural value added. Net real transfers from direct output and input price intervention averaged −7.4 percent a year during 1970–84. Net real transfers from total price intervention averaged −22.2 percent during the same period (−3.5 percent of GDP).

Government intervention in output and input prices led to net price-related transfers out of agriculture during 1970–84, especially during 1973–75 (Table 5-7). In those three years, intervention was aimed primarily at domestic price stabilization, and thus had a substantial adverse effect on the incomes of farmers. ISA-based transfers for the 1960s (not shown) indicate that the country's access to the higher-priced U.S. sugar market during that period was a source of

Table 5-6. Agricultural Budget, Selected Years, 1965–82
(millions of pesos)

Period	Import duty	Export duty/ CSSF levy[a]	Tobacco fee, millers' tax	Others[b]	Total	As a percentage of total tax revenues (1)[c]	As a percentage of total tax revenues (2)[d]
1965	35.0	n.a.	8.3	48.5	91.8	4.8	2.2
1968	30.8	n.a.	10.2	86.3	127.3	4.5	1.4
1971	25.7	286.0	14.6	97.0	423.3	8.6	6.7
1974	27.9	1,596.1	28.7	163.9	1,816.6	13.9	12.6
1977	45.2	1,530.6	44.1	266.3	1,886.2	10.0	8.6
1980	66.2	3,322.5	97.6	539.0	4,025.3	11.7	10.1
1982	38.5	837.4	71.3	712.4	1,659.6	4.3	2.4

Government expenditures in agriculture

	Infrastructure[e]		Research and extension	Agricultural support services[f]	Total[g]	As a percentage of total government expenditures
	With rural roads and bridges	Without rural roads and bridges				
1965	59.3	47.4	51.4	54.5	165.2	7.7
1968	53.3	33.8	49.5	71.7	174.5	5.3
1971	208.8	189.0	72.0	106.8	387.6	8.0
1974	854.0	839.9	229.3	260.8	1,344.2	8.1
1977	1,445.4	1,393.9	375.5	332.7	2,153.6	9.5
1980	2,244.0	2,177.9	557.4	676.6	3,478.0	9.4
1982	2,289.7	2,123.4	719.0	893.0	3,901.6	8.0

n.a. Not available.

a. CCSF levy is the Coconut Consumers' Stabilization Fund levy.

b. "Others" comprise the estimated share of agriculture in economy and taxes; that is, income tax, motor vehicle fees, local tax, and documentary stamp tax.

c. Includes the share of agriculture in economywide taxes (that is, "other taxes").

d. Excludes other taxes.

e. Primarily irrigation, rural roads and bridges, and storage facilities.

f. Includes expenditures of price stabilization and agrarian reform agencies and expenditures for general agricultural administration.

g. Includes expenditures on rural roads and bridges.

Source: Authors' estimates; for more details, see Intal and Power (1989), chap. 5.

Table 5-7. Average Annual Real Transfers: Price-Related Approach
(as percentage of agricultural value added)

| | xup-*based* | | | | isa-*based* | | | |
| | Direct | | Total | | Direct | | Total | |
Period	A	B	A	B	A	B	A	B
Price-related transfers								
1960–64	n.a.	0.3	n.a.	−2.4	n.a.	1.1	n.a.	−1.4
1965–69[a]	−3.1	−0.2	−18.1	−2.8	8.1	1.8	−3.7	−0.2
1970–74	−15.5	−2.4	−33.7	−5.2	−13.6	−2.1	−31.2	−4.8
1975–79	−12.6	−2.0	−35.1	−5.5	−7.0	−1.1	−27.8	−4.4
1980–82	−9.0	−1.4	−25.1	−4.0	−9.1	−1.4	−25.3	−4.2
1980–84	−2.5	−0.4	−17.6	−2.9	−1.7	0.2	−12.4	−2.1
1960–84[b]	−10.1	−1.1	−28.3	−3.9	−5.7	−0.2	−22.6	−2.8
Net transfers: Price-related transfers plus nonprice transfers[c]								
1960–64	n.a.	0.7	n.a.	−2.0	n.a.	1.6	n.a.	−1.0
1965–69[a]	−1.0	0.1	−16.0	−2.4	10.3	2.2	−1.5	0.2
1970–74	−10.4	−1.6	−28.4	−4.4	−8.5	−1.3	−25.9	−4.0
1975–79	−5.0	−0.8	−27.4	−4.3	0.6	0.1	−20.1	−3.2
1980–82	−2.4	−0.4	−18.3	−2.9	−2.5	−0.4	−18.6	−2.9
1960–82[d]	−5.5	−0.4	−23.9	−3.2	−1.0	0.5	−18.2	−2.1

n.a. Not available.

Note: Figures under A denote the shares to agriculture value added, defined as the gross value added from agricultural crops and livestock at constant 1982 prices. Figures under B are the shares to GNP at constant 1982 prices.

  a. For figures under A, average for 1967–69 only.

  b. For figures under A, average for 1967–84 only.

  c. The computations include the estimated share of agriculture to economywide taxes as part of the transfers out of agriculture and the estimated government expenditures on rural roads as part of transfers into agriculture.

  d. Average for 1967–82 only for figures under A.

Source: Intal and Power (1989), chap. 6.

substantial transfers into the agricultural sector. Indirect intervention accounted for about two-thirds of net transfers during 1970–84.

The net transfer to agriculture—that is, the sum of output and input price-related transfers and nonprice transfers—is also presented in Table 5-7. It appears that the government's agricultural policy during the late 1960s and 1970s was a combination of net transfers out of agriculture (which were due to output and input price intervention) and positive transfers into agriculture (due to nonprice intervention). Although positive nonprice transfers moderated the negative price-related transfers, they did not offset them. The overall direct transfers were negative (though small), averaging −1 percent during 1970–84. Overall total transfers, however, averaged −15.7 percent during the same period. That was a significant loss of income.

**Table 5-8. Effects of Direct and Total Price Intervention
on Consumer Real Income, Average, 1966–86**
(percent)

Income class	Direct	Total
All Philippines		
Poor	−0.96	5.48
Lower middle	−0.60	3.83
Upper middle	−0.37	2.75
Rich	−0.20	1.36
Rural		
Poor	−1.03	5.76
Lower middle	−0.73	4.28
Upper middle	−0.48	3.32
Rich	−0.34	2.54
Urban		
Poor	−0.10	5.26
Lower middle	−0.05	3.90
Upper middle	−0.04	2.82
Rich	0.02	2.00
Metropolitan Manila		
Poor	0.21	3.83
Lower middle	0.13	3.01
Upper middle	0.11	2.20
Rich	0.06	1.39

Source: Intal and Power (1989).

Income Distribution

The Philippines has an uneven distribution of income and a high incidence of poverty, neither of which has improved perceptibly during the past 30 years. The Gini ratio hovered around 0.50—which is high by international standards (Table 5-8). The top 20 percent of the population has a higher income share and the bottom 20 percent a lower share than the corresponding groups in the Republic of Korea and Taiwan. The richest 20 percent of the population had 56.5 percent of the total income in 1961 and 52.1 percent in 1985. The income share of the poorest 40 percent rose slightly over the same period—from 12.1 percent in 1961 to 14.3 percent in 1984. Estimates of families in poverty in the Philippines have ranged from 41 percent to 51 percent, and by 1985 the incidence of poverty may have risen as high as 60 percent. Poverty is higher in rural areas than in urban areas, and possibly as many as 70 percent of the bottom 30 percent of poor families depend on agriculture for their livelihood. Indeed, the highest rates of poverty occur among farmers, agricultural laborers, and fish-

ermen. Rice farmers generally are better off, whereas corn and coconut farmers are among the worst off (see Abrera 1976).

The poorest regions are Eastern Visayas, Bicol, the Cagayan Valley,
and Ilocos. In the two "upper middle-income" regions (Central and
Western Visayas), nearly 50 percent of the families are in the nation's
bottom 30 percent income bracket, which suggests a highly unequal
distribution of income. In contrast, less than 6 percent of the families
in metropolitan Manila belonged to the bottom 30 percent in 1985.
Thus, poverty in the Philippines is primarily a rural problem.

Although we estimated the instantaneous, short-run, and cumulative effects of government intervention on the income of farmers in
each region, we present only the instantaneous effects on both nominal and real income for the Philippines as a whole (for the other
results, see Intal and Power 1989). Nominal income effects are defined
as the impact of output and input prices on value added, while real
income effects also incorporate the impact of price policies on the
cost-of-living index.

The income effects at the national level for each crop were measured
as a percentage of GDP (Table 5-9). The results indicate that the nominal and real incomes of sugar and coconut farmers were adversely
affected by direct price intervention, whereas the nominal and real
incomes of corn farmers were favorably affected. The annual average
of direct nominal effects on income during 1971–84 was about −0.5
percent of GDP for sugar and coconut farmers, −0.2 percent for rice
farmers, and 0.1 percent for corn farmers. Direct real income effects
during the same period averaged about −0.2 percent of GDP for sugar
and coconut farmers, 0.1 percent for rice farmers, and 0.4 percent for
corn farmers. The income effect across crops is typical of the pattern
observed in other developing countries. Income losses caused by direct price intervention were lowest among the nominally protected
import-substitute crops, such as corn (where income actually increased), and were highest among traditional export crops, such as
sugar and coconut.

A comparison of the direct effects on real income and on nominal
income reveals the importance of the cost-of-living factor (Table 5-9).
During 1971–79, rice and coconut farmers experienced (on average)
nominal income losses but real income gains; sugar farmers had large
nominal income losses but smaller real income losses; and corn farmers had small nominal income gains but larger real income gains. The
disparity between nominal and real effects can be traced to the nominal disprotection of coconut, sugar, and rice during the 1970s, which
led to a lower cost of living. Moreover, welfare gain from the reduction
in the cost of living, compared with the nonintervention case, was
substantial enough for rice and coconut to outweigh their nominal
income losses in those years. Conversely, in the years when crops

Table 5-9. Instantaneous Income Effects of Direct and Total Price Interventions by Crop
(percentage of GNP)

Period	Rice	Corn	Sugar	Copra	Total
Nominal direct					
1971–74	−0.41	0.11	−0.80	−0.33	−1.43
1975–79	−0.91	0.10	−0.68	−0.45	−1.22
1980–84	−0.11	0.11	−0.20	−0.65	−0.85
1971–84	−0.22	0.11	−0.54	−0.49	−1.14
Real direct					
1971–74	0.05	0.53	−0.37	0.09	0.30
1975–79	0.31	0.59	−0.17	0.06	0.79
1980–84	−0.03	0.18	−0.13	−0.58	−0.56
1971–84	0.11	0.43	−0.21	−0.16	0.17
Nominal total					
1971–74	−0.96	−0.17	−1.22	−0.94	−3.29
1975–79	−0.83	−0.26	−1.22	−1.48	−3.79
1980–84	−0.58	−0.25	−0.52	1.47	0.12
1971–84	−0.78	−0.23	−0.97	1.32	−0.66
Real total					
1971–74	−3.54	−2.76	−3.83	−3.54	−13.67
1975–79	−2.71	−2.13	−3.09	−3.39	−11.32
1980–84	−2.97	−2.64	−2.91	−3.89	−12.41
1971–84	−3.04	−2.49	−3.23	−3.61	−12.37

Source: Intal and Power (1989).

such as rice and corn had large positive nominal protection (for example, 1971), the domestic price level was higher than the nonintervention case, and the price effect was substantial enough to make the welfare loss from reduced purchasing power overshadow the nominal income gains of the farmers.

When the indirect effects of intervention on real income are considered, the positive real income effects of direct price intervention for corn and rice farmers—which averaged 0.4 percent and 0.1 percent of GDP, respectively, during 1971–84—become large negative income effects averaging −2.5 percent and −3.0 percent (Table 5-9). Similarly, the negative real income effects of direct intervention for sugar and coconut farmers become even larger when overvaluation is taken into account. The income losses were large because the producers not only were earning less but also were paying more for protected nonagricultural products.

The real income losses due to direct price intervention were largest in Western and Eastern Visayas, regions that were hard hit, respectively, by the decline in the world price of sugar and by volatility in the world price of copra. Although direct intervention brought regions such as Central Mindanao real income gains, largely because of the positive protection on corn, all regions suffered real income losses from direct and indirect price intervention.

Agrarian insurgency in the Philippines has been closely correlated with land tenure conflicts, poverty, and income disparity. From the 1930s to the early 1960s, the insurgency was concentrated in Central Luzon, but during the 1970s this rice-growing region benefited from government irrigation projects, and the core of resistance shifted to Visayas, Bicol, and Southern Mindanao, areas adversely affected by direct price intervention and by fluctuations in the international market for sugar and coconut. The tie between insurgency and poor agricultural performance was particularly evident in the sugar-producing province of Negros Occidental in Western Visayas, where resistance had been dormant during the sugar boom of the 1960s and early 1970s, and then flared up during the sugar crisis of the 1980s.[7]

Agricultural laborers constitute a substantial proportion of the agricultural population, possibly about 33 percent of rural households, and are among the poorest in this group. The instantaneous real income effect of agricultural pricing policies on these laborers, calculated considering laborers solely as consumers of agricultural products, indicates that their real income rose 0.5 percent a year as a result of direct intervention and 6.5 percent as a result of total intervention during the period 1970–86.

These calculations were based on the assumption that the rural wage rate and rural employment were not affected by pricing policies, which, however, may affect wages over time because of changes in the rural and urban demand and supply of labor and because of internal migration. Real wage rate regressions indicate that agricultural policies did not have a significant effect on real wages in the short run, probably because an improving commodity price environment in a labor surplus situation served more to increase employment than to raise wages. The impact of the pricing policies on employment are not captured in the effects on farm worker income.

To estimate the effects of direct and total price intervention on real income, we classified the consumers identified in the 1971 and 1985 Family Income and Expenditure Surveys into four categories (poor, lower middle class, upper middle class, and rich) and three locations (rural, metropolitan Manila, and other urban). The estimates are presented in Table 5-9.

Direct intervention had the greatest impact on the poor and the smallest impact on the rich. This is not surprising in view of the larger expenditure weights of the four commodities among the poor.

From 1966 to 1986, consumers in rural areas, other urban areas, and the Philippines as a whole were adversely affected by direct intervention. In contrast, consumers in Manila were favorably affected. Although the income effects over time were generally negative for all income groups and all locations during the late 1960s and early 1980s, they were positive during much of the 1973–81 period, probably because of the government's treatment of rice. The rural poor were the ones most vulnerable to domestic price intervention (Table 5-9). They benefited most from total price intervention during 1966–86. This reflects the greater expenditure weight of agricultural products among the poor and the comparative disprotection of agricultural commodities by total price intervention.

In sum, total intervention (see Table 5-9) contributed to poverty in the rural areas because it depressed farmers' real incomes. But total intervention also benefited the consuming poor—especially the net consuming farmers and landless laborers at the bottom of the economic ladder (see Table 5-9). Regions with the most unequal distribution of income or higher rates of poverty were the ones most severely affected by intervention and by declining or unstable world commodity prices.

Price Variability and Stabilization

The Philippine government has intervened in agricultural trading primarily to minimize the presumed adverse impact of price shocks on Filipino consumers and producers. This was precipitated by "crises" of supply or sharply rising world prices (during 1973–74 for coconut and sugar) and has modified the transmission of price shocks between domestic and world prices, and between producer and consumer prices.

A simple test of the government's success at stabilizing domestic prices is to compare the variability in domestic prices (at the producer or consumer level) with that at the corresponding border price (either at the official exchange rate or the free-trade equilibrium exchange rate).

During 1961–86, domestic relative prices showed less variability (measured by their variance) than did border relative prices (Table 5-10). Moreover, the ratio of domestic price variability to border price variability was generally lower during 1973–86 than during 1961–72. Thus the Philippine government obviously gave more attention to price stabilization during the later, more turbulent period. The above results indicate that domestic prices were moderated relative to border prices during the 1960s, and especially during the 1970s. Although there can be structural reasons for such price moderation, price stabilization has been an expressed objective of government intervention in the Philippines.

Table 5-10. Variance of Relative Prices, 1960–82

Period	P/P_{NA}	P'/P_{NA}	P^*/P_{NA}
Relative producer prices			
Rice			
1961–72	0.0072	0.0117	0.0160
1973–86	0.0155	0.1224	0.1557
1961–86	0.0120	0.0783	0.1066
Corn			
1961–72	0.0030	0.0042	0.0054
1973–86	0.0050	0.0145	0.0200
1961–86	0.0044	0.0111	0.0165
Sugar			
1961–72	0.0118	0.0832 (0.0247)	0.1217 (0.0399)
1973–86	0.0268	0.4097 (0.2848)	0.6001 (0.4291)
1961–86	0.0204	0.2944 (0.1752)	0.4427 (0.2713)
Copra			
1961–72	0.0073	0.0160	0.0291
1973–86[a]	0.1328	0.1315	0.2015
1961–86	0.0727	0.0805	0.1289
Relative consumer prices			
Rice			
1961–72	0.0126	0.0234	0.0349
1973–86	0.0291	0.2557	0.3242
1961–86	0.0214	0.1662	0.2276
Corn			
1961–72	0.0072	0.0098	0.0124
1973–86	0.0077	0.0300	0.0392
1961–86	0.0089	0.0245	0.0364
Sugar			
1961–72	0.0109	0.1482 (0.0399)	0.2174 (0.0618)
1973–86	0.0026	0.7897 (0.4291)	1.1488 (0.7951)
1961–86	0.0067	0.5382 (0.3061)	0.7999 (0.4673)

Note: Figures in parentheses are the variance of the border price of sugar using unit value of exports. P/P_{NA} is the relative actual domestic price; P'/P_{NA} is the relative price of the border price at the official exchange rate adjusted to the producer or retail level; and P^*/P_{NA} is the relative price of the border price at the equilibrium exchange rate adjusted to the producer or retail level.

a. Using the Z-statistic, the variability of the domestic relative price of copra is less than the variability of its relative border price.

Source: Intal and Power (1989).

History and Political Economy of Agricultural Pricing Policies

Agricultural pricing policies in the Philippines have passed through four phases since the early 1900s, which correlate more or less with the following periods in its history: American colonialism (1900–34), the Commonwealth period (1935–45), the early years of independence 1946–71, and the period of martial law under Marcos (1972–81).

Phases of Intervention

During the American colonial period from 1900 to 1934, intervention was minimal. The Philippines followed a conservative fiscal and monetary policy under the gold exchange standard, with a peso/dollar rate largely in equilibrium.

When the Commonwealth government took office in 1935, the Philippines began to exercise more active control over crop pricing. The government gained the authority to administer its sugar export quota to the United States under the U.S. Jones-Costigan Act of 1934, although the quota was not explicitly designed to stabilize domestic prices during this time. Specific action with regard to rice and corn occurred early in the Commonwealth period when bad weather caused a crop shortfall. In responding to the ensuing crisis, the government in 1936 established the National Rice and Corn Administration (NARIC), which set price floors and retail ceilings for the two commodities. It maintained these prices through domestic purchases and virtual monopoly control of imports and exports. In contrast, the coconut industry was more or less ignored.

The Philippines gained political independence with the founding of the Republic in 1946. The country then adopted a more aggressive policy toward industrialization, primarily through exchange controls (during the 1950s) and tariff protection (during the 1960s). During these two decades trade distortions caused the peso to become overvalued. The government also intervened on the input side by encouraging the growth of rural banks and by providing fertilizer subsidies and temporary spurts of credit.

The country followed a republican form of government in electoral politics until September 1972, when President Marcos declared martial law and dissolved the legislature. Under martial law the government had considerably more leeway to intervene in prices, and it did so through the New Society program.

A stimulus to intervention during this period was a 17 percent drop in rice production during 1971–73 and a sharp rise in the world price of rice, corn, sugar, and coconut in 1974. The government responded by introducing price controls rationing, and by mixing rice and corn to keep the domestic rice price below the world price. The government also sponsored a production, credit, and extension program—the so-called Masagana-99 program—that aimed at reestablishing self-sufficiency in rice by promoting the use of high-yielding varieties. By the late 1970s this program had met with some success, and the Philippines was producing a marginally exportable surplus for the first time in a century.

Under martial law, NARIC gained the exclusive right to import wheat, and to procure domestically and import soybeans, mungbeans, and other feed ingredients. The government also established the Food Terminal, Inc., a large processing and marketing complex charged with selling low-priced basic foodstuffs in poor urban areas at its own retail outlets. In 1980 the Food Terminal and outlets were subsumed under NARIC, which then became the National Food Authority (NFA), with cabinet status and expanded personnel.

The development of high-yielding rice varieties by the International Rice Research Institute and the University of the Philippines provided an impetus for an ambitious government effort to pave the way for development by providing roads, irrigation, fertilizer, and credit facilities. The fertilizer subsidy was short-lived because of a drop in world prices, which was not matched domestically. The credit program also failed because of the poor repayment rate and the more stringent monetary policies made necessary by the crises of 1983–85.

During the 1970s and early 1980s the government intervened much more actively in the agricultural export sector, most notably in sugar and coconut. The first step was taken in 1970, when explicit export taxation was introduced to stabilize prices and produce more revenue. After sharp increases in the world prices of sugar and coconut in 1973–74, the government imposed a flexible export premium and exerted both direct and indirect control over trading in the two commodities. A government sugar monopoly established new refineries, operated sugar centrals, and acquired leading enterprises for the transport, storage, and handling of sugar and cane for export.

The government also imposed a tax on coconut producers that was to provide revenue for a consumer subsidy for coconut-based products such as cooking oil and soap, which were under price control. The levy was later used to foster controversial replanting and vertical integration programs. The latter aimed at making farmers the owners "in principle" of coconut trading and processing firms by creating United Coconut Mills, Inc. (UNICOM), a government-controlled coconut oil mill.

With the economic crisis of 1983–85, the pressure for reform increased, and the 1986 revolution sparked a movement toward political and economic liberalization, especially in agriculture. Agricultural export taxation (except on logs) and the sugar and coconut monopolies were abolished, and the National Food Authority was reduced to controlling rice and corn, which had been NARIC's function.

Characteristics of the Political Economy

Perhaps the most notable characteristic of Philippine politics as it has affected agriculture has been its power structure, which has been based on individual loyalties and patron-client relationships rather than on the interests of specific economic groups (see Abueva and de Guzman 1969). The two main political parties that emerged in the 1950s and 1960s were supported by similar conglomerations of patrons and clients, and in the absence of salient ideological platforms, party loyalties became associated with predominantly personal considerations. Party membership also became highly unstable as popular leaders shifted allegiances, carrying groups of clients with them.

Now and then, organized economic groups in the Philippines— particularly rice landlords, sugar planters, and coconut producers— have promoted their interests effectively on specific issues. So have labor organizations, associations of small farmers, and the chambers of commerce and industry. But no political party has developed an ideological consensus or enduring basis for a workable political coalition, and the patron-client pattern has endured. Although leaders at the national level have tried to create a consensus, the well-entrenched client-centered system often has led legislators with virtually identical constituencies—from the point of view of economic interests—to take widely divergent positions on such issues as exchange rates or import controls.

The Philippine political system has made it possible for the narrower, individual interests of particular client groups to gain attention. Philippine leaders have been able to rationalize such policies only on nebulous grounds of national interest and "balance." Leaders have taken particular care to appear moderate and to avoid policies that appear to strongly favor one economic interest over another. Even when leaders have taken a strong position on pricing issues, they have retreated quickly in the face of negative public reaction.

The price intervention that has worked against agriculture probably has been largely unintentional—the effect, for example, of cronyism in coconuts, poor management of the government trade monopoly in rice, and manipulation of the premium from the U.S. quota in the case of sugar. Even the positive protection enjoyed by yellow corn during much of the period under discussion was due as much to the need of the government grains trading agency to make a profit on its import monopoly of corn as to the drive for import substitution in corn.

Two important exceptions must be made to the general theme of the unsystematic nature of the bias against agriculture. First, indirect intervention has been dominated by the industrial protection system, which carried with it a systematic bias for industry and hence against agriculture. Yet even here the magnitude of the penalty imposed on agriculture by industrial protection has been poorly understood. Only in 1986 did the Ministry of Agriculture publicly acknowledge the serious adverse effects of the industrial protection regime of the past 30 years.

Second, Philippine political leaders come from an elite social class that has evolved from a landed aristocracy but has long been involved in industry, commerce, finance, and the professions. Hence, the elite represents a broad group of the often self-serving rich. Their rhetoric may suggest they support populist causes, but their actions, such as their successful opposition to land reform and to the development of a strong labor movement, suggest otherwise.

Another important factor to consider is the large role of the central government in the economy, which was approved by the Commonwealth constitution itself. President Manuel Quezon announced in 1936 that he was opposed to "laissez-faire," and he proceeded to establish government corporations, arguing that indigenous entrepreneurship would prevent foreign capitalists from dominating the economy (Gopinath 1987, pp. 116, 121–27). In fact, many still fear that the Philippine market might become dominated by outsiders, particularly Chinese traders or multinational corporations. The Filipino people continue to believe that the government, and not the market, is responsible for ensuring them an adequate supply of essentials at affordable prices.

Nevertheless, economic policies have been greatly influenced by external groups, notably the U.S. government, the International Monetary Fund, and the World Bank. U.S. influence was in effect built into the trade act that the Philippines was obliged to ratify as a condition for receiving rehabilitation aid after World War II, but links with the United States and lending agencies were prolonged by the Philippines' own desire to maintain an attractive climate for development aid and foreign capital. The relationship has been marked by periodic balance of payments crises, culminating in the structural adjustment loans of the early 1980s and the debt crisis of 1983–85.

With the declaration of martial law and the abolition of Congress in 1972, the Philippines embarked on a new political-economic path. The patron-client relationships that had previously linked Manila to the provinces were virtually destroyed. Power shifted to the president, who sought personal wealth and fame along with economic development.

When the Philippine Congress and the legal political opposition were disbanded and replaced by technocrats not directly accountable to the public, international organizations came to have an even greater say in Philippine policy. The end of the martial law regime thus appears to portend significant changes in the country's relations with international lending agencies as the convening of a new Congress exposes Philippine borrowing policy to fuller public scrutiny.

Political Economy of Direct and Indirect Intervention

With certain important exceptions, little effort has been made to coordinate policy decisions respecting direct and indirect intervention in the Philippines. Consequently, the instruments, motivations, and agencies responsible for the specific policies have all been different. Hence, direct and indirect intervention for each crop are discussed separately.[8]

DIRECT PRICE INTERVENTION. The government's effort at direct intervention has been mainly concerned with stabilizing domestic prices of food items, especially of rice and corn, in the face of variable border prices. The principal objective of agricultural pricing policy has been to maintain a balance between producer and consumer interests, and to insulate each from internal or external shocks. Accordingly, intervention has been most prominent in times of crises in domestic supply, such as the 1935–36 "rice crisis" or the "sugar and cooking oil crises" of 1973–74. The pursuit of price stability was intended also to protect the poorest consumers, who spend a large proportion of their income on food products.

The pattern of protection or disprotection of rice and sugar illustrates the income-distribution goal. The producer price of rice remained close to the border price during 1960–86, probably because the government was fully aware of the political power of rice farmers and the importance of rice as a food commodity for Filipinos. The domestic producer price of sugar was lower than the border price of sugar exports but was by and large higher than the ISA price, especially during the 1960s. The differential stemmed from the efforts of the government to transfer part of the U.S. price premium to domestic sugar consumers by not allowing the domestic price to rise to the level of the border export unit value. Again, this has reflected the tendency of the government to distribute benefits equitably.[9]

The domestic producer price of copra hewed closely to the border price during the 1960s, but with the imposition of the CCSF levy and the establishment of UNICOM, the producer price dropped significantly below the border price. This suggests that for copra, government intervention since the latter 1970s was biased against producers and in favor of consumers. In fact, however, government intervention after the cooking oil crisis was presented as a short-term taxation of producers in exchange for ostensible long-term benefits through restructuring of the ownership base of the processing and marketing sector and through productivity increases in coconut farming.

In contrast, the government's pricing policy for corn has been biased in favor of producers and against consumers. This positive price protection has reflected the government's drive for self-sufficiency and the need for the NFA to generate profits. The policy also redistributes income to poor corn farmers.

Estimates of real transfers demonstrate the Philippine government's apparent lack of bias either for consumers or for farmers as a whole. The estimates indicate that net price-related transfers caused by direct price intervention averaged −1.1 percent of GNP per year during 1960–82. Including nonprice transfers, net transfers averaged only −0.4 percent. According to the ISA-related estimates, net price-related transfers caused by direct price intervention and net transfers averaged −0.2 percent and 0.5 percent of GNP per year, respectively, during the period. Thus, direct intervention and nonprice transfers were largely policy neutral for producers vis-à-vis the consumers of agricultural products.

Two interrelated factors have influenced intervention in agriculture: a bias against "monopolistic" traders and a desire to "Filipinize" domestic and international trading. The notion that the profits from domestic agriculture go to middlemen—largely foreign middlemen—has prompted the government to take various measures to divest ethnic Chinese of their control of the retail and wholesale trade, milling, and warehousing of rice and corn. During the control period of the 1950s, Filipinos were also given priority in the allocation of import licenses.

Intervention in export crops, especially sugar and coconut, has been justified in part as a means of strengthening the position of the Philippines vis-à-vis multinational firms that were thought to control world markets. In the case of coconut, a substantial share of copra trading and coconut oil manufacturing was controlled by foreigners, so that the government's attempt to establish cooperatives during the 1960s was partly aimed at increasing the control of Filipinos in coconut trading. The use of the coconut levy to purchase coconut oil mills, establish coconut marketing centers, and build coco-based chemical plants–ostensibly in the name of coconut farmers–was basically an effort to "dealienize" the coconut trading and processing sectors.

Some recent studies have identified political control and rent seeking as motives for price intervention during the 1970s. Selective quotas or tariffs were imposed and exclusive franchises granted, they suggest, because power fell into the hands of a few individuals close to the president, especially in the coconut and sugar sectors (see Canlas and others 1985; Ferrer 1986; McCoy 1983; Intal 1987; de Luna 1986, p. 11).

Another reason for imposing export taxes was the need to increase government revenue. During the 1960s the Philippine tax effort was obviously less successful than that of other countries, so that export taxes and premia became vital supplements to the tax regime in the 1970s. Although export taxes are declining in importance for economic reasons, they remain important for revenue, and the Ministry of Finance has sought to maintain them.

Certain aspects of intervention in each crop merit close attention. Rice, as the most important food crop, has always been politically important. Because the Philippines remained an importer of rice until the late 1970s, the government sought to keep domestic rice prices low for important reasons of macroeconomic policy—most notably to keep overall inflation down and to avoid foreign exchange disequilibria. Thus the general price level declined during the early 1950s and only inched up during the late 1950s. This overall stability was punctuated by crises of substantial negative nominal protection rates, as in 1962–63, and declining profitability to producers, which became an issue in the campaign that won Marcos the presidency in 1965.

During his second year in office, Marcos launched a program that encouraged farmers to plant high-yielding varieties. This program enabled the country to achieve self-sufficiency in rice within three years and thus paved the way for Marcos's reelection in 1969. But floods, crop diseases, and pricing problems in the early 1970s triggered a substantial decline in the real producer price. Production then fell off, and the Philippines again became an importer of rice. Nominal protection rates from direct intervention rose, and real producer prices followed. The government did not allow the domestic retail price to fully reflect the high world prices of 1973–74, however, and NPRS turned negative. The government again pressed for increased production by subsidizing fertilizer, providing credit, and intensifying extension services. Thus by the late 1970s and early 1980s the country had built up marginal export surpluses. But its position as an exporter of rice remained tenuous, and after the droughts of 1983 and 1987 the nation became a net importer, as real rice prices, credit, and government expenditures on irrigation all declined.

In sum, there is no evidence of a persistent or strong bias in rice pricing policy in favor of either producers or consumers.[10] During 1967–86 real transfers averaged -1.1 percent of agricultural value added (0.5 percent excluding 1973–74). The cumulative effect of direct intervention on rice output in 1985 was zero.

The policy for corn was concerned principally with the availability and price of white corn, a staple food for about 10 percent of the population. White corn is not traded by the Philippines, and so when domestic output fell short, yellow corn was imported as a substitute for animal feeds.

With the expansion in hog and poultry production and shifts from backyard to commercial production in the late 1960s, corn import policy became an important issue in the 1970s. A sharp rise in feed corn imports in the early 1970s spurred the government to push for self-sufficiency in yellow corn. The NPR_D for corn averaged 32 percent a year between 1967 and 1986, promoting growth and meeting the profit expectations of the government monopoly importer, the National Grains Authority (which used the profits from corn and other imports to support rice prices).

Of the four principal commodities, only corn showed a positive cumulative output effect as a result of direct price intervention. Transfers to corn farmers averaged 1.3 percent of agricultural value added in the 1967–86 period. It is difficult to gauge the extent of preference to producers over consumers of corn, however, because the high prices served longer-term self-sufficiency objectives and had some positive income distribution effects for poorer corn farmers and disfavored higher-income consumers of livestock products.[11]

Positive NPRDS encouraged the production of domestic yellow corn. As a result, the harvested area in corn rose from 55 percent of the harvested area in rice in 1960 to more than 100 percent by the mid-1980s. At present, the nation appears to be on the verge of self-sufficiency in corn.

Feed millers and livestock firms have resented the rising protection for corn and have become particularly irked by recent pressures from the World Bank to allow imports of meat and meat products. To meet the needs of the domestic livestock industry, the Philippine government may have to reduce corn protection while maintaining production by increasing efficiency and by supporting its infrastructure.

Sugar producers were perhaps the strongest interest group in Philippine politics before martial law. Because of the relatively small number of producers, the large share of plantations in production, and the export premium from the U.S. sugar quota, sugar planters and millers enjoyed considerable power. The public viewed wealthy sugar families as arrogant, ostentatious, and reactionary, but their political power declined under martial law, particularly after the U.S. quota was terminated in the 1970s. The old sugar elite found itself subjected to the control of the Marcos government and its appointed sugar administrator. The fluctuating world sugar prices of the late 1970s and early 1980s left planters and millers heavily mortgaged to the Philippine National Bank, owned by the government, and to the Republic Planters Bank, controlled by cronies of Marcos.

The nominal rate of protection caused by direct intervention (using the adjusted ISA price as the relevant border price) oscillated from an annual average of 101 percent during 1960–71, to −16 percent during 1972–81, to an average of 67 percent during 1982–86. If the export unit value is used as the relevant border price, the nominal rate of protection worsened from an annual average of −14 percent to −21 percent to −25 percent in the same respective periods.

During the 1960s the domestic price of sugar was below the border price and above the ISA price because sugar producers had to satisfy domestic sales quotas at less than export prices to reduce the adverse price effect on domestic consumers of the export premium from the U.S. sugar quota. The price stabilization pursued by the government favored consumers during the early 1970s and producers during the late 1970s. Government control of domestic and export trading was the primary method of intervention, but the performance of the government monopoly was poor, and sugar producers had to shoulder substantial losses through lower government buying prices. Thus planters and millers opposed government intervention and the monopoly.

The volatile and declining price of sugar on the world market of the 1970s and early 1980s surprised Philippine producers and policy-makers, who had become used to a regime of relative certainty. After the U.S. quota was terminated in 1974, planters and the government had to face not only the problematic world market conditions but also the complexities of expanding domestic output in the face of declines in farm productivity and processing efficiency.

Intervention, most notably the opportunism of the government trading monopoly in the 1970s and early 1980s, added to the structural adjustment problems of the industry, as did the rent-seeking behavior of the sugar monopoly. This was caused, in part, by the layering of the domestic distribution network with a proliferation of "paper traders" who generated rents from government-granted quota rights to make purchases and who supplanted industrial users and wholesalers as buyers. Under the Aquino administration, sugar trade has reverted to the private sector, but the basic problems of productivity and diversification remain.

Coconut pricing and marketing were not significantly affected by government intervention until after the 1970s. Intervention was bound to be controversial because nearly 20 percent of Filipino farmers grow coconuts (whereas only 1 percent are in sugar). Intervention gave rise to a parastatal but legally private bureaucracy that worked largely outside the purview of government auditors and whose finances remained generally inaccessible to public scrutiny. In addition, intervention (largely in the form of short-term taxation) was designed to pay for the long-term objectives of crop replanting and industry restructuring, although it provided substantial opportunities for rent seeking.

The government's replanting program was meant to improve stagnating coconut productivity by introducing a hybrid, the seednuts of which came from a farm owned and controlled by the government's coconut administrator, a business associate of Marcos. Although there was some logic in the idea of introducing a higher-yielding variety, it seemed short-sighted to rely on one variety exclusively to increase productivity because two regions of the country were beset by a more serious problem—aging coconut trees. In addition, the returns to the seednut farm may have been excessive because of government expenditures on development costs (funded from the levy) and because of favorable contract prices (Sacerdoti 1982; Institute for Labor and Manpower Studies 1983).

The vertical integration policy was based primarily on a program pushed by the Philippine Coconut Producers Federation (COCOFED) in the late 1960s. In theory, the program was designed to increase the farmers' share in value added through indirect control of processing industries. As part of the integration, a quasi-parastatal coconut oil milling firm, UNICOM, was created to make the processing of raw copra more profitable and to exploit what was presumed to be a degree of monopoly power in world trade.

Processing appears to have been the more important objective for policymakers, since the government set a lower export tax on coconut oil than on copra and banned copra exports to support domestic milling. Moreover, the government actively promoted oil manufacture in the late 1970s. Here again, however, the flow of resources to development may have been diluted by private pecuniary motives. Key policies providing opportunities to collect monopoly rents were made and implemented by a small group of individuals close to Marcos. For example, there appears to have been significant rent seeking in the United Coconut Planters Bank (UCPB) and UNICOM on the part of the individual co-owners, mostly associates of the president, who enjoyed disproportionately higher equity participation than equity contribution.

The government's expenditures on irrigation have benefited primarily the rice industry. Some irrigation investment took place during the mid-1950s as part of President Ramón Magsaysay's social amelioration program for tenants. A second period of investment during the 1970s and early 1980s was both a response to a severe rice crisis and an expression of the economic and electoral strategies of President Marcos. In recent years, the Philippine government has tried to keep water prices to rice farmers below the returns needed to recover the costs of operating and maintaining the irrigation systems, and thus has had to provide subsidies for the National Irrigation Authority.

Fertilizer subsidies devolved from government efforts to bolster food production. The subsidies began with a program for rice and corn farmers in the late 1950s. By the early 1970s, with the establishment of the Fertilizer Industry Authority (later the Fertilizer and Pesticide Authority, FPA), government intervention had expanded to embrace price controls, production, and the marketing of fertilizer and farm chemicals. This expansion was most pronounced during 1973–75, a period of sharply higher world prices, when the government controlled domestic prices for fertilizer for rice and corn and provided budgetary subsidies for domestic fertilizer producers and importers, to cover their losses from price control. In addition, the FPA protected the domestic industry by capping imports at a predetermined level.

Although fertilizer subsidies continued into the early 1980s, the program was criticized for supporting fertilizer producers and importers while hurting farmers. At the same time, the lack of domestic raw materials made it impossible to encourage domestic production of nitrogen fertilizers. In response, the Aquino government liberalized completely the importation of urea and other nonphosphatic fertilizers in 1986, which brought domestic prices for these products to near-border prices. The type of policy desirable for the government's partly owned phosphatic fertilizer firm is still at issue.

Credit has been a focus of input policy in the Philippines. In the early 1950s a system of institutional credit was set up under the auspices of the Agricultural Credit and Cooperative Financing Administration (ACCFA) to reduce farmers' dependence on "usurious" informal credit sources. The program was administered by Farmers' Cooperative Marketing Associations (FACOMAS). With government encouragement, rural banks also began to appear during this period. Then in the 1970s, the government introduced the ambitious Masagana-99 program for rice farmers, a large package of extension services and credit. Similar packages were developed for fisheries, vegetable farmers, and producers of other commodities. Financing for these ventures was to come from banks, which were required to allocate at least 25 percent of loanable funds to agricultural credit through direct loans to farmers or through purchases of eligible government securities or commercial agricultural paper.

Despite the effort that has gone into the various agricultural credit programs, they have not performed well. Repayment problems crippled or killed many of the FACOMAS and bankrupted the ACCFA. Because of loan delinquency, the volume of Masagana-99 loans has dropped continuously, from a peak of almost P1.3 billion, covering 54 percent of all rice farmers in 1974–75, to only P224 million, covering only 6 percent of farmers in 1982–83. Furthermore, many of the commercial and thrift banks have invested in securities rather than the agricultural sector. Consequently, the share of agricultural loans in total bank credit declined from 18 percent in 1966 to 8.0 percent in 1983.

Credit subsidies have failed to offset the effects of other government policies that unduly taxed agricultural production. The main problem here has been the generally low interest rates resulting from administered nominal interest rates, inflation, and peso overvaluation, all of which added to the risks of agricultural lending. The Aquino government has followed an essentially market-oriented interest rate and agricultural credit policy and has eschewed subsidization. In the face of recent credit shortages and drought, however, the government has come under fire for failing to recognize the need for temporary subsidization and intervention, for example, in the form of agricultural loan restructuring.

INDIRECT PRICE INTERVENTION. In general, indirect intervention has had a greater impact on agriculture than direct intervention has. Of the two sources of indirect intervention—protection of the domestic market for manufactures and current account deficits—the former has predominated.

The protection system took shape during the 1950s as a response to the problems of independence. Under the policy of reciprocal free trade with the United States in the pre–World War II period, the Philippines became heavily dependent on the U.S. market for its exports of sugar, copra, and other primary products, and thus was discouraged from diversifying its production. The free entry of U.S. manufactures continued after independence in 1946 under the terms of the Bell Trade Act, which provided for 8 years of continued reciprocal free trade, followed by 20 years of gradually diminishing preferences. The Bell Act also limited Philippine sovereignty in economic policymaking by proscribing export taxes and requiring the government to obtain the permission of the U.S. president in order to alter peso/dollar valuation and convertability.

In the late 1940s the Philippines was faced with a war-torn economy. U.S. aid was therefore applied to the country's large trade deficits, and foreign exchange was used more to support basic consumption than to promote development. By 1949 the nation found itself in the midst of a severe balance of payments crisis, caused by a sharp drop in U.S. expenditures, a steep fall in the price of copra, a recession in the United States, domestic election spending, and capital flight arising from speculation about devaluation of the peso. With the approval of the International Monetary Fund (IMF) and President Harry S Truman, the Philippine Central Bank instituted foreign exchange controls to protect reserves. In 1953, after Congress refused to extend a 1950 import control law, the Central Bank began foreign exchange licensing and hence control of imports, a policy that extended to the end of the decade.

A fundamental cause of the disequilibrium in the balance of payments was that the peso/dollar exchange rate had been kept at the prewar level despite high inflation. The exchange rate made the Philippines appear uncompetitive even in its strongest primary exports without preferences such as reciprocity with the United States. Investors failed to respond to subsidies intended to develop new industries, not because they perceived the exchange rate as a problem but because they attributed the uncompetitiveness of Philippine products to economic backwardness.

Why did policymakers fail to recognize the seriousness of these problems? For one thing, the provision in the Bell Act that required U.S. permission for changes in the rate may have inhibited adjustments. Although Philippine policymakers sought permission to alter the rates for exchange control, they may have hesitated to press the issue for fear of jeopardizing the value of existing U.S. investments in the Philippines—presumably the reason for the original stipulation. Furthermore, Philippine leaders may have wanted to maintain an image of stability for investment. Thus, even when the provision was eliminated in a 1955 revision of the Bell Act, the Central Bank made no move to devalue the peso, and some businesses even feared that repeal would induce monetary instability or inflation.

The Philippine government continued to overvalue the peso until near the end of the decade, defending it via import controls, the only reasonable form of protection, under the arrangements for phased-down reciprocal free trade with the United States. Thus, import controls, which began as an immediate response to the balance of payments crisis and continued as a stabilization policy, became a form of industrial protection. Industrial protection was never rationalized as a development plan, however, but remained a concomitant of foreign exchange policy. The import control regime was administered to restrict goods on the basis of their "essentiality." That is, "essential" producer goods were allowed entry and "semiessential" and "nonessential" consumer goods were not. In effect, this policy discriminated against domestic consumer goods by disprotecting them and encouraging the production of consumer goods with the least proportion of domestic value added.

As industrialization proceeded, the political strength of vested interests increased. The system was also increasingly marked by corruption, smuggling, and underreporting of export earnings. A tightening of controls impeded expansion of new exports. It also displeased consumers, who saw import licensing as a means of denying them access to cheaper foreign goods. A political cycle developed in the control regime, with incumbent administrations—both Nationalists and Liberals—relaxing controls to attract popular support around election time.

The fixed exchange rate policy soon began to erode. The government allowed traders to use certain export earnings to pay for imports outside the parameters of the control system. Margin deposit requirements on import letters of credit were established, and direct fees and taxes were levied on the sale of foreign exchange. Thus a system of multiple exchange rates developed, and the government adjusted the system in response to political and balance of payments pressures. This system failed to solve the balance of payments problem, however. The new Philippine industries depended on imports and were extremely inefficient in saving foreign exchange. Consequently, they placed an ever greater burden on the primary exporting sector. By the end of the decade there was no further room for tightening restrictions on nonessential imports (see Baldwin 1975, chap. 2; International Labour Office 1974, chap. 1).

As the weaknesses of the fixed exchange rate system became apparent, the U.S. government and the IMF apparently began to press the Philippine government to decontrol imports and devalue the peso. No action was taken until 1962, when, after an election in which corruption in the controls system was a major issue, the new Philippine president, Diosdado Macapagal, implemented immediate and full decontrol, stabilizing the exchange rate at P3.90 per U.S. dollar.

With the devaluation, the Philippine tariff system became the principal instrument of intervention. On balance, though, protection in the domestic market was weakened. Nevertheless, there was still a strong bias toward import substitution and against exports, and industrial growth remained sluggish.

In the second half of the 1960s the Marcos regime adapted expansionary policies that again brought the balance of payments under pressure. Some modest import controls were reinstituted, and external borrowing rose sharply. Marcos promised no devaluation in his election campaign of 1969, but when a consortium of lenders made the floating of the peso a condition for loans, Marcos freed the rate, which quickly rose to P6.40.

By the late 1960s Philippine technocrats could see that the nation's development effort was being hampered by the inability of the industrial sector to earn sufficient foreign exchange through exports. An Investment Incentives Act, quickly followed by an Export Incentives Act, contained tax concessions for nontraditional exports. In addition, the government established an export processing zone and a system of bonded warehouses. Growth began in garment exports and later in semiconductors, although this growth was less than in some other countries of the region and was also heavily dependent on imported inputs.

Philippine technocrats saw the new encouragement of exports as a form of trade liberalization—that is, as a substitute for thorough reform of the protection system. But the modest encouragements did little to offset the pervasive bias against exports, or to improve the inefficient allocation of investment that characterized the import control system of the 1950s. Moreover, the economy remained excessively dependent on a few primary exports (Bautista, Power, and others 1979).

Deficits in the Philippines' current account, which became a serious issue in the late 1970s, were another focus of intervention. The first oil price shock of 1973–74, came at a time when the Philippines' external reserves were ample and its external debt modest. Policymakers opted for countercyclical spending in the face of the world recession, thereby adding to the current account deficit. Under this strategy, the government continued to borrow recycled petrodollars from commercial banks, and the ratio of investment to GNP reached an all-time high of about 30 percent.

The second oil shock of 1979–80 found the Philippines with a high external debt and a much weaker reserve position. Perhaps emboldened by earlier successes, the technocrats opted again to maintain growth. This time, however, the recession was more lasting and the rise in real interest rates more substantial. In addition, the government had been unable to diversify the economy or to reduce its dependence on sugar, coconuts, and other primary exports, while the investment allocation remained inefficient. Excessive protection of the domestic market and a bias against export diversification, overambitious foreign borrowing, and imprudent investment guarantees all contributed to an economic debacle, followed by an attempt at reform at the end of the 1970s. In 1978 a presidential decree empowered the Philippine Tariff Commission to review and reform the tariff structure, and talks were held in 1979 with World Bank representatives on the possibility of making reform part of a structural adjustment program and loan package. A gradual removal of import controls was to complement the tariff reform, the first phase of which was implemented despite the crises of the early 1980s.

But the fate of reform is no longer in the hands of the technocrats of the Marcos regime. The Congress elected in May 1987 will be the primary influence on Philippine economic policy and the reform process, and it is too early to say whether it will be able to correct the policy mistakes of the past, given the weight of the powerful vested interests and 35 years of excessive protection and peso overvaluation.

Conclusion

The 1986 revolution that led to the exile of President Marcos after 20 years in office underscored the crucial role that economic factors have played in shaping political events in the Philippines. Marcos, the only president ever to win reelection, was also the first president ever to be forcibly ousted from office. Although electoral fraud triggered the revolution, it came on the heels of rapid inflation (1984) and declines in output and income (in 1984 and 1985), the only instances of negative growth in the Philippines during the post–World War II period.

After the Philippines gained political independence from the United States in 1945, it gradually lost its favored position in the protected American market. This, together with a stubborn bias against correcting a greatly overvalued peso, led policymakers to believe that the Philippines must veer away from dependence on primary exports, whose earnings were subject to the vagaries of world price fluctuations, and encourage industrialization geared to the domestic market. The import control system that was adopted to effect this transformation served a nationalist purpose through the Filipinization of the import trade.

Similarly, the government's direct interventions in coconut and sugar trading during the 1970s were, in part, attempts to reduce non-Filipino domination of agricultural trading and processing. However, the interventions were misguided and wasteful, and thereby aggravated the structural adjustment problems that the coconut and sugar industries faced because of volatile world prices and the growing world use of substitutes. Coconut and sugar plantings and output, which reacted favorably to the sharp rise in world prices during the early 1970s, suffered worsening international competitiveness and declining output in the early 1980s in the face of depressed world prices.

Underpinning the government's direct interventions in rice and corn were the drive for self-sufficiency and stable food prices. The government's direct interventions, primarily price protection for corn and nonprice support services (including irrigation) for rice, contributed to sustained growth in rice and corn output during the 1970s and early 1980s.

Overall, the government's direct interventions in agriculture during the early 1970s and early 1980s favored corn and irrigated rice farmers, disfavored coconut and sugarcane farmers, and largely ignored land tenure problems in coconut, sugar, and plantation agriculture. It is not surprising that the Philippine insurgency shifted from the rice-growing Central Luzon area to the coconut, sugar, and plantation regions south of Manila during the late 1970s and early 1980s.

More than direct intervention, however, indirect intervention had a pervasive effect on the agricultural sector through the real exchange rate. Industrial protection and the concomitant overvaluation of the peso made farming less profitable. Thus Philippine manufacturing expanded during the study period on the backs of the Filipino farmers, so to speak.

During its first months, the Aquino government put an end to trading monopolies in sugar and coconut and abolished export taxes on agricultural exports. It has started to implement a comprehensive land reform program that includes sugar, coconut, and other crops, and it continues to emphasize investments in infrastructure. The challenge of building an efficient and competitive manufacturing sector remains.

Notes

1. The real exchange rate is defined here as the nominal rate multiplied by the ratio of the world price index to the Philippine nonagricultural price index.

Note that the real free-trade equilibrium exchange rate is the nominal free-trade equilibrium rate multiplied by the ratio of the "world" price index to the Philippine nonagricultural price index that would have been operative under free-trade conditions. The divergence between the real free-trade equilibrium rate and the real actual rate as a percentage of the real actual rate is caused by the trade protection regime and the current account imbalances. As Table 5-1 indicates, the divergence is greatest before a peso devaluation and decreases afterward. Table 5-1 also shows that the exchange rate divergence was greater and lasted longer during 1975–82, a portent of the serious payments, economic, and political crisis that followed.

2. The difference between NPR$_{ST}$ and NPR$_{LT}$ is that the latter includes the impact of the exchange rate on the price level in the nonagricultural sector.

3. In estimating NPRS, the domestic wholesale and retail prices used were the prices for Manila, the major consumer and trading market. Producer prices for rice, corn, and copra, which are widely produced, were averages for the nation; prices for centrifugal sugar were the millgate prices (before 1974). Although the four crops merit emphasis because they dominate the agricultural economy, focusing on them limits evaluation of the Philippines' dependency on those crops and of the effect of changes in the real exchange rate on agricultural diversification.

4. Total price intervention is the total of direct and indirect intervention. The cumulative output effect assumes a Nerlovian partial output adjustment to prices changes.

5. Annual nominal rates of protection were used to estimate the output effects, the assumption being that farmers consider such annual price changes to be permanent, and thus are encouraged to increase supply. Of course, farmers may regard some price shocks as temporary, and to that extent Table 5-3 may overestimate the true value of the output effects.

6. Note that the estimates in Table 5-3 are based on the assumption that wages remained constant despite the increase in output that would occur if the government shifted to a free-trade, nonintervention regime. If wages did increase, the output effects would be less than those given. Still, in view of the substantial underemployment of Philippine labor, the wage rate effect might not be large enough to undermine the rigor of the estimates given in Table 5-3.

7. Note, however, that an ethnopolitical insurgency also erupted in the 1970s in Western and Central Mindanao, Muslim-dominated areas that registered the highest rates of growth in per capita real income.

8. However, each major devaluation has been accompanied by new or higher export taxes as a means of dampening the domestic prices of the major exportables. Moreover, rice and corn pricing were also designed to temporarily offset the effects of devaluation.

Direct intervention is registered through a divergence of domestic prices, suitably corrected for marketing costs, from border prices. The sources are the pricing policies of the government marketing or regulatory agencies; various export taxes and levies; and pricing, tax, and trade policies affecting agricultural inputs such as fertilizer. Indirect intervention is registered through departures from the free-trade equilibrium exchange rate. Its sources are the current account deficit and, more importantly for the Philippines, the protection system that has persistently defended an overvaluation of the Philippine peso.

9. It can be argued that without the U.S. sugar quota the Philippines in the 1960s could have contracted sales at prices between the two alternative border prices for sugar—that is, at prices closer to actual domestic prices than either of the alternative prices. Seen in this light, the domestic producer price of sugar did not depart drastically from the border price for extended periods.

10. One group did suffer from the rice pricing policies of the 1970s—the rainfed farmers, who were unable to realize benefits in productivity comparable to those gained by irrigated rice farmers of the lowlands. Hence, national rainfed rice hectarage declined during the early 1980s.

11. The Philippine corn policy also illustrates the way in which the political-economic situation runs counter to an interest-group analysis. Although corn farmers are the second most numerous in the Philippines, they are geographically dispersed and least organized. In contrast, firms in feed milling and livestock and the middle- and upper-class consumers of chicken and pork are wealthier, more organized, and more powerful; still, as NPRDs for corn indicate, policy has favored the corn farmers.

Bibliography

The word "processed" describes works that are reproduced from typescript by mimeograph, xerography, or similar means; such works may not be cataloged or commonly available through libraries, or they may be subject to restricted circulation.

Abrera, A. 1976. "Philippine Poverty Thresholds." In M. Mangahas, ed., *Measuring Philippine Development*. Development Academy of the Philippines.

Abueva, José V., and Raul P. de Guzman. 1969. *Foundations and Dynamics of Filipino Government and Politics*. Manila: Bookmark.

Baldwin, R. 1975. *Foreign Trade Regime and Economic Development: The Philippines*. New York: Columbia University Press.

Bautista, E. 1987. "Rural Labor Market Adjustment to Differential Technical Change in Favorable and Unfavorable Rice-Based Villages in the Philippines." Agricultural Economics Department Workshop Paper. International Rice Research Institute, Los Baños.

Bautista, R., J. Power, and others. 1979. *Industrial Promotion Policies in the Philippines*. Manila: Philippine Institute for Development Studies.

Bouis, H. 1982. "Rice Policy in the Philippines." Ph.D. dissertation, Stanford University, Stanford, Calif.

Canlas, D., and others. 1985. *An Analysis of the Philippine Economic Crisis*. Manila: University of the Philippines.

Clarete, R., and J. Roummaset. 1983. "The Philippine Coconut Industry." Philippine Institute for Development Studies Working Paper. Manila.

Cruz, C., R. Siy, and W. Cruz. 1987. "Issues in Irrigation Water Management in the Philippines." *Policy Issues on the Philippine Rice Economy and Agricultural Trade*. UPLB-CDEM-CPDS.

David, C. C. 1983. "Economic Policies and Philippine Agriculture." Philippine Institute for Development Studies Working Paper 83-02. Manila.

———. 1984. "The National Food Authority." International Rice Research Institute, Los Baños. Processed.

David, C., R. Barker, and A. Palacpac. 1984. "Productivity in Philippine Agriculture." International Rice Research Institute, Department of Agricultural Economics, Los Baños.

de Luna, N. 1986. "The Reality of the Cojuangco Empire." *Business Day*, April 17, p. 11.

Drilon, J. 1967. "Rice Price Stabilization and the Rice and Corn Administration." *Journal of Philippine Public Administration*, July, pp. 230–43.

Ferrer, R. 1986. "Some Notes on Rent Seeking." University of the Philippines, School of Economics, Quezon City. Processed.

Golay, F. 1961. *The Philippines: Public Policy and National Economic Development.* Ithaca, N.Y.: Cornell University Press.

Gopinath, A. 1987. *Manuel L. Quezon: The Tutolary Democrat.* Quezon City: New Day.

Hooley, R. 1984. *Productivity Growth in Philippine Manufacturing: Retrospect and Future Prospects.* Manila: Philippine Institute for Development Studies.

Institute for Labor and Manpower Studies. 1983. *The Coconut Subsidy Program: Who Pays, Who Benefits?* Manila.

Intal P., Jr. 1987. "Government Interventions and Rent Seeking." Department of Economics Discussion Paper 87-04. University of the Philippines, Los Baños.

Intal, Ponciano S., and John H. Power. 1989. *Trade, Exchange Rate, and Agricultural Pricing Policies in the Philippines.* A World Bank Comparative Study. Washington, D.C.

International Labour Office. 1974. *Sharing in Development: A Program of Employment, Equity and Growth for the Philippines.* Geneva.

Ledesman, A. 1982. *Landless Workers and Rice Farmers: Peasant Subclasses under Agrarian Reform in the Philippines.* Los Baños: International Rice Research Institute.

Macaranas, F. 1975. "Development Issues Concerning the Impact and Incidence of Agricultural Taxation in the Philippines." Ph.D. dissertation, Purdue University, West Lafayette, Ind. Processed.

Marcos, F. 1967. "Sugar Industry Crisis. Self-Perpetuating." Speech to the National Federation of Sugarcane Planters. February 18.

———. 1976. *Notes on the New Society. II.* Manila: Marcos Foundation.

———. 1980. "A Climate of Stability of the Sugar Industry." Paper read at the 17th Congress of the International Society of Sugarcane Technologists, February 4. *Sugar News*, February.

McCoy, A. 1983. "In Extreme Unction: The Philippine Sugar Industry." In *Political Economy of Philippine Commodities.* Quezon City: University of the Philippines, Third World Study Program.

Mears, L., and others. 1974. *Rice Economy of the Philippines.* Quezon City: University of Philippines Press.

NEDA (National Economic and Development Authority). 1986. "Study on Government Assistance to Low Income Groups with Inadequate Access to Institutional Credit." Processed.

Nelson, G., and M. Agcaoili. 1983. "Impact of Government Policies on Philippine Sugar." Philippine Institute for Development Studies Working Paper 83-04. Manila.

Oshima, H., and others. 1986. "Rising National Income Per Worker and Falling Real Wages in the Philippines in the 1970s." Paper read at the Conference on Development Alternatives and Prospects, University of the Philippines, Quezon City, December 5–6.

Quisumbing, A. 1985. "Estimating the Distributional Impact of Food Market Intervention Policies on Nutrition." Ph.D. dissertation, University of the Philippines, Quezon City. Processed.

Rama, N. 1967. "Rice, Presidents and Politics." *Philippine Free Press,* August 5, p. 5.

Sacerdoti, G. 1982. "Cracks in the Coconut Shell." *Far East Economic Review,* January 8, pp. 42, 48.

Sangalang, J. 1975. "The Coconut Replanting Program." Center for Policy and Development Studies Working Paper 85-09. Los Baños: University of the Philippines.

Sicat, G. 1984. "A Historical and Current Perspective of Philippine Economic Problems." Paper read at the 21st Annual Meeting of the Philippine Economic Society. December. Processed.

Tan, E. 1980. "Philippine Monetary Policy and Aspect of the Financial Market: A Review of the Literature." In PIDS *Survey of Philippine Development Research I.* Manila: Philippine Institute for Development Studies.

Tan, N. A. 1979. "The Structure of Protection and Resource Flows in the Philippines." In R. Bautista, J. Power, and others, eds., *Industrial Promotion Policies in the Philippines.* Manila: Philippine Institute for Development Studies.

———. 1986. "The Philippines: The Structure and Causes of Manufacturing Sector Protection." In C. Findlay and R. Garnaut, eds., *The Political Economy of Manufacturing Protection: Experiences of ASEAN and Australia.* Sydney: Allen and Unwin.

Technical Board for Agricultural Credit. 1985. *Agricultural Credit Study.* Manila.

Tidalgo, R., and E. Esguerra. 1982. "Philippine Employment in the 1970s." Philippine Institute for Development Working Paper 82-02. Manila.

Treadgold, M., and Hooley, R. 1976. "Decontrol and the Redirection of Income Flows: A Second Look." *Philippine Economic Journal.*

Villegas, E. 1984. *Studies in Philippine Political Economy.* 2d ed. Manila: Silangan.

World Bank. 1984. *World Development Report 1984.* New York: Oxford University Press.

6 Sri Lanka

Surjit Bhalla

Like most developing countries, Sri Lanka relies on agriculture as a primary source of surplus for economic growth. The government of Sri Lanka has intervened in agricultural markets ever since the country gained its independence in 1948. These interventions have included (a) protection for domestic production of rice, a staple crop; (b) taxation of plantation crops like tea and rubber and, to a lesser extent, coconut; (c) food subsidies to consumers, mostly in the form of rice rations sold in government shops but also in the form of price subsidies for wheat and sugar; (d) large subsidies for rice production, primarily in the form of public irrigation; and (e) subsidies to and rationing of agricultural inputs, such as fertilizer. Some of these policies were reversed, however, when a liberalization strategy was initiated in 1978.

The central question posed in this chapter is what would have happened, and who would have gained or lost, if Sri Lanka had adopted a policy of nonintervention? That is to say, what were the intended and unintended effects of the policies that were followed, and what were their underlying costs and benefits?

One of the most striking features of the agricultural sector in Sri Lanka is that it consists of two distinct parts, rice and nonrice, the latter being dominated by tea producers. Another feature is its ability to function within a truly democratic framework, a rarity in developing countries. A third is the political and economic importance of food subsidies. Any attempt to explain Sri Lanka's economy must take into account the above three characteristics.

A suggested political economy framework with testable hypotheses would proceed as follows. Assume that the highly productive tree sector was taxed and the revenues used to create a welfare state in a relatively poor economy. It sometimes pays for a politician or policymaker to meet revenue demands by increasing the rate of taxation. Such increased taxation does not affect short-run output (because of low supply elasticity), and therefore the politician or policymaker does not immediately face the potentially dangerous consequences of higher taxes. Additional revenues are obtained, but producer profits decline. Over time, long-term supply elasticities come into play, and the decline in profits leads to a decline in output, which is followed by a decline in revenues. In other words, the "golden goose" (for example, Sri Lanka's estate sector) is slowly killed. When that happens, it becomes difficult to perpetuate welfare policies because no "easy"sources of revenue are available to pay for subsidies.

If the above is an accurate description of what happened in Sri Lanka, one needs to explain the passivity of the country's estate producers in the face of high taxes. And since lower prices are likely to be passed on to workers in the form of lower wages, one also needs to explain the passivity of estate workers toward a decline in wages.

For the moment, only simple and incomplete explanations are possible. One explanation is that about a third of the tea sector was in the hands of foreign companies at the time of independence. Since an avowed goal of various political parties in Sri Lanka was nationalization of the tea estates, the political cost of alienating such companies was not perceived to be high. Further, there was little short-run cost in reducing the living standards of estate workers, chiefly Tamil migrants from India who had yet to be granted the status of citizens. Thus the hypothesis is that economic and political realities conspired to lead Sri Lanka toward destruction of the estate sector and made reform inevitable. These reforms did arrive, albeit belatedly, in the late 1970s.

This chapter begins by presenting an economic and political overview of the economy. The role of the agricultural sector is then taken up, followed by an analysis of the results of agricultural protection (rice) and agricultural taxation (tree crops). The results of indirect intervention (for example, through exchange rate overvaluation) are also presented. Next, a simple model of price determination is offered for each of the four crops considered (rice, wheat, sugar, and tea). Given that the domestic prices of these crops are set by the government, the model can be termed a "bureaucratic model of price determination." This model yields several results—for example, identifying the pressures that led to higher prices. The model also helps explain tariff/tax rates in agriculture.

The chapter continues by analyzing the welfare effects of past policies. The evolution of agricultural and nonagricultural incomes is examined in order to identify gainers and losers. In addition, the macroeconomic effects of agricultural pricing policies are examined, particularly the link between food subsidies, deficit financing, and inflation. The role of government food subsidies in improving consumer welfare is also analyzed. Contrary to expectations, it turns out that large food subsidies did not materially increase consumer welfare, especially during 1971–77. This result occurred because food subsidy expenditures involved large transfers to domestic rice producers. At the end of the chapter, conclusions are offered.

Economic and Political Background

Sri Lanka is a large island situated close to the southern tip of India. At the time it achieved independence from Britain in February 1948, the country (then known as Ceylon) had a population of almost 7 million. This grew to about 10 million in 1960 and at present is slightly in excess of 16 million.

Most of the population lived in rural areas in 1948, and by 1980 the population was still 80 percent rural. The latter figure included the 7 percent of the population who lived on agricultural estates. Agriculture accounted for 46 percent of total employment in 1980. Almost equal amounts of land are used to raise tea and rubber, but tea employs almost three times as many people as rubber and has somewhat less than three times the output. Because of a higher tax rate on tea (discussed in detail later), tea accounts for almost three times the export earnings of rubber.

Unlike tea and rubber production and yield, coconut production and yield have not remained constant since 1960. Between 1953 and 1985 the value of coconut output increased from 40 percent to two-thirds that of tea and rubber. The increasing importance of rice is highlighted by most indicators. Land area, output, and yields have all shown a significant increase. Rice area has doubled in size, and output has increased more than fivefold since 1953. Whether in terms of rice subsidies for consumers, protection for producers, or massive irrigation programs, rice has been central to the affairs of the nation.

Beginning in 1839, the British imported large numbers of Tamils from India to work on Ceylon's coffee, tea, and rubber estates. It is not clear why the local population was not recruited, but one reason may be that the native Sinhalese refused to work on the plantations (presumably because of low wages).

Statistics on such things as income levels, school enrollment, and mortality rates show that Sri Lanka (Ceylon) was a rich agricultural country in the late 1940s. As such, its postindependence growth was not expected to be constrained by structural factors. The high literacy rate (75 percent in 1963) meant that human capital bottlenecks, which may have restrained other developing countries, did not seem likely to be a problem. Nor was foreign exchange a problem, given the presence of the large tree crop sector.

The postindependence experience can be divided into seven periods (see Table 6-1). The first, under the leadership of the founding United National Party (UNP), lasted from 1948 to 1956. These years

Table 6-1. Phases of Development in Sri Lanka

Period	Years	Ruling party	Prime Minister/ President	Comment
1	1948–56	UNP	Mr. Senanayake[a]	First period after independence; surplus from tree taxes; low to rising consumer subsidies; low import tariffs and essentially free trade. Low protection to rice producers, approximately 50 percent on average.
2	1956–60	SLFP (coalition)	Mr. Bandaranaike[a]	State intervention begins; policy import substitution initiated; tree taxes continue but they begin to provide a reduced surplus; food subsidy expenditures begin to accelerate. Rice protection increases, peaking at 144 percent in 1958.
3	1960–65	SLFP (coalition)	Mrs. Bandaranaike	State intervention continues; import tariffs increase and imports begin to be controlled. Food subsidy expenditures increase and account for 19.4 percent of government revenue in 1964.
4	1965–70	UNP (coalition)	Mr. Senanayake	Interventionist policies continue, but "mini-liberalization" attempted in 1967; exchange rate devalued from 4.78 rupees in 1966 to 5.93 rupees in 1968; no reform of tree crop taxes; indeed extra taxation of traditional exports through an indirect multiple exchange rate scheme (FEEC); growth and rice production accelerate.

5	1970–77	SLFP (coalition)	Mrs. Bandaranaike	Land reform in 1972 and 1975; reimposition of trade controls; implicit tariff on imports reach 162 percent in 1976 (more than 250 percent for nonagricultural goods). Sri Lanka not able to profit from the international commodity boom as tree crop producers are involved in land reform; growth is reduced to negative levels, and inflation reaches high levels with an average rate of 12 percent during 1971–77 (GDP deflator); a virtual breakdown of the economy.
6	1977–88	UNP	Mr. Jayawardene	The UNP wins an overwhelming share of seats with a majority vote. Large reforms introduced in 1978 toward decontrol or "liberalization" of the economy; foreign aid solicited and received in large amounts for an expansionary domestic investment program in agriculture (Accelerated Mahaweli Development Program); sustained increases in tree crop prices; rice output expands and real price of rice to producers and consumers declines; universal eligibility for food subsidies is ended and a food stamp program primarily for the bottom half of the population is introduced in 1980. Presidential system of government introduced in 1982.
7	1988–present	UNP	Mr. Premadasa	—

— Not applicable.
a. Not in office during all years listed.

were characterized by a reasonable growth rate, low inflation, and free trade (trade taxes averaged between 15 and 20 percent). Export earnings came mainly from tea, with rubber and coconut providing the remainder. The economy was therefore vulnerable to the vicissitudes of international events. The Korean War and the subsequent boom in worldwide commodity prices left Sri Lanka richer, but the ensuing bust left it poorer. Through it all, another inheritance of the British period—food rationing/subsidies—was kept intact. The wealth obtained from tree crop exports was seen as a justification for, and the basis of, food subsidies.

The second period (1956–60) witnessed some important changes in direction. The Sri Lanka Freedom Party (SLFP) won the election in 1956 and embarked on an industrialization program via import substitution, under the leadership of the state. In the third period (1961–65), effective import tariffs reached an average 49 percent, up from an average of only 16 percent during 1956–60. Agriculture was neglected during this third period, and welfare expenditures expanded. Nevertheless, economic growth was reasonable, and inflation remained low.

In 1966 the opposition UNP returned to power and a "miniliberalization" strategy was put into motion. Paddy production received renewed support, and agricultural as well as overall growth accelerated. The fourth period was marked by the consolidation of intervention policies, public sector expansion, and an increase in food subsidies and welfare expenditures.

The fifth period (1971–77), under the SLFP, saw a breakdown of the Sri Lankan economy. Since output growth, consumption growth, and equity were at record levels during the preceding five years, there is no easy explanation for the change in political leadership in 1970. The period was characterized by an intensification of government involvement in the economy as well as nationalization of the tea estates in 1972 and the rubber estates in 1975. Import tariffs rose to an average of 106 percent, peaking at 162 percent in 1976.[1] This was also a period of worldwide inflation. The net effect of both internal and external shocks during this period was to reduce the growth rate to a crawl and induce high inflation (almost 12 percent annually, according to the GDP deflator). Low to negative growth, food shortages, oil shock, large budget deficits, and high inflation all contributed to create the ensuing crisis.

This crisis helped bring about a sea-change in Sri Lankan policies in the election of 1977. The United National Party was brought back by the voters. It had campaigned on a platform of economic reform, and soon after assuming power it initiated a liberalization strategy. The exchange rate was doubled, and quantitative restrictions on imports were eliminated. The tariff structure was liberalized and reduced, and government investment in agriculture was radically increased. The implicit tariff rate for the period 1978–85 declined to 48 percent, and during 1984–86 the rate ranged from 17 to 29 percent. Further, the long-standing policy of food subsidies for the entire population was changed: both magnitude and coverage of the subsidies were reduced.

Sri Lanka has now entered a seventh phase of development (1988–present), but it is too early to summarize the economic policies of this period.

Macroeconomic Developments, 1948–85

Although rates of growth and inflation are useful summary statistics, the rate of growth per se is not indicative of the success or failure of a government's policies because it is also affected by exogenous shocks. Nevertheless, over the long term, economic growth is the most important yardstick for measuring the overall impact of a policy. If growth occurs, everything (usually) is seemingly forgiven. If growth does not occur, even good policies get a bad name.

According to the available figures on growth and inflation, Sri Lanka experienced an average annual per capita growth rate of 2.5 percent during the postindependence period (Table 6-2). Each time the SLFP came to power (in 1956 and 1970), however, the growth rate fell drastically. During the 17 years the SLFP was in control, the per capita growth rate averaged 1.44 percent; for the 20 years the UNP was in power, the per capita growth rate averaged 3.5 percent.

Data on private consumption (deflated by the official consumer price index) show a different pattern. Apart from an overall growth rate in per capita consumption that is substantially higher (3.6 percent versus 2.5 percent for GDP), the figure for 1971–77 is surprisingly high at 7.7 percent a year, almost twice the rate for any other period. This would suggest that Sri Lanka was able to withstand the external and internal shocks of most of the 1970s extremely well. Consequently, SLFP's loss of the 1977 election seems a mystery at first glance.

Part of the mystery is explained by the fact that the official CPI is an inadequate indicator of inflation (see Bhalla and Glewwe 1985). One reason that the official price series produced downward-biased estimates of inflation (especially in the 1970s) was because the index was computed on the basis of subsidized rather than market prices. An alternative consumer price index based on data supplied by the Department of Census and Statistics for selected years between 1969 and 1982 was constructed by Bhalla and Glewwe and is used in this chapter. If this index is used to deflate consumption expenditures, the pattern of real per capita consumption growth is similar to the pattern of real per capita income growth observed with the GDP de-

Table 6-2. Income, Consumption, Inflation, and Trade Taxes, 1951–85

Item	1951–55	1956–60	1961–65	1966–70	1971–77	1978–85	1951–85
Real GDP per capita[a]							
Rate of growth (percent)[b]	1.3	−0.5	1.9	4.6	1.5	4.8	2.5
Level (millions of rupees)[c]	776	780	835	970	1,136	1,528	1,057
Private consumption per capita, adjusted CPI							
Rate of growth (percent)[b]	0.2	0.4	−0.9	4.4	0.1	3.2	1.3
Level (millions of rupees)[c]	453	442	445	507	522	633	515
Private consumption per capita, official CPI							
Rate of growth (percent)[b]	−0.4	1.6	−0.7	4.1	7.7	5.0	3.6
Level (millions of rupees)[c]	442	449	464	530	738	1,219	703
GDP deflator	1.1	1.6	−0.5	3.9	11.9	13.2	6.3
Adjusted CPI (PCPIA)	n.a.	1.8	1.9	4.1	14.1	15.9	8.0
Official CPI	0.2	0.6	1.7	4.2	5.7	13.7	5.5
Estimated import tax rate	21.2	15.7	48.5	62.6	106.1	48.2	55.3
Estimated export tax rate	14.8	19.2	18.3	27.0	39.8	20.4	23.2

n.a. Not available.

a. The GDP figures have been revised twice, in 1959 and 1970. Further, two sets of GDP figures exist—those compiled by the Department of Census and Statistics and reported in the International Monetary Fund's *Financial Statistics*, and those compiled by the Central Bank of Sri Lanka and reported by the World Bank. The figures here are from the former.

b. Annual averages for each period.

c. 1956 prices.

Source: National Accounts; Bhalla (forthcoming).

flator. (The rate itself, 1.3 percent, is somewhat lower than the GDP growth rate of 2.5 percent. Part of this result is due to a near doubling of the investment rate during 1978–85.)

The new consumption deflator (hereafter referred to as the adjusted consumer price index, or PCPIA) indicates that instead of increasing at a rate of 7.7 percent during 1971–77, as suggested by the official CPI, the per capita consumption growth rate was in essence zero, and inflation was 14 percent, in contrast to the official 5.7 percent.

The discrepancy that arises when different price deflators are used is striking and worrisome. Depending on the deflator, the assessment of welfare and of policy impact is reversed. Detailed tests carried out for both price series indicate that the adjusted consumption deflator matched the exogenous market data more closely than the official one. Therefore the alternate price data are used in the rest of this chapter.

The figures in Table 6-2 may be thought to reflect the reasons for UNP's landslide victory in 1977. That conclusion would be somewhat unwarranted, however, since economic determinism was not always apparent in earlier years.

Politics and Institutions

Agricultural pricing policies in Sri Lanka cannot be analyzed without a comment on the political and institutional framework. Sri Lanka is one of the relatively few functioning democracies in the developing world, and that makes the analysis difficult, since an intuitive ranking of interest groups is not obvious.

Any number of candidates from any number of parties can contest an election in Sri Lanka. A candidate who gets a plurality of the votes cast wins the election. There are no runoffs. The country inherited this "first-past-the-post" system from the British. A casual interpretation of the workings of this system would suggest that the party with the most votes gets the most seats, but this need not be and, indeed, most often is not the case. In a multiparty system like this one, it is difficult to interpret election results as a judgment on economic policies and performance.

Two examples illustrate the anomalies that can occur. In 1960 two elections were held in Sri Lanka within a space of four months. In an election in March, the UNP gained a plurality of the votes (that is, about 29 percent, not a majority) and formed a governing coalition. After a vote of no confidence in the UNP coalition, another election was held, and the UNP garnered 38 percent of the votes, or 5 percent more than the SLFP. Nonetheless, it was the SLFP that managed to put together a governing coalition. A second example is the 1970 election. Although the UNP won a plurality of the votes (37.9 percent, compared with 36.8 percent for the SLFP), it won only 17 of the 129 seats contested, compared with 91 for the SLFP.

The 1977 election, on the other hand, might have been a true indicator of "the people's choice." The SLFP had been in power for seven years because of constitutional changes in 1972 and entered the election after presiding over a period of political and economic disturbance. (A state of emergency had been declared in April 1971 and was not lifted until February 1977.)

The July 1977 election resulted in a landslide victory for the UNP, led by one-time Finance Minister J. R. Jayewardene. The UNP gained a majority of the votes cast (50.9 percent) and 140 of the legislature's 168 seats. Although the SLFP managed to win 30 percent of the popular vote, it gained only 8 seats. The UNP had pledged to achieve "democratic socialism," and in fact the most significant policy changes in Sri Lankan history occurred in the post-1977 years.

The Role of the Agricultural Sector

The crops of primary importance in Sri Lanka are tree crops and rice. Tree crops (mainly tea, but also rubber and coconut) accounted for more than 90 percent of the value of total exports in 1951–55 and in each succeeding five-year period until 1970. Tree crop taxation accounted for an average 28 percent (Rs 161 million) of total government revenues during the 1951–55 period, while net average food subsidies were Rs 48 million. Thus, after consumer subsidies were paid for the entire population, a "surplus" of Rs 113 million was left for other purposes each year (Table 6-3). During 1971–77, however, tree crop exports fell to an average of 78 percent of all export revenues, and in the most recent period (1978–85) they accounted for only 55 percent.

Rice has been a favored agricultural sector in Sri Lanka. The political reasons are not hard to find. Rice is a staple of the economy, comprising about one-third of the consumer basket (a share that has not changed much over the years). Almost half of the agricultural work force is employed in paddy. Both the UNP and the SLFP have wooed the rice sector over the years, but there has been one main difference in their approach. The UNP has concentrated on the production side, whereas the SLFP has worried more about the consumers. These attitudes toward the paddy sector are a reflection of overall ideologies— that is, UNP's concern with production, in contrast to SLFP's concern with distribution.

Even so, until 1977 every Sri Lankan government followed broadly similar policies with respect to the procurement, distribution, and consumption of rice. The policies were set in the years following World War II, and any change in their parameters became a major event with potentially large political costs.

Table 6-3. Food Imports, Tree Crop Exports, and Tree Crop Taxes 1951–85

Item	1951–55	1956–60	1961–65	1966–70	1971–77	1978–85	1951–85
Food imports							
Value (millions of rupees)[a]	709	716	674	800	830	1,059	824
Share of all merchandise imports[b]	48.1	40.8	42.8	44.2	42.2	15.2	38.0
Tree crop exports							
Value (millions of rupees)[a]	1,617	1,526	1,616	1,476	1,380	2,430	1,722
Share of all merchandise exports[b]	91.4	91.4	93.4	91.7	77.6	54.5	81.4
Tree crop taxes							
Total[c]	267	320	316	432	706	908	542
Share of government revenue[b]	28.0	25.6	20.1	21.8	29.7	23.3	24.9
Share of GDP[b]	5.7	5.6	4.5	4.6	6.0	5.4	5.3

a. All values are in real terms. Deflator is GDP, 1956 = 100.
b. Ratios are averages of the ratios for the individual years.
c. Includes FEEC taxes.
Source: Central Bank of Ceylon, *Annual Review*, various issues; Bhalla (forthcoming).

Since a decline in consumption levels imposed political costs, the consumption level was given "exogenously." Domestic production levels then dictated the level of imports. It was here that ideology affected food policy. The UNP viewed food imports as a constraint to development, because they displaced capital imports. Thus a primary goal of the government was to accelerate the production of rice. In contrast, the SLFP considered industrialization via import substitution a high priority and deemed production incentives for rice to be of secondary importance.

The net effect in both cases was a steady food supply. Although quantity was determined by this approach, prices could theoretically be handled in a number of ways. To protect producers, the government might have paid a producer price that was higher than the import price. But it was hard for each incoming government to raise the consumer price in nominal, let alone real, terms. Thus Sri Lankan governments were able to achieve some flexibility only through arrangements involving free rice, subsidized rice, and market-priced rice.

It would not be an exaggeration to say that the consumer price of rice has had a large impact on policymaking in Sri Lanka for three decades, and that it was not until the system virtually broke down (because of extremely high inflation and negative growth rates) that reform, via the elimination of food subsidies, became possible in 1978. To understand the forces at work in these years, consider for a moment what happens when the international price of export crops increases. This produces a windfall gain for the government through higher tax revenues, which it can accumulate in the form of reserves, invest, or use to pay for more imported rice. If the last option is taken and more rice becomes available, the consumer pays a lower price.

Now suppose that revenues from export taxes fall, either because of a decline in the output of export crops or because of a decline in international prices. In the latter case, the government may decide to increase the tax rates on export crops, an option the Sri Lankan government did exercise in 1965 and 1969. But an increase in tax rates means a disincentive to producers.

Another option is to raise consumer prices, but this usually entails political costs, as the newly installed UNP realized in 1966 when it sought to decrease expenditures for consumer subsidies without losing popular support. The government's solution was to reduce the periodic ration for each consumer from 4 pounds to 2 pounds, while also reducing the ration price from 12.5 cents to 0.0 cents. The result was a 15 percent increase in consumer expenditure (based on per capita per week consumption of 4 pounds), from Rs 2.26 to Rs 2.58. Even though the real cost to the consumer rose, the government could claim that it was providing free rice.

The various components of the food subsidy in Sri Lanka cannot be delineated without some idea of the effective producer price (PRCF) and consumer price (PRCC) for rice. The former is relatively easy to calculate. It is a weighted price, the weights being the government's share of purchases and the open market's share. Computing the effective consumer price is somewhat more complicated. This problem is akin to finding an index number—that is, to determining the normal quantity purchased. Consumer surveys suggest that a consumption level of 4 pounds per capita per week is normal.[2] If this level is considered to be intramarginal (but close to overall purchases under most relative prices), the cost per pound of these 4 pounds may be the "effective" price. That is the assumption made in this chapter.

Four points can be made about the rice prices in Table 6-4. First, there are vast differences between the open market price, the ration-shop price, and the effective consumer price. These differences suggest that calculations of consumer subsidies based on the open-market price or the ration-shop price can be called into question. Second, the average protection to rice producers was 60 percent or more for all periods except the early postindependence period (1951–55) and the liberalization period (1978–85). Third, consumers received large subsidies, especially in the 1960s. Consumer subsidies for the entire 1951–85 period averaged about 14 percent. Fourth, and contrary to popular perception, the "end" of food subsidies in Sri Lanka came not with liberalization in 1978 but rather with the SLFP regime of 1970–77. The consumer cost of rice was 78 percent of the import price in 1970. Two years later, this ratio reached 100.6 percent. External shocks, low domestic production due to adverse weather, and the lack of imported fertilizer, among other things, made it more difficult to subsidize the consumer. As a result, consumer prices averaged 20 percent above import prices during 1973–77.

Types of Intervention

Government intervention in Sri Lanka has taken several forms, including subsidies for food, direct and indirect taxation, and subsidies for fertilizer and irrigation.

The Food Stamp Program

Universal rice rationing was in force until 1980, when the government decided to replace rationing with an eligibility criterion. This criterion stipulated that only households of five persons or more earning less than Rs 300 per month would be eligible for rice subsidies in the form of food stamps. The value of these food stamps was about Rs 18 per

Table 6-4. Rice Prices and Subsidy/Protection Rates on Rice Consumption/Production, 1951–85

Item	1951–55	1956–60	1961–65	1966–70	1971–77	1978–85	1951–85
Consumer price							
Ration shop price[a]	0.22	0.18	0.13	0.00	0.00	n.a.	n.a.
Openmarket price	0.97	0.88	0.88	1.07	1.54	1.04	1.09
Effective price[b]	0.59	0.37	0.26	0.47	0.84	0.95	0.63
Effective price[b] (for poor consumers)	0.59	0.37	0.26	0.47	0.84	0.64	0.56
Producer price							
Farmer price[c]	1.03	0.95	0.91	1.00	1.21	1.04	1.04
Import price[c]	0.71	0.47	0.50	0.63	0.72	1.04	0.71
Rate of subsidy/protection[d]							
Rice production	47.0	104.9	88.2	63.7	80.8	3.7	60.4
Rice consumption	15.9	20.2	46.4	24.6	−13.1	4.7	13.8

n.a. Not available.

Note: All prices have been deflated by the GDP deflator, 1956 = 100.

a. The ration price is the price for the first "purchase" of rice; consequently, it is zero in those years when some rice was provided free.

b. The effective price is defined as the cost per pound of the *first* 4 pounds of purchase of rice per capita per month. Such prices for poor consumers incorporate the income transfers implicit in the food stamp program started in 1980.

c. The import and farmer prices have been made comparable by adjusting for transportation, retail margins, and so on.

d. The subsidy rate for the consumer is based on the effective price of rice and is relative to the import price of rice. The same comparator is used to calculate the subsidy/protection to rice producers. Negative subsidy levels mean a positive amount of taxation.

Source: Agricultural Statistics of Sri Lanka.

capita per month (see Edirisinghe 1985). (Their nominal value was kept constant, and thus their real value was somewhat less.)

With the shift from rice rationing to food stamps, the distinction between the market price of rice and the equivalent consumer cost has virtually disappeared. And because of the steep fall in the international price of rice between 1982 and 1986, the nonpoor consumers (or, more accurately, those who do not qualify for food stamps) pay more than the international price of rice.

In 1987 the government adopted a sliding scale based on family size to determine eligibility. All members of a household receive stamps if the family income is below Rs 300 per month, but only two members receive stamps if the income falls in the range of Rs 600–700 per month. According to a World Bank country report for 1988, the number of stamp recipients has stayed approximately the same (about 7.3 million), although targeting appears to have improved somewhat.

Direct and Indirect Taxation of Agriculture

Like other developing countries, Sri Lanka taxes agriculture both directly and indirectly. The degree of direct taxation can be estimated by comparing product prices (domestic and international) at the same point in the distribution chain. It takes somewhat longer to assess indirect taxation because the equilibrium exchange rate must be included in the calculations.

The equilibrium exchange rate (E^*) is defined as the rate that balances the current account in the absence of any trade taxes (see the appendix to this volume for details on the construction of E^*). Therefore, this rate cannot be calculated without estimating trade taxes. In this study the export taxes imposed on tree crops, after adjustment for transport costs and retail margins, among other factors, were obtained from official documents. No such estimates were available for taxation on imports (mostly industrial goods). In view of the many policies that governments employ to protect industry (tariffs, bans, quantitative restrictions), it is extremely difficult to estimate the *net* protection provided by such policies. During the liberalization year of 1979, the average rate of import protection was 26 percent (Cuthbertson and Khan 1981). Some interesting data have also been obtained on effective tariff rates (t_M) for the years 1956–85 (Bhalla forthcoming). The methodology used applies an errors-in-variables approach to the residuals obtained from a (misspecified) import demand equation (Schiff and Valdés 1986).

To begin with, this exercise demonstrated that the import-substitution industrial strategy and the licensing and import controls introduced in 1961 increased the five-year average tariff rate to 49 per-

Table 6-5. Exchange Rate, 1956–85

Item	1956–60	1961–65	1966–70	1971–77	1978–85	1956–85
"Equivalent" trade taxes						
Imports[a]	15.7	48.5	62.6	106.1	48.2	55.3
Nonfood imports	26.5	83.3	112.3	182.4	58.4	90.2
Exports	19.2	18.3	27.0	39.8	20.4	23.2
Nominal exchange rate						
Official (rupees/						
dollar)	4.76	4.76	5.51	7.07	20.49	9.62
PPP[b]	4.85	5.18	5.39	7.07	22.30	10.17
Equilibrium (E^*)[b]	5.01	5.59	6.51	8.28	23.91	11.16
Equilibrium real exchange						
rate (e^*)[c]	4.79	4.68	5.19	5.08	9.13	6.06
Overvaluation (percent)						
PPP	1.84	8.01	−1.94	−0.12	7.82	3.38
Equilibrium	5.01	14.40	15.12	14.20	14.49	12.94

Note: Price levels are averages within a period and are based on 1956 = 100. The consumer price index for Sri Lanka is the adjusted price index.

a. Trade taxes for imports are estimated through an import demand equation; see text.

b. The real PPP rate is assumed to be 4.79 rupees/dollar (1956 base) for 1956–77 and 15.6 rupees/dollar (1978 base) for 1978 to the present. See text for definition and methodology of computing the PPP and equlibrium exchange rates.

c. Real exchange rate is obtained by deflating the nominal exchange rate by a price index that reflects how removal of trade taxes affects the price of nonagricultural goods.

Source: Central Bank of Ceylon, *Review of the Economy*; Bhalla (1988a).

cent from the "free trade" average of 16 percent that prevailed in the late 1950s (Table 6-5). A devaluation in 1967 accompanied by partial liberalization in 1968 reduced the tariff rate from 83 percent in 1967–68 to 55 percent in 1969. Explicit inward-looking policies adopted in 1970 are captured by an increase in effective import tariffs to 87 percent during 1971–73. The oil price shock and the resulting squeeze on imports drove t_M to a peak of 162 percent in 1976 and to an average level of 122 percent during 1974–77.[3] The large-scale liberalization introduced in 1978 is also clearly reflected in the estimates of t_M. Except for the second oil shock year of 1980, the average tariff rate was estimated to be 48 percent. From 1984 through 1986, the rate ranged from 17 percent to 29 percent.

These estimates of trade taxes allow one to estimate the equilibrium exchange rate in the absence of trade taxes.[4] Purchasing power parity

(PPP) can also be used to estimate E^*. If the real exchange rate for a particular year is known and an adjustment made for the differential between domestic and international prices, one can estimate the actual exchange rate that keeps the real exchange rate constant. The PPP method can be used only if one knows when the current account was in balance.[5] For Sri Lanka, such a period occurred in the early to mid-1950s. Trade taxes were in the teens, and import controls were virtually nonexistent. Consequently, the year 1956 has been chosen as a period when the current account and the exchange rate were in equilibrium.

When the overvaluation of the exchange rate is estimated by these two methods, the results tend to be somewhat lower with the PPP, although neither method yields particularly large estimates of overvaluation (Table 6-5). The largest estimate (15 percent) was obtained for the 1966–70 period; the highest single-year estimate is for 1980, when overvaluation reached 27 percent. Thus, on average, the exchange rate overvaluation of about 13 percent was not a predominant form of agricultural taxation in Sri Lanka, especially when compared with the effect of the equivalent tariff on nonfood imports, which averaged 90 percent (see Table 6-5).

FERTILIZER SUBSIDIES. Between 1978 and 1985 fertilizer subsidies were about three times their average 1971–77 level. After peaking at Rs 782 million in 1980, these subsidies declined to only Rs 369 million in 1986. Containment of the fertilizer subsidy is also reflected in data on the relative price of rice to fertilizer. This relative price decreased in the postliberalization period and in recent years was about 25 percent below its (peak) 1971–77 level.

Fertilizer use in Sri Lanka's rice fields rose from 43,000 tons in 1961–65 to an average 75,000 tons annually during the 1965–70 period, and from 93,000 tons in 1971–77 to 166,000 tons in 1978–85. From 1985 to 1987, consumption was 217,000 metric tons a year.

IRRIGATION SUBSIDIES. The largest cost incurred by Sri Lanka in achieving rice self-sufficiency has been its irrigation subsidies. One of the biggest projects in the world, the Mahawelli irrigation project, was initiated in the late 1960s and accelerated by J. R. Jayewardene soon after he assumed the presidency in 1977. Expenditures on irrigation in 1979 exceeded a billion rupees, a tenfold increase over the 1977 level of Rs 150 million. Such expenditures reached a record level of Rs 7.2 billion in 1982, or more than twice the amount collected through taxes on tree crops. In real terms, irrigation expenditures averaged Rs 5.6 billion a year during 1978–85. The amount of land under irrigation increased from 514,000 acres in 1977 to 700,000 acres in 1984 and 771,000 acres in 1987.

Measures of Agricultural Protection

Several measures can be used to assess discrimination agriculture. The most common measure is the direct nominal protection rate (NPR_D), which is the ratio of the domestic price to the international price minus one. As is well known, this measure does not control for variations in input prices. Consequently, a preferred measure is the effective rate of protection (ERP).

These rates measure the effect of direct intervention. But it is also necessary to measure indirect intervention (NPR_I), which reflects the impact of the exchange rate and industrial protection policies on agricultural incentives (relative to P_{NA}, an index of nonagricultural prices; see the appendix to this volume for details). What is noteworthy about NPR_I is that it is independent of the crop being analyzed.

Estimates of NPR_D, NPR_I, and total nominal protection (NPR_T), as well as ERP for rice, tea, rubber, and coconut, are reported in Table 6-6 (see also Krueger, Schiff, and Valdés 1988 and the appendix to this volume). Six results stand out:

1. Indirect taxation, which averaged 27 percent from 1953 to 1985, increased markedly after the 1950s. After reaching an average of 12 percent in 1956–60, it hit a peak of 39 percent during 1971–77. Between 1978 and 1985 it declined to 30 percent, and in 1984 and 1985 it dropped to 19 percent or less.

2. Tea, rubber, and coconut show high negative levels of direct protection, averaging more than 20 percent. The period 1978–85 witnessed a sharp increase in the direct taxation of tea and rubber, largely as a result of the close to 100 percent devaluation that took place in 1978.

3. Tax rates for coconut follow a similar pattern, except for the 1981–85 period. The lower level of taxation for coconut was a clear signal that policymakers wanted production to increase. For rubber, direct taxation rose from 9 percent in 1956–60 to 25 percent in the 1970s, thereby achieving a rough parity with taxation of tea and coconut in those years.

4. In contrast to the export crops, rice showed a positive rate of protection for most of the study period. Until 1977 the level of protection for rice ranged from 46 to 105 percent. However, the average level of nominal direct protection did not exceed 4 percent between 1978 and 1985.

5. Since NPR_I is negative (an indirect tax), the total protection rate NPR_T is less than NPR_D for all products. For tea, rubber, and coconut, the average tax over the 1953–85 period increased from about 27, 21, and 23 percent for NPR_D to about 47, 41, and 43 percent for NPR_T, while for rice the rate of protection fell from about 61 percent to 19 percent. For the period 1978–85, NPR_D equaled 3.7 percent for rice, while NPR_T

equaled 26.6 percent, so that rice was in fact taxed when the impact of both direct and indirect policies is taken into account.

6. The pattern of direct and total ERP is similar to that of the direct and total NPR, with the ERP values being usually larger than the respective NPR values (both for positive and negative protection).

Agricultural Pricing Policies

Sri Lanka's agricultural pricing policies can best be explained by looking at real farmgate prices, production incentives, and the resulting changes in output.

Real Farmgate Prices

The evolution of real producer prices tracks well the fortunes of Sri Lanka's export crops.

TEA AND RUBBER. Tea and rubber show a sharp decline in real prices from the early 1950s through 1977. The real price of tea, even during the years of high commodity prices in the 1970s, was only two-thirds of the price in the 1950s. Replanting and fertilizer subsidies did not do much to improve tree crop profitability. Rubber prices show a similar decline. Therefore it is not surprising that production of the two crops stagnated in the 1960s and 1970s. Tea yields in 1976 were not much different from those of 1960, and tea production reached its peak level in 1968. For all three tree crops, the area under cultivation has stayed relatively constant; hence, changes in production levels correspond to changes in yields. During the commodity boom years of 1974–75, production was 3 percent less than it was on average during the previous five years.

The fortunes of tea and rubber changed during the liberalization period from 1978 to 1985. Although tax rates rose to record levels, real farm prices also increased sharply, with the result that the average tea price for the period was the highest ever—Rs 4.8 per kg (in 1956 prices), compared with Rs 4.6 during 1952–55 and Rs 3.3 in 1971–77. The increase in rubber prices from 1971–77 to 1978–85 was close to 60 percent. These prices remained high despite declining international prices because of an apparent recognition that declining profits had been responsible for the stagnation of the tree crop sector. The decline in profits was exacerbated by the disastrous land reform laws of 1972 and 1975, which transferred land from private companies to public sector units (see Fernando 1980).

COCONUT. Coconut prices followed a somewhat different course. Real prices remained constant until 1975 and then show an upward move-

Table 6-6. Rates of Protection 1953–85
(percent)

Rate	1953–55	1956–60	1961–65	1966–70	1971–77	1978–85[a]	1953–85	1984[b]	1985[b]
Nominal rate of protection (NPR_D)[c]									
Tea	−18.5	−25.3	−23.8	−25.7	−21.1	−40.6	−27.3	−33.1	−35.1
Rubber	−10.4	−8.9	−13.9	−11.8	−24.9	−38.8	−20.9	−36.5	−15.8
Coconut	−26.2	−21.5	−21.0	−26.4	−22.4	−20.7	−22.6	10.3	−20.3
Rice	46.0	104.9	88.2	63.7	80.8	3.7	61.1	19.1	26.5
Rate of indirect protection (NPR_I)	−10.7	−11.8	−27.0	−30.2	−38.6	−30.0	−26.9	−14.9	−19.0
Total protection rate (NPR_T)[d]									
Tea	−27.6	−34.2	−44.4	−48.2	−51.6	−58.3	−46.8	−43.1	−47.4
Rubber	−20.3	−19.8	−37.1	−38.7	−53.5	−56.7	−41.4	−46.0	−31.7
Coconut	−34.5	−30.7	−42.5	−48.9	−52.3	−43.5	−43.3	−6.1	−35.4
Rice	31.8	81.0	37.8	15.1	12.4	−26.6	19.4	1.4	2.5

Effective rate of protection, direct

Tea	n.a.	−26.7	−28.7	−35.8	−35.2	−46.6	−35.8	−35.2	−38.3
Rubber	n.a.	−6.6	−16.5	−19.5	−40.0	−44.3	−28.3	−38.9	−15.1
Coconut	n.a.	−22.5	−25.2	−34.4	−33.8	−23.5	−27.8	13.1	−21.3
Rice	n.a.	128.5	101.4	65.6	77.9	2.0	67.9	25.4	33.6

Effective rate of protection, indirect

Tea	n.a.	−35.4	−47.9	−55.1	−60.2	−62.3	−53.7	−44.9	−50.0
Rubber	n.a.	−17.7	−38.8	−44.1	−62.6	−60.3	−47.5	−48.0	−31.2
Coconut	n.a.	−31.7	−45.4	−54.5	−59.2	−45.1	−47.8	−3.7	−36.2
Rice	n.a.	101.9	47.8	16.7	11.0	−27.3	23.0	6.7	8.3

n.a. Not available.

a. The figures for 1978–85 are biased upward due to the (temporarily) high rate of taxation in the immediate years after the large devaluation in 1978.

b. The individual-year data for 1984 and 1985 are indicative of the change in tax rates after the effects of the devaluation have been "passed through."

c. Data are at official exchange rates.

d. Data are at equilibrium exchange rates and in the absence of protection to industrial imports.

Source: Bhalla (forthcoming).

ment. The average for the 1978–85 period was 38 cents per nut, almost 300 percent more (in real terms) than the price in the early 1950s. Coconuts have risen in price partly because they are a popular domestic consumption item. According to a 1969–70 consumer survey, coconuts and coconut by-products account for 8 percent of the consumption basket in Sri Lanka.

RICE. If prices are any indication, rice producers have not been favored by the government. The real price of rice in 1985 was identical to the price in the early 1950s. In 1967 the government raised the procurement price by 17 percent after it had stayed constant in nominal terms for years. The next significant increase occurred in November 1977, when the price went up from Rs 33 a bushel to Rs 40 a bushel, an increase of 21 percent.

These periodic price increases have not been reflected in real farmer prices. The real producer price in 1986 was almost 20 percent below the low price of 1977. However, the amount of land devoted to rice cultivation, the use of modern inputs, and yields have all risen over the years, bringing Sri Lanka close to self-sufficiency in rice production. (This is in striking contrast to the stationary yields of the plantation crops.) In other words, technological change and other factors have shifted the supply curve to the right. Thus, even though the real output price fell, profits for rice farmers have increased.

Production Incentives and Output Response

One conclusion that emerges from the preceding discussion is that changes in protection rates are inadequate indicators of changes in policy, as are real prices, especially where technological change and subsidized inputs are present. However, the fact that Sri Lanka's subsidies for tea and rubber producers remained more or less unchanged suggests that the incentive structure was biased against tree crops. In contrast, the output prices of rice oscillated with the party in power. Real prices rose strongly in the mid-1970s because of the commodity boom, but they also declined sharply in 1977.

The heavy subsidy to rice production made such production competitive in Sri Lanka in 1978. This new competitiveness was helped by the large devaluation in that year. From 1978 to 1981 the rice sector was also (effectively) taxed at about Rs 600 million a year. Even though rice prices have continued to fall in real terms since then, production subsidies to rice turned positive in 1982 because of an even larger decline (40 percent) in the international price of rice.

One prediction—a significant increase in tree crop production—has not been realized. Coconut production has increased, but tea and rubber appear to be lagging. Tea output reached 214,000 tons in 1984, which was up from an average level of 192,000 tons in 1980–83 and 197,000 in 1959–61.

Determination of Domestic Farm Prices

The model offered to explain the movement in farmgate prices, Pf, is a simple one. It is based on the assumption that the primary concern of every farmer is to ensure the continuation of the real price. While increases are to be preferred, it is even more important that real prices (and by implication, real profits) do not decline (see Krishna and Rayachaudhuri 1980).

Changes in international prices will obviously affect the lobbying goal, and the "fair" price. Border price increases should lead to domestic price increases as the perceived comparative advantage changes, and declines in border prices should lead to corresponding reductions in domestic prices.

The domestic rate of inflation will also affect farmgate prices. Thus, a simple model of price determination would be as follows:

$$(6\text{-}1) \qquad Pf_z = a + b_1 Pi_z + b_2 Px_z$$

where z refers to first differences in logs multiplied by 100 (or percentage change), Pf = farmgate price, Pi = domestic inflation (proxied by the price of nonagricultural goods), and $Px(Pm)$ = border prices for exports (imports).

Equation 6-1 represents the basic model. Two modifications are possible. First, a "catch-up" variable may be introduced. This variable allows producers to recoup past losses. In other words, if the price increase is less than the rate of inflation, farmers can argue for compensation and receive an increase that exceeds the rate of inflation. Alternatively, such a variable (defined as $[Pf_z - Pi_z]_{-1}$, or the gap in price gains lagged one period) allows for lags in the determination of farm prices.

The second modification pertains to the border price. The assumption underlying Equation 6-1 is that positive and negative changes in border prices have an equal impact. This assumption is questionable. In a period of rising prices, decisionmakers may try to mop up excess profits. Therefore, positive changes in Px_z, expressed as Px_{zp}, will lead to correspondingly smaller changes in farm prices, or the coefficient of Px_{zn} will be less than unity. However, when international prices are dropping (denoted by Px_{zn}), revenue considerations will dictate that the pass-through in prices or the coefficient of Px_{zn} must be greater than unity. If international prices drop by 10 percent, for example, the pressure to maintain revenues will imply that the per unit difference between domestic and international prices be held constant. This implies a reduction of more than 10 percent.

The coefficients of the border prices can also be interpreted in terms of tax rates. A coefficient of unity means the tax rate is being maintained, whether the border price changes negatively or positively. A coefficient greater than 1 for Px_{zp} implies a decline in the tax rate, while a coefficient greater than 1 for Px_{zn} implies an increase in the rate.

These modifications suggest the following model:

$$(6\text{-}2) \quad Pf_z = a + b_1 Pi_z + b_2 (Pf_z - Pi_z)_{-1} + b_3 Px_{zp} + b_4 Px_{zn} + e.$$

The b_1 sign is equal to 1 if there is full pass-through of domestic prices and if real prices are maintained. The sign b_2 allows farm prices to rise in step with domestic inflation. The sign is expected to be negative, with a maximum possible magnitude of 1. The terms b_3 and b_4 are equal to 1 (if the tax rate is held constant or a "full" pass-through is assumed) or ≤ 1.

Another factor to consider in determining domestic prices for the export crops is the source of revenue or expenditure. Ordinarily, this is not expected to affect an item of expenditure or revenue. It is generally assumed that governments take a total view of the revenue situation and then decide on expenditures. But this assumption ignores the importance of tea taxes as revenue contributors, and rice subsidies as discretionary expenditure items. Under J. R. Jayewardene, Sri Lanka's finance minister in 1951 (now president), the presumed relationship between consumer subsidies for rice and export taxation became an official policy concern (Fernando 1987).

Can the presumed link between the domestic price of export (tree) crops (and thus tree crop tax revenues) and food subsidy expenditures be demonstrated? It is plausible to suppose that if domestic political considerations dictate expenditures on food subsidies, and if government revenues, excluding tree crop tax revenues, are deficient, tree crops will be taxed more. Conversely, if such revenues are in surplus, tree crops will be taxed less.

This suggests that a variable representing the "burden" of food subsidies is the ratio of such food subsidy expenditures Fd to Rx, where Rx is revenue net of tree crop taxes. This ratio, given by Rb ($Rb = Fd/Rx$), indicates the burden at a point in time. Equation 6-2 estimates changes in farm prices. Correspondingly, the food burden variable is represented by its first difference: $Rbd = Rb - Rb_{-1}$.

If policymakers do try to ease the increased burden of food subsidies by increasing the taxation of tree crops, the coefficient of Rbd should be significantly negative. The greater the absolute magnitude of this coefficient, the greater the attempt to extract short-run revenue from producers of tree crops.

In view of the large devaluation of 1978, a dummy variable representing this event, D78, is also included in the estimation.

Is there any simultaneity between the change in the burden of taxation, *Rbd*, and price change, Pf_z? Such simultaneity is unlikely for the following reasons. First, the burden of taxation is a ratio between food subsidies (which are a function of an exogenous variable, the international price of rice) and revenues from outside of agriculture. Second, the variable used is the change in *Rbd* during the previous period; consequently, any unknown systematic biases are likely to be factored out. And third, a recursive model of decisionmaking is assumed above—that is, the politically important variable, food subsidies, is given a much higher priority than the level of tree crop taxation. Thus, food subsidy levels are exogenous to the farm prices of tree crops.

Results of Price Determination Model

The model used to incorporate the considerations noted above was as follows:

$$(6\text{-}3) \qquad Pf_z = a + b_1 Pi_z + b_2 (Pf_z - Pi_z)_{-1} + b_3 Px_{zp}$$
$$+ b_4 Px_{zn} + b_5 Rbd + b_6 D78 + u.$$

The results from this model (Table 6-7) provide striking confirmation of our bureaucratic model of decisionmaking. The overall explanatory power of the model is high (adjusted R^2 is generally about 0.70 for equations in first differences of logs) and individual t statistics are large. Further, tests on the residuals (the Durbin-Watson statistic is inappropriate because of the presence of a lagged dependent variable) do not suggest serial correlation.

Equation 6-3 is an appropriate vehicle for studying the political economy of agricultural pricing. The nature of lobbying pressure and its success or failure can be discovered by analyzing the variables mentioned above (see Table 6-7).

The two consumer crops (rice and coconut) show a significant coefficient for inflation, whereas the two export crops (tea and rubber) do not. The coefficient for coconut (1.23) is greater than unity, which suggests that the real producer price of coconut may have been allowed to increase over time. Rice producers have a large coefficient for inflation (0.70), but the value is less than unity, which means that the real price of rice declined over time.[6] Both tea and rubber have a small coefficient (0.35 and 0.30), which indicates that the real prices of these crops were allowed to decline.

Some of the lagged effects of inflation are captured through the "compensatory" variable. This variable was highly significant for tea and significant for coconut. Therefore, tea producers were apparently able to partly recapture a decline in real price in subsequent periods.

Table 6-7. Determination of Farm Prices

Variable	Tea	Rubber	Coconut	Rice
Constant	−0.84	−1.36	1.37	−3.86
	(0.38)	(0.35)	(0.29)	(1.10)
Inflation coefficient	0.35	0.30	1.23	0.70
	(1.36)	(0.66)	(2.20)	(2.62)
Compensatory variable	−0.49	−0.17	−0.24	−0.09
	(4.76)	(1.08)	(1.76)	(0.49)
Border prices, positive changes	1.08	0.70	0.60	0.44
	(8.57)	(4.25)	(3.79)	(4.2)
Border prices, negative changes	1.12	0.48	0.93	−0.0
	(3.90)	(1.62)	(3.37)	(−0.02)
Food subsidy burden	−0.69	−0.50	−1.04	n.a.
	(2.99)	(1.21)	(1.93)	n.a.
Dummy (1978 = 1)	−57.1	−14.0	−40.9	−24.2
	(6.34)	(0.91)	(2.42)	(2.04)
R^2	0.86	0.67	0.77	0.64
Durbin-Watson statistic	2.04	1.98	1.94	2.12

n.a. Not available.

Note: Inflation is measured in terms of the price of nonagricultural goods. The dependent variable in all cases is the percentage change (first differences in logs) of the domestic price of the crop. Inflation, catch-up, and border prices are also expressed in terms of first differences in logs. Since a lagged dependent variable appears in the catch-up term, the Durbin-Watson statistics are biased. However, both Durbin-h statistics on regression of residuals on their lagged values showed no serial correlation. Absolute value of *t*-statistics is reported in parentheses.

Source: Author's calculations.

But the magnitude of the lagged gap coefficient for tea (− 0.49) indicates that a secular decline in the domestic price of tea was not averted. Rubber producers appear to have been the least effective group in maintaining profitability of production, while coconut producers were the most effective. Rice producers were able to capture only two-thirds of the increase in inflation.

The main finding of this study is that border prices had an asymmetrical effect on farmgate prices. The magnitude of this asymmetry may be indicative of political pressures. Negative price changes for rice were not passed through (the coefficient is zero, with a large standard error). In other words, if the international price dropped, rice producers successfully argued that it was not in the long-term interests of the economy to follow suit. This most likely reflects the desire of Sri Lankan governments to encourage domestic rice production.

For tea, the coefficient for both positive and negative price changes is approximately equal at 1.1. In other words, in boom periods the tax rate decreased marginally (but revenue increased), and during busts the tax rate increased in order to preserve the level of revenues. This result is partial confirmation of a link between food subsidies and tea taxation.

Revenue pressures also affected coconut, since the tax rate appears to have been maintained despite price declines (the coefficient of Px_{zn} is 0.93). Price increases, on the other hand, were presumably seen as an opportunity to extract additional tax revenues.

Insulation of domestic prices from international price pressure seems to have been a principal goal in rubber pricing. Rubber producers lost when prices increased (increase in tax rate, coefficient = 0.70) and gained when border prices declined (decrease in tax rate, coefficient = 0.48).

The net movements of domestic and international prices appear to have been as follows.

TEA. Domestic inflation was not considered a strong argument for nominal price increases. However, the government did pass along increases in international prices to producers, and made no attempt to mop up excess revenues.

RUBBER. The goal in rubber pricing seems to have been to maintain the domestic price rather than keep tax revenues at a constant level. However, since there was no significant response to domestic inflation, a secular decline in the real price of rubber seems to have been part of policy.

COCONUT. There was definite pressure to increase the real price earned by coconut producers. It appears that governments have had an explicit policy toward a real price increase, independent of the movement in international prices. Tax rates increase when border prices move up, and tax rates do not decline when border prices fall.

RICE. The results obtained with the model strongly support the "known" fact that rice was a favored sector. Almost two-thirds of domestic inflation was passed through to the producers (in addition to large input subsidies). Further, negative price changes in international prices were not translated into domestic price reductions, while almost half of the increases in border prices were passed through. This last result suggests that governments were mindful of the large protection afforded to rice producers, but that political pressures were effective in preventing a rapid decline in the protection rate.

Conclusions about the Price Determination Model

According to the short-term bureaucratic model of price determination, domestic prices are inherited. Short of a structural change, price setting is a matter of balancing revenues and expenditures. Domestic inflation is understood by price-setters, and producers can generally expect to receive price increases in inflationary times. However, pressure groups and "initial conditions" determine whether the price increase is fully compensatory. For example, even though rice has been a favored commodity in Sri Lanka, the high level of protection at the beginning of the study period meant that governments were reluctant to fully compensate rice producers for domestic inflation. The analysis clearly revealed discrimination against tree crop producers. These producers were more affected by international price changes, and in the cases of tea and coconut, declining prices were fully passed through. The net effect of such policies was a long-term decline in tea and rubber prices, which have only recently begun to emerge from their trough.

Gainers and Losers

The two important questions to raise concerning the effects of Sri Lanka's agricultural pricing policy are (a) Whether, and if so by how much, did Sri Lanka lose (or gain) by intervening? and (b) How did agriculture fare with respect to nonagriculture? No discussion of agricultural pricing policies in Sri Lanka would be complete without some mention of the contribution of food subsidies to consumer welfare. According to many analysts, since the removal of these subsidies in 1980, equity has decreased. In particular, the welfare of the poor members of society has decreased absolutely.

Effect on the Economy of Removing Intervention

It is useful to speculate on the changes that would have occurred in Sri Lanka if there had been no government intervention in agricultural prices during the study period. What is expected of such calculations is the correct order of magnitude. Clearly, the existence of a free-trade regime would have meant a structural transformation, and it is not clear what rules would have applied.

OUTPUT. All the tree crops, by definition, have low supply elasticities. The tax rates on these crops were about 15 to 30 percent. If long-term supply elasticity is assumed to be 0.1 to 0.2, the loss in output due to intervention ranged from 1.5 to 6.0 percent. If supply elasticity is assumed to be 0.5 and the protection rate is 80 percent, the removal of intervention would have implied a 40-percent decline in the output of rice. With the parity observed in recent years at conventional exchange rates, movement toward an equilibrium exchange rate would have meant a 5- to 10-percent gain in rice output.

CONSUMPTION. The impact on consumption would have been somewhat greater than the effect on output. Coconut consumption would have been 20 to 40 percent less in most years, although in recent years the losses would have been only 10 to 15 percent. Rice consumption until the late 1960s would have been reduced by large amounts if there had been no intervention. Thereafter, rice consumption would not have changed much.

FOREIGN EXCHANGE. Revenue from tree crop exports would have been considerably higher in the nonintervention scenario, on the order of 50 to 60 percent. This is given by a 30 percent change in price and a 2 percent change in output. Earnings from coconut exports would have gone up owing to a decline in domestic consumption. Since rice imports tended to fluctuate in line with changes in consumer subsidies, rice consumption, and therefore imports, would have been lower until the late 1960s. The changes would have been minor after 1981, once self-sufficiency was achieved.

Overall, Sri Lanka suffered a net loss of foreign exchange because of its policy of price intervention and exchange rate overvaluation. Expressed as a share of actual total export earnings, the gains from a policy of nonintervention would have been about 20 percent in most years. The largest foreign exchange losses occurred during 1978–82, when the government did not pass through all of the real price increase caused by the devaluation of 1978. The gain from a policy of nonintervention in those years would have at times been more than double the actual net earnings from agricultural exports. Although intervention produced gains for producers in 11 years of the study period, the gains were sporadic and not very large.

Transfers to and from Agriculture

Table 6-8 shows the real transfers to agriculture at equilibrium exchange rates. Infrastructure and implicit subsidies (such as the production subsidy to rice farmers) are included in these calculations.

Between 1956 and 1977, transfers to rice producers were consistently smaller than transfers out of tree crops. The share for the period 1953–85 was about 46 percent. After 1978, because of increases in rice productivity combined with devaluation, rice was taxed for the first time ever. For the years 1978–83, the rice tax averaged almost 20

Table 6-8. Transfers to and from Agriculture 1953–85

(millions of rupees)

Transfer	1953–55	1956–60	1961–65	1966–70	1971–77	1978–85	1953–85
Transfers on output prices	−1,603.8	−2,469.4	−4,723.3	−5,139.4	−2,902.0	−15,667.5	−6,428.1
Importables (rice)	1,598.3	2,456.4	2,218.1	2,145.2	2,926.6	−2,032.6	1,306.6
Exportables (tree crops)	−3,202.1	−4,925.9	−6,941.4	−7,284.6	−5,828.6	−13,634.9	−7,734.7
Transfers on purchased inputs (such as fertilizer, irrigation, credit)	n.a.	n.a.	252.6	1,113.8	1,201.9	6,776.4	2,104.7
Production-related transfers (output and input)	−1,603.8	−2,469.4	−4,470.7	−4,025.6	−1,700.0	−8,891.1	−4,323.3
Nonprice transfers	1,707.8	1,978.2	2,356.7	2,654.1	1,877.4	2,139.1	2,131.0
Sum of all transfers	104.0	−491.2	−2,114.0	−1,371.4	177.4	−6,752.0	−2,192.3
Sum of all transfers as share of agricultural GDP	−0.34	−2.24	−9.19	−9.90	−13.63	−20.89	−11.22
Sum of all transfers as share of GDP	−0.10	−0.79	−2.90	−3.06	−3.98	−5.72	−3.26

n.a. Not available.

Note: All transfers are deflated according to the adjusted CPI, 1985 = 100.

Source: Bhalla (forthcoming).

percent of the tree crop tax. The years 1984–86 witnessed net transfers to rice cultivation.

In Table 6-8, transfers are expressed both as a share of agricultural GDP and of total GDP. The figures suggest that agriculture was a net contributor to the economy, with a 1953–85 annual average of around 3.3 percent of GDP and 11 percent of agricultural GDP. This "tax" was paid primarily by tea producers.

A turning point for Sri Lankan agriculture occurred in 1982. In every year before 1982 (except 1954 and 1955), agriculture transferred resources to the rest of the economy. Since 1982, primarily because of large irrigation expenditures and a fall in international rice prices, agriculture has been a net beneficiary (Bhalla forthcoming).

Socioeconomic Groups and Food Expenditures

When the available data are broken down into urban, rural, and estate components, it is possible to obtain some information on income distribution in the occupational categories of government and industrial workers, paddy farmers, and plantation workers, respectively. The results of this exercise indicate that paddy farmers gained and plantation workers lost under the agricultural pricing policies of the past two decades.

Consumer survey data are available for the years 1963, 1969–70, 1973, 1978–79, 1980–81, and 1981–82. Table 6-9 reports on adjusted levels of food expenditure by the different socioeconomic groups.[7] Residents in the estate sector in 1963 enjoyed a 73 percent higher level of food expenditure than other rural residents and a 6 percent higher level than urban residents. As measured by food consumption, estate residents were the richest, but a mere seven years later, consumption in the estate sector was 2 percent less than rural consumption and 25 percent below urban consumption.

In the last year for which data are available (1981–82), the welfare levels of estate workers had improved again, and food expenditures were 13 percent above those of rural residents.[8] However, given that the consumer price of rice had risen by 550 percent and wheat by 860 percent during this period, it is highly likely that the relative welfare level of estate workers did not improve after 1969–70. This decline in the relative welfare of estate residents was exacerbated by a reduction in food subsidies in 1978–79. The new food stamp policy targeted recipients on the basis of self-declared incomes. Given that estate workers' wages were known, and were generally above the threshold level, no "leakage" to them was possible.

Urban residents have also witnessed a large decline in relative food expenditures (and perhaps income) since 1963. In 1981–82 urban res-

Table 6-9. Per Capita Per Month Food Consumption, Selected Years, 1963 to 1981–82

Area	1963		1969–70		1973		1978–79		1980–81		1981–82	
	Rupees	Index	Rupees	Index	Rupees	Index	Rupees	Index	Rupees	Index	Rupees	Index
Urban	30.0	167.0	40.9	122.0	41.0	121.0	102.7	117.6	180.0	118.7	198.7	124.6
Rural	17.94	100.0	33.5	100.0	33.8	100.0	87.3	100.0	151.6	100.0	159.5	100.0
Estate	31.08	173.0	32.8	97.9	37.8	111.8	106.5	122.0	147.1	97.0	179.7	112.7
Entire island	24.46	136.0	34.7	103.6	35.5	105.0	92.5	105.9	156.9	103.5	168.4	105.6
Entire island (real)	31.0	—	34.7	—	27.9	—	27.7	—	32.2	—	28.8	—

— Not applicable.

Note: All expenditures are in current prices except those in the last row. Real expenditures are based on a food price index (1970 = 100) constructed by Bhalla and Glewwe (1985, 1986) using data supplied by the Department of Census and Statistics.

Source: Various consumer survey reports.

idents enjoyed only a 25 percent advantage over rural workers, compared with 67 percent in 1963.

Food Subsidies, Inflation, and Welfare

After 30 years of strong popular support for food subsidies, the government decided in 1980 to drastically reduce these subsidies. Although the move was an unwelcome one, it aroused few protests. Almost everyone recognized that the costs of food subsidies had become too high.

If food subsidies had continued at a high level, investment in physical capital may have declined and thus the growth rate may have slowed. In addition, the inflation rate may have gone up because of the need for deficit financing. Table 6-10 illustrates the linkage between food subsidies (EFSN), tree crop taxes (TXTC), budget deficits, and inflation, and presents a "new" indicator of policy—the ratio of food subsidies to revenue from tree crop taxes multiplied by 100 (EFSNTC).[9] Changes in this ratio indicate the size of the "surplus" available for welfare expenditures. That is, a value of 100 indicates that tree crop revenues were just sufficient to cover food subsidy expenditures, with nothing left over. Correspondingly, a low percentage indicates an easing of expenditures.

A large increase in EFSN in 1952, from Rs 132 million to Rs 247 million, prompted the government to reduce subsidies in July 1953. This met with political protests, and the prime minister was forced to resign. In November 1954 the new government began to increase the subsidies. It is likely that the government was pressured to reduce subsidies because the ratio of subsidies to tree crop tax revenues reached 109 percent.

The EFSNTC again peaked in 1961 and 1962, when it jumped past 75 percent. A finance minister lost his job after the customary food riots, and the government was "forced" to raise food subsidies. The net effect was that 15.5 percent of Sri Lanka's annual revenues during the period 1961–65 were devoted to food subsidies.

The next significant increase in EFSNTC occurred in 1971. In addition to the subsidy of 2 pounds of free rice per capita each week, the government allowed an additional 2 pounds to be provided at a subsidized price of 37.5 cents per pound (the market price being 61 cents a pound). Without a concomitant increase in revenues from tree taxes, the EFSNTC increased from 80 percent in 1970 to 149 percent in 1971. In 1973, with EFSNTC at its all-time peak (171.7), the government attempted to reduce the subsidy. The ration price for 2 pounds was increased from 50 cents to 80 cents in February 1973 (but reduced to 70 cents in March 1973). In October of that year the free ration was cut from 2 pounds to 1 pound. The conditions signified by the high

Table 6-10. Food Subsidies, Tree Crop Taxes, and the Budget, 1950–85
(millions of rupees)

Item	1950–55	1956–60	1961–65	1966–70	1971–77	1978–1985	1951–85
Per capita annual food subsidy	14	13	23	20	34	31	24
National food subsidy (EFSN)	115	121	245	245	449	460	299
Tree crop taxes (TXTC)ᵃ	267	320	316	303	287	908	440
Burden of food subsidy (EFSNTC) (percent)	43.1	38.7	77.1	81.0	158.1	51.7	75.0
Food subsidy as a percentage of revenue	11.6	9.6	15.5	12.6	18.9	12.1	13.6
Food subsidy as a percentage of budget deficit	−21.9	−43.3	−59.3	−41.2	−58.6	−18.3	−40.0
Government revenues	1,014	1,250	1,579	1,944	2,380	4,038	2,226
Government expenditures	1,094	1,509	1,992	2,547	3,207	6,812	3,219
Deficit as a percentage of GDP	−1.5	−4.4	−5.9	−6.6	−7.0	−15.6	−7.6

Note: All variables are in real terms; GDP deflator, 1956 = 100. The last row excludes "'outlier" figures for 1950, 1951, and 1956.

a. Tree crop taxes exclude multiple exchange rate taxes (FEEC) which were levied from 1968–77.

Source: Central Bank of Ceylon, *Review of the Economy*.

levels of the EFSNTC made these reforms inevitable, and in 1978 the figure was brought down to 43.9 percent from 151.6 percent the previous year.

The high levels of the index prior to 1978 imply that the benefits of the 1970s boom in commodity prices were not realized by Sri Lanka. In other words, the larger profits from gains in international commodity prices were apparently used to pay for increased food subsidies. Tea production actually declined in 1976 to its lowest level since 1960, and rubber production in 1974 dropped to its lowest point since 1967. Both the declines in export crop production and the increases in the price of imported rice made it difficult to create a surplus for welfare expenditures.

The Welfare of the Poor

Recent research (Sahn 1986; Anand and Kanbur 1987) has suggested that the cut in food subsidy expenditures after 1978 caused an increase in malnutrition and a reduction in social equity in Sri Lanka. Sahn argues that "while it is not possible to put forth a counter-factual argument as to what would have been the consumption and nutritional consequences if a change in policy regimes had not taken place in 1977, the data available on employment and wages, like the information on nutritional status, calorie intake, and real expenditure levels show that the four lowest expenditure deciles have seen a decline in their food energy intake" (p. 825). Anand and Kanbur attribute this decline mainly to the reduction in food subsidies: "Between 1979 and 1982 real per capita government expenditure on food subsidies fell from Rs 62.29 to Rs 20.72. While it would be difficult, given the many other forces in play,and the data available, to establish a clear and unambiguous link between this cut and food consumption in the population, the results are at the very least suggestive" (p. 20).

Although food subsidy expenditures have played an important role in the Sri Lankan economy, it does not follow that such expenditures governed consumer welfare. For that, one has to look at real incomes and consumer prices. Government subsidies can influence the latter, but movements in this variable can be extremely misleading, as becomes clear from the operation of food subsidies in Sri Lanka. As discussed earlier, rice was imported at a low price and procured from domestic farmers at a high price, with the consumer price always below the procurement price but above or below the import price, depending on budgetary pressures. Movements in these nonconsumer prices could have had an impact on the subsidies without affecting the real price to the consumer, and thus the consumer's welfare.

Although data are not available on the effective consumer price of rice, ration shop and market prices can be used to construct a series yielding a cost per pound based on a consumption norm of 4 pounds per capita per week. This series approximates the consumer price until 1980, when the food stamp program replaced universal subsidies. Consequently, from that date, two prices are observed: one for the recipients of food stamps, another for all other consumers.

Once an effective consumer price is calculated, it is a straightforward procedure to determine movements in real prices (deflated by the GDP deflator) as well as the effective subsidy or tax on consumption. The tax rate is defined as ($[Pc - Pm]$ $100/Pm$), where Pc is the effective consumer price and Pm the import price.

Contrary to the expectations of Sahn and Anand and Kanbur, this exercise reveals a positive correlation between real food subsidies and real consumer prices (0.35) for the period 1951–86. Note, too, that "true" food subsidies (defined as the percentage difference between domestic and international prices) ended not in 1978 but in 1972. Thus, during 1971–77 consumers were not subsidized but were taxed at an average rate of 13 percent a year.

The pattern of real rice prices in more recent years is also revealing. Prices increased during 1980–82, but for the years 1984–86 they stayed steady at almost the same level as that in 1977. In other words, consumers seem to be considerably better off now; real incomes have increased, while rice prices have stayed approximately the same. And food subsidy expenditures have been drastically reduced. Such expenditures declined from Rs 51 per capita in 1978 to only Rs 15 per capita in 1986.

The rice price suggests that the poor are facing the same real price as they did almost 20 years ago. Figures on employment and incomes also suggest that real incomes have gone up, at least since 1973. Thus it is somewhat difficult to accept Sahn's conclusion that welfare for the bottom 30 percent has deteriorated with liberalization.

In addition, there is some direct evidence to support the view that the welfare of the poor has improved since liberalization. As mentioned earlier, estate residents lost in relative terms during the preliberalization period, and the food subsidy program did not cover them in the postliberalization period. However, the decision to increase the real output prices of export crops has allowed the wages of estate workers to increase since 1978.

According to preliminary 1985–86 data, the growth in wages has translated into increased food consumption for estate residents. Rice consumption has gone up by 14 percent and wheat consumption by 54 percent since 1980–81. The nominal food expenditures in 1986 were 34 percent higher than those of rural residents.

Although the poor have become better off, a word of caution is in order. Appealing as the indicator of food consumption may be for welfare purposes during times of food scarcity, it is a considerably less meaningful indicator at other times. Estate residents are still poor, as any overall (food and nonfood) indicator would show.

Conclusion: A New Era

Sri Lanka's recent policies indicate that the government has come to realize that the agricultural sector can play an important role in development. Rice production in 1985 was more than double the average level in 1975–76, and the real prices of tree crops have shown a persistent increase. Protection to industry has been radically reduced, and the exchange rate has been made favorable to exporters.

One of the government's new policies has been to eliminate universal food subsidies and replace them with a targeted food stamp program reaching half the population. Government expenditures on food subsidies often included a large subsidy to domestic rice producers. Indeed, it appears that consumer food subsidies in Sri Lanka ended as early as 1972. Data for 1985–86 indicate that food consumption among the most economically vulnerable groups (estate workers) has increased considerably since the previous peak year of 1969–70. For the population receiving the subsidies, the effective real price of rice is now lower than in any year since 1972 and equal to the levels of 1968–69. For the population at large, the effective real prices of rice are only 10 percent above those recorded in the prereform year of 1977.

Growth rates indicate that the stagnation of the economy has been arrested, although long-term trends are difficult to identify because of the political problems in the country. To what extent tree crops will contribute to the surplus in the future is still unknown.

Notes

1. As discussed earlier, these tariff rates are an estimated average for total imports. Since food imports accounted for about 50 percent of total imports and were not taxed, the average tariff rates on industrial inputs and consumer durables were about twice those noted above.

2. According to a 1969–70 socioeconomic survey, the average per capita consumption per month was 17.45 pounds; the lowest income group (below Rs 200 per month) had a per capita rice consumption of 16.1 pounds per month. This was also the lowest consumption of any income group; the highest consumption was in the range of Rs 400–600 and was equal to 18.9 pounds. In 1985–86 the per capita consumption in one of the poorest areas–the estates–was almost 23 pounds per month.

3. Note that this average level was the estimate after the introduction of a dummy variable (in the import demand regression equation) to capture the

abnormally high level for the oil shock year of 1974. See Bhalla (forthcoming) for details on the estimation technique.

4. See the appendix to this volume for the calculation of E^*. The supply and demand elasticities for foreign exchange were assumed to be 0.75 and -2.0, respectively (Bhalla forthcoming).

5. An implicit assumption of the PPP method is that the structure of the economy and external conditions remain constant over time. In the estimate obtained and reported in Table 6-4, the structure of the economy is assumed to be constant for the period 1956–77. In view of the reforms of 1978, a different (but constant) structure is assumed for 1978 onward.

6. This does not indicate that rice producers have lost in terms of relative profitability. This model of price determination ignores the role of direct subsidies in production, and, as noted earlier, rice producers have obtained large irrigation subsidies. Since other crop producers have received very little in the form of direct subsidies, the model can be considered an accurate representation of the underlying reality for nonrice producers.

7. The assumption here is that expenditures on food are an indicator of welfare. This is heuristically supported by the fact that food consumption can be (relatively) accurately measured and comprises a large proportion of the consumer budget. See Anand and Hariss (1986) for the development of a food expenditure index of poverty.

8. These calculations assume that the basket of goods is the same for all residents. This is patently not the case, especially for rural and estate residents. The former consume more rice, the latter more wheat. Relative prices of these two items will thus partly dictate real welfare levels.

9. It is a moot question whether tree crop taxes should include the FEEC taxes. These taxes were due to the multiple exchange rate policy (low exchange rate for exports) introduced as part of the 1968 reforms. Thus FEEC taxes were essentially an additional tax on tree crops. For behavioral considerations, it might be the case that FEEC taxes were considered general revenues and not part of the explicit revenue gained from pricing. This is the view adopted here. (Also for intertemporal consistency, the ratio net of FEEC taxes is the relevant variable.) In any case, the results of the analysis are unaffected by including or excluding FEEC taxes.

Bibliography

The word "processed" describes works that are reproduced from typescript by mimeograph, xerography, or similar means; such works may not be cataloged or commonly available through libraries, or they may be subject to restricted circulation.

Alailima, P. 1985. "Evolution of Government Policies and Expenditure on Social Welfare in Sri Lanka during the 20th Century." World Bank Development Research Department, Washington, D.C. Processed.

Anand, Sudhir, and Christopher Hariss. 1985. "Living Standards in Sri Lanka, 1973–1981/82: A Partial Analysis of Consumer Finance Survey Data." Central Bank of Sri Lanka Research Project on Living Standards. World Bank, Washington, D.C. Processed.

————. 1986. "Food and Standard of Living in Sri Lanka." Oxford University. Processed.

Anand, Sudhir, and Ravi Kanbur. 1987. "Price Policy and Basic Needs Provision: Intervention and Achievement in Sri Lanka." Discussion Paper 74. University of Warwick, Development Economics Research Centre.

Askari H., and J. T. Cummings. 1976. *Agricultural Supply Response: A Survey of the Econometric Evidence.* New York: Praeger.

Bhalla, Surjit S. Forthcoming. *Trade, Exchange Rate, and Agricultural Pricing Policies in Sri Lanka.* A World Bank Comparative Study. Washington, D.C.

————. 1990. "Economic Policies, Foreign Aid and Economic Development." In Uma Lele and Ijaz Nabi, eds., *Aid, Capital Flows and Development.* San Francisco, Calif.: Institute for Contemporary Studies Press.

————. 1988a. "Does Land Quality Matter: Theory and Measurement." *Journal of Development Economics* (Netherlands), vol. 29 (July), pp. 45–62.

————. 1988b. "Is Sri Lanka an Exception: A Comparative Study of Living Standards." In T. N. Srinivasan and P. Bardhan, eds., *Rural Poverty in South Asia.* New York: Columbia University Press.

————. 1988c. "Sri Lankan Achievements: Fact and Fancy." In T. N. Srinivasan and P. Bardhan, eds., *Rural Poverty in South Asia.* New York: Columbia University Press.

Bhalla, Surjit S., and Paul Glewwe. 1985. "Living Standards in Sri Lanka—Mirage and Reality." Central Bank of Sri Lanka Research Project on Living Standards. World Bank, Washington, D.C. Processed.

————. 1986. "Growth and Equity in Developing Countries: A Reinterpretation of the Sri Lankan Experience." *World Bank Economic Review,* vol. 1.

Central Bank of Ceylon. *Price and Wage Statistics.* Various years. Colombo, Sri Lanka.

————. *Report on the Consumer Finance Survey.* Various years. Colombo, Sri Lanka.

————. *Review of the Economy.* Various issues. Colombo, Sri Lanka.

Chenery, Hollis B., and A. S. Goldberger. 1959. "The Use of Models for Development Policy." Paper prepared for the International Association for Research on Income and Wealth, Rio de Janeiro.

Cuthbertson, A. G., and Zubair Khan. 1981. "Effective Protection to Manufacturing Industry in Sri Lanka." World Bank, Washington, D.C. Processed.

Dahanayake, P. A. S. 1977. *Economic Policies and Their Implications for Foreign Exchange Resource Availability in Sri Lanka, 1956–1972.* Colombo, Sri Lanka: Central Bank of Ceylon.

De Menil, George, and Surjit S. Bhalla. 1975. "Direct Measurement of Popular Price Expectations." *American Economic Review,* vol. 65, March.

De Silva, K. M. 1981. *A History of Sri Lanka.* New Delhi: Oxford University Press.

Edirisinghe, Neville. 1985. "The Food Stamp Program in Sri Lanka: Costs, Benefits, and Policy Options." Washington, D.C.: International Food Policy Research Institute. Processed.

Fernando, Nimal A. 1980. "Continuity and Change in Plantation Agriculture: A Study of Sri Lanka's Land Reform Program on Tea Plantations." Ph.D. dissertation, University of Wisconsin.

————. 1987. "The Political Economy of Agricultural Pricing Policies in Sri Lanka since Independence." Paper prepared for World Bank Project on Agricultural Pricing Policies in Sri Lanka, April.

Forest, D. M. 1967. *A Hundred Years of Ceylon Tea, 1867–1987.* London: Chatto and Windus.

Gavan, James D., and Indrani Chandrasekara. 1979. "The Impact of Public Foodgrain Consumption and Welfare in Sri Lanka." International Food Policy Research Institute Report 13, December. Washington, D.C.

Glewwe, Paul. 1986a. "The Distribution of Income in Sri Lanka in 1969–70 and 1980–81: A Decomposition Analysis." *Journal of Development Economics* (Netherlands), vol. 24.

————. 1986b. "Economic Liberalization and Income Inequality: Further Evidence on the Sri Lankan Experience." *Journal of Development Economics* (Netherlands), vol. 28 (March), pp. 233–46.

————. 1986c. "Trends in Self-Employed Incomes in Sri Lanka, 1969–70 to 1981–82." Geneva: International Labour Office. Processed.

Hartley, Michael J., Marc Nerlove, and R. Kyle Peters, Jr. 1984. *Supply Response for Rubber in Sri Lanka: A Preliminary Analysis.* World Bank Staff Working Paper 657. Washington, D.C.

Jayantha, Dilesh. 1984. "Sri Lanka: The Political Framework (1947–84)." Paper prepared for Central Bank of Sri Lanka Research Project on Living Standards. World Bank, Washington, D.C. Processed.

Krishna, Raj, and G. S. Rayachaudhuri. 1980. *Some Aspects of Wheat and Rice Price Policy in India.* World Bank Staff Working Paper 381. Washington, D.C.

Krueger, Anne, Maurice Schiff, and Alberto Valdés. 1985. "A Comparative Study of the Political Economy of Agricultural Pricing Policies: A Framework for the Country Studies." World Bank, Country Economics Department, Washington, D.C. Processed.

————. 1988. "Measuring the Impact of Sectoral and Economywide Policies on Agricultural Incentives in LDCs. *World Bank Economic Review,* vol. 2 (September), pp. 255–71.

Kuruppu, C. R. 1984a. "Effect of Change in Fertilizer/Crop Price Relationship on Fertilizer Consumption and Crop Production in Sri Lanka." National Fertilizer Secretariat, Colombo, Sri Lanka. Processed.

————. 1984b. *Fertilizer Marketing in Sri Lanka.* Colombo, Sri Lanka: National Fertilizer Secretariat.

Peebles, P. 1984. *Sri Lanka: A Handbook of Historical Statistics.* Boston: G. K. Hall.

Ponnambalam, Satchi. 1980. *Development Capitalism in Crisis—The Sri Lankan Economy, 1948–1980.* London: Zed Press.

Richards, P., and A. Stoutjesdijk. 1970. *Agriculture in Ceylon until 1975.* Paris: Organisation for Economic Co-operation and Development.

Sahn, David E. 1986. "Malnutrition and Food Consumption in Sri Lanka: An Analysis of Changes from 1969 to 1982." International Food Policy Research Institute, Washington, D.C. Processed.

————. 1988. "The Effect of Price and Income Changes on Food-Energy Intake in Sri Lanka." *Economic Development and Cultural Change* (U.S.), vol. 36 (January), pp. 315–40.

Schiff, Maurice, and Alberto Valdés. 1986. "Toward an Empirical Specification of Policy Instrument Behavioral Equations." World Bank, Country Economics Department, Washington, D.C. Processed.

Sri Lanka, Department of Census and Statistics. 1972. *Special Report on Food and Nutritional Levels in Sri Lanka.* Colombo.

————. 1987. *Labour Force and Socio-Economic Survey 1985–1986: Preliminary Report.* Colombo.

Sri Lanka, Ministry of Agricultural Development and Research. 1981. *Agricultural Statistics of Sri Lanka.* Colombo.

Sri Lanka, Ministry of Plan Implementation. 1986. *Food and Nutrition Statistics.* Vols. 1 and 2. Colombo.

Summers, Robert, and Alan Heston. 1984. "Improved International Comparisons of Real Product and Its Composition: 1950–1980." *Review of Income and Wealth* (U.S.), ser. 30, no. 2 (June), pp.207–62.

Tambiah, S. J. 1986. *Ethnic Fratricide and the Dismantling of Democracy.* Chicago, Ill.: University of Chicago Press.

Thorbecke, Erik, and Jan Svejnar. 1987. *Economic Policies and Agricultural Performance in Sri Lanka 1960–1984.* Paris: Organisation for Economic Co-operation and Development.

————. 1952. *The Economic Development of Ceylon.* Baltimore, Md.: Johns Hopkins University Press.

7 Thailand

Ammar Siamwalla
Suthad Setboonsarng

This chapter is about government intervention in the prices of four of Thailand's leading agricultural commodities: rice, sugar, maize, and rubber. The analysis begins with an overview of the economy and agricultural sector, which is followed by a discussion of the policy history of the four commodities, the measures of direct and indirect intervention, and the consequences of intervention.

Overview of the Economy

The Thai economy took an important turn in 1958, when, following a coup, Field Marshal Sarit Thanarat committed Thailand to a path of economic growth based essentially on private ownership of the means of production, an open trading regime, and relatively stable fiscal and monetary policies. Many governments have succeeded Sarit's, but all have maintained the basic economic policies he laid out, although the commitment to stable fiscal and monetary policies has been somewhat frayed at times.

The Thai Macroeconomy, 1960–85

Possibly because of the orthodox economic policies established by Sarit, and certainly because of abundant land resources and heavy public investment in infrastructure, the Thai economy grew at the fairly high rate of 7.2 percent per year between 1960 and 1973 (see Table 7-1). Between 1973 and 1985, however, the Thai rate of growth declined to 6.2 percent, paralleling the instability and declining growth in the world economy. The per capita income growth rate was 4.3 percent for the period 1960–73 and 3.7 percent for the period 1973–85.

Thailand achieved its high growth rates with a relatively low rate of inflation, at least for the period before 1973. This low inflation rate was achieved largely through the exchange rate policies pursued by

Table 7-1. Average Annual Rates of Change in Key Economic Variables, 1960–85
(percent)

Variable	1960–73	1973–79	1979–85
Gross domestic product (GDP)	7.2	7.1	5.3
Population	2.9	2.2	2.1
GDP per capita	4.3	4.9	3.2
Consumer price index (Bangkok)	2.8	11.4	6.9
GDP deflator	3.1	11.3	5.1
Baht/dollar exchange rate	−0.1	−0.5	4.2
Area under cultivation	3.1	2.4	−0.4
Labor force in agriculture	1.8	2.9	2.6
Agricultural production	4.9	4.5	3.0

Note: Rates of change are obtained from trend regression.

Source: Consumer price index—Department of Business Economics, Ministry of Commerce; baht/dollar exchange rate—Bank of Thailand; area under cultivation—Ministry of Agriculture and Agricultural Cooperatives; labor force in agriculture—National Statistical Office; other data—National Accounts Division.

the government and the Bank of Thailand, which kept domestic inflation close to the then-low inflation rate of the dollar. In fact, the baht/dollar exchange rate varied within limits of less than 2 percent from 1955 to 1981. The government maintained this stable exchange rate without recourse to tight import or exchange control regulations. Although the government used protective tariffs, import restrictions, and bans on some items, it never deployed these instruments extensively. The nominal exchange rate remained stable only because of the conservative fiscal and monetary policies of the government and the Bank of Thailand, at least until 1973. In fact, between 1960 and 1972 the rate of increase of the Bangkok consumer price index never exceeded 4 percent per year, and it exceeded 3 percent in only three years.

After 1973, world economic instability and domestic political instability combined to disturb the balance that had become typical of Thailand's economic policymaking. Fiscal deficits began to soar, sustained by the newly found access to foreign commercial bank lending. Foreign indebtedness thus also began to increase steeply (after 1977). The increased volatility of exchange rates abroad made the commitment to a fixed baht/dollar parity increasingly untenable, particularly after 1979, when the dollar began to appreciate against other major currencies. These developments, together with a decision not to increase domestic oil prices following the second oil shock in 1979, led to a run on the baht and forced the government to devaluate by 15 percent in July 1981.

Since 1982 the Thai government, encouraged by the International Monetary Fund (IMF), has quietly returned to the conservative fiscal policy of the pre-1973 period. The government has increased the output prices of some public enterprises to more realistic levels, has postponed some major investment projects, and has limited new foreign borrowing by the public sector, at first to $1.5 billion and later to $1 billion annually. In this way, the government reduced the public sector deficit from 7.7 percent of GDP in 1982 to 5.9 percent in 1985 (the percentage declined further after 1985). So far, however, the government has shown little sign of tightening Thai monetary policy.

The moderately high growth performance of the Thai economy since 1960 has "trickled down" some benefits to the poor. The proportion of the population living below the poverty line has steadily and substantially declined from 57 percent in 1962–63 to 24 percent in 1981. Income inequality has increased in every region, however, and in both urban and rural areas, although the increase has been more pronounced in the rural areas.

The Agricultural Economy, 1960–85

Thailand entered the postwar period with abundant resources of unused land. The nation thus was in a better position than other countries to cope with the high rate of population growth being experienced throughout the developing world (Thailand's annual population growth rate was 3.1 percent in the 1950s but had dropped sharply to 1.8 percent by 1985). Thailand is probably unique among Asian countries in that the land under cultivation per agricultural worker actually was increasing until as late as 1977. Part of the expansion of agriculture may be attributed to the replacement of traditional animal-based draft power by the tractor, which made it possible to cultivate much larger amounts of land per farm, and to heavy public investment in roads, which rendered marketable the produce of large tracts of land.

The expansion of agricultural area in Thailand increased the output of all crops. Production increases occurred in waves emphasizing particular upland crops, for which the new land was most suitable. Maize output grew most rapidly from the late 1950s to the mid-1960s, kenaf in the first half of the 1960s, sugarcane in the late 1960s and early 1970s, and cassava in the late 1960s and throughout the 1970s. Even rice production increased, although rice is not primarily an upland crop. Overall, real value added in agriculture grew at an annual rate of 5.4 percent between 1973 and 1984.

The rapid growth of agriculture during the 1960s and 1970s allowed Thailand to increase its exports considerably. Thai agriculture, already open to the influences of the world market because of its rice surpluses, became even more exposed as production and exports of new crops expanded. Even in 1984, when domestic consumption of agricultural goods had begun to catch up with expanding production, Thailand was still exporting 72.5 percent of its maize, 64.5 percent of its sugar, and nearly all of its cassava and natural rubber. The amount of rice exported amounted to 35.8 percent in 1984. This was a considerable amount, considering that rice is really the only staple food for Thais.

For the government, the export orientation of the agricultural sector has allowed administratively easy and effective intervention when the aim has been to bring prices down. Such a strategy earns revenues, and Thai governments have introduced a variety of taxes and regulations to facilitate it. The only exception to this price strategy has been sugar; the government has sought to boost the domestic producer and consumer prices above the world price. Normally this would entail a fiscal outlay, but because Thai governments have sought to avoid paying direct subsidies, they have devised a different system of intervention.

Agricultural Policies for Four Leading Commodities

Government intervention in Thai agriculture may be better understood through a more detailed historical examination of policies for four key commodities: rice, sugar, maize, and rubber.

Rice

Intervention in rice began just after World War II, when, in response to an Allied demand that Thailand pay its war indemnity in rice, the government imposed a rice export monopoly. Over time, the monopoly form of taxation and a multiple exchange rate system (wherein rice export proceeds have to be sold to the Bank of Thailand at an exchange rate well below that of imports and even other exports) evolved into a specific export tax, the "premium." Other forms of export taxation were added later, so that at its most elaborate, the government system of export barriers included the export premium, collected by the Ministry of Commerce; an ad valorem export duty of 5 percent, collected by the Ministry of Finance (cut to 2.5 percent in 1984); a "rice reserve requirement" for exporters to supply the Ministry of Commerce with rice at below-market prices as a measure to subsidize designated domestic consumers; and quantitative restrictions on exports (Siamwalla 1975).

Although the diverse instruments of intervention in rice prices ultimately had the same effect on the rice market, they were maintained individually because the bureaucracy saw them as having different degrees of flexibility. In addition, the resources generated by the different types of intervention ended up at different agencies and were used for different purposes.

Figure 7-1 shows the movements of the four explicit and implicit taxes (as percentages of the border price) between 1959 and 1986. In the early years of this period, the premium was the intervention of choice because its rates, under the exclusive control of the Department of Foreign Trade of the Ministry of Commerce, could be varied easily, whereas varying the export duty required the approval of Parliament. The Farmers' Aid Fund Act of 1974 shifted some decisionmaking power away from the Commerce Ministry by specifying that changes in the premium now had to be submitted to the cabinet for approval. The act also specified that revenue from the premium was to accrue to a special Farmers' Aid Fund under the control of the Ministry of Agriculture and Agricultural Cooperatives (see Siamwalla 1987). In response, the Commerce Ministry began to prefer the rice reserve requirement over the premium as an instrument of intervention.

Throughout the period, the government's ultimate weapon over exporters was direct quantitative control. The primary objective of such control appears to have been the Commerce Ministry's wish to limit competition among exporters as a strategy for cartelizing the trade and thus for extracting additional monopoly profits from foreign buyers—profits that would accrue mostly to exporters.

More important than the assignment of decisionmaking powers were the intended uses of resources made available by the various taxation measures. First, the Ministry of Commerce's control of the premium rates allowed it to cover any losses it might incur in its own operations in government-to-government (G-to-G) trade. Second, the rice the ministry obtained at below-market prices allowed it to launch a cheap rice program. Third, the establishment of the Farmers' Aid Fund allowed the government to launch price support measures (at the same time that the government was taxing exports) by going to the rural areas and buying paddy at slightly above market prices.

Export taxes had a clear and at times substantial impact on domestic rice prices. They affected producer and consumer prices equally, if appropriate adjustments are made for marketing costs. In contrast, the cheap rice program and price support operations made possible by the export taxes had only a marginal impact on rice prices for producers and consumers. Yet these programs were of enormous importance from a political standpoint. Not only did they represent highly public attempts by the government to help the poor but they generated substantial patronage funds for those in charge of the programs. Indeed, the primary beneficiaries of the cheap rice program were the retail outlets, which were essentially creatures of the bu-

Figure 7-1. Tax Equivalent of Four Government Measures on Rice Exports, 1959–86

Percentage of export price

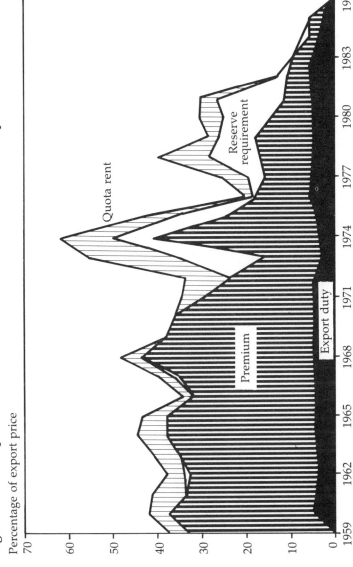

Source: Export duty—Thailand, Ministry of Commerce for tax rates; *Royal Thai Gazette* for assessed price. Premium and reserve requirement—Thailand, Ministry of Commerce, Department of Foreign Trade.

reaucrats of the Ministry of Commerce. The beneficiaries of the producer price support program were the rice mills.

Figure 7-1 also shows that the magnitude of the combined taxes or tax equivalents varied considerably. The factors explaining those changes have also shifted. At the beginning of the period (until 1965), revenues from the premium contributed significantly to the budget (about 10 percent). Because of its importance in the budget, the premium rate could not be varied to stabilize domestic prices. But as the importance of the premium as a source of revenue declined after 1965, its use as a domestic price stabilizer increased.

The strength of price stabilization as a motive in government rice export policies can be seen clearly in Figure 7-2, which shows the real domestic price and the real border price over time.[1] Figure 7-2 also brings out another point: domestic price stability was achieved by a policy that chopped off the price peaks. At no time was the domestic price above the border price. This asymmetry reflected a clear proconsumer bias in the government's rice policies. Not only did the

Figure 7-2. Border and Domestic Paddy Prices, 1960–84

Baht per ton (thousands)

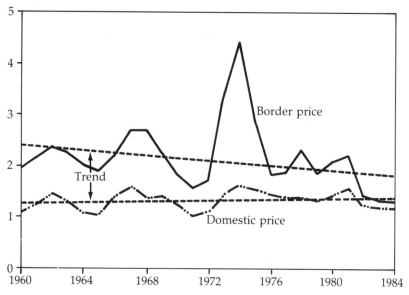

a. Deflated by the rural CPI (1972 = 100).
Source: Siamwalla and Setboonsarng (1989).

export taxes favor consumers, but the government supplemented these policies with a cheap rice sales program with revenues drawn from one of the export taxes. This program was of limited effectiveness and was even counterproductive at times of crisis, as in 1973 and 1974. But different governments found it politically prudent to retain the program.

Beginning in 1975, government policies—or at least government rhetoric—shifted away from the proconsumer slant of the previous years. The government first vitiated the cheap rice program by reducing the quality of the rice it provided and finally did away with the program in 1982.

Another sign of the shift away from consumers was that the government began to establish higher "support prices" to "help" farmers. As suggested, the principal motivation for these programs was to divert resources originating from rice export taxes to the millers, who wielded a large influence over individual members of Parliament as financiers of political campaigns and as controllers of important blocs of votes. As the government's agents in rice purchase operations, the millers reaped a good deal of the benefits of the support programs (Pinthong 1984). Paradoxically, maintaining the export taxes deprived the government of the single most effective way to increase domestic rice prices, because the "supports" were funded from the export taxes, particularly the rice premium. In fact, the Ministry of Agriculture explicitly advocated continuing the rice premium because it was using the funds from the premium to finance its support operations.

In 1983, after a particularly costly "support" program, the government curtailed the diversion substantially and made a serious attempt to liberalize the rice trade. Various export taxes were gradually dismantled, and on January 14, 1986, for the first time since the end of World War II, Thailand's rice exports were free of all restrictions.

Sugar

The Thai government's approach to sugar has been quite different from its approach to rice. Whereas Thailand has exported rice for over a century, it imported sugar as recently as 1960. Under these conditions, the Thai sugar industry became one of the first for which there was a conscious attempt at import substitution, and thus there is a tradition of protecting the industry rather than extracting from it.

The tradition of sugar protection was reinforced even when technological developments transformed Thailand into a large sugar exporter. It was during the 1960s that the country's older, two-tiered method of sugar production gave way to a system of continuous production under one roof.[2] The shift in technology also drastically changed the relationship between the cane growers and the sugar millers (Kirakul 1975). Under the older production system, the growers and millers interacted at arm's length, making spot transactions when the cane was cut and ready to be fed to the mills. Under the integrated mill system, deliveries of cane must be scheduled precisely. Hence, growers who wish to supply cane to a specific mill must contract with the mill in advance to deliver certain quantities of cane at certain times. But this new arrangement, dictated by the technology, did not take into account how the price of cane was to be determined. This uncertainty, combined with earlier grower-miller tensions, quickly led the cane growers to form associations for collective bargaining with the millers. This unionization of the growers may not have led to a better cane price relative to the sugar price, but the advent of the associations certainly changed the political context under which sugar policy was formed in the 1970s and 1980s.

The collective bargaining process made the sugar industry appear wracked by conflict. Between 1969 and 1982, growers and millers had annual confrontations in October over the sugarcane price for the forthcoming crushing season, from mid-November to mid-April. The government was gradually drawn into this conflict to play the role of "milch cow" by providing extra resources to pacify apparently irreconcilable differences between the two parties. In this role, the government temporarily removed or reduced business taxes, provided export subsidies, and negotiated a large loan of US$78 million (in 1982) on behalf of the industry. In the long run, the biggest loser from government intervention in grower–miller affairs was the consumer. The domestic consumer price for sugar for most of the period under study was generally above the world price, sometimes considerably so.

The government's main price policy instrument for the sugar industry, as soon as it became an export industry in the early 1960s, was a "home price" scheme (Corden 1971). Essentially this involved a cross-subsidization from the high-priced domestic market to support losses in the export market. To administer the scheme, the government had to closely supervise the production and distribution of sugar so that no sugar would leak into the more profitable domestic market. The large scale of the modern sugar mills made it possible for the government to implement the scheme. As a result, sugar is now the most heavily protected of the agricultural commodities, despite the fact that it is exported.

The implications of the various measures on sugar prices are shown in Figure 7-3. In contrast to measures for the other commodities, which generally involved only border measures, the measures on sugar caused the prices of sugar for consumers, mills, and growers

Figure 7-3. Sugar Prices, 1962–84

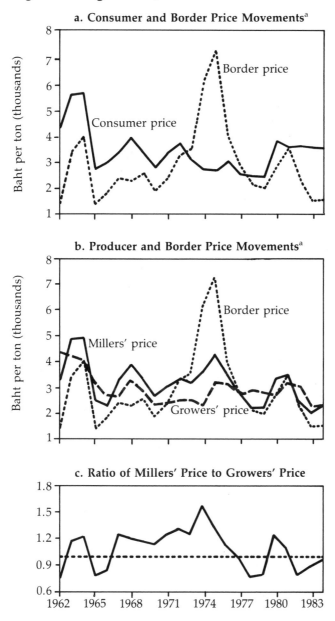

a. Consumer and Border Price Movements[a]

b. Producer and Border Price Movements[a]

c. Ratio of Millers' Price to Growers' Price

a. Border prices are measured at official exchange rates.
Prices are deflated by the GDP deflator (1972 = 100).
Source: Siamwalla and Setboonsarng (1989).

to move separately. Therefore, we had to look at all three price series as well as the series for border prices. Figures 7-3a and 7-3b show the different price series for sugar, all converted to wholesale prices of raw sugar and deflated by the value added deflator for nonagricultural goods with a base year of 1972.

Figure 7-3a indicates that the domestic consumer price generally stayed well above the border price, except between 1973 and 1977, when the world sugar price was extraordinarily high. The higher consumer price allowed the millers to obtain a higher price for their sugar. As the share of exports in total production expanded (it increased from 31 percent in 1971 to 60 percent in 1984), the cross-subsidization possible for a given level of consumer price gradually diminished. Alternatively, the government would have had to increase the consumer price much more to attain a given level of protection for the industry. It is clear that over the years the government has had less room to maneuver, which is why the millers' price in Figure 7-3b comes closer to the border price after 1977.

Figure 7-3c shows the relation between the growers' and the millers' prices for sugar. The formation of the growers' associations in the mid-1960s seems to have had little impact on the relative prices at the two levels. The growing intervention of the government from the mid-1970s onward seems to have had a stronger impact. This analysis confirms the point made earlier that the growers' association has served less as an autonomous institution for collective bargaining (such as a trade union in a developed country) than as a political pressure group that could deliver results to its members only by persuading the government to intervene on their behalf.

Maize

The Thai government intervened in maize between 1965 and 1981, motivated largely by a desire to maintain Thailand's then largest maize markets, Japan and Taiwan, China. Both markets required season-long contracts between exporters and importers. To ensure that the contracts would be fulfilled, the government imposed quantitative restrictions on exports to markets other than Japan and Taiwan. These restrictions implied that the onus of misforecasting the domestic supply situation or the extent of demand outside Japan and Taiwan would fall on domestic suppliers and therefore ultimately on the maize growers. It was possible that in some years the domestic price would be somewhat higher than it would be in a free trade regime, but there was a clear tendency for domestic suppliers to lose out, given the way the quota allocation was managed. In sum, the system generally imposed an implicit tax on maize exports in the form of a quota rent. We calculated that in 1967–81 this implicit tax ranged from 1.6 percent to 9.7 percent. In only two of these fifteen years was there an implicit subsidy.

Over the years, Japanese and Taiwanese markets became less profitable for Thai maize exporters as countries closer to Thailand, such as Malaysia and Singapore, developed their livestock industries and began to demand more maize. Thus, the raison d'être for export intervention began to disappear, and in 1981 the maize trade was completely liberalized.

Rubber

The Ministry of Finance collects two taxes on rubber: a duty entirely for general revenue and a smaller levy to finance a rubber-replanting program. The export duty on rubber is levied at a progressive rate, so that when the world rubber price increases, the tax rate rises according to a preset schedule.

The government has experienced some problems with the system because the effective rate drifts upward with inflation. In the 1960s the tax rate fluctuated between 10 and 16 percent, peaking in 1969. As prices rose in the 1970s, the effective rate also rose, peaking at 26 percent in 1980, a substantial jump considering that rubber prices in real terms were roughly the same in 1969 and in 1980.

The rather simple method of taxing rubber made it unlikely that the matter would appear on the political agenda. There was no export quota to be given out, and rubber alone among Thailand's leading agricultural exports required no licensing. The automatic mechanism of the tax allowed processors and exporters to conduct their business without uncertainty. Moreover, the growers, as in all Thai crops except sugar, were unorganized. Thus it took a sharp fall in rubber prices in 1981 to bring the commodity to public attention, as members of Parliament from the rubber-growing regions of the South pressed for a revision of the tax schedule that brought the effective taxation rate down to the levels prevailing in the 1960s.

Indirect Effects of Nonagricultural Policies on Relative Prices

In addition to implementing policies that have a direct effect on commodity prices, a government may adopt policies that seem unconnected with the agricultural sector and then find that they influence agriculture profoundly. Our analysis here focuses on overall trade policies (that is, all intervention affecting foreign trade) and macroeconomic management (which was chiefly responsible for the current account imbalance that characterized the Thai balance of payments throughout much of the period under study).

The government's trade policies protected the industrial sector and had two negative effects on agriculture. First, industrial protection made the goods purchased by farmers more expensive. Second, and more subtly, trade policies caused the value of the foreign exchange earned by the export sector to be lower than it would have been otherwise. The consequent overvaluation of the domestic currency penalized the agricultural sector, which produces mostly unprotected tradable goods. The penalty can be measured as a wedge, the difference in the relative price between each of the agricultural commodities and nonagricultural goods when compared with what the relative prices would have been in the absence of such trade intervention. This wedge is the indirect effect of intervention on prices. The combined direct and indirect effects on prices are the total effect of intervention. Here, we are assuming that any current account imbalance arises from maladjustments in the real exchange rate. In other words, the correct real exchange rate is the one that will bring the current account balance to zero.[3]

We examined the penalty levied on the agricultural sector in two cases: assuming that the entire current account deficit was unsustainable (requiring adjustment in the real exchange rate) and assuming that it was sustainable (requiring no adjustment in the real exchange rate).

Both trade and macroeconomic policies, in the case in which current account imbalances were assumed unsustainable, shared a pathway—the exchange rate mechanism—by which they made their influence felt on the agricultural sector. We began, therefore, by analyzing how the two types of policies influenced exchange rates.

We derived the impact of trade and macroeconomic policies on the equilibrium exchange rate by using an elasticity approach (for the detailed formulas and calculations, see Siamwalla and Setboonsarng 1989). This approach allowed us to decompose the individual effects of the different policies on the exchange rate. These are reported in Table 7-2, which indicates the effect on the exchange rate if the policies were to be removed. Import tariffs led to an overvaluation of the baht, as expected, as did the protection given the sugar industry, which was not trivial. This overvaluation was offset in part by export taxes on rice and other agricultural products. The overvaluation of the baht resulting from trade policies fluctuated around 10 percent, except in 1974, when very high rates of export taxation imposed to insulate the domestic economy from the commodity boom of 1973–74 almost entirely offset the impact of import duties.

The impact of macroeconomic policies on the exchange rate was much more variable, with a dividing line around the year 1975. The period before 1975 tended to have smaller balance of payment prob-

Table 7-2. Effect on Exchange Rate of Removal of Various Types of Price Intervention, 1960–84
(percent)

Period	Import taxes	Rice taxes	Rubber taxes	Tin royalty	Sugar policies	Maize policies	Other export taxes	Total trade policies	Current account deficit	Total trade and macro policies
1960–64	12.44	−6.72	−0.22	−0.21	3.22	0.00	−0.11	8.39	3.45	11.84
1965–69	14.51	−5.16	−0.14	−0.25	1.62	−0.14	−0.11	10.33	4.67	14.99
1970–74	13.35	−3.97	−0.13	−0.21	1.92	−0.13	−0.10	10.73	5.16	15.90
1975–79	12.40	−2.03	−0.19	−0.29	0.67	−0.12	−0.07	10.37	13.75	24.12
1980–84	9.45	−0.81	−0.13	−0.24	2.58	−0.03	−0.02	10.60	14.73	25.54

Source: Siamwalla and Setboonsarng (1989).

249

lems except for the years 1969–71. The period after 1975 was marked by consistently large balance of payments deficits.

The effect of trade and macroeconomic policies on the exchange rate was passed on to all tradable products, including the four agricultural commodities of interest. As we have noted, direct policies for the individual crops have been liberalized gradually from about 1981 onward. But the benefits of liberalization for agriculture had to await macroeconomic policy reforms that were slower in coming. Unfortunately, the recent reduction in extractions from the agricultural sector has been overshadowed by a steep fall in world agricultural commodity prices.

Adjusting agricultural prices for the exchange rate overvaluation was by itself insufficient. Because we used the index of nonagricultural prices as the deflator for agricultural prices, and because the nonagricultural sector contained a tradable subsector whose prices were affected not only by the exchange rate overvaluation but directly by trade policies, we had to adjust this deflator as well. These adjustments were fairly small—less than 6 percent in absolute value (see Siamwella and Setboosang 1989).

Having made the calculations for the equilibrium exchange rate and the adjusted index of nonagricultural goods prices, we measured the combined impact of commodity-specific government policies, overall trade policies, and macroeconomic policies. The results are reported in Table 7-3, which shows the proportionate change in the actual, observed relative prices of the four selected commodities from what they would have been if all government intervention had been removed. Because removing government intervention in the price of rice would change the world price, that effect was taken into account in defining the border price free of government intervention.

The rates of protection for all commodities other than sugar were substantially negative (Table 7-3). For rice and maize, direct disincentives have declined in more recent years (and by July 1988 had dropped to zero). For these two crops, the disincentive that remained was due to the indirect effect arising from the impact of trade and macroeconomic policies on the exchange rate. The direct effect on rubber in the latter period was high because of an increase in the effective exchange rate in the 1970s. As a result of adjustments made first in 1981 and later in 1984, however, the rate has declined from these levels somewhat. In the case of sugar, domestic prices have tended to be well above border prices, to confirm our conclusion about the effect of the politics of the sugar industry. The degree of protection given to the sector declined substantially in the latter period because of an increase in the ratio of exports to domestic consumption. If the indirect effects of trade and macroeconomic policy were taken into

Table 7-3. Effect of Price Intervention on Relative Producer Prices, 1962–84

(percent)

Commodity and period	Direct	Total (1)[a]	Total (2)[b]
Rice[c]			
1962–72	−0.2922	−0.3713	−0.3922
1973–84	−0.2422	−0.3171	−0.3663
1976–84	−0.1898	−0.2739	−0.3332
Sugar (consumer)			
1962–72	0.8522	0.6518	0.6006
1973–84	0.3595	0.2160	0.1221
1976–84	0.6040	0.4318	0.3113
Sugar (mills)			
1962–72	0.7760	0.5854	0.5359
1973–84	0.0802	−0.0297	−0.1014
1976–84	0.1939	0.0686	−0.0206
Sugar (grower)			
1962–72	0.4155	0.2645	0.2272
1973–84	0.0260	−0.0789	−0.1492
1976–84	0.1984	0.0735	−0.0157
Maize			
1962–72	−0.0108	−0.0785	−0.0992
1973–84	−0.0357	−0.1291	−0.1896
1976–84	−0.0267	−0.1270	−0.1985
Rubber			
1962–72	−0.1016	−0.2012	−0.2270
1973–84	−0.2006	−0.2781	−0.3273
1976–84	−0.2158	−0.2966	−0.3538

Note: Figures represent averages for each period.

a. Assumes current account deficit is sustainable.

b. Assumes current account deficit is not sustainable.

c. Adjusted for export price effect.

Source: Siamwalla, and Setboonsarng, forthcoming.

account, protection in the latter half of the period would disappear entirely.

The magnitude of the trade policy impact, as mentioned, did not stray far from the 10 percent mark for the entire period. The impact of the macroeconomic policy, however, appears to have drifted upward from a level generally below 5 percent to between 5 and 10 percent, so that the combined effect of both trade and macroeconomic policies implies a penalty of 15 to 20 percent for all tradable agricultural commodities.

The emergence of indirect effects as an important factor adversely affecting the agricultural sector remains largely unmentioned in policy discussions both within and outside the Thai government. To the extent that exchange rate adjustments would have made these effects somewhat more transparent, these points could have been raised when the government had to defend its devaluations in 1981 and 1984. Even then, the government did not obtain any support from farmers' groups against the more vocal opponents of devaluation. Exporters, normally influential in agricultural matters, suffered short-term losses—some of them heavy—from their exposure during devaluation, and therefore they could not be relied on to make unbiased judgments at such times. Because the two devaluations took place at a time when the worldwide agricultural market was weak, their favorable effects on agricultural prices were canceled by the continuing slide in dollar prices of the agricultural goods. Thus the two devaluations fell short of being the ideal laboratory experiment that would have demonstrated the main message of Table 7-3.

Consequences of Government Intervention

The consequences of intervention in Thailand can best be understood by examining the changes in output, consumption, and foreign exchange earnings; the fiscal impact of agricultural pricing policies; the impact on resource flows between agriculture and the rest of the economy; and the effects of pricing policies on income distribution.

Output, Consumption, and Foreign Exchange Earnings

We estimated the effects of intervention on output and consumption (except for the effect on sugar output) by applying the elasticity coefficients to the results on price deviations in Table 7-3. We obtained both short- and long-run effects. For the latter, we assumed a simple distributed-lag form. The elasticities and the distributed-lag coefficients were obtained from econometric estimates in the literature. We also used subjective judgment in choosing actual elasticities from a vast array of estimates available from previous work (for the supply elasticities we used mainly the surveys by Thanapornpan 1983 and Kunwatanusorn 1983). In general, we chose elasticities that reflected economic considerations—for example, the ratio between the long- and short-run elasticities was 7 for rubber, 2 for rice, and 1.5 for maize. We also noted that the output elasticities of rice and maize declined linearly between 1960 and 1980, as surplus land was exhausted. Appendix Tables 7-8 through 7-13 show the output effects for both the short run and the long run obtained for all crops except sugar (which we discuss below). Appendix Tables 7-16 through 7-18 show the effects of intervention on consumption of all commodities except rubber, the domestic consumption of which is negligible.

To trace the effect of government intervention on sugar output, we employed a newly estimated econometric model. Specifically, we estimated the following two equations:

(7-1) $\ln Q = -1.5649 = 1.0934.W.\ln.PG - (6.9329D$
$- 0.9529\ D.W.\ln PMe) = 0.5420\ W.\ln CAP = u_1$

(7-2) $\ln CAP = -7.5921 = 0.6655\ \ln PMe$
$= 0.9161\ \ln Q_{-1} = 0.1460\ TX = u_2$

where Q is the quantity of sugar produced; CAP is the total capacity of the mills; PG is the sugar price for the growers, deflated by the index of nonagricultural goods; PMe is the similarly deflated sugar price expected by the millers (in the model and in the simulation this was the forecast with the aid of a second order autoregressive model); D is a dummy variable with a value of 0 between 1961 and 1970 and a value of 1 from 1971 onward; TX is a time trend variable with a value of 0 for 1963 and before, with values of 1,2, . . . 9 for the years 1964–72, and with a constant value of 9 for the years after 1972; and $W = 0.4\ L = 0.3\ L^2 = 0.3\ L^3$, where L is the lag operator.

The idea behind Equation 7-1 was that after the new technology was introduced in the sugar industry, the supply of cane would no longer be decided by the growers but instead would be constrained by the decisions of the mills about how much sugarcane would be required for the next season. Another constraint on the supply of cane was the capacity of the mills. Because this was an economic variable, we estimated Equation 7-2 to explain its movements over time. Because of the presence of the lagged Q in the capacity equation, which is in turn an explanatory variable for Q, the model is essentially autoregressive. We tested it by running a dynamic simulation covering the period of estimation and judged its performance satisfactory, with an R^2 between the predicted and the actual sugar output of 0.86 (for details of the estimation procedures, see Siamwalla and Setboonsarng 1989).

We then used this model to simulate the case in which both the grower price (PG) and the expected mill price (PMe) were determined by the world price. In this way we obtained the effect of government intervention on sugar prices. We defined the short-run effect for any given year as the effect of removing government intervention in that year (and that year alone) without any change in mill capacity. We defined the cumulative effect as that of removing government intervention in 1961. Its effects are embodied in the alternative time path for the capacity.

Appendix Tables 7-14 and 7-15 show the impact of intervention on sugar output. The effect on sugar output was quite substantial, particularly the cumulative effect. According to our analysis, the sugar industry would have shrunk to a quarter of its size in 1984 if the direct policies aiding it had been removed. If the liberalization of the industry had been accompanied by a general trade liberalization, however, the industry would have contracted only slightly more than a third of the 1984 level. If there had been a correction of macroeconomic policies as well, the industry would have contracted to only half the 1984 level.

The impact of government policies on the output and consumption of the different crops can be summarized by examining the impact on foreign exchange earnings of these policies. Tables 7-4 and 7-5 show the short-run and cumulative effects on the foreign exchange earnings of government intervention in the four commodities. In terms of order of magnitudes, rice taxes dominated the picture in the 1960s.[4] The negative effect of intervention on rice and the positive effect on sugar more or less offset each other in the 1970s and 1980s (with the exception of some extraordinary movements in the 1973–75 period associated with the commodity boom). The downward trend in rice taxes plus a relatively steady level of sugar protection led to a slowly rising trend in net impact until in the 1980s it became positive. Note also that the increased diversification of Thailand's exports lessened the impact of intervention as a proportion of total export earnings.

Revenues

Certain government policies—for example, taxes—induce resource flows out of the agricultural sector directly to the national budget. Direct subsidies do the reverse. In addition to supporting policies that we have grouped under the rubric of pricing policies, governments also spend money to benefit the agricultural sector—for example, for irrigation, and agricultural research and extension. What has been the net effect of all these government activities on the agricultural sector? Our calculations may throw some light on this issue. We have added up the tax revenues from the various measures described above, making some adjustments to account for the fact that part of the burden of the export tax falls on foreign buyers of Thai rice. Columns 1 through 4 of Table 7-6 display the results of these calculations.[5] Columns 5 and 6 indicate government expenditures, not only the funds from the central budget but those obtained from extra-budgetary sources, such as the Farmers' Aid Fund and the Rubber Replanting Fund. Because it is hard to say whether government outlays for roads constitute an expenditure on agriculture per se, we have reported figures that both include and exclude road expenditures. All figures shown in Table 7-6 have been deflated by a specially constructed rural consumer price index.

Table 7-4. Short-Run Effect of Government Intervention on Foreign Exchange Earnings, 1960–84

(millions of constant 1972 U.S. dollars)

	Direct effect						Total effect (1)						Total effect (2)					
Year	Rice	Maize	Sugar	Rubber	Total	Percentage of total exports	Rice	Maize	Sugar	Rubber	Total	Percentage of total exports	Rice	Maize	Sugar	Rubber	Total	Percentage of total exports
1960	n.a.	n.a.	n.a.	n.a.	n.a.	n.a.	n.a.	n.a.	n.a.	n.a.	n.a.	n.a.	n.a.	n.a.	n.a.	n.a.	n.a.	n.a.
1961	−128.21	n.a.	n.a.	−3.80	−132.01	−22.74	n.a.	n.a.	n.a.	n.a.	n.a.	n.a.	n.a.	n.a.	n.a.	n.a.	n.a.	n.a.
1962	−141.43	n.a.	n.a.	−4.08	−145.51	−21.71	n.a.	n.a.	n.a.	n.a.	n.a.	n.a.	n.a.	n.a.	n.a.	n.a.	n.a.	n.a.
1963	−111.52	n.a.	n.a.	−3.52	−115.04	−18.05	−141.94	n.a.	n.a.	−5.90	−147.84	−23.19	−149.77	n.a.	n.a.	−6.52	−156.29	−24.52
1964	−124.65	n.a.	n.a.	−3.75	−128.40	−20.07	−150.21	n.a.	n.a.	−5.71	−155.91	−24.37	−167.24	n.a.	n.a.	−7.03	−174.27	−27.24
1965	−148.33	n.a.	n.a.	−3.42	−151.75	−18.80	−170.06	n.a.	n.a.	−5.13	−175.19	−21.70	−175.30	n.a.	n.a.	−5.55	−180.85	−22.40
1966	−164.89	n.a.	n.a.	−3.41	−168.30	−20.19	−195.29	n.a.	n.a.	−5.39	−200.68	−24.08	−199.14	n.a.	n.a.	−5.65	−204.79	−24.57
1967	−164.40	n.a.	46.18	−2.51	−120.73	−13.69	−215.97	n.a.	37.16	−4.34	−183.15	−20.78	−224.64	n.a.	35.64	−4.65	−193.65	−21.97
1968	−129.29	−6.25	21.51	−2.41	−116.44	−13.48	−159.13	−16.92	17.22	−4.04	−162.87	−18.86	−168.18	−20.41	16.08	−4.54	−177.05	−20.50
1969	−146.26	−7.46	52.43	−2.91	−104.19	−13.06	−177.58	−22.90	41.03	−5.71	−165.16	−20.70	−198.03	−34.12	34.73	−7.58	−205.00	−25.70
1970	−81.97	−2.40	21.74	−3.87	−66.51	−8.22	−113.96	−22.94	12.70	−6.67	−130.87	−16.17	−135.34	−38.61	7.01	−8.61	−175.54	−21.69
1971	−56.78	−4.30	65.91	−2.36	2.47	0.32	−85.71	−24.90	56.10	−4.46	−58.97	−7.71	−110.19	−44.77	48.31	−6.30	−112.94	−14.77
1972	−87.03	−2.69	54.39	−1.83	−37.16	−4.33	−127.58	−14.12	46.20	−4.24	−99.75	−11.62	−147.26	−20.27	41.08	−5.44	−131.89	−15.37
1973	−138.27	11.46	104.62	−4.33	−26.52	−2.46	−188.60	−12.46	77.70	−8.98	−132.34	−12.26	−195.95	−16.24	69.18	−9.68	−152.69	−14.14
1974	−352.89	−25.78	148.70	−7.98	−237.96	−16.05	−408.71	−49.77	98.90	−11.86	−371.42	−25.06	−416.68	−53.35	86.91	−12.42	−395.55	−26.68
1975	−267.02	−6.05	−37.80	−5.47	−316.34	−15.14	−278.77	−13.29	−76.06	−6.30	−374.41	−17.91	−284.90	−17.14	−85.40	−6.73	−394.16	−18.86
1976	−137.76	−10.76	−47.94	−6.99	−203.45	−11.80	−160.93	−21.84	−75.45	−9.62	−267.84	−15.53	−197.85	−40.55	−101.46	−13.93	−353.79	−20.51
1977	−62.53	−2.55	44.44	−10.12	−30.77	−1.40	−96.26	−9.97	15.34	−14.32	−105.21	−4.79	−120.61	−15.57	−12.39	−17.42	−165.99	−7.56
1978	−93.17	0.34	67.48	−13.20	−38.54	−1.60	−134.67	−11.94	46.13	−19.46	−119.94	−4.97	−181.26	−26.65	21.09	−26.81	−213.64	−8.85
1979	−141.12	−2.47	121.75	−18.32	−40.15	−1.53	−179.15	−13.87	102.17	−26.07	−116.92	−4.45	−220.49	−26.72	81.01	−34.75	−200.95	−7.65
1980	−104.76	−4.52	130.70	−17.60	3.82	0.12	−142.82	−14.34	107.93	−24.21	−73.44	−2.40	−202.52	−30.22	75.05	−34.97	−192.66	−6.29
1981	−130.20	−4.34	217.38	−14.79	68.05	2.05	−159.48	−10.94	187.61	−19.05	−1.87	−0.06	−212.52	−21.65	141.79	−25.90	−118.28	−3.57
1982	−80.73	−5.93	147.94	−7.73	53.55	1.65	−101.06	−11.88	128.88	−11.16	4.77	0.15	−139.96	−22.07	94.92	−17.07	−84.19	−2.59
1983	−29.70	0.00	117.64	−6.29	81.65	2.70	−53.38	−8.05	103.64	−11.18	31.03	1.03	−68.75	−13.19	90.02	−14.30	−6.21	−0.21
1984	−21.37	0.00	178.09	−9.05	147.67	5.50	−48.59	−10.28	157.37	−14.46	84.04	3.13	−87.37	−24.95	130.66	−22.22	−3.89	−0.14

n.a. Not available.

Source: Siamwalla and Setboonsarng (1989).

Table 7-5. Cumulative Effect of Government Intervention on Foreign Exchange Earnings, 1960–84
(millions of constant 1972 U.S. dollars)

Year	Direct effect						Total effect (1)						Total effect (2)					
	Rice	Maize	Sugar	Rubber	Total	Percentage of total exports	Rice	Maize	Sugar	Rubber	Total	Percentage of total exports	Rice	Maize	Sugar	Rubber	Total	Percentage of total exports
1960	n.a.	n.a.	n.a.	n.a.	n.a.	n.a.	n.a.	n.a.	n.a.	n.a.	n.a.	n.a.	n.a.	n.a.	n.a.	n.a.	n.a.	n.a.
1961	n.a.	n.a.	n.a.	n.a.	n.a.	n.a.	n.a.	n.a.	n.a.	n.a.	n.a.	n.a.	n.a.	n.a.	n.a.	n.a.	n.a.	n.a.
1962	n.a.	n.a.	n.a.	n.a.	n.a.	n.a.	n.a.	n.a.	n.a.	n.a.	n.a.	n.a.	n.a.	n.a.	n.a.	n.a.	n.a.	n.a.
1963	n.a.	n.a.	n.a.	n.a.	n.a.	n.a.	n.a.	n.a.	n.a.	n.a.	n.a.	n.a.	n.a.	n.a.	n.a.	n.a.	n.a.	n.a.
1964	n.a.	n.a.	n.a.	n.a.	n.a.	n.a.	n.a.	n.a.	n.a.	n.a.	n.a.	n.a.	n.a.	n.a.	n.a.	n.a.	n.a.	n.a.
1965	-228.32	n.a.	n.a.	-12.83	-241.15	-41.55	n.a.	n.a.	n.a.	n.a.	n.a.	n.a.	n.a.	n.a.	n.a.	n.a.	n.a.	n.a.
1966	-273.63	n.a.	n.a.	-12.51	-286.14	-42.68	n.a.	n.a.	n.a.	n.a.	n.a.	n.a.	n.a.	n.a.	n.a.	n.a.	n.a.	n.a.
1967	-291.22	n.a.	46.18	-9.68	-254.72	-39.96	-369.02	n.a.	36.79	-16.33	-348.56	-54.67	-379.74	n.a.	35.39	-17.51	-361.86	-56.76
1968	-232.28	n.a.	21.72	-9.09	-219.66	-34.33	-292.03	n.a.	16.97	-15.55	-290.61	-45.42	-302.41	n.a.	15.81	-16.73	-303.33	-47.40
1969	-221.48	n.a.	56.00	-11.64	-177.12	-21.94	-275.14	n.a.	42.81	-21.18	-253.50	-31.40	-293.58	n.a.	36.54	-23.51	-280.55	-34.75
1970	-146.20	n.a.	35.33	-10.56	-121.43	-14.57	-194.52	n.a.	25.99	-19.28	-187.81	-22.54	-215.47	n.a.	21.21	-22.18	-216.43	-25.97
1971	-111.55	n.a.	75.13	-7.98	-44.40	-5.04	-154.69	n.a.	64.92	-14.97	-104.74	-11.88	-180.68	n.a.	57.88	-18.07	-140.86	-15.98
1972	-140.97	-4.37	69.98	-7.41	-82.77	-9.58	-207.60	-27.05	60.93	-15.32	-189.05	-21.89	-235.03	-37.19	56.66	-18.60	-234.17	-27.11
1973	-229.28	9.08	137.85	-16.03	-98.39	-12.33	-331.69	-35.84	104.26	-35.19	-298.45	-37.41	-355.44	-44.48	94.16	-41.36	-347.12	-43.51
1974	-463.34	-22.18	255.62	-21.59	-251.50	-31.08	-596.09	-76.77	183.83	-44.01	-533.05	-65.87	-616.44	-83.07	164.21	-49.52	-584.82	-72.27
1975	-372.63	-12.24	144.37	-16.20	-256.70	-33.56	-425.80	-39.42	60.97	-29.12	-433.36	-56.66	-435.77	-44.10	35.85	-31.95	-475.97	-62.23
1976	-255.84	-13.92	86.58	-23.26	-206.45	-24.06	-297.86	-31.61	16.02	-38.45	-351.90	-41.01	-327.38	-46.19	-15.67	-43.47	-432.71	-50.43
1977	-180.08	-6.28	136.83	-28.88	-78.41	-7.26	-228.76	-17.80	69.32	-43.14	-220.37	-20.41	-257.85	-25.57	35.44	-48.82	-296.81	-27.49
1978	-178.77	-1.58	106.67	-38.75	-112.44	-7.59	-234.34	-15.63	69.95	-54.56	-234.58	-15.83	-280.16	-28.35	44.50	-64.72	-328.73	-22.18
1979	-200.29	-3.02	147.46	-53.44	-109.29	-5.23	-252.50	-17.96	115.91	-73.03	-227.58	-10.89	-298.05	-31.52	92.00	-89.13	-326.70	-15.63
1980	-189.48	-5.37	158.01	-59.70	-96.55	-5.60	-246.82	-18.58	127.03	-81.55	-219.91	-12.75	-310.40	-34.21	93.77	-102.60	-353.43	-20.49
1981	-202.36	-5.53	273.06	-48.38	16.78	0.76	-262.04	-17.62	226.28	-66.59	-119.97	-5.46	-325.34	-28.99	177.29	-83.11	-260.15	-11.84
1982	-130.35	-7.29	214.15	-32.70	43.80	1.81	-172.10	-17.99	183.04	-46.84	-53.89	-2.23	-217.23	-28.77	150.68	-60.06	-155.38	-6.43
1983	-78.97	-2.08	148.67	-35.47	32.17	1.22	-119.73	-13.89	128.79	-53.43	-58.26	-2.22	-147.86	-20.86	113.30	-67.62	-123.05	-4.68
1984	-52.21	-0.64	204.69	-34.10	117.75	3.84	-96.38	-14.83	180.07	-53.36	15.51	0.51	-137.28	-28.18	152.74	-69.39	-82.10	-2.68

n.a. Not available.
Source: Siamwalla and Setboonsarng (1989).

256

Table 7-6. Resource Flows between the Agricultural Sector and the Government, 1960–84

(millions of baht, deflated by rural CPI, 1972 = 100)

Year	Revenues from taxation				Expenditures on agriculture		Net transfer from agriculture to government	
	Rice	Sugar	Rubber	Total	Roads included	Roads excluded	Roads included	Roads excluded
1960	742.66	0.15	399.12	1,141.93	967.76	539.48	174.17	602.45
1961	941.36	0.06	356.46	1,297.87	1,299.63	627.84	-1.76	670.03
1962	692.51	-89.39	306.76	909.58	1,596.25	846.93	-546.17	203.14
1963	793.25	-58.50	298.64	1,033.39	1,787.49	979.34	-636.62	171.54
1964	1,239.79	-25.48	286.99	1,501.30	2,185.96	1,176.42	-627.66	381.88
1965	1,159.81	-125.03	292.54	1,327.31	2,979.78	1,668.93	-1,476.64	-165.79
1966	914.29	0.83	249.59	1,164.71	3,901.92	2,007.67	-2,689.67	-795.42
1967	787.03	0.52	175.23	962.79	4,928.98	2,283.51	-3,966.19	-1,320.72
1968	894.72	0.00	171.22	1,065.94	5,969.62	2,660.03	-4,903.67	-1,594.08
1969	691.59	0.00	413.43	1,105.02	6,257.74	2,726.27	-5,152.72	-1,621.25
1970	370.00	0.00	268.50	638.50	6,583.05	3,161.30	-5,944.55	-2,522.80
1971	239.31	0.00	175.26	414.57	6,748.11	3,230.13	-6,333.54	-2,815.56
1972	248.02	0.00	179.32	427.34	6,495.76	2,821.29	-6,068.43	-2,393.95
1973	221.82	0.00	635.31	857.13	5,459.85	2,498.15	-4,602.71	-1,641.02
1974	1,411.73	385.06	622.61	2,419.40	4,588.58	2,235.57	-2,169.18	183.83
1975	945.46	631.72	360.21	1,937.38	6,483.51	3,640.46	-4,546.14	-1,703.08
1976	586.03	357.90	683.41	1,627.34	7,806.08	4,292.98	-6,178.74	-2,665.64
1977	1,275.46	71.39	785.67	2,132.52	9,058.01	5,078.17	-6,925.49	-2,945.65
1978	877.22	35.50	904.28	1,817.00	8,949.01	5,381.85	-7,132.01	-3,564.85
1979	741.80	33.95	1,358.16	2,133.91	10,004.02	6,171.21	-7,870.21	-4,037.40
1980	784.80	19.41	1,232.27	2,036.48	10,432.10	6,104.32	-8,395.62	-4,067.84
1981	684.39	123.24	680.59	1,489.21	9,630.39	5,908.22	-8,142.18	-4,420.01
1982	543.62	232.23	400.10	1,175.95	10,763.37	6,940.45	-9,587.43	-5,764.51
1983	n.a.	42.10	661.85	n.a.	9,767.21	6,156.66	n.a.	n.a.
1984	n.a.	52.41	598.49	n.a.	n.a.	n.a.	n.a.	n.a.

n.a. Not available.
Source: Siamwalla and Setboonsarng (1989).

The revenue obtained by the government from the agricultural sector appears to have been quite small. The revenue figures showed no clear upward trend, although there was a temporary increase in the mid-1970s, connected with the world commodity boom. The expenditure side, however, showed a strong upward trend. Thus, although the figures on revenues and expenditures were roughly comparable in the early 1960s, two decades later the expenditures (excluding roads) were outpacing revenues by a ratio of six to one.

Resource Flows from Agriculture to the Economy

Resource flows between the agricultural sector and the government capture only a part of the consequences of government intervention. Intervention also induces a flow of resources between agriculture and the larger economy. For example, urban consumers of rice benefited from the cheaper rice resulting from the export tax. To measure this type of flow, we used a different technique from the one used for Table 7-6, where we tracked individual flows. Instead, we asked how real agricultural income was affected by government price intervention.

For the moment, we set aside government expenditures on agriculture. To recalculate real agricultural income, we first calculated nominal income as it would have been if government intervention had been removed throughout the period under study. This involved the effects of government intervention on both prices and output. Because the output effect varies according to the length of the "run," and because we had three "runs"—instantaneous (when output does not vary at all), short, and long—we had three possible results. Here, we report only the instantaneous results. The second step was to calculate the rural deflator as it would have behaved if the government had ceased to intervene and used this alternative deflator to obtain the real income of the agricultural sector in the absence of government intervention.

This method of calculation focused on the·real income of the agricultural sector. Transfers into or out of this sector were then defined as changes in real income. The disadvantage of this method was that it was difficult to identify the individual flows and the beneficiaries (or the sources) of these flows. Against this, there was the important advantage that we could introduce types of price distortion other than government taxation as an explanatory factor for the resource flows. In particular, our analysis stressed the role of exchange rate and trade policies as distorting factors. Note that we included here the impact of exchange rate and trade policy not only on the four selected commodities but also on all other tradable agricultural products. We also included their impact on the rural consumer price index (CPI).

According to our calculations, there was a net outflow from the agricultural sector to the rest of the economy (Table 7-7). The figures do not net out the inflows that occurred because of government expenditures. The net resource flows of these expenditures (including roads), which are taken from column 7 of Table 7-6, are shown in Figure 7-4.

The figures in Table 7-7 show that the resource outflow from the agricultural sector to the rest of the economy was many times larger than that to the government alone (four to five times larger in the instantaneous case and counting only the direct effect). There is a simple explanation for this discrepancy. Many government measures, particularly with respect to rice, led to a large implicit transfer between the agricultural sector and the consumers of its product outside the sector. These were not counted when we examined the receipts and expenditures of the government, but they were picked up in our calculations here. The agricultural sector did bear a heavy burden of support in keeping the price of rice low for nonagricultural consumers. The implicit subsidy of rice consumption clearly dominates the figures: the gross outflow (direct effect only, instantaneous run; see column 1 of Table 7-7) drops sharply, almost to zero, in the 1980s, when there was a sharp lowering of the barriers to rice exports.

The direct effect of the resource outflow net of the inflow through government expenditures slowly declined over time (again except for the "blip" of the mid-1970s), so that by the mid-1980s there was actually a substantial net inflow into the agricultural sector. But if the indirect effects of trade and macroeconomic policies are taken into account, the net resource outflow was quite substantial until as late as 1981. It was only after the macroeconomic policy reforms that began in 1982 that the resource outflow began to drop noticeably.

Income Distribution

To trace the effects of government intervention on the incomes of different households, we used household income and expenditure data from a socioeconomic survey of 1980–81 carried out by the Thai National Statistical Office. These data actually refer to 1980, which was a somewhat untypical year for government policies and also for Thailand's weather pattern. This was the only year for which data were available, but since the survey gives a richly detailed picture of household income sources, we decided to use the results.

We divided all of the households in Thailand into four occupational categories (rice farming, nonrice farming, nonfarming rural, and urban), and three income strata (rich, medium, and poor). The rich households were the top 30 percent of all households, the poor were the bottom 30 percent, and the medium were the remaining 40 per-

Table 7-7. Gross Resource Flows from Agriculture to the Rest of the Economy, 1960–84
(millions of baht, deflated by rural CPI, 1972 = 100)

Year	Instantaneous Direct	Total[a]	Total[b]	Short-run Direct	Total[a]	Total[b]	Cumulative Direct	Total[a]	Total[b]
1960	3,852.09	n.a.	n.a.	n.a.	n.a.	n.a.	n.a.	n.a.	n.a.
1961	4,929.83	n.a.	n.a.	5,384.89	n.a.	n.a.	n.a.	n.a.	n.a.
1962	3,585.67	5,346.50	5,628.03	4,944.64	n.a.	n.a.	n.a.	n.a.	n.a.
1963	4,748.26	6,359.42	6,983.36	5,347.05	7,128.62	7,840.10	n.a.	n.a.	n.a.
1964	5,609.36	7,156.71	7,365.36	6,166.49	7,831.47	8,137.61	n.a.	n.a.	n.a.
1965	4,927.86	6,699.89	6,836.97	6,275.08	8,241.83	8,419.70	6,682.59	n.a.	n.a.
1966	4,562.43	6,913.55	7,170.40	5,368.11	7,957.35	8,256.76	5,787.47	n.a.	n.a.
1967	7,327.74	9,956.98	10,434.92	7,885.94	10,620.34	11,159.14	8,290.76	11,438.86	12,045.50
1968	6,925.32	9,485.47	10,563.71	7,414.38	10,257.10	11,490.25	7,952.63	11,041.03	12,346.32
1969	4,949.52	8,029.43	9,459.99	5,369.12	8,804.96	10,545.63	5,744.76	9,287.34	11,031.80
1970	2,738.22	5,513.14	7,143.44	2,918.06	5,942.64	7,871.37	3,175.24	6,166.40	8,047.86
1971	3,978.05	7,360.16	8,512.18	4,143.24	7,732.10	9,127.86	4,372.44	7,841.30	9,166.21
1972	5,343.50	8,777.54	9,119.28	5,493.42	9,202.59	9,681.77	5,683.58	9,678.30	10,246.13
1973	12,879.76	16,889.33	17,240.23	13,219.76	17,649.42	18,090.88	13,716.05	18,805.11	19,451.53
1974	23,199.53	25,878.89	26,427.98	23,930.22	27,165.38	27,855.23	24,163.93	28,195.84	29,074.73
1975	13,252.86	16,781.60	19,984.38	13,774.62	17,697.77	21,242.94	13,461.55	17,963.56	21,821.61
1976	5,535.32	9,762.49	11,787.19	5,726.75	10,223.67	12,611.83	5,771.94	10,567.72	13,049.26
1977	5,851.46	10,931.85	14,799.45	5,978.45	11,228.90	15,376.81	6,318.85	11,829.87	16,239.29
1978	6,942.46	11,512.99	14,692.41	7,376.50	12,127.65	15,644.43	7,856.47	12,797.96	16,474.18
1979	5,787.55	10,429.13	15,427.18	6,418.05	11,222.00	16,581.43	6,736.66	11,696.76	17,300.34
1980	7,870.15	12,006.87	16,193.85	8,091.30	12,384.87	16,979.40	8,418.87	12,939.26	17,797.20
1981	8,496.23	13,016.65	18,127.92	8,648.80	13,284.30	18,782.35	8,869.80	13,761.86	19,571.41
1982	743.37	4,685.64	6,518.76	1,287.30	5,193.76	7,105.99	1,599.66	5,599.13	7,614.78
1983	603.32	4,790.63	9,267.23	1,032.39	5,194.63	9,690.30	1,269.40	5,566.67	10,342.42
1984	280.68	4,862.10	8,141.35	759.84	5,307.13	8,695.71	947.77	5,609.46	9,127.07

n.a. Not available.

a. Assumes current account deficit is sustainable.

b. Assumes current account deficit is not sustainable.

Source: Siamwalla and Setboonsarng, 1989.

**Figure 7-4. Real Net Resource Flows from Agriculture
to the Rest of the Economy, 1960–84**

Baht (billions)[a]

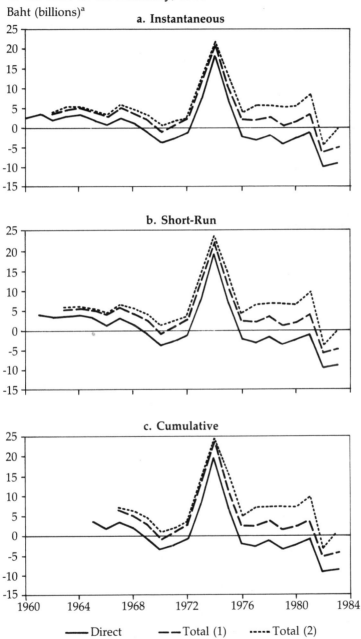

a. Deflated by the rural CPI (1972 = 100).
Source: Siamwalla and Setboonsarng (1989).

cent. Thus when we refer to a rich rice-farming household, we mean that it belonged to that occupational category and was in the top 30 percent in income of all households, not just the top 30 percent of rice-farming households.

The most striking feature of the data is the high level of income in urban areas. Close to 70 percent of Thailand's urban households were in the rich stratum, while very few urban households belonged to the poor stratum, as we defined it. A second point of interest is the size of the rice-farming population in Thailand, which accounts for 38 percent of the total number of households, even though value added from paddy production contributed merely 6.6 percent of GDP in 1980. This disparity between the numbers in the labor force and their contribution to production is explained by the higher proportion (44 percent) of rice farming households classified as poor.

We estimated the impact of government intervention on income distribution by adjusting the real income of each household in the sample in a manner similar to the one we used to aggregate the real income of the agricultural sector. Naturally, we had to make some strong assumptions here. First, we assumed that government intervention had zero impact on nominal wages and on the nominal prices of nontraded goods. Second, although we managed to include the impact of trade policies on the prices of goods consumed by households, we could find no way to assign the benefits of industrial protection (the producer subsidy equivalent) to individual households. Thus, the total effects reported in Figures 7-5b and 7-5c should be read with this problem in mind. Third, the quota rent made possible by government policies was assumed to accrue entirely to the rich urban households. This probably was the least unrealistic of the assumptions.

The change in real income reported in Figure 7-5 is based on a recalculation of household incomes and the change in their cost of living. Because our assumptions were made more palatable if we considered only the instantaneous effect, we have reported only those results. They indicate that the main burden of government intervention was felt by rich rural households, whose income dropped about 3–4 percent as a result of intervention.

The most surprising result was that the main beneficiaries of intervention were the rich urban households. One reason for this result may have been that these urban households were the main beneficiaries of the quota rent, and this was not trivial. Second, we did not include in our analysis the effect of lower rice prices on wages.

Another point to note is the relatively small impact of intervention in producer prices on the income of poor rural households (for a similar result, see Trairatvorakul 1984). This was because the income of poor farmers came from a variety of sources; poor rice farmers, for

**Figure 7-5. Instantaneous Change in Real Income
Owing to Intervention, 1981**

Percent

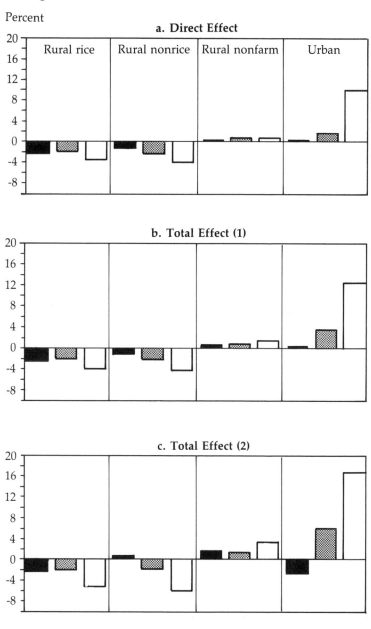

a. Direct Effect

b. Total Effect (1)

c. Total Effect (2)

Poor ▨ Medium ☐ Rich

Source: Siamwalla and Setboonsarng (1989).

example, obtained only half their income from rice sales. A significant part of the income of poor farmers was in off-farm wages, and only a sixth of those off-farm wages appear to have come from the agricultural sector. Hence, removing intervention in the agricultural sector affected poor farmers less than it did their wealthier counterparts.

The results reported above do not appear to change significantly when indirect effects appears are included in the calculations. Part of the reason may be that we were unable to incorporate adequately the effects of nonagricultural policies into our analysis. Doing so probably would have accentuated the results above. That is, the major beneficiaries of intervention would still have been the urban rich (through increased income from import-competing sectors), with the urban poor and middle-income groups gaining somewhat through higher wages at the time the baht was overvalued. In addition, the disparity between the rural and urban income due to the government's agricultural policy would have increased.

Conclusion

In this history of Thai agricultural pricing policies, we have described the policies toward individual crops separately because the policies for each crop evolved independently, both in fact and in the minds of policymakers. There was little spillover effect from one crop policy to another. Our approach seemed particularly appropriate because of the land surplus in Thailand, which veiled the opportunity cost of supporting one crop via the lost output of another. Moreover, since rice is the principal staple, there are rather small consumption substitution effects among the three food crops treated here.

The separate policies were reflected in the separate politics of each crop. Because of the structure of the sugar industry and the concentration of cane farmers around the mills, this segment of Thailand's agricultural sector has become organized into two main pressure groups: growers and millers. Although ostensibly adversarial, the two groups have been effective in using the threat of conflict between them to wring concessions from the government. In turn, the government has passed along the burden of these concessions (mostly to the domestic consumer) because concentration in the sugar industry has made the administration of a home-price scheme feasible.

Such a scheme cannot be envisaged for the other three crops. The processing and handling of these other crops have not spawned extra-bureaucratic organizations that exert independent pressure on government behavior. Consequently, their politics have remained internal to the bureaucracy. This has been particularly true for rice. Because rice is important to the economy and the legal framework that guides policymaking has become increasingly complex, decisionmaking has become diffused among different ministers. By the end of the study period, interdepartmental horse-trading had become the norm, and the resources available in the contending departments had begun to shape policy. With maize and rubber, decisionmaking powers have remained more concentrated—in the Ministries of Commerce and Finance, respectively—and this has made for somewhat greater stability in policies.

For all farm crops except sugar, the organizations representing growers have been fairly weak, and therefore they have been unable to build up much pressure for a price. But when an elected parliamentary system has been in operation, as has generally been the case since 1973, the members of Parliament have pressed actively for measures to help farmers in their districts. Significantly, the members have seldom campaigned to eliminate export taxes, which would have benefited farmers growing those crops. Instead, they usually have preferred to have the government engage in support operations in their districts, because that was the best way for them to obtain patronage money.

More powerful than the farmers as political pressure groups have been the exporters. Paradoxically, they have been powerful precisely because most government measures have occurred at the point of export. Before introducing trade measures, bureaucrats and ministers have found it prudent to consult exporters on various technical aspects of the intervention. This naturally has given the latter an entrée to the policymaking process that no farmer could aspire to achieve. This entrée has been particularly valuable for the exporters in that inside information has allowed them to obtain large speculative profits on their trading.

Much of the debate surrounding price intervention took place at the time a specific measure was to be implemented. Did the consequences of a particular intervention have an impact on the policies? Probably not. The Thai government was driven mostly by a desire to influence prices directly, generally with an awareness that tampering with prices would affect farmers' incentives to produce. The government probably was less sensitive to the incentive effect in the case of rice, but then the actual elasticity of supply for rice was small. In any case, even if less rice was produced as a consequence of the government's extractive policies, the government was not penalized in any way. For importing countries, a shortfall in domestic production of the staple cereal would imply many hard decisions about the allocation of foreign exchange to food imports. But in Thailand in most years, the government has considered surplus rice a nuisance because it has had to make an effort to sell the rice in the world market.

For sugar, where the policies have been designed to boost rather than to depress prices, the government again has been fully aware that Thailand is overproducing a commodity for which the world will pay only a low price. Despite the sometimes severe problems involved in administering its sugar policy, the government has been unable to resist political pressure to continue its support of the industry.

If we define *liberalization* as action taken with the knowledge that trade distortions have become counterproductive and that therefore reducing them would improve economic welfare, only the dismantling of the barriers to maize trade and the sharp reduction in export duties on rubber in the early 1980s can be construed as liberalization measures. The same cannot be said for the dismantling of the rice trade barriers that occurred at about the same time. Rather, it was a response to sharply deteriorating world market conditions and was in step with the government's traditional practice of adjusting the level of export barriers to stabilize domestic prices.

This brings us to one of the main problems in analyzing the liberalization of agricultural goods as distinct from the liberalization of industrial goods: world markets are much more volatile for the former than for the latter. Agricultural price policies therefore must gyrate in response. Consequently, not much learning can take place, because the experience of any given year is almost unique. Only when the average distortion has become very large, as it did for rubber in the early 1980s, has there been a movement toward correction.

If, however, we look at the attitudes of Thai governments toward the agricultural sector as a whole rather than toward liberalization per se, then clearly there has been a discernible change. Transfers out of agriculture to the rest of the economy have by and large declined (allowing for fluctuating world prices), not only because of the reduction in trade barriers but also because of the infusion of more and more government funds and the growth of subsectors such as the sugar industry, whose organization has allowed it to draw in resources from the rest of the economy. Here, quantitative results are in line with prevailing political rhetoric, which increasingly has emphasized rural development. We would like to stress, however, that this shift in political attitudes is an autonomous event and is not a response to the effects of previous policies.

The beneficial effect of the increasing infusion of resources into agriculture has been offset by a much more lax fiscal policy that began in the mid-1970s. The tax system in Thailand, which has proved rather difficult to reform, has left government revenues stuck at about 14 to 15 percent of GDP, whereas expenditure needs have been inching up toward 18–19 percent. Large public sector deficits became the norm in the late 1970s, with inevitable consequences for the balance of payments. This led to an increase in the overvaluation of the baht, from 14 percent during the 1960s to about 25 percent in the 1980s. The overvaluation implied a transfer out of the agricultural sector.

There were many reasons for the profligate macroeconomic policies of the late 1970s and early 1980s. First came the second oil price increase and the ready availability of petrodollars to finance a postponement of needed adjustments. Second, sharp political conflicts in Southeast Asia in the mid-1970s led to a heavy increase in Thailand's military expenditures, financed again by foreign loans. Third, in the early 1980s an erroneous decision was made to keep the baht linked to the dollar even though the latter was appreciating rapidly. This was another case in which the ready availability of foreign funds made possible an unwise decision. It is highly probable that real wages (and urban incomes in general) thereby remained at an unsustainably high level, although the lack of adequate research on wage behavior means that this conclusion is far from certain. But this artificial maintenance of urban wages (if it took place) implies that the agricultural sector was again penalized. There was no clear voice from within the agricultural sector on these macroeconomic policy moves, not even in 1981 and 1984, when devaluations of the baht should have established the link between macroeconomic policies and agricultural incomes in people's minds. The second devaluation, which appears to have achieved its mostly macroeconomic objectives, took place against the backdrop of a rapid decline in agricultural prices worldwide, so that the beneficial effect of the devaluation on agriculture was not readily apparent and did not gain the sector's political support.

Appendix Table 7-8. Short-run Effect of Price Intervention on the Output of Rice, 1960–84
(tons)

Year	Actual production	Direct effect		Total effect (1)		Total effect (2)	
		Production without intervention	Proportionate difference	Production without intervention	Proportionate difference	Production without intervention	Proportionate difference
1960	7,873,140	n.a.	n.a.	n.a.	n.a.	n.a.	n.a.
1961	9,111,499	10,660,008	-0.1453	n.a.	n.a.	n.a.	n.a.
1962	9,509,565	11,102,273	-0.1435	n.a.	n.a.	n.a.	n.a.
1963	9,882,705	11,194,271	-0.1172	11,589,120	-0.1472	11,693,203	-0.1548
1964	10,650,699	12,234,050	-0.1294	12,588,974	-0.1540	12,831,009	-0.1699
1965	10,976,792	12,913,538	-0.1500	13,226,833	-0.1701	13,303,530	-0.1749
1966	10,718,698	12,475,483	-0.1408	12,837,463	-0.1650	12,884,091	-0.1681
1967	13,895,361	15,375,099	-0.0962	15,892,114	-0.1256	15,981,338	-0.1305
1968	11,192,024	12,483,899	-0.1035	12,818,640	-0.1269	12,922,632	-0.1339
1969	12,033,958	13,792,266	-0.1275	14,226,141	-0.1541	14,519,271	-0.1712
1970	13,462,690	14,724,129	-0.0857	15,283,124	-0.1191	15,675,579	-0.1412
1971	13,856,000	14,802,683	-0.0640	15,329,523	-0.0961	15,797,138	-0.1229
1972	14,236,196	15,478,515	-0.0803	16,111,142	-0.1164	16,429,645	-0.1335
1973	12,412,674	13,504,467	-0.0808	13,958,699	-0.1108	14,027,386	-0.1151
1974	14,760,521	16,889,692	-0.1261	17,283,642	-0.1460	17,341,112	-0.1488
1975	13,818,788	16,237,847	-0.1490	16,362,891	-0.1555	16,428,701	-0.1589
1976	15,558,872	17,053,383	-0.0876	17,328,593	-0.1021	17,780,646	-0.1250
1977	15,482,101	16,105,085	-0.0387	16,456,223	-0.0592	16,716,178	-0.0738
1978	13,997,331	14,783,211	-0.0532	15,162,827	-0.0769	15,609,500	-0.1033
1979	17,039,587	18,455,741	-0.0767	18,868,644	-0.0969	19,331,851	-0.1186
1980	15,790,538	16,677,758	-0.0532	17,019,820	-0.0722	17,576,698	-0.1016
1981	17,368,094	18,494,002	-0.0609	18,763,214	-0.0744	19,265,139	-0.0985
1982	17,774,323	18,907,075	-0.0599	19,207,973	-0.0746	19,800,467	-0.1023
1983	16,878,516	17,312,765	-0.0251	17,671,097	-0.0449	17,909,225	-0.0576
1984	19,548,943	19,892,158	-0.0173	20,341,054	-0.0389	21,003,149	-0.0692

n.a. Not available.
Source: Siamwalla and Setboonsarng (1989), Appendix Table A-16.

268

Appendix Table 7-9. Short-run Effect of Price Intervention on the Output of Maize, 1960–85
(tons)

Year	Actual production	Direct effect		Total effect (1)		Total effect (2)	
		Production without intervention	Proportionate difference	Production without intervention	Proportionate difference	Production without intervention	Proportionate difference
1960/61	543,900	n.a.	n.a.	n.a.	n.a.	n.a.	n.a.
1961/62	598,276	n.a.	n.a.	n.a.	n.a.	n.a.	n.a.
1962/63	727,892	n.a.	n.a.	n.a.	n.a.	n.a.	n.a.
1963/64	932,328	n.a.	n.a.	n.a.	n.a.	n.a.	n.a.
1964/65	912,385	n.a.	n.a.	n.a.	n.a.	n.a.	n.a.
1965/66	1,159,594	n.a.	n.a.	n.a.	n.a.	n.a.	n.a.
1966/67	1,225,829	n.a.	n.a.	n.a.	n.a.	n.a.	n.a.
1967/68	1,298,739	n.a.	n.a.	n.a.	n.a.	n.a.	n.a.
1968/69	1,416,550	1,518,982	−0.0674	1,694,165	−0.1639	1,751,582	−0.1913
1969/70	1,713,500	1,829,061	−0.0632	2,069,270	−0.1719	2,244,425	−0.2366
1970/71	1,938,160	1,973,476	−0.0179	2,276,485	−0.1486	2,508,854	−0.2275
1971/72	2,300,000	2,367,477	−0.0285	2,691,926	−0.1456	3,005,988	−0.2349
1972/73	1,315,000	1,362,882	−0.0351	1,568,007	−0.1614	1,679,208	−0.2169
1973/74	2,339,000	2,216,108	0.0555	2,472,957	−0.0542	2,513,525	−0.0694
1974/75	2,500,000	2,715,600	−0.0794	2,917,842	−0.1432	2,948,175	−0.1520
1975/76	2,863,168	2,917,846	−0.0187	2,983,486	−0.0403	3,018,417	−0.0514
1976/77	2,675,195	2,792,720	−0.0421	2,914,527	−0.0821	3,121,712	−0.1430
1977/78	1,676,518	1,707,726	−0.0183	1,798,960	−0.0681	1,868,300	−0.1027
1978/79	2,790,575	2,786,280	0.0015	2,941,366	−0.0513	3,129,580	−0.1083
1979/80	2,863,201	2,888,840	−0.0089	3,008,433	−0.0483	3,145,216	−0.0897
1980/81	2,997,882	3,040,635	−0.0141	3,134,659	−0.0436	3,289,756	−0.0887
1981/82	3,448,538	3,506,960	−0.0167	3,596,155	−0.0410	3,741,414	−0.0783
1982/83	3,002,304	3,085,706	−0.0270	3,170,528	−0.0531	3,318,352	−0.0952
1983/84	3,552,391	3,552,391	0.0000	3,667,954	−0.0315	3,742,345	−0.0508
1984/85	4,225,572	4,225,572	0.0000	4,373,451	−0.0338	4,588,712	−0.0791

n.a. Not available.
Source: Siamwalla and Setboonsarng (1989), Appendix Table A-17.

Appendix Table 7-10. Short-run Effect of Price Intervention on the Output of Rubber, 1960–84
(tons)

Year	Actual production	Direct effect		Total effect (1)		Total effect (2)	
		Production without intervention	Proportionate difference	Production without intervention	Proportionate difference	Production without intervention	Proportionate difference
1960	170,800	n.a.	n.a.	n.a.	n.a.	n.a.	n.a.
1961	186,100	189,513	-0.0180	n.a.	n.a.	n.a.	n.a.
1962	195,400	201,471	-0.0301	n.a.	n.a.	n.a.	n.a.
1963	198,300	203,575	-0.0259	207,425	-0.0440	208,430	-0.0486
1964	210,600	216,182	-0.0258	219,645	-0.0412	221,981	-0.0513
1965	217,400	221,934	-0.0204	224,995	-0.0338	225,739	-0.0369
1966	218,100	223,711	-0.0251	227,507	-0.0413	227,992	-0.0434
1967	219,300	224,503	-0.0232	229,049	-0.0426	229,827	-0.0458
1968	257,800	262,893	-0.0194	267,277	-0.0355	268,630	-0.0403
1969	281,800	283,260	-0.0052	288,978	-0.0248	292,805	-0.0376
1970	287,200	294,927	-0.0262	302,345	-0.0501	307,499	-0.0660
1971	316,300	325,943	-0.0296	333,900	-0.0527	340,892	-0.0721
1972	336,900	342,865	-0.0174	352,817	-0.0451	357,785	-0.0584
1973	367,700	373,643	-0.0159	382,912	-0.0397	384,307	-0.0432
1974	382,100	390,547	-0.0216	397,536	-0.0388	398,552	-0.0413
1975	348,700	366,073	-0.0475	368,327	-0.0533	369,512	-0.0563
1976	393,000	405,522	-0.0309	410,968	-0.0437	419,883	-0.0640
1977	431,000	447,668	-0.0372	456,144	-0.0551	462,403	-0.0679
1978	467,000	494,455	-0.0555	505,985	-0.0770	519,517	-0.1011
1979	534,300	559,670	-0.0453	571,589	-0.0652	584,945	-0.0866
1980	465,200	491,275	-0.0531	501,351	-0.0721	517,755	-0.1015
1981	507,700	546,648	-0.0712	555,878	-0.0867	570,748	-0.1105
1982	576,000	610,508	-0.0565	621,646	-0.0734	640,821	-0.1012
1983	593,900	611,453	-0.0287	624,643	-0.0492	633,060	-0.0619
1984	617,200	642,129	-0.0388	657,025	-0.0606	678,411	-0.0902

n.a. Not available.
Source: Siamwalla and Setboonsarng (1989), Appendix Table A-18.

Appendix Table 7-11. Cumulative Effect of Price Intervention on the Output of Rice, 1960–84

(tons)

| | Direct effect | | | Total effect (1) | | Total effect (2) | |
Year	Actual production	Production without intervention	Proportionate difference	Production without intervention	Proportionate difference	Production without intervention	Proportionate difference
1960	7,873,140	n.a.	n.a.	n.a.	n.a.	n.a.	n.a.
1961	9,111,499	n.a.	n.a.	n.a.	n.a.	n.a.	n.a.
1962	9,509,565	n.a.	n.a.	n.a.	n.a.	n.a.	n.a.
1963	9,882,705	n.a.	n.a.	n.a.	n.a.	n.a.	n.a.
1964	10,650,699	n.a.	n.a.	n.a.	n.a.	n.a.	n.a.
1965	10,976,792	14,328,975	−0.2339	n.a.	n.a.	n.a.	n.a.
1966	10,718,698	14,103,184	−0.2400	n.a.	n.a.	n.a.	n.a.
1967	13,895,361	17,017,570	−0.1835	17,954,719	−0.2261	18,083,273	−0.2316
1968	11,192,024	14,004,017	−0.2008	14,857,012	−0.2467	14,997,579	−0.2537
1969	12,033,958	15,148,783	−0.2056	16,057,021	−0.2505	16,343,042	−0.2637
1970	13,462,690	16,221,018	−0.1700	17,263,991	−0.2202	17,696,159	−0.2392
1971	13,856,000	16,126,948	−0.1408	17,077,431	−0.1886	17,636,782	−0.2144
1972	14,236,196	16,567,747	−0.1407	17,804,209	−0.2004	18,321,883	−0.2230
1973	12,412,674	14,629,871	−0.1516	15,844,718	−0.2166	16,153,899	−0.2316
1974	14,760,521	17,943,344	−0.1774	19,147,934	−0.2291	19,340,202	−0.2368
1975	13,818,788	17,789,838	−0.2232	18,568,443	−0.2558	18,703,167	−0.2612
1976	15,558,872	19,009,324	−0.1815	19,646,517	−0.2081	20,019,644	−0.2228
1977	15,482,101	17,791,488	−0.1298	18,401,771	−0.1587	18,760,298	−0.1747
1978	13,997,331	15,903,787	−0.1199	16,516,035	−0.1525	16,995,338	−0.1764
1979	17,039,587	19,342,432	−0.1191	19,995,064	−0.1478	20,549,439	−0.1708
1980	15,790,538	17,753,585	−0.1106	18,372,734	−0.1405	19,021,203	−0.1698
1981	17,368,094	19,428,822	−0.1061	20,119,736	−0.1368	20,795,991	−0.1648
1982	17,774,323	19,917,971	−0.1076	20,683,745	−0.1407	21,445,972	−0.1712
1983	16,878,516	18,360,030	−0.0807	19,118,198	−0.1171	19,662,924	−0.1416
1984	19,548,943	20,588,660	−0.0505	21,447,597	−0.0885	22,188,943	−0.1190

n.a. Not available.

Source: Siamwalla and Setboonsarng (1989), Appendix Table A-19.

271

Appendix Table 7-12. Cumulative Effect of Price Intervention on the Output of Maize, 1960–85
(tons)

Year	Actual production	Direct effect		Total effect (1)		Total effect (2)	
		Production without intervention	Proportionate difference	Production without intervention	Proportionate difference	Production without intervention	Proportionate difference
1960/61	543,900	n.a.	n.a.	n.a.	n.a.	n.a.	n.a.
1961/62	598,276	n.a.	n.a.	n.a.	n.a.	n.a.	n.a.
1962/63	727,892	n.a.	n.a.	n.a.	n.a.	n.a.	n.a.
1963/64	932,328	n.a.	n.a.	n.a.	n.a.	n.a.	n.a.
1964/65	912,385	n.a.	n.a.	n.a.	n.a.	n.a.	n.a.
1965/66	1,159,594	n.a.	n.a.	n.a.	n.a.	n.a.	n.a.
1966/67	1,225,829	n.a.	n.a.	n.a.	n.a.	n.a.	n.a.
1967/68	1,298,739	n.a.	n.a.	n.a.	n.a.	n.a.	n.a.
1968/69	1,416,550	n.a.	n.a.	n.a.	n.a.	n.a.	n.a.
1969/70	1,713,500	n.a.	n.a.	n.a.	n.a.	n.a.	n.a.
1970/71	1,938,160	n.a.	n.a.	n.a.	n.a.	n.a.	n.a.
1971/72	2,300,000	n.a.	n.a.	n.a.	n.a.	n.a.	n.a.
1972/73	1,315,000	1,394,843	−0.0572	1,814,024	−0.2751	2,001,093	−0.3429
1973/74	2,339,000	2,242,301	0.0431	2,730,111	−0.1433	2,824,236	−0.1718
1974/75	2,500,000	2,682,892	−0.0682	3,163,161	−0.2097	3,218,144	−0.2232
1975/76	2,863,168	2,978,665	−0.0388	3,240,233	−0.1164	3,283,342	−0.1280
1976/77	2,675,195	2,830,942	−0.0550	3,032,467	−0.1178	3,189,833	−0.1613
1977/78	1,676,518	1,759,444	−0.0471	1,907,552	−0.1211	2,007,220	−0.1648
1978/79	2,790,575	2,814,427	−0.0085	2,995,330	−0.0684	3,154,361	−0.1153
1979/80	2,863,201	2,895,904	−0.0113	3,060,688	−0.0645	3,206,455	−0.1071
1980/81	2,997,882	3,051,311	−0.0175	3,187,931	−0.0596	3,339,831	−0.1024
1981/82	3,448,538	3,524,286	−0.0215	3,693,187	−0.0662	3,848,105	−0.1038
1982/83	3,002,304	3,110,827	−0.0349	3,283,678	−0.0857	3,442,464	−0.1279
1983/84	3,552,391	3,588,583	−0.0101	3,769,669	−0.0576	3,876,129	−0.0835
1984/85	4,225,572	4,237,531	−0.0028	4,459,013	−0.0524	4,649,620	−0.0912

n.a. Not available.
Source: Siamwalla and Setboonsarng (1989), Appendix Table A-20.

Appendix Table 7-13. Cumulative Effect of Price Intervention on the Output of Rubber, 1960–84
(tons)

Year	Actual production	Direct effect		Total effect (1)		Total effect (2)	
		Production without intervention	Proportionate difference	Production without intervention	Proportionate difference	Production without intervention	Proportionate difference
1960	170,800	n.a.	n.a.	n.a.	n.a.	n.a.	n.a.
1961	186,100	n.a.	n.a.	n.a.	n.a.	n.a.	n.a.
1962	195,400	n.a.	n.a.	n.a.	n.a.	n.a.	n.a.
1963	198,300	n.a.	n.a.	n.a.	n.a.	n.a.	n.a.
1964	210,600	n.a.	n.a.	n.a.	n.a.	n.a.	n.a.
1965	217,400	240,529	-0.0962	n.a.	n.a.	n.a.	n.a.
1966	218,100	242,160	-0.0994	n.a.	n.a.	n.a.	n.a.
1967	219,300	243,415	-0.0991	259,980	-0.1565	262,937	-0.1660
1968	257,800	282,449	-0.0873	299,934	-0.1405	303,150	-0.1496
1969	281,800	305,943	-0.0789	325,719	-0.1348	330,563	-0.1475
1970	287,200	315,483	-0.0897	338,846	-0.1524	346,617	-0.1714
1971	316,300	346,559	-0.0873	373,070	-0.1522	384,804	-0.1780
1972	336,900	367,692	-0.0837	400,559	-0.1589	414,195	-0.1866
1973	367,700	399,864	-0.0804	438,289	-0.1611	450,681	-0.1841
1974	382,100	421,652	-0.0938	462,740	-0.1743	472,842	-0.1919
1975	348,700	392,807	-0.1123	427,977	-0.1852	435,698	-0.1997
1976	393,000	441,385	-0.1096	472,968	-0.1691	483,405	-0.1870
1977	431,000	489,819	-0.1201	518,877	-0.1694	530,448	-0.1875
1978	467,000	537,884	-0.1318	566,796	-0.1761	585,383	-0.2022
1979	534,300	616,891	-0.1339	647,169	-0.1744	672,052	-0.2050
1980	465,200	556,376	-0.1639	589,730	-0.2112	621,878	-0.2519
1981	507,700	611,283	-0.1695	650,268	-0.2192	685,639	-0.2595
1982	576,000	680,342	-0.1534	725,441	-0.2060	767,646	-0.2497
1983	593,900	689,465	-0.1386	737,874	-0.1951	776,120	-0.2348
1984	617,200	711,093	-0.1320	764,123	-0.1923	808,255	-0.2364

n.a. Not available.
Source: Siamwalla and Setboonsarng (1989), Appendix Table A-21.

Appendix Table 7-14. Short-run Effect of Price Intervention on the Output of Sugar, 1960–84

(tons)

		Direct effect		Total effect (1)		Total effect (2)	
Year	Actual production	Production without intervention	Proportionate difference	Production without intervention	Proportionate difference	Production without intervention	Proportionate difference
1960	428,968	n.a.	n.a.	n.a.	n.a.	n.a.	n.a.
1961	462,852	n.a.	n.a.	n.a.	n.a.	n.a.	n.a.
1962	342,582	n.a.	n.a.	n.a.	n.a.	n.a.	n.a.
1963	271,244	n.a.	n.a.	n.a.	n.a.	n.a.	n.a.
1964	407,033	n.a.	n.a.	n.a.	n.a.	n.a.	n.a.
1965	436,364	n.a.	n.a.	n.a.	n.a.	n.a.	n.a.
1966	385,241	n.a.	n.a.	n.a.	n.a.	n.a.	n.a.
1967	329,280	212,912	0.5466	233,871	0.4080	237,724	0.3851
1968	204,631	132,686	0.5422	146,148	0.4002	149,116	0.3723
1969	378,320	278,082	0.3605	308,467	0.2265	321,899	0.1753
1970	438,795	362,476	0.2105	406,335	0.0799	434,418	0.0101
1971	566,384	193,516	1.9268	219,559	1.5796	241,348	1.3468
1972	509,599	217,227	1.3459	250,590	1.0336	274,817	0.8543
1973	818,100	429,814	0.9034	494,443	0.6546	527,581	0.5507
1974	1,087,076	656,394	0.6561	744,467	0.4602	770,585	0.4107
1975	1,153,556	989,306	0.1660	1,074,603	0.0735	1,093,217	0.0552
1976	1,642,520	1,579,464	0.0399	1,691,159	−0.0288	1,789,260	−0.0820
1977	2,244,123	1,887,241	0.1891	2,030,081	0.1054	2,177,868	0.0304
1978	1,628,944	1,082,916	0.5042	1,200,462	0.3569	1,347,127	0.2092
1979	1,768,205	862,193	1.0508	966,931	0.8287	1,086,026	0.6281
1980	1,103,093	519,192	1.1246	583,497	0.8905	678,998	0.6246
1981	1,707,415	848,309	1.0127	941,736	0.8131	1,092,409	0.5630
1982	2,597,200	1,308,326	0.9851	1,446,354	0.7957	1,701,624	0.5263
1983	2,099,037	917,536	1.2877	1,017,879	1.0622	1,150,408	0.8246
1984	2,052,775	759,507	1.7028	851,901	1.4096	981,712	1.0910

n.a. Not available.

Source: Siamwalla and Setboonsarng (1989), Appendix Table A-22.

Appendix Table 7-15. **Cumulative Effect of Price Intervention on the Output of Sugar, 1960–84**
(tons)

Year	Actual production	Direct effect		Total effect (1)		Total effect (2)	
		Production without intervention	Proportionate difference	Production without intervention	Proportionate difference	Production without intervention	Proportionate difference
1960	428,968	n.a.	n.a.	n.a.	n.a.	n.a.	n.a.
1961	462,852	n.a.	n.a.	n.a.	n.a.	n.a.	n.a.
1962	342,582	n.a.	n.a.	n.a.	n.a.	n.a.	n.a.
1963	271,244	n.a.	n.a.	n.a.	n.a.	n.a.	n.a.
1964	407,033	n.a.	n.a.	n.a.	n.a.	n.a.	n.a.
1965	436,364	n.a.	n.a.	n.a.	n.a.	n.a.	n.a.
1966	385,241	n.a.	n.a.	n.a.	n.a.	n.a.	n.a.
1967	329,280	212,912	0.5466	236,618	0.3916	239,587	0.3744
1968	204,631	130,989	0.5622	148,264	0.3802	151,367	0.3519
1969	378,320	250,701	0.5091	294,779	0.2834	307,979	0.2284
1970	438,795	208,821	1.1013	256,046	0.7137	273,859	0.8023
1971	566,384	108,455	4.2223	138,147	3.0999	153,002	2.7018
1972	509,599	117,725	3.3287	156,543	2.2553	175,330	1.9065
1973	818,100	262,044	2.1220	360,337	1.2704	401,450	1.0379
1974	1,087,076	365,663	1.9729	513,549	1.1168	560,385	0.9399
1975	1,153,556	544,035	1.1204	739,668	0.5596	796,864	0.4476
1976	1,642,520	965,939	0.7004	1,273,973	0.2893	1,397,966	0.1749
1977	2,244,123	1,301,036	0.7249	1,687,597	0.3298	1,874,358	0.1973
1978	1,628,944	758,412	1.1478	1,003,206	0.6237	1,153,216	0.4125
1979	1,768,205	636,731	1.7770	846,431	1.0890	989,659	0.7867
1980	1,103,093	350,380	2.1483	465,426	1.3701	563,287	0.9583
1981	1,707,415	554,557	2.0789	737,711	1.3145	905,142	0.8864
1982	2,597,200	709,473	2.6607	956,447	1.7155	1,197,290	1.1692
1983	2,099,037	497,968	3.2152	677,865	2.0965	835,727	1.5116
1984	2,052,775	391,123	4.2484	537,513	2.8190	675,847	2.0373

n.a. Not available.
Source: Siamwalla and Setboonsarng (1989), Appendix Table A-23.

Appendix Table 7-16. Effect of Price Intervention on the Consumption of Rice, 1960–84

(tons)

Year	Actual consumption	Direct effect		Total effect (1)		Total effect (2)	
		Consumption without intervention	Proportionate difference	Consumption without intervention	Proportionate difference	Consumption without intervention	Proportionate difference
1960	6,050,758	n.a.	n.a.	n.a.	n.a.	n.a.	n.a.
1961	6,723,623	6,406,616	0.0495	n.a.	n.a.	n.a.	n.a.
1962	7,583,773	7,221,843	0.0501	n.a.	n.a.	n.a.	n.a.
1963	7,734,716	7,428,343	0.0412	7,345,297	0.0530	7,324,028	0.0561
1964	7,777,581	7,426,437	0.0473	7,355,979	0.0573	7,309,432	0.0640
1965	8,105,242	7,666,032	0.0573	7,603,285	0.0660	7,588,227	0.0681
1966	8,434,531	7,994,600	0.0550	7,914,301	0.0657	7,904,180	0.0671
1967	11,649,494	11,228,609	0.0375	11,094,373	0.0500	11,071,809	0.0522
1968	9,573,562	9,189,311	0.0418	9,098,579	0.0522	9,071,052	0.0554
1969	10,483,861	9,944,767	0.0542	9,826,245	0.0669	9,748,972	0.0754
1970	11,851,151	11,434,085	0.0365	11,264,927	0.0520	11,151,257	0.0628
1971	11,444,812	11,136,065	0.0277	10,976,072	0.0427	10,840,444	0.0558
1972	11,034,964	10,646,299	0.0365	10,465,085	0.0545	10,377,652	0.0633
1973	11,126,739	10,717,559	0.0382	10,561,128	0.0536	10,538,113	0.0559
1974	13,221,703	12,424,478	0.0642	12,292,961	0.0756	12,274,141	0.0772
1975	12,377,486	11,455,245	0.0805	11,413,142	0.0845	11,391,174	0.0866
1976	12,568,886	12,005,509	0.0469	11,909,792	0.0553	11,757,421	0.0690
1977	11,017,807	10,793,347	0.0208	10,672,568	0.0323	10,585,650	0.0408
1978	11,562,858	11,223,417	0.0302	11,069,267	0.0446	10,895,354	0.0613
1979	12,801,907	12,230,997	0.0467	12,077,328	0.0600	11,911,108	0.0748
1980	11,552,244	11,179,488	0.0333	11,044,131	0.0460	10,832,835	0.0664
1981	12,774,180	12,301,719	0.0384	12,195,511	0.0474	12,003,864	0.0642
1982	12,040,773	11,602,607	0.0378	11,493,208	0.0476	11,285,608	0.0669
1983	11,611,122	11,435,493	0.0154	11,295,791	0.0279	11,205,434	0.0362
1984	12,551,181	12,420,796	0.0105	12,255,597	0.0241	12,022,309	0.0440

n.a. Not available.

Note: The consumption without intervention (C_1) is computed from actual consumption (C_0) from $C_1 = C_0(PB/PD)^{-E}$ where PB is the border price, PD is the domestic price, and E is the elasticity of demand.

Source: Siamwalla and Setboonsarng (1989), Appendix Table A-24.

276

Appendix Table 7-17. Effect of Price Intervention on the Consumption of Maize, 1960–85
(tons)

Year	Actual consumption	Direct effect		Total effect (1)		Total effect (2)	
		Consumption without intervention	Proportionate difference	Consumption without intervention	Proportionate difference	Consumption without intervention	Proportionate difference
1960/61	24,969	n.a.	n.a.	n.a.	n.a.	n.a.	n.a.
1961/62	3,475	n.a.	n.a.	n.a.	n.a.	n.a.	n.a.
1962/63	5,816	n.a.	n.a.	n.a.	n.a.	n.a.	n.a.
1963/64	9,735	n.a.	n.a.	n.a.	n.a.	n.a.	n.a.
1964/65	16,295	n.a.	n.a.	n.a.	n.a.	n.a.	n.a.
1965/66	27,275	n.a.	n.a.	n.a.	n.a.	n.a.	n.a.
1966/67	45,652	n.a.	n.a.	n.a.	n.a.	n.a.	n.a.
1967/68	76,412	n.a.	n.a.	n.a.	n.a.	n.a.	n.a.
1968/69	127,898	125,552	0.0187	121,971	0.0486	120,897	0.0579
1969/70	210,600	206,741	0.0187	199,636	0.0549	195,091	0.0795
1970/71	261,062	259,631	0.0055	248,586	0.0502	241,341	0.0817
1971/72	201,316	199,412	0.0095	191,170	0.0531	184,362	0.0920
1972/73	253,280	250,065	0.0129	237,852	0.0649	232,103	0.0912
1973/74	147,698	150,848	−0.0209	144,516	0.0220	143,599	0.0285
1974/75	530,672	512,039	0.0364	496,390	0.0691	494,177	0.0739
1975/76	521,468	516,728	0.0092	511,208	0.0201	508,343	0.0258
1976/77	532,815	520,433	0.0238	508,424	0.0480	489,683	0.0881
1977/78	367,465	363,216	0.0117	351,488	0.0455	343,204	0.0707
1978/79	617,166	617,874	−0.0011	593,447	0.0400	566,660	0.0891
1979/80	721,038	715,218	0.0081	689,324	0.0460	662,016	0.0892
1980/81	856,872	842,832	0.0167	813,413	0.0534	768,850	0.1145
1981/82	238,387	233,760	0.0198	227,010	0.0501	216,761	0.0998
1982/83	844,664	818,089	0.0325	792,612	0.0657	751,574	0.1239
1983/84	679,430	679,430	0.0000	654,522	0.0381	639,368	0.0627
1984/85	1,162,260	1,162,260	0.0000	1,116,541	0.0409	1,055,676	0.1010

n.a. Not available.

Note: The consumption without intervention (C_1) is computed from actual consumption (C_0) from $C_1 = C_0(PB/PD)^{-E}$ where PB is the border price, PD is the domestic price, and E is the elasticity of demand.

Source: Siamwalla and Setboonsarng (1989), Appendix Table A-25.

Appendix Table 7-18. Effect of Price Intervention on the Consumption of Sugar, 1960–84
(tons)

Year	Actual consumption	Direct effect		Total effect (1)		Total effect (2)	
		Consumption without intervention	Proportionate difference	Consumption without intervention	Proportionate difference	Consumption without intervention	Proportionate difference
1960	423,245	n.a.	n.a.	n.a.	n.a.	n.a.	n.a.
1961	461,315	n.a.	n.a.	n.a.	n.a.	n.a.	n.a.
1962	299,563	n.a.	n.a.	n.a.	n.a.	n.a.	n.a.
1963	218,421	636,552	−0.6569	585,079	−0.6267	572,492	−0.6185
1964	358,125	623,069	−0.4252	580,077	−0.3826	553,108	−0.3525
1965	352,530	536,773	−0.3432	504,685	−0.3015	497,237	−0.2910
1966	330,383	656,593	−0.4968	608,717	−0.4572	602,903	−0.4520
1967	314,267	546,031	−0.4245	498,935	−0.3701	491,374	−0.3604
1968	204,579	312,226	−0.3448	289,834	−0.2942	283,322	−0.2779
1969	362,218	664,361	−0.4548	607,227	−0.4035	572,315	−0.3671
1970	382,547	552,017	−0.3070	493,633	−0.2250	457,478	−0.1638
1971	391,813	627,037	−0.3751	562,545	−0.3035	512,458	−0.2354
1972	102,098	156,998	−0.3497	138,031	−0.2603	129,613	−0.2123
1973	542,695	682,676	−0.2050	611,396	−0.1124	601,474	−0.0977
1974	643,229	616,875	0.0427	569,554	0.1294	563,047	0.1424
1975	558,122	301,478	0.8513	293,267	0.9031	289,059	0.9308
1976	518,546	236,863	1.1892	223,061	1.3247	202,527	1.5604
1977	590,724	515,789	0.1453	474,043	0.2461	445,843	0.3250
1978	588,895	601,791	−0.0214	542,499	0.0855	481,745	0.2224
1979	578,387	740,029	−0.2184	673,079	−0.1407	606,633	−0.0466
1980	651,397	875,537	−0.2560	799,092	−0.1848	691,315	−0.0577
1981	588,776	876,364	−0.3282	812,759	−0.2756	721,721	−0.1842
1982	390,960	440,203	−0.1119	405,809	−0.0366	353,956	0.1045
1983	562,146	970,910	−0.4210	882,002	−0.3626	830,443	−0.3231
1984	810,816	1,983,930	−0.5913	1,789,411	−0.5469	1,549,211	−0.4766

n.a. Not available.

Note: The consumption without intervention (C_1) is computed from actual consumption (C_0) from $C_1 = C_0(PB/PD)^{-E}$ where PB is the border price, PD is the domestic price, and E is the elasticity of demand.

Source: Siamwalla and Setboonsarng (1989), Appendix Table A-26.

Notes

1. We are here slurring over the fact that eliminating the various export taxes will affect the border price somewhat, because Thailand is not a small country as far as the world rice market is concerned. But the point here is that the Thai government's primary objective is to stabilize the domestic price of rice.

We have also calculated the variance of the logarithms of the domestic and border prices as measures of the instability of the two price series. We found that for the subperiods 1966–74 and 1975–84 the instability of the domestic price was less than one-fourth that of the border price (see Siamwalla and Setboonsarng 1989, Table 2-8).

2. In the older method, the cane was crushed and the juice boiled to extract *muscovado*, a sweet, sticky substance that was then taken to another plant, where it was centrifuged and transformed into granulated sugar. The new method involved crushing the cane and then boiling the juices and crystallizing the sugar in a centrifuge in a single, continuous process.

3. This is not always an appropriate assumption, because a current account deficit can be covered by a capital inflow that may be sustainable in the long run. To find out how much capital inflow is sustainable requires an intertemporal macroeconomic model that would specify the optimal borrowing path given the information available at the beginning of each planning period. Such a task is well beyond the scope of the present exercise, however, and lacking such a refined model, we used the simpler method described above.

4. The estimate of the foreign exchange impact of the government intervention on rice already takes into account the effect of the policy on the level of the border price caused by Thailand's position as a larger exporter.

5. Maize does not show up as a contributor of tax revenues in Table 7-6 because the only intervention engaged in by the government is quantitative restrictions, which do not generate revenue.

References

Corden, W. M. 1971. *Theory of Protection*. Oxford: Clarendon Press.

Kirakul, Krisada. 1975. "Sugar Cane Procurement in the Eastern and Western Regions of Thailand." Master's thesis, Faculty of Economics, Thammasat University, Thailand.

Kunwatanusorn, Suthep. 1983. "Supply Response of Certain Agricultural Commodities: A Survey of Knowledge." *Warasan Setthasat Thammasat*, vol. 1, no. 1 (March), pp. 189–222.

Pinthong, Chirmsak. 1984. "The Distribution of Benefits and Burden of the Rice Market Intervention by the Marketing Organization for Farmers, 1982/83" (in Thai). *Warasan Thammasat*, vol. 2 (June).

Siamwalla, Ammar. 1975. "A History of Rice Policies in Thailand." *Food Research Institute Studies*, vol. 14, no. 3.

_____. 1987. "The Farmers' Aid Fund Act of 1974: Its Genesis and Aftermath." Paper prepared for an Economic Development Institute Senior Policy Seminar held in Korea by the World Bank, November 9–13.

Siamwalla, Ammar, and Suthad Setboonsarng. 1989. *Trade, Exchange Rate, and Agricultural Pricing Policies in Thailand*. A World Bank Comparative Study. Washington, D.C.

Thanapornpan, Rungsan. 1983. "Are Thai Farmers Economic Animals? A Survey of Knowledge on Rice Supply Response" (in Thai). *Warasan Setthasat Thammasat*, vol. 1, no. 1 (March), pp. 148–88.

Trairatvorakul, Prasarn. 1984. *The Effects on Income Distribution and Nutrition of Alternative Rice Price Policies in Thailand*. International Food Policy Research Institute Research Report 46 (November). Washington, D.C.

Appendix

Anne O. Krueger
Maurice Schiff
Alberto Valdés

We provide here a summary of the principal concepts and measures used in the eighteen country studies. For the country chapters of this volume, authors selected the most relevant material from their country studies, so all chapters do not necessarily cover in the same detail all the items presented here.

The first part of the appendix discusses concepts used in measuring the impact of sector-specific and economywide policies on incentives. The second part describes concepts used for measuring the effects of these policies on output, consumption, foreign exchange, the budget, transfers between agriculture and the rest of the economy, and rural and urban income distribution. The relationship between price policy and government investment is then addressed, and in the final section price variability is discussed.

The Impact of Policies on Incentives

The agricultural sector consists of hundreds of products in most countries. To make the research manageable, authors were asked to identify key agricultural products for their studies. Authors generally covered crops that were important to trade and to domestic consumption, although they also considered the degree to which the crops chosen for analysis were representative of agriculture as a whole.

Sector-Specific Pricing Policies

Most agricultural crops are tradable, and most countries have so small a share in world trade that the prices at which they can buy or sell these commodities are given. In such cases, the border prices of the commodities examined can be used as reference prices to measure the impact of sector-specific or direct price interventions on agricultural prices. To be sure, border prices must be adjusted for transport costs and other factors to make them comparable to producer prices.

Nonetheless, it is a reasonable assumption that in most unregulated markets, producer prices would be closely related to border prices, plus or minus the margins for transport, storage, differences in quality, and handling costs.

The following analysis deals with nominal protection measures, but effective rates of protection were also computed in those countries where the required data were available.

The domestic producer price P_i of an exportable product i is given by:

$$(A-1) \qquad P_i = P_i^W E_0(1 - t_i) - C_i$$

where P_i = domestic producer price, P_i^W = foreign-currency border (f.o.b.) price, E_0 = nominal official exchange rate, t_i = export tax ($t_i > 0$) or subsidy ($t_i < 0$), and C_i = adjustment for differences in quality, location (transport), time (storage), and other margins.

If a different exchange rate E' is applied to the exports of product i, then the official exchange rate E_0 should be replaced by E' in Equation A-1.

The export tax t_i may be explicit (as in the case of Argentina), or it may be implicit, as when there is an export quota or prohibition, or when output is procured by a government agency at a price below what would have prevailed in the absence of direct intervention.

The producer price in the absence of direct intervention is given by

$$(A-2) \qquad P_i' = P_i^W E_0 - C_i'$$

where C_i' = adjustment for quality, transport, storage, and other margins, all measured under competitive conditions.

Similarly, for importables the corresponding expressions are:

$$(A-3) \qquad P_j = P_j^W E_0(1 + t_j) - C_j$$

and

$$(A-4) \qquad P_j' = P_j^W E_0 - C_j'$$

where P_j^W = foreign-currency border (c.i.f.) price, and t_j = import tariff ($t_j > 0$) or subsidy ($t_j < 0$).

We are interested in determining t_i and t_j. These are not always explicit. Data may be available on P_i and P_j, as well as on P_i^W and P_j^W, but not on the hypothetical prices P_i' and P_j'. Border prices P_i^W and P_j^W must first be adjusted for C_i' and C_j' to obtain P_i' and P_j', which are comparable to the actual producer prices P_i and P_j, in order to determine the direct protection rate.

Uncontroversial as they may appear, these adjustments between domestic prices and the relevant border prices have often not been considered in much of the literature that reports nominal rates of protection to agricultural tradables. Taxes or subsidies on agriculture are often calculated by simply comparing border prices and producer prices. Some exceptions are Beenhakker (1987), Ahmed and Rustagi (1985), and Westlake (1987). However, not all differences between $P_i(P_j)$ and $P_i^W E_0(P_j^W E_0)$ result from intervention; the differences may partly reflect actual "competitive" costs or compensating differentials.

For example, producing areas may be located far from the ports or consumption centers, so adjustments must be made for transporation costs. Also, the time of import may differ from harvest time, so storage costs must be included. Moreover, the border price of tradable products (such as powdered milk) influence the domestic price of the nontradable related products (fluid milk) and the relation between these two prices through processing margins must be considered in the calculations. Finally, in taking these factors into account, the actual marketing and distribution costs often need adjustment for products whose transportation is subsidized or whose marketing is done primarily by parastatals with costs that differ significantly from competitive margins.

The nominal protection rate NPR$_D$ for direct price policies affecting product A is given by

$$(A-5) \qquad \text{NPR}_D = \frac{P_A/P_{NA} - P_A'/P_{NA}}{P_A'/P_{NA}} = \frac{P_A - P_A'}{P_A'}$$

where P_{NA} is a price index of the nonagricultural sector.

As can be seen from Equation A-5, the impact is calculated relative to the price that would have prevailed in the absence of intervention. This is done throughout the study.

P_{NA} is not affected by direct (sector-specific) price interventions, so the direct measures of intervention related to P_A or P_A/P_{NA} are identical.

For a nontradable product, calculating the impact of price policies on its price is more difficult because we need to know the impact on both demand and supply, and for that we need to know the elasticity of those functions with respect to all their arguments. This task is much simpler when the product is a close substitute for a tradable product in production or consumption.

Economywide Policies

Relative agricultural prices P_A/P_{NA} are also affected by trade policies affecting nonagricultural products (mostly industrial goods) and by policies affecting the real exchange rate. Agriculture tends to be more tradable than the nonagricultural sector, which includes such nontradables as public and private services (retail, transportation, banking), housing, construction, and so forth. Consequently, P_A/P_{NA} will vary with the level of the real exchange rate.

The price index in the nonagricultural sector (P_{NA}) consists of P_{NAT} (price index of the tradable component of the nonagricultural sector) and P_{NAH} (price index of the nontradable component of nonagriculture), with

$$(A-6) \qquad\qquad P_{NA} = \alpha P_{NAT} + (1 - \alpha)P_{NAH}$$

where α = share of tradables in nonagriculture.

Exchange-rate policies will affect both P_A and P_{NAT} relative to P_{NAH}. Also, trade policies on nonagriculture will affect P_{NAT}.

To capture the exchange-rate effect, a simple three-sector model (exportables, importables, and nontradables) was constructed to estimate the equilibrium real exchange rate e^* in the absence of interventions, which for a given price of the nontradable sector P_{NAH} corresponds to the equilibrium nominal exchange rate E^*. E^* is defined as the exchange rate that equilibrates the current account (or leads to a current account deficit that is sustainable in the long run)[1] in the absence of tariffs and quotas on imports (t_M) and in the absence of export taxes and other export restrictions (t_x) for a given price of nontradables P_{NAH}. E^* is given by

$$(A-7) \qquad\qquad E^* = \left(\frac{\Delta Q_0 + \Delta Q_1}{\epsilon_s Q_s + \eta_D Q_D} + 1\right) E_0$$

where ΔQ_0 = nonsustainable part of the current account deficit, ΔQ_1 = current account deficit that would result from removing trade taxes t_M and t_x at exchange rate E_0, $Q_s(Q_D)$ = quantity supplied (demanded) of foreign exchange, $\epsilon_s(\eta_D)$ = elasticity of supply (demand) of foreign exchange with respect to the real exchange rate e (η_D is defined as being positive), $E^*(E_0)$ = equilibrium (actual) nominal exchange rate, which corresponds to e^* (e) for a given P_{NAH}, and ΔQ_1 is given by

$$(A-8) \qquad\qquad \Delta Q_1 = \frac{t_M}{1 + t_M} Q_D \eta_D - \frac{t_x}{1 - t_x} Q_s \epsilon_s$$

where t_M = average equivalent tariff (including effect of quotas) and t_x = average equivalent export taxes.[2]

Changes in monetary or fiscal policies will tend to be reflected in ΔQ_0, in ΔQ_1, or in E_0, and will therefore be captured by E^* in Equation A-7. The same is true of changes in terms of trade, world interest rates, and other exogenous shocks. For example, an increase in government expenditures financed through money creation will lead to an increase in ΔQ_0 if trade taxes and E_0 are unchanged. If the rate of protection, t_M, is increased, it will lead to an increase in ΔQ_1. Alternatively, the government may decide to raise E_0. Possibly, a combination of these three adjustments will occur. In any case, the change in policy will be reflected in E^*.

Similarly, an increase in the world price of importables (for example, oil) will lead to an increase in ΔQ_0, or in ΔQ_1 if tariffs and quotas are used to reduce imports, or possibly in E_0, or in a combination of the three, and it will lead to an increase in E^*.

The nonagricultural price, P_{NA}, in the absence of trade taxes, t_{NA}, on nonagricultural tradables and at the equilibrium exchange rate E^* is given by

$$(A-9) \qquad P_{NA}^* = \alpha \frac{E^*}{E_0} \frac{P_{NAT}}{1 + t_{NA}} + (1 - \alpha) P_{NAH}$$

where t_{NA} = effect of trade policies on the price of nonagricultural tradables.

t_{NA} differs from t_M becaust t_M applies to all importables, while t_{NA} applies to nonagricultural tradables (importables and exportables).

Elimination of trade taxes as well as a change from E_0 to E^* will affect P_{NAH} over time because of substitutions in production and consumption leading to a reallocation of factors of production between the tradable and nontradable sectors. However, we are interested in the effect of these policies on P_A/P_{NA} before the reallocation of resources occurs, and we therefore abstract from the effect on P_{NAH}.[3]

Indirect or economywide policies will change P_A/P_{NA} to $(E^*/E_0) P_A/P_{NA}^*$, so that the indirect effect is given by

$$(A-10) \qquad \text{NPR}_I = \frac{P_A/P_{NA} - \dfrac{E^*}{E_0} P_A/P_{NA}^*}{\dfrac{E^*}{E_0} P_A/P_{NA}^*} = \frac{1/P_{NA} - \dfrac{E^*}{E_0} /P_{NA}^*}{\dfrac{E^*}{E_0} /P_{NA}^*}$$

$$= \frac{P_{NA}^*}{P_{NA}} \frac{E_0}{E^*} - 1.$$

The indirect effect measured by NPR$_I$ is due to (a) the official exchange rate (E_0) not being at its equilibrium value E^* (in the absence of trade policies), which affects both P_A and P_{NAT}, and (b) t_{NA}, which affects P_{NAT}. As can be seen from Equation A-10, the indirect effect is independent of the specific tradable product analyzed; that is, it is the same for all tradable agricultural products and depends only on E^*/E_0, on t_{NA}, and on α. If the product is not tradable, then the indirect effect is due exclusively to the effect on P_{NA}.

The sum of the direct and the indirect effects, or the total effect, on P_A/P_{NA} is given by

(A-11)
$$\text{NPR}_T = \frac{P_A/P_{NA} - \dfrac{E^*}{E_0} P'_A/P^*_{NA}}{\dfrac{E^*}{E_0} P'_A/P^*_{NA}}.$$

NPR_D had to be adjusted to npr_D so that $\text{npr}_D + \text{NPR}_I = \text{NPR}_T$. npr_D is defined as $\text{npr}_D = \text{NPR}_D(1 + \text{NPR}_I)$. This is equivalent to replacing the denominator P'_A/P_{NA} in Equation A-5 by the denominator $(E^*/E_0)P'_A/P^*_{NA}$ in Equation A-11. Since NPR_I in Equation A-10 can also be written as

(A-12)
$$\frac{P'_A/P_{NA} - \dfrac{E^*}{E_0} P'_A/P^*_{NA}}{\dfrac{E^*}{E_0} P'_A/P^*_{NA}}$$

it follows that npr_D, NPR_I, and NPR_T have the same denominator, and $\text{npr}_D + \text{NPR}_I = \text{NPR}_T$. The measure of direct intervention reported in this volume is npr_D.

The total effect of price policies on P_A/P_{NA} is due to sector-specific or direct price interventions (resulting in P_A instead of P'_A), to the exchange-rate effect, and to the trade policies t_{NA} affecting the non-agricultural sector (mostly industrial protection).

Wherever the data were available, the same was done for effective rates of protection (ERP), measuring the impact of those policies on value added for the agricultural products and, in the case of Chile, also for the nonagricultural sector.

The Effect of Policies on Economic Variables

Throughout the studies, both the direct (sector-specific) and the total (direct plus indirect or economywide) effects on output (short- and long-run), consumption, foreign exchange, budget, intersectoral transfers, and income distribution are reported. We start with the effects on output.

Output

The matrix of own- and cross-elasticities of output with respect to the prices of the products analyzed and of variable inputs was derived from the estimation of a system of supply functions or was borrowed from other studies.

Assuming all variables are in logs, we have for any product i (using a Nerlovian approach):

(A-13) $\quad Q_i = a_i + \sum_j a_{ij}P_{j,-1} + \sum_k a_{ik}P_{k,-1} + b_iQ_{i,-1}$

where $Q_i(Q_{i,-1})$ = output of product i in period t (period $t-1$); $P_{j,-1}(P_{k,-1})$ = price of product j, including product i (input k) relative to P_{NA} (at $t-1$); $a_{ij}(a_{ik})$ = elasticity of Q_i with respect to $P_{i,-1}(P_{k,-1})$; and b_i = coefficient of adjustment.

Assume $\hat{X}$ = dlog X. For small changes:

(A-14) $\quad \hat{Q}_i = \sum_j a_{ij}\hat{P}_{j,-1} + \sum_k a_{ik}\hat{P}_{k,-1} + b_i\hat{Q}_{i,-1}.$

For large changes, the new values for $P_{j,-1}$, $P_{k,-1}$ and $Q_{i,-1}$ must be inserted in Equation A-13 to obtain the new value for Q_i ($Q'_{i,SR}$ for the short-run direct effect, $Q^*_{i,SR}$ for the short-run total effect, and Q'_{iC} or $Q^*_{i,C}$ for the corresponding long-run, cumulative effects).

In the short run (where product prices change at $t-1$ but are assumed to be unchanged before that), $Q_{i,-1}$ is assumed to be given (that is, $\hat{Q}_{i,-1} = 0$ in Equation A-14) so that for direct intervention the short-run output effect $\hat{Q}'_{i,SR}$ is

(A-15) $\quad \hat{Q}'_{i,SR} = \sum_j a_{ij}\mathrm{NPR}_{D(j,-1)} + \sum_k a_{ik}\mathrm{NPR}_{D(k,-1)}$

and for total intervention it is

(A-16) $\quad \hat{Q}^*_{i,SR} = \sum_j a_{ij}\mathrm{NPR}_{T(j,-1)} + \sum_k a_{ik}\mathrm{NPR}_{T(k,-1)}.$

The Nerlovian long-run effect on Q_i is obtained by dividing all elasticities a_{ij} and a_{ik} by $1-b_i$. This measures the effect on Q_i of the price intervention NPR at $t-1$ being constant indefinitely, and provides little insight on the long-term effect of price intervention.

An alternative measure is the cumulative effect, which measures the effect on $Q_{i,t}$ of the prices being at their nonintervention value since $t=1$, the first year of the sample period. In this case, we are measuring the alternative, dynamic path that Q_i would have followed if the interventions had been removed at $t=1$ and prices had followed a nonintervention path.

We assume that interventions were removed at $t=1$ but were not announced at $t=0$, so that the impact on Q_i at $t=1$ is zero. At $t=2$, the short-run and cumulative output effects are the same, since $\hat{Q}_{i,t=1} = 0$. At $t=3$, $\hat{Q}_i$ will depend both on $\hat{P}_j$ and $\hat{P}_k$ at $t=2$ and on $\hat{Q}_i$ at $t=2$. At $t=4$, $\hat{Q}_i$ will depend on $\hat{P}_j$ and $\hat{P}_k$ at $t=3$ and on $\hat{Q}_i$ (cumulative) at $t=3$, which depends on $\hat{P}_j$ and $\hat{P}_k$ at $t=2$

and on $\hat{Q}_i$ at $t = 2$. It can be shown that the cumulative effect on Q_i is given by Equation A-14 if $\hat{Q}_{i,-1}$ is reinterpreted as the cumulative effect at $t - 1$.[4] The direct cumulative effect, $\hat{Q}'_{i,c}$, is obtained by replacing $\hat{P}_{m,-1}$ by $\text{NPR}_{D(m,-1)}$, where $m = j, k$. For the total cumulative effect, $\hat{P}_{m,-1}$ is replaced by $\text{NPR}_{T(m,-1)}$.

If the elasticities a_{ik} are not available, and data on value added for products j are available, then a measure of $\hat{Q}_i$ can be obtained from Equation A-17:

$$(A\text{-}17) \qquad \hat{Q}_i = \sum_j c_{ij}\hat{v}_{Aj,-1} + d_i\hat{Q}_{i,-1}$$

where VA = value added; $c_{ij} = a_{ij}(\text{VA}_{j,-1}/P_{j,-1})$, or the elasticity with respect to VA_j; and d_i may or may not be equal to b_i in Equation A-14.

In some studies, the long-term process of investment and labor migration underlying the long-run supply response was explicitly incorporated, including the allocation of investment between agriculture and nonagriculture. An application of such an approach is presented in the study on Chile.

Consumption

We assumed that short-run effects are equal to cumulative effects; that is, that the effect of $\hat{P}_j$ (consumer price of any j) at t on consumption of $i(Q_i^c)$ occurs entirely at t, and there are no lagged effects as in output. This assumption is not entirely valid for consumer durables, nor in the case of endogenous tastes depending on past consumption, but we believe it provides a good approximation in the case of food products. The consumption effect is

$$(A\text{-}18) \qquad \hat{Q}_i^c = \sum_j f_{ij}\hat{P}_j$$

where f_{ij} = elasticity of $Q_{i,t}$ with respect to $P_{j,t}$.

The direct and total effects on Q_i^c are obtained by replacing $\hat{P}_j$ by $\text{NPR}_{D,j}$ and $\text{NPR}_{T,j}$, respectively.

The income effect on Q_i^c has been ignored except when the income change relative to GDP of eliminating the interventions is large enough to affect Q_i^c, or when income elasticities are available by income group, and changes in income or the elasticities vary by income group.

Foreign Exchange

Four effects on foreign exchange were calculated, related to the four effects on output (direct, total, short-run, and cumulative). The foreign exchange effects include the change in excess supply for each product multiplied by the border price and summed over all products analyzed, as well as the change in value of imported inputs accompanying the changes in output.

Two comments are in order. First, some products may have switched categories after the removal of interventions. For instance, in the case of an imported product, it may remain as an imported good and the foreign exchange effect is calculated at the c.i.f. border price; it may become a nontraded good because of excess supply at the c.i.f. price and excess demand at the f.o.b. border price; or it may become an exported product because of excess supply at the f.o.b. border price. These considerations were taken into account for the effects on foreign exchange. Second, in the case of total intervention, only the effect on agricultural foreign exchange was taken into account. For instance, the effect of the removal of restrictions on industrial imports was not included.

Budget

In this section, an estimate was made of the effect on the budget of direct price policies on agricultural products and inputs. These include taxes or subsidies on output, exports, imports, inputs, consumption, marketing, and processing, including the profits and losses of parastatals involved in these activities. Wherever possible, data on actual expenditures or revenues, rather than the announced tax or subsidy rates, were used.

Intersectoral Real Income Transfers

The purpose was to estimate whether the agricultural sector gained or lost from the set of direct and total price interventions as well as from nonprice transfers. Nonprice transfers include the subsidy element of government expenditures specific to agriculture (for example, on irrigation, research and extension, and rural transportation), as well as transfers out of agriculture, such as tax revenues specific to agriculture but not included in the price transfers (for example, land taxes).

The price-related transfers measure the effect of the price policies on agricultural GDP. These differ from the effects on the budget for several reasons. First, some of the gains (or losses) to producers are often captured by the consumers, with only a part going to the government. An extreme case would be a control on the price of a food product, which would tax producers and subsidize consumers but have no effect on the budget. Similarly, some input subsidies may be captured by the industries producing those inputs rather than by the agricultural sector. Second, the measure of real income transfers includes the effect of intervention not only on nominal income but also on the cost of the consumption basket of rural households. For that purpose, authors of the individual studies estimated the impact on the consumer price index (CPI) of removing direct intervention (CPI') and removing total intervention (CPI*).

CPI, CPI', and CPI* are defined as follows.

(A-19)
$$\text{CPI} = \sum \beta_i P_i + (1 - \sum \beta_i) P_{\text{NA}}$$

where β_i = share of agricultural product i in the rural CPI, and $1 - \sum \beta_i$ = share of nonagricultural goods and services in the rural CPI.

(A-20)
$$\text{CPI}' = \sum \beta_i P_i' + (1 - \sum \beta_i) P_{\text{NA}}$$

where CPI' reflects the cost of the consumer basket in the absence of direct intervention.

(A-21)
$$\text{CPI}^* = \sum \beta_i (E^*/E_0) P_i' + (1 - \sum \beta_i) P_{\text{NA}}^*$$

where CPI* reflects the cost of the consumer basket in the absence of total intervention.

Income Distribution

STATIC EFFECTS. Urban consumers were classified by income groups. Their real income is affected because direct and total intervention influence the cost of their consumption basket. The effect varies by income group because of differences in the weights of the various products in each group's consumption basket. When data permitted, other classifications were used, such as the effect on the urban functional distribution of income.

Rural household classification in each country depended on the structure of production, on the political influence of various rural groups, and on the availability of data. In some countries households were classified according to whether members were large-scale farmers, small-scale farmers, farm laborers, or rural nonagricultural laborers. In other countries, where farmers tend to grow one product and where farm size is associated with the product grown (for example, estates producing an export crop and small-scale farmers producing a food crop), the classification was by product. In other cases, the effect on the functional distribution of income was estimated.

The real income effect of direct and total intervention for each group was obtained by calculating the effect on nominal income (value added) and on the cost of the consumer basket. Some small-scale farmers may have been net buyers of the food product grown and may have used off-farm income to acquire the additional food. Where data on off-farm income were available, an effort was also made to estimate the effect of intervention on that source of income.

For hired labor, the static income effect was estimated based on the assumption that nominal income remained unchanged. This assumption was relaxed for the dynamic effects.

DYNAMIC EFFECTS. Over time, income of farm labor may change because of changes in the demand for and supply of labor. The supply of labor may vary because of changes in hours worked and because of migration, which depends in part on the relative returns to labor in urban and rural areas.

From a model of migration and of demand for and supply of labor in rural and urban areas, a reduced-form equation for real income for rural labor was derived as a function of current and lagged values of agriculture's domestic terms of trade and real urban labor income, and of the unemployment rate. Equations of that type were estimated in those countries for which data were available. Using the empirical results, it was then possible to assess the dynamic effect of intervention on the real income of rural labor.

Government Investment and Expenditure Index

It has been claimed that taxation of agriculture was compensated by increased public expenditures on agriculture. To verify this, authors calculated indexes of government investment and total expenditures for agriculture.

The index of government investment bias (GIB) is defined as the share of agriculture in government investment relative to the share of agriculture in GDP:

$$(\text{A-22}) \qquad\qquad \text{GIB} = \frac{\text{AGI/GI}}{\text{AGDP/GDP}}$$

where AGI = agricultural public investment expenditures, GI = total public investment expenditures, and AGDP = agricultural GDP (evaluated at prices in the absence of direct interventions).

Two questions of interest arise. First, what is the relation over time between GIB and agricultural price policy and incentives? Second, is government investment biased in favor of or against the agricultural sector, or is it neutral?

The answer to the second question depends on the criterion used. If a neutral policy is defined as one under which the share of agriculture in public investment expenditures equals the share of agriculture in GDP, then a value of GIB larger (smaller) than 1 indicates a bias in favor of (against) agriculture. If efficiency is used as a criterion, then a neutral policy is one under which the marginal social returns to public investment in agriculture and in nonagriculture are equalized, and a higher (lower) return in agriculture indicates a bias against (in favor of) agriculture.

An index of government expenditure bias was also calculated as

(A-23) $$\text{GEB} = \frac{\text{AGE/GE}}{\text{AGDP/GDP}}$$

where AGE = agricultural government expenditures, and GE = total government expenditures.

Price Variability

Three indexes of price variability were calculated: the standard deviation, the coefficient of variation (equal to the standard deviation of the price relative to the average price), and the Z-statistic.

The Z-statistic is defined as

(A-24) $$Z = \left(\frac{\displaystyle\sum_{t=2}^{n} (P_t - P_{t-1})^2}{n - 1} \right)^{1/2}$$

where P is the price of any product relative to P_{NA}.

The standard deviation (SD) of the price series is the square root of the average squared deviation of the price from the sample mean. The Z-statistic is the square root of the average squared deviation of the price from its value lagged one period (or of the first difference in the price). The two statistics SD and Z are thus directly comparable.

Producers may be more concerned with annual changes in their prices than with the deviation from the sample mean. Moreover, two very different price series may have the same SD value even though one would be considered more stable than the other, and this would be reflected in the Z value. For example, assume $P_1 = 100$ for ten periods and then rises to 200 for ten additional periods, whereas P_2 varies annually from 100 to 200. That is,

(A-25) $$P_{1t} = \begin{cases} 100, & 0 \le t \le 9 \\ 200, & 10 \le t \le 19 \end{cases}$$

and

$$P_{2t} = \begin{cases} 100, & t = 2n, \ 0 \le n \le 9 \\ 200, & t = 1 + 2n, \ 0 \le n \le 9. \end{cases}$$

Both series have the same mean of 150 and have the same standard deviation, $SD = 50$, but P_{1t} has a much smaller Z value. $Z = 100$ for P_{2t} and $Z = 23$ for P_{1t} (approximately). Thus the Z-statistic seems to better reflect the relative stability of the two series, in the sense that P_{1t} experiences only one change over the period whereas P_{2t} changes every year.

The calculations of the various measures of intervention and of their effects were then used as a quantitative basis for the analysis of the political economy of agricultural pricing policies in each country.

Notes

1. The sustainable current account deficit may be positive because of long-run commitments on foreign aid, worker remittances, foreign investment, and so forth.

2. In some cases (for example, Chile) a real exchange rate equation was also estimated as a function of the terms of trade, trade policies, and other variables reflecting absorption and wage policy.

Equations A-7 and A-8 are correct for small changes and are good approximations for larger changes. The exact solution for large changes with constant elasticities is shown in the study of the Dominican Republic, and the difference between the two solutions is small even for large t_M, t_x, and ΔQ_0. Derivation of Equations A-7 and A-8 and methodologies for estimating the equivalent tariff, t_M, are available from the editors of this volume.

3. In a few studies (for example, Chile) the effect on P_{NAH} is taken into account.

4. The solution is found in the methodological memoranda, which are available from the editors of this volume.

References

Ahmed, R., and N. Rustagi. 1985. "Agricultural Marketing and Price Incentives: A Comparative Study of African and Asian Countries." International Food Policy Research Institute, Washington, D.C.

Beenhakker, Henri L. 1987. "Issues in Agricultural Marketing and Transport Due to Government Intervention." Discussion Paper, Transportation Issues Series, Report TRP7 (May), World Bank, Washington, D.C.

Westlake, M. J. 1987. "The Measurement of Agricultural Price Distortion in Developing Countries." *Journal of Development Studies*, vol. 23 (April), pp. 367–81.